# CITIES
# AND
# MARKETS

## *Studies in the Organization of Human Space*

Presented to

**Eric E. Lampard**

Edited by

**Rondo Cameron**
**Leo F. Schnore**

**University Press of America, Inc.**
**Lanham • New York • Oxford**

**Copyright © 1997 by**
**University Press of America,® Inc.**
4720 Boston Way
Lanham, Maryland 20706

12 Hid's Copse Rd.
Cummor Hill, Oxford OX2 9JJ

**Library of Congress Cataloging-in-Publication Data**

Cities and markets : studies in the organization of human space / edited
by Rondo Cameron, Leo F. Schnore.
Presented to:
Eric E. Lampard
p.    cm.
Includes bibliographical references.
1. Urban economics  2. Economic history.  3. Cities and towns--
History.  I.  Cameron, Rondo E.  II.  Schnore, Leo Francis.
HT321.C534  1996   330.9173'2--dc20    96-41461 CIP

ISBN 0-7618-0522-2 (cloth: alk. ppr.)
ISBN 0-7618-0523-0 (pbk: alk. ppr.)

♾™ The paper used in this publication meets the minimum
requirements of American National Standard for information
Sciences—Permanence of Paper for Printed Library Materials,
ANSI Z39.48—1984

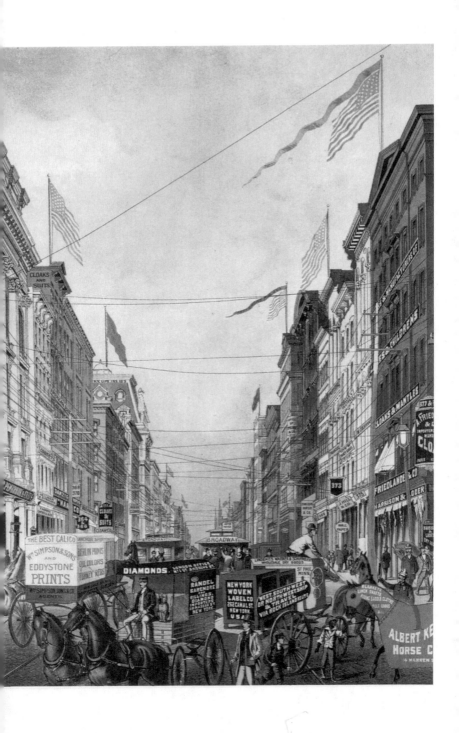

# Contents

# Contributors

**Peter G. Buckley**
Assoc. Professor of History,
The Cooper Union for the Advancement of Science and Art
New York, New York.

**Rondo Cameron**
Kenan University Professor, Emeritus,
Emory University

**Kathleen N. Conzen**
Professor of History
University of Chicago

**Jospeh L. Garonzik**, Editor
Genealogical Publications
Baltimore, Maryland

**H. Thomas Johnson**
Retzlaff Professor of Quality Management
School of Business Administration
Portland State University

**Jacob M. Price**
Professor of History, Emeritus
University of Michigan

**Paul L. Robertson**
Professor, Department of Economics and Management
University of New South Wales

**Morton Rothstein**
Professor of History, Emeritus
University of California, Davis

**Leo F. Schnore**
Professor of Sociology, Emeritus
University of Wisconsin

***Marc J. Stern***
Assistant Professor of History
Bentley College

***Margaret Walsh***
Reader in American and Canadian Studies
University of Nottingham

***Sam Bass Warner, Jr.***
Professor of History and Environmental Studies, Emeritus
Brandeis University

# Part One

*Industrialization and the Dynamic of Technological Progress Reconsidered*

The essays in this volume, although at first sight a disparate lot, possess a collective unity that is belied by the individual titles. The authors are mostly former colleagues or students of Eric E. Lampard, and it is his insights and seminal contributions that have inspired them. The essays range widely in subject matter, but they are all concerned with the organization--or reorganization--of human space. From the market structure of the colonial Chesapeake to the design of transportation systems in the American Midwest, from the growth of modern industry to concern with the environment, they all deal with the ways in which people and policy makers reacted to changes in the size and distribution of human populations, in technology, in institutions, and in the organization of cities and markets. They thus cover a wide range of problems in urban and economic history, disciplines that Lampard did so much to shape and inform.

That being the case, the editors have invited Lampard himself to provide a preview of the chapters. The remaining paragraphs of this Preface and Preview are his.

## *Chapter 1*

The great divide between "modern" and all that went before is the late-Victorian notion of "the industrial revolution." It is an almost indispensable datum in the social sciences and has become part of the intellectual furniture of literary and cultural "theorists" who otherwise show little acquaintance in their work with economic history. It separates us from our "preindustrial" past. Chapter 1 by Rondo Cameron confronts the issue of conceptualizing recent economic change directly with his essay: "Misunderstanding the Industrial Revolution" --he does not even need a subtitle. The idea of "revolution" was propagated by Arnold Toynbee in his *Lectures on the Industrial Revolution of the Eighteenth Century* given at Oxford in 1880-81 and published posthumously in 1884. Although the metaphor of "industrial revolution" dates back in various contexts through Marx, Mill, Engels, and Blanqui to French writers who had used it with reference to the displacement of domestic linen manufactures by cottons in certain localities of France *c.* 1800, it was Toynbee's formulation which gave the term its historiographical *éclat*. Four or five "mechanical discoveries" between 1769 and 1792 were harnessed by textile entrepreneurs to power from James Watt's steam engines to "mark the introduction of the factory system." Toynbee's account became Holy Writ for socially conscious writers of the time and, in the words of his celebrity nephew, Arnold J. Toynbee, he "created the frame within which all subsequent work on the Industrial Revolution has been carried out." A remarkable accomplishment indeed for a young teacher who was stricken down at the age of 30.

Toynbee's identification of "industry" with manufacturing and factory organization became part of an enduring stereotype. Reorganization of work and ways of living in the new mill towns destroyed the earlier intimacy that had imbued the relations of masters and men: "a 'cash nexus' was substututed for the human tie." Environments deteriorated in the congested factory towns and newly enclosed countryside, while working men and women were exposed to the bitter "exploitation" and distress which henceforth accompanied recurrent fluctuations in "the state of trade." "The effects of the Industrial Revolution," Toynbee concluded "prove that free competition may produce wealth without producing well-being. We all know the horrors that ensued in England before it was restrained by legislation and combination."

Rondo Cameron makes clear that industrial developments in the aggregate since the 18th century were notably more "evolutionary" than "revolutionary". After a review of recent discussions of this issue he notes that there is still no consensus among scholars on the approximate dates at which the putative "revolution" began or ended. Altogether a light-hearted screed, Cameron's central point is, nevertheless, deadly serious: in our attempts to make sense of the past, we often become victims of our favorite historiographical metaphors. Economists, eager to maintain a notional "industrial revolution" as a singular moment in the history of resource productivity may also be, unwittingly, resuscitating Toynbee's somewhat frayed story of its doleful impact on working people's lives. That, after all, remains the chief interest of noneconomic scholars and the caring public in the idea of the "industrial revolution." It may be instructive for those who tend to see things in clear images that the only economist whom Toynbee revered was Adam Smith.

## *Chapter 2.*

Whether rising average real incomes or sustained increases in ratios of capital to other productive resources are regarded as key indicators (motivators?) of the industrialization process, there can be little doubt that high returns to innovators in the market place furnish a potent incentive to change (abnormal profits) -- until they are eroded by competitors. While they last, such economic "rents" constitute an essential fuel of technological and organizational progress. Nevertheless, as Paul L. Robertson explains in Chapter 2, "Inertia and Industrial Change," not all branches of manufactures or, by implication, other sectors are equally "state of the art." At any time, an economic observer is confronted by "the coexistence of a variety of competing technologies and organizational forms" within particular industries or regions at similar levels of development; what A.P. Usher, the economic historian of mechanical inventions, once dubbed "the contemporaneity of the non-contemporaneous."

The processes of economic and social transformation under industrialism unfold in piecemeal fashion, with markedly divergent rates of change over time. Despite investments in steam-powered machinery by some firms in Britain's early cotton manufacturing districts, for example, firms in other locations profitably adhered to the extant water-powered engines, even improved water-powers, for many decades thereafter. Nor did steam power--one of the mainstays of the industrial revolutionary flag--spread rapidly to most other industries, only becoming general throughout Britain's manufacturing centers about 1870. Much the same phenomena were seen in the American northeast during antebellum decades.

Robertson underlines this feature of industrialization with copious other examples and seeks an explanation for such uneven and prolonged transitions in technology and organization (which, incidentally, often run counter to expectations founded on neoclassical economic theory). An array of factors and conditions underlies this "inertia" which is by no means identifiable with economic stagnation, even when it can be associated with slower rates of growth or diminishing returns, no less. There may be "rational" economic explanations for the persistence of older modes of production. Among usual suspects assembled are resource deficiencies, entrepreneurial failures, labor intransigence, governmental ineptitude, so-called "cultural incompatibilities," but Robertson is especially concerned with what he calls "institutional variables," both inside and outside the firm. Not all organizations or, for that matter, regions possess the requisite capabilities or adequate routines to take up the latest innovations (which themselves come intermittently in 57 varieties); hence the persistence of the obsolescent alongside emergent novelty--although eventual changes in manufacturing leadership become probable. Once-dominant firms, industries, even nations (Britain, Germany, the U.S., Japan) may become followers in certain instances or retreat from competition altogether.

## *Chapter 3*

The secular growth of nations and regions, as well of localities, is always affected by the "mix" of productive activities and their variable contributions to the *composition* of output and incomes. Over time there is a continuous shift among the several sectors--agriculture, mineral extraction, forestry and logging, manufactures, transport, and communications, distribution, etc.--as well as in the contributions made by leading industries to net investment and output within the conventional sectors. Within manufacturing, for example, some old industries may be declining (e.g.,cotton goods), some are either stable or only slow growing (e.g., lumber products, men's clothing), while others, particularly those introducing new products or novel technical processes, may be growing rapidly (e.g., steel, electric machinery). In 1860, 1910, and 1960 the following census industries were the half-a-dozen largest in the U.S. in declining order of value-added by manufacture:

| 1860 | 1910 | 1960 |
|------|------|------|
| 1. Cotton Goods | 1. Machinery | 1. Non-Electric Machinery |
| 2. Lumber & Products | 2. Lumber & Products | 2. Electrical Machinery |
| 3. Boots & Shoes | 3. Printing & Publishing | 3. Motor Vehicles |
| 4. Flour & Meal | 4. Iron & Steel | 4. Steel |
| 5. Men's Clothing | 5. Malt Liquors | 5. Aircraft |
| 6. Iron | 6. Men's Clothing | 6. Basic Chemicals |

In short, alterations in the structure of output in an economy--the "mix" of activities and products--inhere in dynamic industrial societies and are ultimately registered *via* markets by changes in final demand. The course of industrialization--as indicated in Part I of this volume — does not run smoothly and neither the theory of the firm nor the neoclassical model of perfect competition can account for disruptions and lags that occur in the histories of particular industries or regions (even when they are non-revolutionary).

Robertson's analysis of "inertia" amid pervasive innovation complements and extends Cameron's critique of *the* "industrial revolution". In Chapter 3, Marc J. Stern's narrative of the potteries of New Jersey offers another very different perspective on industrialization: "Organization on the 'Periphery,': Market Restrictions and Workplace Control in Trenton, New Jersey's Sanitary Pottery Industry, 1900-1929", which highlights the role of skilled labor. This industry underwent fairly steady expansion in a particular locality and, from the 1880s, shifted into a very different type of ceramic product, sanitary ware, *without* benefit of fuel-burning machines (other than steam pumps and wheels), technical innovations, "horizontal" and "vertical", integration, or other paradigmatical strategy to achieve notionally-necessary economies of scale.

The location in Trenton around midcentury--already home to the nation's largest ironworks, Cooper-Hewitt--reflected the availability of essential clays, fuel for kilns, and transportation access to major urban markets, especially New York City, the nation's principal wholesale distribution emporium. Both master and operative potters were in-migrants to the city, if not always foreign born. The potteries were generally small undertakings (mostly partnerships or proprietaries), with low entry costs and limited capitalization, producing flexible, batch-sized (as distinct from "bulk" or "continuous") outputs of mainly finished goods. Initially they made general ware for household and institutional users rather than fine china but, with only minor adaptations of skills, techniques, and materials, were increasingly driven by competitive pressures into sanitary ware for the urbanizing populations of the American Northeast. American cities needed plumbing facilities as well as sewage-disposal systems, as Paul de Roussiers was told at the time by unemployed journeymen in London contemplating emigration.

Stern's tale of pottery transformation presents a very different view of industrialization from the earlier examples of textiles, heavy industry, coal mining, or steam railroads. He is among scholars who affirm the economic importance of the many small-scale "unoligopolized" branches of manufacture-- what the business historian, Thomas K. McCraw, labeled "peripheral markets"--as opposed to oligopolized "core" markets, such as petroleum, meatpacking, cigarettes, steel, where *price* competition ("unfair," "cut throat," "unbridled," "wasteful," among less printable epithets) had come to threaten the huge overhead investments (fixed costs) of integrated corporations. Insofar as the potteries remained essentially capitalizations of labor skills, Stern reminds us that--as Toynbee had insisted--history happens to people: industrialization always had a grimy human face.

The Trenton potteries were founded mostly by descendents of 18th-century English potters, who were themselves among the first cohorts of the old "industrial revolution" (who, nevertheless, passed by unnoticed by Toynbee). The master potter, Josiah Wedgewood, had changed the face of "the old peasant craft" in the 1760s by reorganizing his work processes into a hierarchical division of labor skills and installing the specialized operatives in his new "Etruria" pottery at Hanley. There he went on improving the materials and methods for producing low and high quality ware and had employed the services of artists, such as Flaxman, to embellish the attractiveness of his designs. To sustain such an intensive and expensive degree of specialization in his highly-controlled work environment, Wedgewood at the outset had entered into his fruitful partnership with the Liverpool merchant, Thomas Bentley, in order to maintain a sufficient level of demand, especially in the London and Home Counties' markets.

Almost a century later the early Trenton potters hoped to enter and enlarge the domestic share of the home market for general ware, hitherto dominated by the English exporters. From the beginning they confronted heavy competition from foreign aud domestic potters (chiefly their "cousins" In East Liverpool, Ohio), alike vulnerable to recurring fluctuations in levels of demand. Price wars among competing pottery firms and districts led frequently to reductions in wages and in the operatives' customary autonomy and expectations, mitigated only by successful lobbying for higher tariff protection.

Stern explains the shift of Trenton's resources into the less competitive and more buoyant market for sanitary ware in the setting of a collusive turn-of-the-century regimen jointly contrived by the employers' trade association and the operatives' trades union. An ill-timed strike against the potteries and a politically-motivated federal anti-trust suit (U.S. *v* Trenton Potteries *et al.*, 1923) combined--during the chaotic market adjustments after the first Great War--to destroy the prevailing *modus vivendi* and thereby open up the sanitary ware market to oligopolization by large plumbing supply houses, able to exploit the new technics of tunnel kilns and casting processes (bulk production) as a substitute for the labor skills on which the earlier capitalization of the industry had been based.

# 1

# Misunderstanding the Industrial Revolution

## Rondo Cameron*

A simple but hallowed view of the industrial revolution suggests a cataclysm followed by a catastrophe: a violent social upheaval bringing misery in its train. It began about the year 1760 when steam power was harnessed to new textile machinery in English factories. The outcome was a century of exploitation and unrest as tens of thousands were uprooted from a quiet country existence and herded into "dark satanic mills." There they were compelled to work very long hours for pitiably small reward in vile conditions which were not substantially remedied before the second half of the nineteenth century through the militant activity of trade-unions and the passage of benevolent factory laws.

— Eric E. Lampard[1]

Eric Lampard was not the first scholar to question the accuracy or validity of the term "industrial revolution." His teachers — T. S. Ashton, H. L. Beales, and especially A. P. Usher — had already done that, Usher as early as 1920.[2] But Lampard, invited by the American Historical Association's Service Center for Teachers of History to prepare a pamphlet for use by secondary school teachers, sought to steer his prospective readers away from the then still prevalent notion that the so-called revolution was "a cataclysm followed by a catastrophe." He did so by suggesting that the traditional industrial revolution should be studied as an early example of economic growth — growth studies were very much in fashion in the l950s — but, anticipating later critics of such studies, he further asserted that historians should carry their arguments "beyond a limited framework such as 'economic growth' to the ultimate reference of culture.... The cultural framework... enables the historian to treat *the* industrial revolution and the emergence of urban-industrial society as a whole, in all its interrelated aspects — technical, socioeconomic, and intellectual." [3]

Since that early and promising beginning Lampard departed economic history in the strict sense to pursue urbanization, historical demography, and other more fashionable specialties, leaving to me, his erstwhile colleague at Wisconsin, the thankless task of persuading an obtuse profession to forego misleading its students and the general public with meaningless terminology.[4]   My efforts have gone unheeded but not unnoticed. David Landes called me "quixotic";[5] presumably mine is one of "the shriller voices calling for excision of the concept [industrial revolution] from our textbooks and scholarly papers" that "can safely be ignored."[6]

Before proceeding with my probably futile attempt at conversion, I wish to recapitulate what seem to me to be the major issues. If, in the process, I repeat some of my earlier statements, I beg forgiveness on the grounds that no one has paid any attention to them.

*I*

(1) In the first place, the controversy is about terminology.  Earlier I wrote, "This is not a question of pedantry, semantics, or fashion but of scientific accuracy and correct understanding."[7]   I now believe that it is a question of semantics in terms of the first dictionary definition of that word: "the study of meanings: . . . the historical and psychological study and the classification of changes in the signification of words or forms viewed as factors in linguistic development and including such phenomena as specialization and expansion of meaning, meliorative and pejorative tendencies, metaphor, and adaptation."[8]   The term industrial revolution, as is well known, came into widespread use after the posthumous publication of Toynbee's lectures.[9]  It was inaccurate from the beginning, "a catchphrase popularized by a youthful, naive social reformer, not a scholar, who wanted to draw attention to the causes of what he regarded as the moral degradation of the British working classes."[10]   Toynbee's purpose in coining the phrase was to justify state intervention, not only in the workplace — factory legislation — but also in the home — subsidized housing for the poor. He argued explicitly, "First, that where individual

rights conflict with the interests of the community, there the State ought to interfere; and second, that where the people are unable to provide a thing for themselves, and that thing is of *primary social importance*, then again the State should interfere and provide it for them."[11]

Although the term quickly won popular acceptance, scholarly analysis and criticism was slower in coming; Usher's critique (1920) was the first serious assessment of the term, thirty-five years after it had gained currency.[12] In 1928 Beales criticized it, but wrote that "to try to discredit it now seems pedantic."[13] In 1957, however, that same Beales wrote, "A new phase in the historical interpretation of this so-called revolution is surely called for now when its historians admit that it is a misleading term and yet refuse to try to invent another."[14]

To bolster my crusade I tried to enlist E. A. Wrigley, an editor of the *Economic History Review*. He replied, "On the substance of the matter (about the industrial revolution) we are largely in agreement, I think. On the use of the term, you may be right & I have been too timid. Certainly if the term did not exist it is hard to believe that it would now gain currency. But, given that it does exist, the case is more uncertain. One might simply avoid using the term, as Clapham largely did which would be honest but would not be likely to reduce its general usage significantly. Or one might attack it head on, as has been done fairly often in recent years. I suppose this might eventually lead to its disuse but better, though harder, is to find something that comes easily off the tongue and is not misleading — a preferable substitute. The terminology I used ["advanced organic economy" and "mineral-based energy economy"] may be accurate but it is cumbersome and inelegant."[15]

Wrigley's response is typical of many others that I have received: yes, we agree that the industrial revolution wasn't really revolutionary, but what else would you call it? Nothing could be simpler. The Danish economist Svend Aage Hansen, in his study of *Early Industrialisation in Denmark*, wrote "A new and valuable contribution to this refining of concepts has been made recently by the studies of 'the early stages of industrialisation' carried out by Rondo Cameron and his colleagues. In fact the concept of 'early industrialisation' as defined by Cameron is more precise, and therefore a far better tool to work with, than the term 'industrial revolution', which has been the one most commonly employed hitherto in the debate on Danish industrialisation."[16]

(2) Secondly, the controversy is about the substance of the events that constitute the so-called revolution. There is general agreement that the American Revolution, the French Revolution, and the Russian

Revolution (among others) were historical *realities*. They had identifiable beginnings and endings (even if there is some disagreement on the precise dates), and the participants were very much aware of their involvement. In contrast, there is no agreement on the dates of the so-called industrial revolution. Toynbee was invited to lecture on the reign of George III (1760-1820). It is not clear why Ashton chose 1760-1830 — perhaps it was suggested by his publisher — but Ashton himself was quite clear on "the essential fact of continuity": "The word 'revolution' implies a suddenness of change that is not, in fact, characteristic of economic processes. The system of human relationships that is sometimes called capitalism had its origins long before 1760, and attained its full development long after 1830."[17] Beales, uneasy with the dates as well as the general idea, opted for a longer period — a century, 1750-1850 — and other authors have had still other dates. McCloskey prefers 1780-1860.[18]   According to A. E. Musson, "The older view . . . clearly is no longer tenable. . . . the extent of industrial changes before the mid-nineteenth century have [sic] been greatly exaggerated"; his figures show a tenfold increase in steam power between 1870 and 1907, fully a century after the conventional dating.[19]

Did contemporaries know they were involved in an industrial revolution? A couple of English scholars who want to "rehabilitate" the (old) industrial revolution insist that "Radical change was obvious to contemporaries, but it has been obscured in recent historiography. . . ," but their evidence is laughably skimpy and unrepresentative.[20]   Adam Smith, who used an unmechanized pin factory to demonstrate the advantages of the division of labor, was completely unaware of anything resembling an industrial revolution.[21]   Ricardo reluctantly added a chapter on machinery to the third edition of his *Principles*, but it is hopelessly muddled logically, and betrays not one scintilla of evidence of actual experience with machinery. In Wrigley's view, "the classical economists were not merely unconscious of changes going on about them that we now term an industrial revolution: they were in effect committed to a view of the nature of economic development that ruled it out as a possibility."[22]

If the general public was aware of rapid industrial change one would expect to find it reflected in the literature of the time, but one can read the novels and poetry of Jane Austen, William Blake, Charlotte and Emily Bronte, Robert Burns, Lord Byron, John Keats, Sir Walter Scott, Percy Shelley and others and discover no hint of industrial upheaval. William Wordsworth was well aware of the French Revolution, which he extolled, but of the industrial revolution he had no clue.

In short, the industrial revolution was not a historical reality, but an abstraction — one could even say a fiction — dreamed up by persons long after the events that purportedly constituted it.

(3) In the third place, why should we be concerned? After all, any economic historian familiar with recent literature — Crafts, Harley, etc.[23] — knows that growth was slower than that depicted in the early, impressionistic literature. So what? As I have said before, industrial revolution is probably the only phrase in the economic historian's lexicon that is widely recognized by the general public — and almost universally misunderstood. The misunderstandings refer to the pace of change ("sudden, discontinuous," "radically discontinuous"), the dates or length of the period ("the English Industrial Revolution took place within a space of about four decades, having . . . run its course by around 1820," "in England in 1837, *after* the industrial revolution . . ." [emphasis added]), and to the supposed consequences (the purported decline in the standard of living). Nor are these misunderstandings confined to the general public; the quotations above are by reputable scholars. (I have deliberately not cited the sources in order to avoid embarrassing them. After all, *they* are not to blame if we economic historians misled them.)

The noted biologist and paleontologist, Stephan Jay Gould, tells of an analogous situation in his field. "Natural selection" is the key phrase in the Darwinian theory of evolutionary change. Gould is aware that "the theory has a history of misuse almost as long as its proper pedigree. . . . But most false expropriations of our chief phrase have been without our knowledge and against our will." Gould, however, was quite unprepared to encounter *natürliche Auslese* in the Wannsee Protocol, the document drawn up by Adolf Eichmann as the "final solution" to the Nazis' Jewish problem. "To think that the key phrase of my professional world lies so perversely violated in the very heart of the chief operative paragraph in the most evil document ever written!"[24] The chief difference in the misuse of the key phrase of evolutionary biology and that of economic history is that in the latter case the economic historians themselves are the principal culprits.

## *II*

Most economic historians of my acquaintance agree with me that the term is a misnomer but, like Wrigley, their consciousnesses not having been raised by exposure to the paragraph above, they regard it as harmless and continue to use it from force of habit. Patrick O'Brien, for example, wrote me that "I'm afraid the term Industrial Revolution will last as long as the term Renaissance."[25] Although I am not a Renaissance scholar, I am aware that it, too, is a misnomer; but I doubt that its use does as much positive harm as that of the industrial revolution.[26] O'Brien himself, in his otherwise admirable inaugural lecture as Professor of Economic History and Director of the Institute of Historical Research in the University of London,[27] uses the term five times (three with initial capitals, two uncapitalized); in this case no positive harm results but, on the other hand, use of the term adds nothing of substance to his sentences. In contrast, I will quote a model sentence where the term might have been used but was not, showing how easily we can replace it: "Meanwhile industrialization progressed in an economy 'afflicted' by ever increasing 'burdens' of taxation."[28]

Use of the term may have been encouraged by the belief that, as an 1896 textbook put it, "The change . . . was sudden and violent."[29] Although Usher and Ashton tried to alter that notion, most writers continued to emphasize the element of discontinuity. Walt Rostow, perhaps the most influential scholar to deal with the subject since Ashton, greatly strengthened it with his concept of the "take-off," which he dated precisely in England as 1783-1802.[30] Alexander Gerschenkron eloquently criticized Rostow at the Konstanz conference of the International Economic Association,[31] but agreed with him on the question of discontinuity, which Gerschenkron called "a great spurt": "The 'great spurt' is closely related to W. W. Rostow's 'take-off'. . . . Both concepts stress the element of specific discontinuity in economic development; great spurts, however, are confined to the area of manufacturing and mining, whereas take-offs refer to national output. Unfortunately, in the present state of our statistical information on long-term growth of national income, . . . there is hardly any way of establishing, let alone testing, the take-off hypothesis."[32] Simon Kuznets, whose critique of the take-off hypothesis at the Konstanz conference can only be characterized as devastating,[33] remarked dryly, "the data are not adequate for testing hypotheses concerning the time patterns of growth rates. But they do not provide support for W. W. Rostow's 'take-off' theory . . . nor . . . the Gerschenkron hypothesis."[34]

Although most economic historians use the term from force of habit, two who do not are Joel Mokyr and R. M. Hartwell. We might call them the leading fundamentalists (in the religious sense) of economic history.

Mokyr has written a very good book on the history of technology, but he almost spoiled it by insisting on treating the industrial revolution as a historical reality.[35] (He also tried to deify it by writing it with initial capitals.) Analogizing technological change with biological evolution, he borrows the idea of "punctuated equilibria" from paleobiology. In this theory evolution endures long periods of stasis during which only micromutations occur, but occasionally experiences rapid change as a result of multiple macromutations. Accordingly, "New techniques can thus evolve in two ways. One is through a sudden macroinvention, followed by a series of microinventions that modify and improve it to make it functional without altering its concept. The other is through a sequence of microinventions that eventually lead to a technique sufficiently different from the original one as to classify it as a novel technique rather than an improved version of the original one."[36] Mokyr then argues that in the period after 1750, which he calls "years of miracles," Britain (but not continental Europe) witnessed a number of macroinventions such as to merit the appelation industrial revolution.

There are a number of difficulties with this interpretation. In the first place, as Mokyr himself admits, analogies can only be suggestive, not conclusive. Morover, by setting his *annus mirabilis* in 1750 he cuts out a number of candidates for the role of macroinventions, such as coke-smelting of iron ore (1709) and the Newcomen steam engine (1712). More fundamentally, according to this analogy, whatever the period chosen for the revolution, whether 1750-1850 or 1760-1830, it would have to be followed by another period of stasis, which clearly it was not. Although our devices for counting or measuring technological change are very crude, it seems likely that technological change has been increasing at an accelerating rate — i.e., exponentially — from some time in the distant past, perhaps the high middle ages, perhaps the origin of civilization, perhaps the origin of the species *homo sapiens*.

At the 1987 meeting of the Social Science History Association I organized a panel on the so-called industrial revolution. Max Hartwell and I gave the principal papers, which were subsequently published.[37] C. K. Harley, David Landes, and J. G. Williamson had been invited to comment on Hartwell's and my papers, although in fact they gave papers of their own; to the best of my knowledge they have not been published, at least in the form there presented, and I do not now recall their substance, except that none of them addressed the issues I raised. Hartwell, of course, answered the question in his title in the affirmative; but before discussing the substance of his paper I wish to digress slightly.

Hartwell's and my papers had been circulated in advance. Using his paper as a basis, I wrote a little skit that I called "The Drama of the Industrial Revolution," the transcript of a counterfactual conversation between R. M. Hartwell and the Great Interrogator. It has never been published but, in all modesty, I believe it merits the attention of posterity. Charles P. Kindleberger, the session chairman, played the role of the Great Interrogator and *I* (not Hartwell) played his role:

> G.I.: Do you agree that the pace of change of industrialization was slower than suggested by Toynbee, Gibbins, and later writers up to and including Deane and Cole?
>
> R.M.H.: Yes, see my paper, page 2.
>
> G.I.: Do you agree that the process of industrialization was not "sudden, rapid, catastrophic, dramatic, massively destructive of old structures, quickly transforming, and nationally comprehensive"?
>
> R.M.H.: Yes, see page 10.
>
> G.I.: Do you agree that the process of industrialization was characterized by continuity?
>
> R.M.H.: Yes, see page 9.
>
> G.I.: Do you agree that the process was incomplete in 1850?
>
> R.M.H.: Yes, see the same page.
>
> G.I.: Do you agree that the term "industrial revolution" is a misnomer?
>
> R.M.H.: NO!
>
> G.I.: Why, in view of your answers to the first four questions, do you answer the last in the negative?
>
> R.M.H.: Because the phrase occurs in the titles of all my books.

To his credit, Hartwell clapped louder and laughed more heartily than anyone else.

I shall now rephrase Hartwell's answer to the last of the Great Interrogator's questions, based on the substance of his paper. In his view, the term is justified because life today is different from what it was in the first half of the eighteenth century. The question, "was there an industrial revolution?" "is absurd because it is counterintuitive — intuition based on the obvious differences between developed and underdeveloped economies, between industrial and agricultural areas, between cities and villages, between factories and farms, between industrial workers and peasants, differences which point unambiguously to the revolutionary nature of industrialization. . . ."[38] But to contrast the character of post-industrial society with that of pre-industrial society by reference to an industrial revolution inevitably confuses the nature of the changes with the pace of change, which is quite another matter.

In contrast to Hartwell, Mokyr, and others who see economic change in England in the latter half of the eighteenth century as the beginning of world-wide modern economic growth, Eric Jones has detected what he calls "intensive growth" (i.e., growth in per capita incomes) in regions as distant geographically and chronologically as Sung China, early modern Europe, and Tokugawa Japan.[39]  In his view, the *impulse* for growth is universal, or at least very widespread.  What prevented it from realizing itself in the past was reactionary political regimes that seized surplus income as rent and dissipated it in military adventures and monumental architecture.

As an explanation of economic change in both the past and present, I find Jones's argument superior to those of the one-industrial-revolution variety; yet it is not wholly satisfactory.  Although rent-seeking has certainly characterized many societies in the past as well as the present, that alone is scarcely sufficient to stifle growth altogether.  Instead, physical constraints in the form of diminishing marginal returns to the scarce factors of production, especially land, appear to have been the major determinant.[40] The introduction of new sources of energy (or power), coal at first, other fossil fuels later, gradually overcame those constraints, but it was a long drawn-out process, by no means "revolutionary."  Wrigley's terminology is appropriate:  "The transition from an advanced organic economy to an energy-based mineral economy was . . . under way in Tudor times. . . .  If real income is treated as the key defining characteristic of the industrial revolution, then it follows that the latter was not unambiguously established until the second half of the nineteenth century."[41]

In conclusion, I return to Stephen Jay Gould's predicament when he discovered the Nazis' misuse of natural selection.  "Science, as a profession, does have a little something to answer for, or at least something to think about. . . .  German evolutionists did not raise a chorus of protest against Hitler's misuse of natural selection, dating to *Mein Kampf* in 1925. . . .  A scientist's best defense against such misappropriations lies in a combination . . . [of] vigilance and humility."[42]  Economic history, as a profession, also has a responsibility.  Economic historians should be vigilant in rooting out humbug and false analogies and metaphors, and humble in their search for true facts and correct interpretations and perspectives, as Lampard advised us more than thirty five years ago.

\* Charles P. Kindleberger, Donald N. McCloskey, Patrick O'Brien, Pat Richardson, Richard Sylla, and E. A. Wrigley gave me the benefit of their comments and suggestions on an earlier draft. Neither they nor Eric Lampard are responsible for the way I have used their words and ideas.

1. *Industrial Revolution: Interpretations and Perspectives* (Washington, D.C.: American Historical Association Service Center for Teachers of History, l957), p.l.

2. Abbott Payson Usher, *An Introduction to the Industrial History of England* (Boston: Houghton Mifflin Company, 1920); H. L. Beales, *The Industrial Revolution, 1750-1850: An Introductory Essay* (London: Longmans, Green & Co.: 1928; reprinted with a new introductory essay, Frank Cass & Co, 1958); id., "Was There an Industrial Revolution?" *Listener*, 21 February 1957; T. S. Ashton, *The Industrial Revolution, 1760-1830* (London: Oxford University Press, 1948).

It is ironic that Ashton, who had no special fondness for the term, allowed his publisher to pin it and the equally misleading dates on his influential little book because, as a result of criticisms by such scholars as George Unwin, Herbert Heaton, John U. Nef, and Joseph Schumpeter, it had fallen out of favor by the 1940s and was scarcely used by serious scholars.

3. Lampard, *Industrial Revolution*, p. 35.

4. Rondo Cameron, "The Industrial Revolution, a Misnomer," in Jügen Schneider, ed., *Wirtschaftskräfte und Wirtschaftswege: Festschrift für Hermann Kellenbenz*, vol. 5 (Stuttgart: Klett-Cotta, 1981), 367-76; revised version in *The History Teacher*, 15 (May 1982), 377-84; "La révolution industrielle manquée," *Social Science History*, 14:4 (Winter 1990), 559-65. See also my *Concise Economic History of the World from Paleolithic Times to the Present* (New York: Oxford University Press, 1989; 3rd ed. forthcoming, 1997), pp. 128-30, "Mercantilism: A Misnomer," and pp. 163-65, "The Industrial Revolution: A Misnomer."

5. In discussion of "A New View of European Industrialization" at a meeting of the Council for European Studies in Washington in 1983.

6. Joel Mokyr, "Was There a British Industrial Evolution?" in Joel Mokyr, ed., *The Vital One: Essays in Honor of Jonathan R. T. Hughes* (Greenwich, CT: JAI Press Inc., 1991), p. 254.

7. "La révolution industrielle manquée," p. 560.

8. Webster's Third New International Dictionary of the English Language Unabridged (Springfield, MA: G. & C. Merriam Co., 1968), p. 2062.

9. Arnold Toynbee, *Lectures on the Industrial Revolution in England; Popular Addresses, Notes, and Other Fragments* (London: Rivington, 1884). The edition I consulted is entitled *Toynbee's Industrial Revolution* (New York: Augustus M. Kelley, Publishers, 1969); it is a reprint of the original edition, with a new introduction by T. S. Ashton.

10. Cameron, "La révolution industrielle manquée," p. 559.

11. Toynbee, *Lectures*, p. 216, emphasis in the original. The quotation is from one of his "popular addresses" entitled "Are Radicals Socialists?" It is ironic that a scholar of the status of R. M. Hartwell argues strongly for the legitimacy of the term in view of its origins; see below, pp. 14-15.

12. See above, n. 2.

13. Beales, *Industrial Revolution*, p. 27.

14. H. L. Beales, in *Listener* (n. 2), p. 310, quoted in Lampard, *Industrial Revolution*, p. 1.

15. Wrigley to Cameron, 6 June 1990.

16. Svend Aage Hansen, *Early Industrialisation in Denmark* (Copenhagen: G. E. C. Gads Forlag, 1970), p. 10.

17. *Industrial Revolution*, p. 2.

18. Roderick Floud and Donald McCloskey, *The Economic History of Britain since 1700* (2nd ed. Cambridge: Cambridge University Press, 1994), vol. I, chap. 10.

19. A. E. Musson, *The Growth of British Industry* (New York: Holmes and Meier, 1978), pp. 8, 61, 167-8.

20. Maxine Berg and Pat Hudson, "Rehabilitating the industrial revolution," *Economic History Review*, 45 (Feb. 1992), 24-50.

21. Cf. Charles P. Kindleberger, *Historical Economics: Art or Science?* (Berkeley and Los Angeles: University of California Press, 1990), chap. 5, "The historical background: Adam Smith and the industrial revolution." (Originally published in Thomas Wilson and Andrew S. Skinner, eds., *The Market and the State: Essays in Honour of Adam Smith* [Oxford: Clarendon Press, 1976]).

22. Wrigley to Cameron, 13 May 1992.

23. C.K. Harley, "British industrialization before 1841: Evidence of slower growth during the industrial revolution," *Journal of Economic History*, 42 (June 1982), 267-89; N.F.R. Crafts, *British Economic Growth during the Industrial Revolution* (Oxford: Oxford University Press, 1985); N.F.R. Crafts, S.J. Leybourne, and T.C. Mills, "Trends and cycles in British industrial production, 1700-1913," *Journal of the Royal Statistical Society*, ser. A, 152 (1988), 43-60; id., "Britain," in Richard Sylla and Gianni Toniolo, eds., *Patterns of European Industrialization: The Nineteenth Century* (London and New York: Routledge, Chapman & Hall, 1991), pp. 109-52. In the never-ending cycle of revision R. V. Jackson has recently reworked the statistics of all of the above and concludes that "industrial activity grew faster and accelerated more sharply after 1780 than is apparent in either the Harley or the CLM estimates," but then admits that, "Like its predecessors, the index is conjectural and rests on a slight foundation"; "Rates of industrial growth during the industrial revolution," *Economic History Review*, 45 (Feb. 1992), 1-23; the last sentence is from the article summary.

24. Stephan Jay Gould, "The Most Unkindest Cut of All," *Natural History*, May 1992, p. 8.

25. Personal communication, 1 October 1991.

26. Richard Sylla, whose perceptive comments have helped me improve this paper in several places, adds "I think you need to explain why IR does 'positive harm'... and is not the harmless term that so many of your correspondents allege" (Sylla to Cameron, 20 May 1992). The statements by reputable scholars quoted on the previous page are the evidence. If we are misleading other reputable scholars — some of them economic historians, though not of England or Britain — what are we doing to our students, and the general public?

27. Patrick K. O'Brien, *Power with Profit: The State and the Economy, 1688-1815* (London, 1991).

28. Ibid., p. 25.

29. H. de B. Gibbins, *Industry in England, Historical Outlines* (10th ed., London, 1920), p.342.

30. W. W. Rostow, "The Take-off into Self-Sustained Growth," *Economic Journal*, 66 (1956), 25-48; id., *The Stages of Economic Growth: A Non-Communist Manifesto* (New York: Cambridge University Press, 1960; 2nd ed., 1971).

31. "The Early Phases of Industrialization in Russia: Afterthoughts and Counterthoughts," in W. W. Rostow, ed., *The Economics of Take-Off into Sustained Growth* (London: Macmillan & Co. Ltd., 1963), pp. 151-69.

32. Alexander Gerschenkron, *Economic Backwardness in Historical Perspective* (Cambridge, MA: The Belknap Press of Harvard University Press, 1962), pp. 353-4, n.1.

33. "Notes on the Take-off," in Rostow, ed., *Economics of Take-off*, pp. 23-43.

34. Simon Kuznets, *Economic Growth of Nations: Total Output and Production Structure* (Cambridge, MA: The Belknap Press of Harvard University Press, 1971), pp. 41-2.

35. Joel Mokyr, *The Lever of Riches: Technological Creativity and Economic Progress* (New York: Oxford University Press, 1990). See my review in *American Historical Review*, 96 (Oct. 1991), 1164-65.

36. Mokyr, *Lever*, p. 294.

37. R. M. Hartwell, "Was There an Industrial Revolution?" *Social Science History*, 14:4 (Winter 1990), 567-76; Cameron, "La révolution industrielle manquée."

38. "Was There an Industrial Revolution?" p. 567.

39. E. L. Jones, *Growth Recurring: Economic Change in World History* (Oxford: Clarendon Press, 1988).

40. Cf. E. A. Wrigley, *Continuity, Chance and Change: The Character of the Industrial Revolution in England* (Cambridge: Cambridge University Press, 1988), pp. 17-18.

41. Wrigley, *Continuity, Chance and Change*, p. 95.

42. Gould, "The Most Unkindest Cut," *Natural History, May* 1992, pp. 8, 10.

# 2

# Inertia and Industrial Change[1]

## Paul L. Robertson

### *INTRODUCTION*

One of the most persistent debates surrounding economic change is whether it is incremental or revolutionary in nature; whether, for instance, a period of change that lasted anywhere from seventy to one hundred years may be properly termed an industrial *revolution*.[2] Regardless of the terminology used, however, it is clear that technological transitions in industrialized economies have frequently been prolonged and uneven. Despite the early adoption of the steam engine in the cotton textile industry, for example, the switch to steam power was for many decades confined to a few sectors in Britain and only became general after 1870.[3] But the failure to adopt new technologies does not necessarily indicate stagnation. Although other sectors of the British economy retained traditional technologies and forms of organization well into the nineteenth century,[4] in many cases they underwent significant changes involving the *adaptation* of their existing technologies and organizational arrangements that, over time, led to significant growth in productivity in the period of early industrialization.[5]

Similarly, the 'climacteric' after 1870, when Britain's relative economic lead was eroded, was a period of unevenness in change. Although dominance in newer sectors such as organic chemicals, electrical products, and steel was secured by American or German producers, the British retained their lead in most of the older areas including textiles and the manufacture of textile machinery, shipbuilding, and electrical cable production. Again, as in the period of early industrialization, the older sectors - those in which Britain preserved its supremacy after 1870 - did not stagnate, because technological change grounded primarily in adaptations of existing technologies remained capable for many years of delivering improvements in technology.[6]

A further example of uneven and extended adjustment is the growing economic leadership of the United States in the 1920s which reflected an earlier adoption of capital-intensive technologies and greater efficiencies stemming from superior organization of production than occurred in Western Europe. Only after the Second World War did European firms begin on a large scale to adopt these innovations, and as late as 1960 Western European firms had, on average, not totally achieved the levels of output per worker that prevailed in the United States in 1925.[7] More recently, the poor performance of some established industries such as automobiles in the United States since the 1960s has derived in part from the retention of older technologies and organizational forms in America after they had been superseded in Japan.[8]

In the world of neoclassical economics, older, and apparently less-productive, technologies or organizational forms should not coexist for extended periods with newer technologies or ways of organization. Perfect knowledge and instantaneous adjustment should induce producers to adopt improvements as soon as they become available. But in practice, adjustment is frequently prolonged, perhaps for several decades. The spread of electrification took nearly a century, for instance, and today, more than 45 years after the invention of the transistor, new uses for microprocessors are being found at a rapid (and perhaps still accelerating) pace.[9]

In this chapter the reasons for prolonged adjustment are considered and a model is proposed to indicate circumstances under which the retention of seemingly outdated capital equipment or practices (which I term inertia) *may* be economically rational. Four hypotheses concerning inertia are then considered in the light of a variety of historical examples.

## INSTITUTIONS, CAPABILITIES, AND INERTIA

There is a range of explanations of inertia. One set is the "real" or, in the narrow sense, "economic" explanations that look to abstract variables like demand levels, factor endowments, and relative prices to justify the failure of some organizations to change. A second reason for inertia is simple incompetence, when managers are either too stupid or too idle to adopt desirable new methods. This is a popular explanation of Britain's relative economic decline after 1870[10] and is also consistent with recent comments on American businessmen attributed to Japanese leaders. Alternatively, there may be cognitive or informational problems. Managers may not have access to new knowledge or they may not recognize improvements that do not fit their pre- conceptions.[11] Another set of explanations for inertia relies on cultural incompatibilities. For example, Wiener[12] claims that the structure of British society since the end of the nineteenth century has discouraged entrepreneurship and innovation.

Here, we concentrate on the influence of institutional variables on inertia.[13] Institutions may either retard or encourage innovation. If the institutional structure is unsuited to a new technology and inert, change will be difficult to implement. When existing institutions are flexible or well-adapted to the requirements of an innovation, however, change will be accomplished relatively easily. As innovating firms may be affected by different sets of institutions, it is possible that one group may be impeded in its attempts to innovate while another group has a "head start" because it has already gained access to some of the necessary institutions for other reasons.

Overall, when it is present inertia exerts two principal influences on the ability of firms to cope with innovation. (1) Inertia is often a product of successful adaptation to earlier innovations, as a firm develops ways of operating that appear to be so well suited to its internal and external environment that it sees no reason to change. In many instances, this adaptation may prove so effective that the firm can retain a total cost advantage for a prolonged period despite using an outdated technology because it can still capitalize on its mastery of compatible support and ancillary operations, while firms adopting a new, and technically more efficient technology, are still wrestling with the expensive process of acquiring the endogenous and exogenous institutional backup necessary to gain full value from the innovation.[14]

(2) When inertia retards the learning process necessary to deal with a subsequent important innovation, however, firms that are otherwise in a position to make the eventual transition to a new technology may be so

slow in coming to grips with change that dominance shifts to new entrants who are unencumbered by prior developments, learn new adaptive procedures more quickly, and are able, therefore, largely to appropriate the market by the time the established firms have learned to cope with the innovation. The obstacle in this case may be termed "lockout", as leaders using the old technology find that they cannot successfully make the transition when there is a significant innovation.[15]

Routines and capabilities are at the heart of both of these aspects of inertia.

From the standpoint of the internal operations of a firm, the adoption of an innovation may be conceived of as a form of diversification. The Wrigley and Rumelt classifications of the degree of diversity or relatedness of intrafirm operations are based on the extent to which technological or marketing activities are shared across operations.[16] The adoption of a radically new product or process technology for an existing product would lead a firm into unfamiliar, albeit still related, territory, in the same way as would diversification into a new product which shared marketing or technological bases with other products of the firm. The ability of the firm to master such a change would then depend on whether it possessed the technical and organizational flexibility to cope with an extended range of activities.

Three decades ago, in what is arguably still the richest treatment of the subject, Edith Penrose outlined a number of conditions that might induce a firm to undertake a strategy of diversification, which can be extended to cover innovation. According to Penrose, firms have a tendency to acquire surplus quantities of both material and human resources. Firstly, because of indivisibilities, firms may obtain excess amounts of one or more inputs. Resources must often be purchased in bundles and, except in the relatively rare situations in which the inputs needed for the amount produced happen to coincide with the "least common multiple" of the bundles, there will be surpluses. Secondly, the efficiency of human resources tends to increase over time as personnel become more knowledgeable and more adept at dealing both with the external environment and with the administration of the firm itself.[17]

The firm has a clear incentive to make good use of these excess resources. The way in which it employs its surpluses, however, will vary according to the firm's strengths. Not only will the varieties of resources differ among firms, but many of the most important types of resources are heterogeneous. In particular, human resources involving entrepreneurship, management, or research are not standardized, rendering each firm unique because it has kinds and combinations of resources different from those of other firms.

Penrose believes that this heterogeneity of resources will have a strong endogenous influence on the strategy adopted since each firm should attempt to make the best use of its surpluses given the qualitative nature of its own strengths. While there may be a range of uses to which a particular combination of excess resources can be put, the firm will tend to choose those that fit most closely with the types of knowledge and scope of operations that have evolved from earlier experience because these are likely to prove most profitable.

Although her terminology differs, Penrose anticipated many of the most important ideas later elaborated by other writers. In particular, Richardson introduced the useful term *capabilities* to refer to the skills, experience, and knowledge that a firm possesses. He concludes that firms "would find it expedient, for the most part, to concentrate on similar activities," that is on those that require common capabilities.[18] Ansoff and Panzar and Willig employed a wider definition than Richardson of the attributes that firms may build on in choosing the scope of their activities. These include excess capacity in marketing, production, raw material procurement, and finance, as well as managerial or entrepreneurial knowledge, skills, and experience. For convenience, however, we will follow Teece in using "capabilities" to refer to all of these attributes.[19]

Another aspect of capabilities that has recently received a great deal of attention is organizational culture. In practice, not all organizations may be equally able to cope with change, as existing patterns of behavior involving both executives and subordinates may be resistant to change. Organizations develop collective habits or ways of thinking that can be altered only gradually. To the extent that a given culture is either flexible or consistent with a proposed change in product or process technology, the transition to the new regime will be relatively easy. If, however, the culture is incompatible with the needs posed by the change and is inflexible, the viability of the change will be threatened.[20]

Nelson and Winter have formulated an economic analogue of capabilities, including organizational culture. "Routines," as they put it, "are the skills of an organization."[21]  In the course of its development, a firm acquires a repertoire of rountines that derives from its activities over the years.  To the extent that these routines are efficient and difficult to come by, they are a most important asset, but they also induce inertia because they are difficult for the firm to change once in place.[22]

Teece discusses the positive aspects of such routines: That they may contribute to a capability that enables a firm to undertake new activities that are compatible with its current activities.[23]  Teece neglects the negative side of Nelson and Winter's analysis, however, and fails to note that the inflexibility, or inertia, induced by routines and the capabilities that they generate can raise to prohibitive levels the cost of adopting a new technology or entering new fields.  Such inertia can develop to the extent that existing rules are both hard to discard and inconsistent with types of change that might otherwise be profitable.

In adopting a product or process innovation, therefore, firms must look for a total-cost solution by weighing up possible increases in transaction costs caused by a departure from their existing capabilities and routines against savings or profitable marketing opportunities and routines against savings or profitable marketing opportunities brought about by the change in technology.  Moreover, the ensuing transaction costs may have two components, (1) those that derive from disruption of existing operations and (2) those that result from the need to learn a new set of capabilities appropriate to the new product or process technology.

Technological change, as we have shown, comes in a variety of forms that affect the likelihood of it being assimilated into existing firms.  First, it is necessary to distinguish between minor and radical changes.  A technological change may be characterized as "a bit-by-bit cumulative process until it is punctuated by a major advance."  In general, these frequent *minor* changes can be assimilated in passing, and characterize the equilibrium stage.  This is not true, however, of *major* innovations of the revolutionary stage of punctuated equilibrium,[24] which are "advances so significant that no increase in scale, efficiency, or design can make older technologies competitive [in direct cost terms] with the new technology."[25]  Assuming that the adoption of a major innovation is feasible, the speed of adjustment will depend on the compatibility between the capabilities required by the old and new technological regimes.  Some innovations are "competence destroying" whereas others are "competence enhancing" for particular organizations. Whereas major competence-enhancing innovations may, in time, be assimilated, the creation of entirely new organizations may be needed to deal with innovations that undermine the capabilities or competences of existing firms. Alternatively, there may be existing firms in other fields that are better able to cope with the innovation because it demands capabilities that, perhaps fortuitously, are compatible with their existing routines.[26]

## *LEARNING AND INERTIA*

Learning is the antidote to inertia because it allows organizations to switch paths by augmenting their routines and capabilities. Organizations that learn quickly, cheaply, and accurately therefore have a degree of flexibility that is denied to organizations that can only learn slowly or at great expense, or that cannot learn at all. Thus, while "[i]nertia is . . . a profoundly functional organizational characteristic in stable/predictable environments",[27] it is ultimately destructive when it impedes learning at times of significant change.

Stiglitz distinguishes between learning by doing and learning by learning. Under the familiar concept of learning by doing,[28] organizations improve their efficiency and effectiveness through experience. Stiglitz applies this notion to the learning process itself. As he explains,[29]

> Just as experience in production increases one's productivity in producing, so experience in learning may increase one's productivity in learning. One learns to learn, at least partly in the process of learning itself. . . . By specialization in learning, one may improve one's learning skills.

But learning is not an all-embracing process. Rather, it is localized in that learning about one field of study may not yield significant increases in an organization's ability to learn about other fields.[30] There may be some spillovers that result simply from the process of learning how to question, but specific knowledge about a technology in a given industry may be of little value in dealing with a particular innovation in the same industry but with unfamiliar characteristics.[31] Recently, Stiglitz's observations on learning by learning have received some support from

Kelly and Amburgey who show that prior experience in dealing with a similar type of change increases the chances of an organization coping successfully with subsequent changes, but experience in dealing with dissimilar changes does not.[32]

Some types of learning can also be picked up externally, by watching and benefiting from the experience of others. Learning by learning remains important, however, because some knowledge is tacit and cannot be verbalized and transferred to outsiders, while other knowledge is proprietary and not available to the public at large. The ability of an organization to overcome inertia by learning is therefore limited by the timing of the learning effort and the method of learning that is chosen. Both Spence and Silverberg, Dosi, and Orsenigo have shown through simulations that lack of learning presents substantial barriers to entry.[33]

In large part, this is because organizations can readily pick up knowledge in the public domain but will be less efficient than experienced competitors if they cannot tap their own sources of tacit and proprietary knowledge. As the only way that an organization can learn the latter[34] is through learning by doing, the later the organization enters a new field or adopts an innovation, the further behind it is likely to be in efficiency. In such cases, established firms faced with mastering an innovation may encounter barriers to entry in the same way as new entrants to the industry. They may therefore find it hard to make the transition from the old to the new technology if they delay for very long.

Cohen and Levinthal call the ability of a firm to pick up information from external sources (and thus to fend off inertia to a degree) its "absorptive capacity". They contend that an organization's absorptive capacity for external knowledge is a function of its existing knowledge. Thus organizations that already have some background in a given area may find it quicker and cheaper to acquire new related knowledge than do organizations with no prior experience in the area. Cohen and Levinthal point to basic, or generalized, R & D activities as an important way to improve a firm's chances of spreading its external nets widely in acquiring useful knowledge from its surrounding environment. But, as it is not feasible to have a basic background in all areas, the problem is still to determine which fields are likely to prove sufficiently fertile in the future to justify an investment in basic background knowledge now.[35] Firms that do not make the correct decisions ( that do not know how to learn what they specifically need to learn) may lose irrevocably. In the words of Cohen and Levinthal:[36]

> A firm without a prior technological base in a particular field may not be able to acquire one readily if absorptive capacity is cumulative. In addition a firm may be blind to new developments in fields in which it is not investing if its updating capability is low. Accordingly ... firms may not realize that they should be developing their absorptive capacity due to an irony associated with its valuation: the firm needs to have some absorptive capacity already to value it appropriately.

Furthermore, as Penrose noted, some organizations have better initial learning capabilities than others.[37] Each organization is unique and its ability to acquire the knowledge necessary to adopt a significant innovation successfully differs from that of existing or potential competitors. If the innovation is competence destroying, the inertia generated by mastery of an older technology may preclude the rapid acquisition of knowledge that will permit the transition. Competence-enhancing innovations, on the other hand, can benefit either existing firms or new entrants depending on whether the competences that are strengthened are related to or distinct from those associated with the old technology.

## THE POPULATION DYNAMICS OF MARKET DOMINANCE

As vital elements of internal learning are needed, first to determine which capabilities a change demands, and then to master them, inertia will be strong and the adoption of major competence- or capabilities-destroying innovations can be expected to be gradual. In the interim, the industry may be composed of two sets of firms, the representatives of the older technology who will gradually wither, and those of the new technology who, as will be shown, may or may not gain the momentum required to establish themselves permanently. The survival of the older technology rests on the mastery of appropriate capabilities by existing firms who have learned to make the most efficient use of their resources under existing conditions. If capabilities for the new technology have not yet been worked out, therefore, a prolonged period may follow in which the total cost of production of the representatives of the old technology is less than that of the newer because the transaction cost savings arising from the use of efficient routines more than offset the direct savings in production costs that can be attributed to the new technology.[38] In fact, under certain circumstances, it may pay firms to continue to invest in a dying technology even though they would incur an accounting loss as a result.[39]

But, within any given population of firms, the withering of the representatives of the old technology and their replacement by firms that have  adopted the innovation are not symmetrical processes.  This is because there may be competition *between* as well as *within* populations. It is conceivable that there may be different endowments of capabilities and other resources that make the firms in one population, for  example the  producers in  an  industry  in a particular country, better able to adopt the new technology than producers elsewhere.  An obvious example would be an endowment of some vital mineral that is highly localized, expensive to transport, and unnecessary under the old technological regime.  If an innovation rendered this mineral necessary, not only would firms using the old technology in locations distant from the mineral deposits be at a severe cost disadvantage if they innovated, but distant new entrants would also face a severe handicap.

Equally  importantly,  there  may  be  artificial differences among populations that lead to differential rates of success in adopting the new technology.   This could arise, for instance, if one nation had, for independent reasons, already invested in a set a capabilities needed for the efficient use of an innovation, say those associated with technical education, but other nations had not.  If this nation's firms were thus enabled to achieve rapid control over the new technology, they could potentially appropriate the innovation and gain a lasting market dominance.[40]

A second, and more pervasive, artificial means of gaining market dominance is through the use of tariffs.  Assume that, under an existing technology, production in an industry is controlled by firms in a single country who have gained an early lead.  These firms have used their cost advantages, based in large part on the efficient use of learned capabilities, to blanket domestic and export markets to such an extent that there are few foreign competitors.[41]   When a major new technology is developed that dramatically reduces direct costs of production, many of the existing firms are initially reluctant to adopt the innovation because their capabilities still give them an overall cost advantage. A few pioneers, however, venture into the new technology and slowly develop the capabilities necessary to use it at its most efficient level. After a period of time, the capabilities of the representatives of the old technology are no longer great enough to compensate for higher direct costs of production and these firms are obliged either to adopt the new technology belatedly (a risky and probably futile gesture[42]) or to quit the field.

In the meanwhile, a second country, which has not had a successful group of firms using the old technology, imposes a tariff (or equivalent trade barrier) to protect local firms that adopt the innovation. Because of the tariff, these firms do not have to compete against the foreign first movers whose mastery of capabilities associated with the old technology still gives them an advantage in the early stages of adoption. Furthermore, if the pioneering nation gives no tariff protection to its own producers, firms in the follower country are able to compete on equal, or nearly equal, terms with the representatives of both the old and new technologies in the pioneer's home market. If the market in the follower nation is large enough to accommodate available economies of scale, firms adopting the new technology there are able to move down their learning curves much faster than similar firms in the pioneering nation that face competition from imports as well as from the local firms that have retained the old technology. Under this scenario, it is entirely plausible that the adopters of the innovation in the follower nation are able to learn so much more quickly that they can appropriate the greater part of the market by the time the older firms in the pioneer nation finally succumb, and that the adopters of the innovation in the pioneer will have been relegated to a minor role or eliminated altogether.[43]

Nevertheless, the retention of the old technology by the pioneering firms may be rational. For example, a discounted cash flow analysis could show that the pay-off to "harvesting" the existing operation, by reducing investment and letting it run down to the point of extinction, is greater than that from shifting to a new technology because of the much higher profits to the old technology in the early years, when capabilities appropriate to the innovation are still under development. David gives a good example of harvesting in the defense of DC electrical power that

Edison mounted during the Battle of the Systems.[44] According to David, Edison was not being quixotic when he took elaborate, and sometimes bizarre, steps to contain the spread of an AC power system that even he must have known was superior in many ways. Edison needed funds for experimentation in new areas and had neither the patents nor the financial resources to enter AC transmission himself. What he really wanted to accomplish was an orderly transition that would permit him to liquidate his substantial investments in the DC technology at a good price so that he could get on with his new work. By resisting until the rotary converter was perfected, which allowed AC power to be converted to DC and thus ensured the viability of the existing DC network,[45] Edison was able to sell out at a greater profit than if he had either sold during the earlier period when the continued viability of DC was uncertain or shifted to AC as a follower. The diagram in Figure 1 illustrates graphically the possibility of harvesting and a consequent shift in leadership among firms. The solid lines are experience curves[46] for two different basic technologies for producing the same good. The downward slope of the curves derives not only from learning by doing, but from such factors as economies of scale and minor competence-enhancing innovations. Indeed, the curves are drawn on a double-log scale, which emphasizes that, in the early stages, relatively small increases in cumulative output lead to relatively large decreases in production costs, but after the product matures much larger increases in cumulative output are needed to generate the same absolute decreases in production costs.

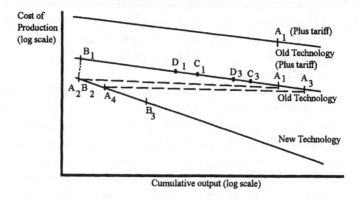

Figure 1

Initially, there are four firms employing the old technology: an experienced and relatively low-cost producer at $A_1$, an inexperienced and relatively high-cost producer at $B_1$, and two intermediate firms at $C_1$ and $D_1$. Firms A, C, and D are in one nation and firm B in another. Assume now that there is a major innovation that, if implemented, shifts a producer to a new and lower experience curve.[47] Both firm A and firm B have equal capabilities to adopt the innovation and would therefore be at the same point on the new experience curve $(A_2, B_2)$. Firm B would find the innovation desirable and adopt it, but firm A would face inertia because it is already producing at far lower cost. Not only would firm A endure lower profits if it adopted the innovation, but it might even face extinction if other domestic producers using the established technology (Firms C and D) declined to innovate and instead engaged in stiff price competition. Because of its higher initial cost structure, firm B, of course, would not be able to survive during this transition phase unless it were somehow insulated from competition. This, however, is perfectly feasible if B is in a different country and can be protected by a tariff.

After a period of time (years, or perhaps even decades) in which both firms have gained experience on their respective curves, A will have moved to $A_3$ and B to $B_3$, at which points their production costs are equal. But B's costs will be falling faster. If firm A wishes to change to the new technology now, however, the best it can hope for is to enter at $A_4$ because, although it will have access to publicly-available knowledge concerning the innovation, A will not be able to tap the tacit and proprietary knowledge that firm B has gained. C and D will be at a similar disadvantage. Thus, the leading firms when the old technology was dominant will become the followers after the new technology takes hold because they will always have less knowledge and therefore relatively higher costs if they do not innovate initially at the same time as Firm B. Under such circumstances, if the transition period is long and the initial cost differential high, the rational course for firms A, C, and D is to harvest their investments by collecting higher profits over the period of transition even though the eventual result is to become followers or perhaps be driven from the industry when the innovative technology has become established.

The same basic mechanisms can operate either for entire national industries, as illustrated here, or for leading firms within a particular national economy that are less well-equipped than some domestic competitors to cope with a significant innovation.[48]

The evolutionary explanation presented here should be distinguished from the now-familiar notion of technological lock-in.[49] In the broadest sense, we are, of course, arguing for a kind of lock-in. Because of the continuing possibility of learning along a particular technological or organizational path, there are, in effect, transaction costs impeding movement to a new path. This is very much a matter of path-dependency. But the cause of the lock-in is not (necessarily) increasing returns arising from the presence of network externalities or from fixed costs in complementary activities. Rather, the dependence on path arises simply from the persistence of routines. In a neoclassical world of fully informed actors, one needs a specific nonconvexity to achieve lock in. In a more believable world of ignorance and bounded rationality, the following of rules — as a necessary tool of cognition — is enough to do the trick.

## FOUR HYPOTHESES

The analysis we present suggests a class of explanations that help to predict which firms will appropriate the benefits from an innovation. Here, we illustrate four hypotheses with a variety of historical and modern examples.

*Hypothesis 1.* A firm that is adept at employing an existing technology will be less likely to adopt a new technology that is incompatible with its current capabilities than will a firm that is less adept at using the existing technology, even if the new technology offers the prospect of long-run increases in profits for both firms.

This is the hypothesis with which we are most concerned. It is illustrated in Britain after 1870 by electricity generation and electrical machinery and, perhaps most paradigmatically, by cotton textiles. The relatively stunted development of the electrical products industry in Britain is a reflection of an older legacy, in this case in the use of gas for lighting and of steam, pneumatic, and hydraulic tools in industry. The electrical-machinery branch of the industry was especially weak in Britain, but British firms had trouble in competing even in simple items. Imports of electric lamps in 1908 were nearly as large as total domestic production in 1907, and imports of incandescent light bulbs were half again as large as domestic production. The older telegraphic equipment branch, and in particular cable manufacturing, was somewhat stronger, but in general the British produced less sophisticated varieties of equipment for home consumption and for export to the underdeveloped areas of the globe.[50]

In large part, the failure of the British to attain greater success in electrical products manufacturing can be traced to the slow adoption of electricity for lighting, traction, and power purposes in the United Kingdom. Many of the reasons for this were political. By 1913, there were only a few large generating stations in both Chicago and Berlin, serving centralized power and light systems in each city. By contrast, "Greater London had sixty-five electrical utilities, seventy generating stations averaging only 5,285 kw. in capacity, forty-nine different types of supply systems, ten different frequencies, thirty-two voltage levels for transmission and twenty-four for distribution, and about seventy different methods of charging and pricing."[51] This failure to consolidate was based on legislation that gave each municipality effective control over both public and private supply within its boundaries. Moreover, as late as 1912, the majority of electrical power used in Britain was actually generated by users rather than purchased from generating stations, further increasing the fragmentation of supply.[52]

In several important respects, however, the slow adoption of electrical power can be traced directly to the existing provision of other types of power in Britain which were not matched by developments in the U.S.A. or Germany. In contrast to the United States, inexpensive gas lighting was available in many British cities before electric lighting was feasible. Even in the early years of the twentieth century, electrical power was more expensive relative to gas in Britain than in the U.S.A.[53] The use of electricity for industrial purposes in Britain was retarded in two ways by existing structures. Many firms were already using steam or other forms of power, and the slow rate of expansion of the economy left less scope than in Germany or the U.S.A. for the construction of entirely new plants that could be laid out to make the best use of electrical power rather than, as in the past, built around a central steam power plant that optimized the use of shafts and belting but did not take advantage of the flexibility that electricity could provide. In addition, the structure of the economy itself reduced the spread of electrification since cotton textiles and coal mining, which were of greater importance in Britain, were less susceptible to conversion to electrical power than many fast growing industries in America and Germany.[54]

Nonetheless, it remains the case that the institutions retarding change in the electrical industries were in large part quasi-exogenous governmental ones. For this reason, the cotton textile industry provides a purer example in which the principal "institutions" retarding change were the endogenously developed skills and capabilities of firms and workers.

Mass and Lazonick have recently provided a thorough summary of the debate on the British cotton industry in which they have been prominent participants.[55] Their analysis of the sources of British dominance in the industry draws in most respects on a set of facts that are not broadly in dispute, even if these authors place their own interpretation on them. The facts are these. Combining their early capabilities in the premechanical textile trades with mechanical innovativeness, the British developed a set of productive capacities in mass-produced cotton textiles ahead of any other nation. These capabilities arose in an extremely decentralized manner that partook of Marshallian external economies. Among these capabilities was a highly developed market in cotton fiber. Technologically, these capabilities came to center around the self-acting mule and the power loom, which guided incremental innovation and conditioned the skills of the labor force. Although the exact productivity figures may be in dispute, it is clear that these competences in the British economy allowed the industry to follow an experience curve like those in Figure 1. And Britain was further along this curve than all others.

In the 1890s, however, a new technological paradigm emerged with the development of the automatic loom by Draper in the U.S.A. This device allowed for higher throughput and required less-skilled operatives. In order to benefit from its advantages, however, one needed yarn more resistant to breakage (for a given count) than that produced by the mule. The ring frame, which also required less labor skill and which, quite rationally, was little used in skill-rich Britain, thus became an important complement to the automatic loom, as it produced the needed stronger yarn. Coupled with new techniques for blending grades of cotton for ring spinning, the combination of the automatic loom and the ring offered a technological trajectory different from the one on which Britain had embarked. The U.S.A., Japan, and others speedily adopted these techniques behind tariff walls. In the Mass and Lazonick account,[56] Japan was particularly adept at honing the labor skills complementary to this new technology. And after World War I, that country led a pack of low-wage countries — all of which depended on ring spinning and automatic looms — in a successful assault on British dominance. Britain attempted belatedly to adopt the new technologies, but found itself perennially behind on the experience curve.

Hypothesis 1 is also consistent with the experiences of a number of modern firms in mature industries that face a low level of price elasticity. There is little incentive for established firms to sponsor innovations if lower prices (or *de facto* lower prices as when extra longevity more than compensates for higher sticker prices) will lead to decreased total revenue as a result of inelastic demand. Innovation will be favored, however, by new entrants which stand to gain market share at the expense of existing concerns if they can exploit better product or process technologies. This helps to explain, for example, why it was Wilkinson Sword rather than Gillette that introduced stainless steel razor blades, and why American tire manufacturers were reluctant to produce the long-life steel-belted radial designs promoted by Michelin.[57]

The deterioration of the position of American automobile manufacturers in recent decades is also a function of inertia, in this case in the face of important changes in process technologies by Japanese firms. These changes, which to a large extent involve organizational innovations, are based on a total rethinking of the nature of mass production in the light of improvements in quality monitoring mechanisms in recent decades. By linking low costs in mass production to high quality output — in contrast to the Taylor-Ford premise that there is a trade-off between cost and quality — Japanese automobile manufacturers have been able simultaneously to gain a significant advantage in costs of production and a marketing advantage sustained by a reputation for high quality. Despite eventual adjustments by U.S. and European automobile producers, it appeared for a time that a substantial share of the market had been permanently ceded to the Japanese.[58]

*Hypothesis 2.* If there is no major innovation in an industry, the incumbent leaders will probably retain leadership.

It is well-established that firms that gain market dominance are likely to hold onto it unless there is a major technological change.[59] To reverse the examples cited under Hypothesis 1, the following firms all held market leadership under relatively stable conditions for several decades until challenged by major innovations: Gillette in razor blades; Goodyear, Firestone, and Uniroyal in tires; and General Motors, Ford, and Chrysler in automobiles. Similar examples of long-term dominance in mature markets apply in typewriters, electrical products, and many other industries.

In the late nineteenth and early twentieth centuries, British industries were also able to retain their market dominance when there were no major innovations, even when firms in related industries were being supplanted by foreign competition. British cottons maintained their dominance of diverse international markets until well into the twentieth century, particularly in piece goods. Imports failed to penetrate the home market and, despite increased foreign competition, there was seldom any absolute decrease in exports except in the case of yarns.[60] In engineering the older sectors such as cotton-textile machinery also kept their international dominance. The ring frame may have been a competence-destroying innovation from the point of view of the British spinners, but it was competence-enhancing from the point of view of the machinery firms, who strengthened their position through production.[61] The market for British locomotives and rolling stock held up as well, especially in the Empire and South America. In boilers and prime movers, Britain exported more than the United States or Germany in 1913, and in agricultural machinery, more than Germany.[62]

*Hypothesis 3.* If there is a major innovation, but it is highly compatible with existing capabilities (i.e., it is competence-enhancing), the incumbents will probably retain leadership.

In their discussion of the automobile industry, Abernathy and Clark[63] list a number of innovations that were highly significant but nevertheless competence-enhancing. Moreover, they note that, since a firm can have importance competences in several areas, an innovation that is destructive of one competence can bolster others. Thus the introduction of the inexpensive V-8 engine and steel bodies eroded some of the technical competences of major firms but allowed them to enhance their existing marketing competences.

A further example in Britain is the advent of the steel hull for oceangoing merchant vessels in the 1870s. This innovation reduced hull weights by as much as 15 per cent in comparison to iron hulls and offered improved strength and flexibility. It was, however, a change that fitted in well with the capabilities of both existing shipbuilders and steel makers in Britain. By the 1890s, virtually all major ships were built of steel and Britain had retained its leadership.[64]

*Hypothesis 4.* If the innovation is, for all practical purposes, entirely new (that is, there is no significant existing industry), then the benefits of the innovation will be appropriated by the population of firms that already has the best access to the most important relevant capabilities. These may be either entirely new firms or incumbent firms in related fields.

EMI's experience with the CT scanner illustrates the problems a technical pioneer can encounter if it does not possess complementary capabilities.[65] Although EMI had the technical sophistication to develop the scanner, the device required a higher standard of training, servicing, and support than hospitals had needed until then. EMI was not in a position to provide these services, but GE and Technicare, two firms that were similarly sophisticated in electronics, were also established medical suppliers. As Teece reports the final result:[66]

> By 1978 EMI had lost market share leadership to Technicare, which was in turn quickly overtaken by GE. In October 1979, Godfrey Houndsfield of EMI shared the Nobel prize for invention of the CT scanner. Despite this honor, and the public recognition of its role in bringing this medical breakthrough to the world, the collapse of its scanner business forced EMI in the same year into the arms of a rescuer, Thorn Electrical Industries, Ltd. GE subsequently acquired what was EMI's scanner business from Thorn for what amounted to a pittance. . . Though royalties continued to flow to EMI, the company had failed to capture the lion's share of the profits generated by the innovation it had pioneered and successfully commercialized.

Mitchell[67] has since shown that incumbent firms with related capabilities in other branches of medical diagnostic imaging are also more likely to enter new fields in imitation of pioneers than are incumbent firms without related capabilities.

Another early example of Hypothesis 4 is the substitution of iron hulls and steam propulsion for wooden-hulled sailing vessels around 1850.[68] These changes thoroughly undermined the distinctive competence of North American shipbuilders, which lay in their sources of cheap timber, and instead placed a premium on access to iron plates and steam boilers, both fields in which Britain had already established the basis for leadership. Similarly, Britain developed a strong bicycle industry at the end of the nineteenth century, based in large part on the country's strong external economies in the manufacture of mechanical parts.[69]

In other cases, late Victorian and Edwardian Britain did not possess the right capabilities to capture the benefits of wholly new innovations. In some electrical and chemical industries, for example, countries with systems of technical education more developed than that in Britain were in a better position to appropriate the benefits of innovations that relied on the use of technically-trained labor. As in the case of other types of education, it was difficult to align the costs and returns from technical training and, as the government and potential students were less willing to pay in Britain than in some other countries, technical education there was stunted.[70] Firms in Britain, which could rely on their initial capabilities arising from a stock of skilled labor, were confirmed in their reliance on manual skills and became less able as technologies evolved to make the transition to more highly technical routines. This, in turn, determined not only the work practices of firms in older industries but helped to steer British entrepreneurs away from industries where technical knowledge was vital because they knew that suitable workers would be expensive to hire. In Germany, the U.S.A., and Switzerland, a readily expandable pool of technically-educated workers was already available when the electrical and chemical industries began to take hold. As these foreign firms had many of the necessary capabilities for innovation on hand before the innovations were actually adopted, they were able to learn other routines much more quickly and to seize market share before British firms could become meaningful competitors.

The model presented here is intended as only one explanation among many for the coexistence of a variety of competing technologies and organizational forms even in nations at similar stages of development. Other factors such as deficiencies in real resources, limited markets, labor intransigence, or entrepreneurial failure may also have been important factors influencing technological choice. Furthermore, the model does not, at first glance, explain some of the more interesting cases of inertia. For example, one appealing working hypothesis is that the existence of strong pig and wrought iron industries in Britain before the advent of Bessemer steel would have retarded vertical integration and put British steel manufacturers at a disadvantage in comparison to integrated German and American competitors who could convert hot pig iron directly, without reheating. Elbaum has pointed out, however, that Bessemer firms in Britain were as highly integrated as those elsewhere and that the problems can be traced to the subsequent early conversion of the British to open hearth technology at a time when economies of scale offered by the Siemens-Martin process were too small to justify vertical integration. On this reading, the origins of fragmentation were technical and cannot be easily traced to an early start and subsequent inertia.[71] Also, although (as our analysis would predict) German steelmakers seem to have benefited from having tariff protection at a time when their competitors did not,[72] the effects of cartels and control by the banks may have been more ambiguous. Because separate cartels were organized for each major stage of production, they created an artificial barrier between the pig iron and steel producers that, in at least one important case, inhibited vertical integration.[73] Before a firmer conclusion can be reached, more detailed studies of the steel and iron industries in the three countries will be needed. It is nevertheless clear that institutional factors, especially those embodied in capabilities and routines, can both improve the ability of a firm to exploit an existing technology and make it more difficult to innovate by generating an inertia that is hard to overcome. Not all organizations are equally well equipped to adapt to change, however, and firms that are adept at using an existing technology may have fewer of the capabilities required to cope with innovation than a new entrant or a firm that was less successful under the old regime. When this is true, a change in industrial leadership is probable, with the hitherto dominant firms becoming either followers or leaving the industry altogether because they are no longer competitive. From this perspective, the slow and uneven pace of technological change across sectors and among nations since the middle of the eighteenth century becomes a little easier to understand.

1. An earlier version of this paper, co-authored with Richard N. Langlois, was presented at the Boulder meeting of the Economic History Association in September, 1991. I am grateful to Dick Langlois for his many substantive comments and suggestions and, in particular, for his contribution to the section on the cotton textile industry. I am also grateful for comments on the earlier version by Tim Hatton, Paul Johnson, John Lyons, and Bernard Elbaum. Responsibility for any errors, of course, remains mine.

2. Rondo Cameron, "Misunderstanding the Industrial Revolution", elsewhere in this volume; David S. Landes, "Introduction: On Technology and Growth", in Patrice Higonnet, David S. Landes, and Henry Rosovsky, eds., *Favorites of Fortune: Technology, Growth, and Economic Development since the Industrial Revolution*, Cambridge, Ma., 1991, p. 13.

3. A. E. Musson, 'Industrial Motive Power in the United Kingdom, 1800-1870', *Economic History Review*, vol. XXIX, 3, 1976, pp. 415-439.

4. By organization, I mean both internal firm organization and market-based relationships between producers and their suppliers and customers.

5. Donald McCloskey, "The Industrial Revolution 1780-1860: A Survey", in Roderick Floud and Donald McCloskey, eds., *The Economic History of Britain since 1700*, vol. 1, Cambridge, 1981, pp. 115-117; Maxine Berg and Pat Hudson, "Rehabilitating the Industrial Revolution", *Economic History Review*, vol. XLV, 1992, pp. 34-37; Pat Hudson, *The Industrial Revolution*, London, Edward Arnold, 1992, ch. 4.

6. Recently, several writers of whom the most prolific is William Lazonick, have argued that the tendency of British producers to adapt existing technologies rather than adopt new ones has been one of the principal causes of Britain's relatively poor economic record since the 1870s. William Lazonick, *Competitive Advantage on the Shop Floor*, Cambridge, Ma., 1990; *idem., Business Organization and the Myth of the Market Economy*, Cambridge, 1991; Bernard Elbaum and William Lazonick, eds., *The Decline of the British Economy*, Oxford, 1986.

7. Edward F. Denison, *Why Growth Rates Differ*, Washington, 1967; Richard R. Nelson and Gavin Wright, "The Rise and Fall of American Technological Leadership: The Postwar Era in Historical Perspective", *Journal of Economic Literature*, vol. XXX, 1992, pp. 1931-1964. See also, H.T. Johnson, Ch. 7 below, for an accounting perspective.

8. The literature on this subject has become enormous in recent years. See, for example, Michael L. Dertouzos, Richard K. Lester, and Robert M. Solow, *Made in America: Regaining the Productivity Edge*, Cambridge, MA., 1989.

9. Paul A. David, "The Dynamo and the Computer: An Historical Perspective on the Modern Productivity Paradox", *American Economic Review*, vol. 80, no. 2, 1990, pp. 355-361.

10. Derek H. Aldcroft and Harry W. Richardson, *The British Economy 1870-1939*, London, 1969.

11. Connie J. G. Gersick, "Revolutionary Change Theories: A Multilevel Exploration of the Punctuated Change Paradigm", *Academy of Management Review*, vol. 16, 1991, p. 18.

12. M. J. Wiener, *English Culture and the Decline of the Industrial Spirit, 1850-1980*, Cambridge, 1981.

13. Although general cultural variables such as "national character" are also institutions in the sense meant here, they are not considered in this chapter because of the difficulties in establishing criteria and finding usable data.

14. Michael T. Hannan and John Freeman, *Organizational Ecology*, Cambridge, MA, 1989.

15. Wesley M. Cohen and Daniel A. Levinthal, "Absorptive Capacity: A New Perspective on Learning and Innovation", *Administrative Science Quarterly*, vol. 35, 1990, p. 137.

16. Bruce R. Scott, "The Industrial State: Old Myths and New Realities", *Harvard Business Review*, vol. 51, 1973, pp. 133-48; Richard P. Rumelt, *Strategy, Structure, and Economic Performance*, Boston, 1974.

17. Edith T. Penrose, *The Theory of the Growth of the Firm*, Oxford, 1959.

18. G. B. Richardson, "The Organisation of Industry", *Economic Journal*, vol. 82, 1972, p. 895.

19. H. Igor Ansoff, *Corporate Strategy*, Harmondsworth, 1965; J. C. Panzar and R. D. Willig, "Economies of Scope", *American Economic Review*, vol. 71, 1981, pp. 268-72; David J. Teece, "Economies of Scope and the Scope of the Enterprise", *Journal of Economic Behavior and Organization*, vol. 1, 1980, pp. 223-47.

20. John P. Kotter and James L. Heskett, *Corporate Culture and Performance*, New York, 1992; Paul L. Robertson, "Economies of Scope, Organizational Culture, and the Choice of Diversification Strategies", Economics and Management Working Paper No. 2/1990, Department of Economics and Management, University College, University of New South Wales; Richard N. Langlois, "Transaction-Cost Economics in Real Time", *Industrial and Corporate Change*, vol. 1, 1992, pp. 99-127; Colin Camerer and Ari Vepsalainen, "The Economic Efficiency of Corporate Culture", *Strategic Management Journal*, vol. 9, special issue, 1988, pp. 115-126.

21. R. R. Nelson and S. G. Winter, *An Evolutionary Theory of Economic Change*, Cambridge, Ma., 1982, p. 124. Note that *routines* refer to what an organization actually does, while *capabilities* include what it may do if its resources are reallocated. Thus a firm's routines are a subset of its capabilities that influence but do not fully determine what the firm is competent to achieve.

22. Moses Abramovitz makes a similar point at the level of the national economy. "Catching Up, Forging Ahead, and Falling Behind", *Journal of Economic History*,

vol. XLVI, 1986, pp. 402-405.

23. David J. Teece, "Towards an Economic Theory of the Multiproduct Firm", *Journal of Economic Behavior and Organization*, vol. 3, 1982, pp. 39-63.

24. For a general discussion of punctuated equilibrium, see Gersick, "Revolutionary Change Theories".

25. Michael L. Tushman and Philip Anderson, "Technological Discontinuities and Organizational Environments", *Administrative Science Quarterly*, vol. 31, 1986, p. 441.

26. *Ibid.*, pp. 439-465.

27. Michael L. Tushman and Elaine Romanelli, "Organizational Evolution: A Metamorphosis Model of Convergence and Reorientation", in L. L. Cummings and B. M. Staw, eds., *Research in Organizational Behavior*, vol. 7, 1985, p. 195.

28. Devendra Sahal, *Patterns of Technological Innovation*, Reading, Ma., 1981, pp. 108-110.

29. Joseph E. Stiglitz, "Learning to Learn, Localized Learning and Technological Progress", in Partha Dasgupta and Paul Stoneman, eds., *Economic Policy and Technological Performance*, Cambridge, 1987, p. 130.

30. *Ibid.*, pp. 126-30.

31. From our standpoint, Stiglitz seems to reverse the time dimension involved in change. He writes, for example, that "the basic concept of 'weaving' is involved in virtually all textile production, but much of the technical knowledge associated with modern automated factory production is inapplicable to hand-loom weaving." *Ibid.*, p. 127. It seems far more relevant, however, that the knowledge of the hand-loom weavers was not readily transferable to later technologies.

32. Dawn Kelly and Terry L. Amburgey, "Organizational Inertia and Momentum: A Dynamic Model of Strategic Change", *Academy of Management Journal*, vol. 34, 1991, p. 606.

33. A. Michael Spence, "The Learning Curve and Competition", *Bell Journal of Economics*, vol. 12, 1981, pp. 49-70; Gerald Silverberg, Giovanni Dosi, and Luigi Orsenigo, "Innovation, Diversity and Diversion: A Self-Organisation Model", *Economic Journal*, vol. 98, 1988, pp. 1032-1054.

34. This is particularly true of tacit knowledge since proprietary knowledge may be obtained through industrial espionage or other surreptitious methods.

35. Cohen and Levinthal, "Absorptive Capacity"; *idem.*, "Innovation and Learning: The Two Faces of R & D", *Economic Journal*, vol. 99, 1989, pp. 569-96.

36. "Absorptive Capacity", p. 138.

37. Penrose, *Growth of the Firm,* p. 150.

38. Hannan and Freeman, *Organizational Ecology*, ch. 4.

39. Ming-Je Tang, "An Economic Perspective on Escalating Commitment", *Strategic Management Journal*, vol. 9, special issue, 1988, pp. 79-92.

40. Abramovitz, "Catching Up", p. 388.

41. Although somewhat exaggerated, this is a fair description of Britain's position following the Napoleonic Wars.    David S. Landes, *The Unbound Prometheus: Technological Change and Industrial Development in Western Europe from 1750 to the Present*, Cambridge, 1969, ch. 3.

42. A number of studies all indicate that the ability of existing firms to adjust to radical product or process innovation is highly limited.  Arnold C. Cooper and Dan Schendel, "Strategic Responses to Technological Threats", *Business Horizons*, February, 1976, pp. 61-69; Richard N. Foster, "Timing Technological Transitions", in Mel Horwitch, ed., *Technology in the Modern Corporation: A Strategic Perspective*, New York, 1986; Tushman and Anderson, 'Technological Discontinuities'.

43. Tariffs are only one means that a late mover can use to assist its firms in achieving control over a major innovation.  Other tools include regulations that make it difficult for foreign firms to become established in the follower nations, as is alleged to happen in Japan, the use of "safety" regulations to discriminate against imports, and campaigns to encourage local customers, especially governments, to buy locally-produced goods.

44. Paul A. David, "The Hero and the Herd in Technological History; Reflections on Thomas Edison and the Battle of the Systems", in Patrice Higonnet, David S. Landes, and Henry Rosovsky, eds., *Favorites of Fortune: Technology, Growth, and Economic Development since the Industrial Revolution*, Cambridge, Ma., 1991, pp. 72-119.

45. DC power was still supplied in sections of major cities at least as late as the 1960s.

46. Derek F. Abell and John S. Hammond, *Strategic Market Planning*, Englewood Cliffs, N.J., 1979.

47. In fact, an alternative definition of a major innovation is one that requires a shift to a different experience curve since minor innovations are among the factors that contribute to a movement down a particular curve.

48. In the initial stages, before the necessary capabilities to deal with the innovation have been developed and total costs are higher for innovators than for users of the older technology, preferential government policies would probably not be available for innovators in the same economy as the current leaders under the earlier technological regime.  Other devices to "protect" the innovators would be possible, however, such as the cross-subsidization of innovating divisions by other parts of diversified firms.

49. Paul A. David, "Clio and the Economics of QWERTY", *American Economic Review*, vol. 75, 1985, pp. 332-337; Thorstein Veblen, *Imperial Germany*, New York, 1915, pp. 126-127.

50. A. S. Byatt, *The British Electrical Industry 1875-1914*, Oxford, 1979;

*idem.*, "Electrical Products", in Derek H. Aldcroft, ed., *The Development of British Industry and Foreign Competition 1875-1914*, London, 1968, pp. 238-273.

51. Thomas P. Hughes, *Networks of Power: Electrification in Western Society 1880-1930*, Baltimore, 1983, p. 227.

52. Byatt, *British Electrical Industry*, ch. 6; Hughes, *Networks of Power*, pp. 227-238, 249-250.

53. Byatt, *British Electrical Industry*, p. 24.

54. *Ibid.*, chs. 3-5.

55. William Mass and William Lazonick, "The British Cotton Industry and International Competitive Advantage: The State of the Debates", *Business History*, vol. 32, 1990, pp. 9-65.

56. For alternative views, see the following works: Lars G. Sandberg, *Lancashire in Decline*, (Columbus, 1974); and, in particular, Gary R. Saxonhouse and Gavin Wright, "New Evidence on the Stubborn English Mule and the Cotton Industry, 1878-1920", *Economic History Review*, vol. XXXVII, 1984, pp. 507-19; and *idem.*, "Stubborn Mules and Vertical Integration: The Disappearing Constraint", *Economic History Review*, vol. XL, 1987, p. 87-94.

57. Although Michelin was an established tire manufacturer in Europe, it had an insignificant share of the U.S. market and, like a new entrant to the field in general, had little to lose if the innovation were rejected in America but a great deal to gain if it were successful.

58. James P. Womack, Daniel T. Jones, and Daniel Roos, *The Machine that Changed the World*, New York, 1990; Michael J. Smitka, *Competitive Ties: Subcontracting in the Japanese Automotive Industry*, New York, 1991.

59. Marvin B. Lieberman and David B. Montgomery, "First-Mover Advantages", *Strategic Management Journal*, vol. 9, special issue, 1988, pp. 41-58.

60. R. E. Tyson, "The Cotton Industry", in Derek H. Aldcroft, ed., *The Development of British Industry and Foreign competition 1875-1914*, London, 1968, pp. 100-127.

61. Saxonhouse and Wright, "New Evidence".

62. S. B. Saul, "The Engineering Industry", in Derek H. Aldcroft, ed., *The Development of British Industry and Foreign Competition 1875-1914*, London, 1968, pp. 186-237.

63. William J. Abernathy and Kim B. Clark, "Innovation: Mapping the Winds of Creative Destruction", *Research Policy*, vol. 14, 1985, pp. 3-22.

64. Sidney Pollard and Paul Robertson, *The British Shipbuilding Industry, 1870-1914*, Cambridge, Ma., 1979.

65. David J. Teece, "Profiting from Technological Innovation: Implications for Integration, Collaboration, Licensing, and Public Policy", *Research Policy*, vol. 15, 1986, pp. 285-305.

66. *Ibid.*, pp. 298-299.

67. Will Mitchell, "Whether and When? Probability and Timing of Incumbents' Entry into Emerging Industrial Subfields", *Administrative Science Quarterly*, vol. 34, 1989, pp. 208-230.

68. Pollard and Robertson, *British Shipbuilding*.

69. A. E. Harrison, "The Competitiveness of the British Cycle Industry", *Economic History Review*, vol. XXII, 1969, pp. 287-303.

70. Paul L. Robertson, "Employers and Engineering Education in Britain and the United States, 1890-1914", *Business History*, vol. XXIII, 1981, pp. 42-58.

71. Bernard Elbaum, "The Steel Industry before World War I", in Elbaum and Lazonick, *Decline of the British Economy*, pp. 54-55.

72. Steven B. Webb, "Tariffs, Cartels, Technology, and Growth in the German Steel Industry, 1879 to 1914", *Journal of Economic History*, vol. XL, 1980, pp. 309-329.

73. P. Barrett Whale, *Joint Stock Banking in Germany*, London, 1930, pp. 53, 62.

# 3

# Organization on the Periphery?:
## Market Restrictions and Workplace Control in Trenton, New Jersey's Sanitary Pottery Industry, 1900-1929[1]

## Marc Stern

Late nineteenth and early twentieth-century America witnessed momentous economic changes as manufacturers attempted to create, serve, and control an emerging national economy. Mergers established large, vertically integrated corporations that dominated many industries, mechanized production, and standardized products to cut unit costs and increase their market share. Most increased throughput, the speed and volume of the flow of goods through the production process, driving down unit costs. Vertical integration of resource acquisition and product distribution further reduced transaction costs. "Managed" firms and markets partially replaced raw-edged competition. Price leadership, product competition, and brand loyalty increasingly supplanted price competition. The survivors--many failed--heralded a new, oligopolistic industrial environment. Business historian Alfred D. Chandler, Jr., stresses the role of markets, technology, and federal antitrust policy in this process. At the same time, he all but ignores labor-management relations as an aspect of these changes.[2]

Chandler acknowledges, however, that these large, vertically-integrated mass production firms did not dominate every industry. Small, owner-managed firms remained important in industries that did not move into mass production. Technological changes provided a crucial precondition to shifts in managerial and corporate organization.

Following on Chandler's argument, historian Thomas McCraw analyzes the unoligopolized fields. Unlike "core" oligopolized industries such as oil, steel, or cigarette manufacture, these "peripheral" sectors remained locked into cycles of competition and the limitations imposed by antitrust laws.[3]

In recent years, Philip Scranton and others have shown that these "peripheral" industries remained vital to economic development during the early twentieth century, despite their lack of vertical integration and mechanization. Various "paths to profit and accumulation," notes Scranton, coexisted, and many trades prospered by retaining productive flexibility and "batch" production. Short runs of specialized goods worked to order or in anticipation of short-term demand often defied mechanization and the deskilling of the trade. Small to medium-sized family firms and partnerships dominated batch-oriented industries, though many large companies also retained this system. Localized geographic centers of specialized production geared to the availability of raw materials, support services, skilled labor pools, and market connections often emerged. Significantly, Scranton, unlike Chandler and McCraw, stresses the central role of labor-capital relations in analyzing these batch-oriented, skill-intensive trades.[4]

Bulk manufacturers, on the other hand, prospered by making staple goods for sale from inventory. Some of these products were intermediate, standardized components that served as parts of finished goods. Anticipation of demand and easy substitution of specific articles and grades of work led firms to maintain warehouses for rapid response to orders. But even here, companies avoided vast inventories. Bulk-oriented firms made goods in large quantities although many still relied on skilled handwork which left considerable power in labor's hands. They were, Scranton notes, forced to innovate to cut their costs.[5]

Batch and bulk shops remained within competitive market structures, but did not lack alternatives to price competition. Firms--and trade associations--sometimes divided markets at established prices by type and grade of good until high profits lured competitors. Price fixing, however, left them vulnerable to antitrust action. Indeed, Chandler suggests that "cartels of small, 'family firms' . . . might well have continued into the twentieth century" if not for antitrust legislation.[6] Actually, they did.

This essay considers the path of the U.S. sanitary pottery industry and its trade association, the Sanitary Potters Association (SPA) from 1900 to its dissolution in 1923. Such organization of batch and bulk producers provided much the same stability that large corporations created in mass-production industries. Centered in Trenton, New Jersey, sanitary potteries produced bathroom and kitchen ware including sinks, bathtubs, toilets. Agreements among these independent, single-function firms prevailed while contracts with their skilled workers preserved labor peace without price wars. This essay will, therefore, demonstrate the importance of expanding Chandler and McCraw's factor matrix to include labor and will suggest the continued importance of such batch and bulk oriented firms in early twentieth-century American economic life.

### The Pottery Industry, 1850-1914

With few exceptions, imported English pottery dominated American markets prior to 1850. With some few exceptions, small U.S. potteries manufactured cheap earthenware for domestic and industrial use. The industry grew in two centers thereafter: East Liverpool, Ohio, and Trenton, New Jersey. In the latter, skilled English immigrant potters[7] found a location convenient to raw materials, markets, transportation, and partners with capital. Large shops employed over two hundred workers--many of them Anglo-American--by 1870, and Trenton's thirty-seven potteries employed 4,235 workers by 1890.[8]

Custom and skill remained more important than managerial authority in this labor and skill-intensive trade. Operatives worked to customary earning levels enforced by the manufacturers. If earnings rose beyond the norm, rates fell; workers therefore restricted output. Piece rates thus affected both the pace of shop life and the workers' community standing and condition.[9]

Jobbers marketed pottery products nationally, but potteries also sold directly to retailers.[10] Output included bulk, staple whiteware that was often indistinguishable--save for quality--from one firm to the next. Warehouses held undecorated stock in reserve by the 1880s to speed response to orders. But most establishments feared inventories of finished goods, since ornamentation and design shifted rapidly, and batch orders remained common.

Trenton manufacturers both competed and cooperated. They understood that success as a pottery center required a critical mass to guarantee ready access to raw materials, labor, support for tariffs, and recognition as a production center.[11] These pottery owners also had to deal with their workmen. Trenton's Manufacturing Potters' Association (MPA), formed in response to their workers' unionization, broke unions in 1865, 1869, and 1877. But unity was conditional, and wage cuts failed in 1874 and 1885 because some shops held hefty inventories while others faced bare warehouses and feared shutdowns.[12]

The association also sought to shift from price taking to price making by controlling price and discount lists for whitewares. But national competition required national controls. Founded in 1875, the United States Potters' Association (USPA) served that purpose,[13] although its attempts at price fixing failed prior to 1881 as declining transportation barriers, cheap imports, and regionally divergent production systems undercut trade solidarity. Ohio potteries mechanized, lowered piece rates, and began making "schemeware," cheap bulk goods designed for variety stores, mail order houses, and as premiums for brand name consumers. Price fixing returned by 1890.[14]

Caught between low-cost Ohio production and inexpensive European imports, Trenton's difficulties increased when the 1893 depression and falling tariffs sparked price and wage reductions. Innovation and cost cutting might have allowed Trenton to compete once the depression ended, but low profits discouraged renovations. While Ohioans negotiated amicable agreements with the East Liverpool-based National Brotherhood of Operative Potters (NBOP) in 1897, Trenton workers insisted on comparable facilities as a precondition for (lower) Ohio rates and increased output. These were not forthcoming, and Trenton generalware was increasingly marginalized by 1900. Trenton workers even withdrew from the NBOP in 1900 rather than accept the reductions standard national wage rates might have entailed.[15] Uniform rates and formal contracts arrived in the west while Eastern conditions deteriorated.[16] In 1904, however, the NBOP determined to enforce the list in Trenton regardless of shop conditions.[17] Formal and informal agreements among firms then maintained price stability until 1914 with the support of the trade's larger shops.[18]

These contracts demonstrated that shop and price stability went hand-in-hand in this skill-intensive trade. Price wars presaged rate cutting which brought strikes and low profits, while associationism and covenants begat peace and high returns. The move to scheme production and institutional purchasing[19] certainly promoted this policy. Stable production mattered in dealings with tea companies or five-and-dimes, for corporate consumers had become these potters' market. Bulk and batch production put a premium on labor peace and trade agreements.

## The Sanitary Trade, 1872-1900

As cutthroat competition ate into profits and destabilized firms after 1870, some Trenton shops diversified their product mix with belleek china, hotel china, and industrial porcelain. Another line emerged in 1873 when Thomas Maddock experimented with sanitary ware for the expanding urban market. Increased concern for sanitation offered Trentonians the chance to compete with imported appliances and domestic enameled iron.[20] Trenton's proximity to major cities, its pool of skilled operatives, and access to raw materials gave the locale an advantage over competitors if they could make an acceptable product.

Seven Trenton sanitary potteries--and one Baltimore pottery --employing almost one thousand workers sold staple and specialty goods through jobbers, catalogs, and showrooms by 1890.[21] Their trade association (c.1884) experimented with price lists, but prior to 1890, domestic competition soon undid each compact.[22] Unlike generalware, they competed successfully with imports and, by 1890, controlled 90 percent of the market.[23] These developments paralleled the emergence of staple, or industry standard, ware, but firms still crafted diverse pieces, including their staples, in batch runs, and sought to avoid large inventories.

Skilled male pressers worked clay into mold sections which they fused together and finished. While regular pressers made staple goods, especially skillful workers pressed specialty items. Each clayman made a set number of pieces per day with rates and limits fixed by "playing off" the time it supposedly took to press various pieces and the income normally earned by the potters as skilled journeymen. This process involved a delicate balance of community norms and the power held by either side during negotiations.[24]

Teams of skilled kilnmen "placed" pieces in kilns for the first of up to three firings, after which ware was glazed and refired before being shipped out in crates made by a skilled packer.[25] Unskilled laborers also worked in the shops, but a ratio of roughly 2.5 skilled workmen to one less skilled employee prevailed. Unlike generalware, where journeymen employed less-skilled helpers, sanitary workers hired few assistants.[26]

The price wars temporarily ceased when the Plumbers' Earthenware Manufacturing Association (PEMA) organized *circa* 1889. Prices rose, and journeymen supported this virtual monopoly by discouraging migration to other regions. With the market under control, however, the PEMA turned on its journeymen and broke their union in 1891. Rates fell, output rose by a third, and charges for defective work increased.[27]

Market and shop control encouraged Trenton, New York and Philadelphia manufacturers and financiers to attempt a monopoly of Trenton producers. Five of seven Trenton sanitary shops merged to form the Trenton Potteries Company (Tepeco) in 1892, but two family firms--including Maddock--remained independent. High profits eluded Tepeco, as vertically integrated, rationalized, bulk production came slowly. Former owners initially retained control of their shops, handwork continued, and generalware's decline drew shops to sanitary, increasing competition. This provoked Tepeco to cut prices by one-third in December 1892, but increased competition and depression almost doubled reductions by 1895, and repeated efforts to restore prices failed.[28]

With technology stable, price wars inspired rate cutting. The new Sanitary Pressers' Union (SPU) unilaterally reduced its list wages to enroll off-list pressers in June 1895 and struck for higher, standardized wages hoping this would "remove the temptation toward discountism" among both the workers and, it appears, the manufacturers. Victory transformed the union into the Sanitary Pressers' National Union (SPNU), but labor activism quickly reunited the manufacturers, and a November lockout broke the workers' spirit, if not their organization, and pre-strike conditions returned.[29]

The lockout implied renewed cooperation in the trade, and twelve sanitary shops formed the American Sanitary Association (ASA) in March 1896 to stabilize market prices. This collapsed when nonmembers undercut prices. Predictably, they rejected an SPNU offer to enforce price agreements by striking offending firms in exchange for recognition and industrywide conditions.[30] Whatever their disagreements, the manufacturers would not accept their workers' unions as a presence in their shops. Not until 1899, when the nearly-destitute, 450-member SPNU joined the NBOP as Local Union (LU) 45, did conditions begin to change.[31]

The post-1897 economic revival, meanwhile, brought increased construction and demand for sanitary pottery. This drew more competitors from the generalware trades, and prices fell as firms bid for market share. But price competition meant wage cuts and workers responded with walkouts. As a leading potter, Archibald Maddock, later recalled, "only those who have lived through a rugged economy of unbridled competition, can understand its frustrating aspect." Personal hostilities among the employers exacerbated the chaos.[32]

### The Sanitary Potters' Association

Industrial expansion after 1900 brought more than twenty more firms (in and outside Trenton) to join the trade, and by 1916, sanitary formed one-quarter of the nation's pottery production and almost three-fifths of Trenton's clay output. Manufacturing spread to Indiana, West Virginia, Pennsylvania, Illinois, and California. Tepeco even expanded to Canada (1905) under the Canadian Trenton Potteries Company label. New products including lavatories, flush tanks, seats, and urinals helped firms compete with enameled iron manufacturers, and Tepeco devoted entire potteries to particular products.[33] Meanwhile, the purchase of a sanitary pottery by the giant Standard Sanitary Manufacturing Company (1913), the construction of a new Trenton plant and pottery by the J.L. Mott Company (1905), and the purchase of a Trenton shop by the L. Wolff Manufacturing Co. (1905) brought clayshops into vertically integrated plumbing supply houses. Still, the trade largely remained independent, as staple and specialty batch goods flowed out of Trenton.[34]

Unlike the large, mass production firms described by Chandler, most potteries remained small: eleven of fourteen Trenton companies in 1915 employed 250 or fewer workers. The largest single shop, Thomas Maddock's Sons, only claimed 450 workers, while the tiny Economy Pottery boasted 15 employees. Pottery manufacture generally remained an intimate process based on personal control,[35] and 'management' usually meant a supervising partner and two or three foremen for two hundred workers.[36]

Positive experiences in generalware led to yet another sanitary trade association. Not surprisingly, Tepeco General Manager John Campbell promoted this effort. Leading the industry's only large corporation, Campbell understood his firm's stake in avoiding damaging price wars, but unlike mass production oligopolies, Tepeco could neither introduce continuous production techniques nor control market prices.[37]

With "no constitution and no by-laws" or annual reports, the SPA met "only when business required it" and distributed bulletins to members regarding policy, but the association monitored the market closely. Federal sources suggest that monthly gatherings drew delegates from almost every shop in the land by 1912.[38] Members relied on their memories of competition and overcapacity to keep the peace. Where recall failed, fines usually succeeded. Those few who refused all accommodation withdrew from the organization.[39]

The SPA was remarkably stable. Only two men, both Trenton-based, served as president: Campbell (1900-1911) and A.M. Maddock, II (1911-1923) of Thomas Maddock's Sons. They led the trade's largest independent firms and benefitted from reasonable profits generated, along with products, at a steady pace. Cooperation meant stability for both. They would have survived conflicts, but why risk losses?

Two men also served as secretaries: J.J. Dale (pre-1916), and George Dyer (1916-1923). As the only salaried officer, they kept meeting minutes, conducted SPA business, and worked closely with the president. They communicated with members, other trade associations, and the SPA's lawyers. Protests about violations of trade agreements went through their office, and they investigated and resolved conflicts whenever possible.[40]

The SPA experimented with a variety of price-fixing techniques, including a collective selling company and patent pool prior to 1906, and continued experimenting as time went on.[41] The new cartel initially set prices and market shares based on kilnspace, and price and discount lists remained an important feature of the trade for the next two decades. Smaller shops received "relatively larger allotments" to compensate for their relatively higher fixed costs, and larger shops accepted this. Similarly, small shops were sometimes permitted free to set their rates roughly 5 percent below the association's list to attract business. Such practices were apparently tolerated in the interests of avoiding even more destructive price wars.[42]  The SPA also set packing, credit, and shipment fees.  The cartel approached "dissolution and an open market" several times but held.[43]

SPA regulation even garnered federal endorsement during World War I when authorities asked for industrywide prices on 200,000 items destined for military cantonments.  The association fixed prices below prevailing lists though "some manufacturers complained and refused to accept orders at those lower figures."  Patriotism aside, this list allowed more efficient firms to capitalize on scale and standardized bulk production to gain federal custom during a building slump.  The SPA met again at war's end and fixed new, lower lists to stimulate business.[44]

These lists dominated SPA practices as the potters struggled to control competition without violating the Sherman Act.  They began gathering and charting regional price variations in 1916.  Against the advice of counsel, who warned that setting price lists based on written reports on prices received by firms, might violate the Sherman Antitrust Act, the association joined other open price associations which emerged following the Supreme Court's 1911 "rule of reason."[45]  Advocates claimed open pricing promoted reasonable trade, and cartel members believed reasonable prices kept them within the law.  Reason, historian Martin Sklar suggests, became the opposite of what was "prejudicial to the public interest," and devastating, demoralizing price wars with their rate cutting and strikes were not in the public interest.[46]

The SPA also believed it could determine whom to sell to and what to sell: members sold only to legitimate jobbers, not plumbers masquerading as merchants.  Archibald Maddock argued that members supported this system because wholesalers "had established the importance and necessity of the function they performed."  Wholesale purchases, after all, reduced the need for the potters to hold costly inventory.  The SPA even cooperated with the jobbers' trade group to flush out plumbers passing as wholesalers.[47]  Finally, the SPA endorsed the long-held practice of excluding seconds, or "B" goods, from domestic markets.  Their sale undercut "A" pieces and diminished everyone's reputation.[48]  Both practices boosted the cost of goods to consumers by increasing the number of transactions through middlemen and restricting access to low-cost seconds.

Did SPA lists work?  Many firms abided by agreements, but

competition still affected prices. Jobbers shopped around and sometimes obtained goods off list. Furthermore, SPA prices could not safely exceed free market prices since independent and smaller association firms anxious to capture market share could cut lists searching for profits attendant to steady production and increased scale. Unusual profits would also lure competitors into the field, and the SPA worked hard to avoid this. Even government officials prosecuting the association for antitrust violation quickly dropped their claim that SPA prices were unreasonable.[49]

Prior to 1914, however, SPA officials rarely complained of internal price cutting; most came from outsiders and ironmongers. Successful controls prior to 1906 actually allowed six or seven new shops--"pirates," Campbell called them--to cut prices and claim a piece of the market. Older firms bound by SPA agreements fought to retain their market and taught newcomers the advantages of associationism.[50] "Lame ducks" occasionally violated the rules, but the compact held. Rampant price warfare ended.[51]

### SPA-NBOP Relations

Price fixing and trade agreements relied on standardized costs, and labor was the largest of these.[52] Some workers understood their role in pricing and argued that "it is essential that we control the labor market in order that the employer can determine to a great degree what the selling price shall be."[53] Many other manufacturers' associations opted instead for the National Association of Manufacturers' open shop,[54] but the potter's arrangement was not unique. Other skill-dependent bulk and batch-oriented trades, e.g., glassmaking, maintained contracts.[55] Competition and production processes often determined if firms negotiated with their unionized workmen.

Labor agreements thus facilitated the cartel's success: contracts preserved market peace and acknowledged control's bilateral nature. As Campbell informed Congress in 1914, the bosses had "wider liberty" before 1902 than after, but strikes disrupted their world. "While you might be entirely independent, at the same time you were certainly in hot water a good portion of the time. . . . You paid for your independence."[56] The SPA and NBOP negotiated their first contract in June 1902, agreeing to rate increases for pressers on staple goods, apprentice-journeyman ratios, and fixed apprenticeship terms. Agreements covered ovenmen and packers by 1903.[57] Most sanitary porcelain firms outside Trenton, including the vertically integrated plumbing supply company, Standard Sanitary Manufacturing Co., eventually affiliated to take advantage of SPA-NBOP contracts.[58]

"The first and cardinal principle" said Campbell in 1914, was "that there should be no strikes or lockouts." Systematic negotiation soon replaced strikes, and national and regional union bureaucrats helped repress wildcats.[59] The union also discouraged legal strikes, requiring a *90 percent* vote to legitimate a walkout before 1904. Even grievous abuses rarely provoked such unanimity, and sanitary pressers argued the rule "prevents the possibility of the use of the main weapon of organized labor." National leaders eventually concurred, but the shift to three-fourths, and later two-thirds, still left strikes unlikely, and, occasional wildcats aside, an aversion to conflict by SPA and NBOP leaders kept the trade walkout-free until 1922.[60]

Most dealings concerned wages, shop conditions, and trade practices. Contracts evolved from open-ended (1902) to two-year agreements (1908) approved by negotiating committees without a vote by either SPA or NBOP members.[61] Each side regularly withdrew contentious proposals which might stalemate proceedings. Conferees turned special conditions over to the standing committee whenever possible rather than deadlock negotiations.[62]

### *Negotiations and the Standing Committee*

Both sides agreed: negotiations were better than shutdowns. Using generalware's standing committee as a model, the SPA and NBOP established a joint committee after a crisis in 1903 nearly provoked a strike. This council resolved problems which emerged between contracts and forestalled strikes or lockouts. The SPA initially lobbied for the right to strike or lock out with two-weeks notice should an issue deadlock their discussions, but NBOP negotiators rejected such a compromise. The no shutdown rule prevailed.[63]

John Campbell chaired the committee's monthly meetings from 1903 to 1914. It resolved tie votes without an arbitrator, and unlike generalware, where many disagreements returned to the shop for settlement, the committee resolved most issues. It defined shop rights and obligations and set rates when shop committees failed to come to terms with employers. Workers grudgingly labored under protest while the committee pondered a case, and vindication brought restitution.[64]

Both sides initially saw the committee as a venue for industrywide issues, but it soon became the general court of last resort, and the caseload increased with time. NBOP President Hughes noted worker impatience with delays as early as 1907, and conditions deteriorated further thereafter. This tendency eventually drove Campbell from the panel in 1915 and led the NBOP to assign Eastern Executive Board members, including Vice President Frank Hutchins, as ex officio panelists to expedite matters.[65]

The committee included three NBOP members and three SPA manufacturers. While employers served for many years, NBOP delegates elected by locals or appointed by the union president changed more frequently. Many workers began their tenure as hardliners, but experience, increased trade knowledge, and familiarity with their adversaries led most to more moderate postures and, eventually, their removal by dissatisfied benchmates.[66] Union delegates usually tried to stand above everyday conflict and preserve smooth relations with the manufacturers even if it angered other operatives.[67] Hutchins, for example, frequently dismissed charges of harassment by fired union activists and agreed that firms let these men go for cause. That the discharged sometimes included Socialists or militant shopmen undoubtedly tempered Hutchins's desire to pursue the issue, since they were the bane of his existence. This attitude compromised relations between local and national unionists.[68] Nevertheless, the committee system largely ended strikes and lockouts, and even Hutchins acknowledged that few committeemen failed to do their duty.[69]

Still, the agreement was never foolproof. Workers sometimes walked out over committee decisions,[70] and the odd lockout embittered the operatives. The latter usually occurred when firms departed the SPA to go it alone, since SPA jurisdiction left with the firm. Where members reneged on obligations, however, as in 1910, Campbell vowed that the association would "make good on it." In all, he conceded in 1914 that the workers honored the agreement "quite as well as the manufacturers have respected theirs."[71]

## Mechanization: Casting, Kilns and Cooperation

Most potteries accepted SPA-NBOP authority, but several remained aloof. Predictably, innovation began among these outsiders competing for market share by lowering per unit costs, increasing worker productivity, and employing less-skilled workers. SPA shops, on the other hand, innovated slowly for technical and economic reasons. Experience with overcapacity and unregulated markets, after all, had taught SPA men that stability benefitted the trade. The skilled operatives' resistance to mechanization exacerbated the SPA's problems.

Technological experimentation occurred on several fronts,[72] but slip casting and tunnel kilns were the most important. Slip casting spread from Germany (1905) to England (1907), and entered American shops (1908) when New Castle, Pennsylvania's Universal Sanitary Manufacturing Company introduced the technique. Casting with liquid clay slip was relatively simple and less skill-intensive than pressing, but it initially damaged costly molds and failed with higher quality, vitreous clay bodies, so manufacturers only cast cheap goods.[73]

Unable to find enough skilled, nonunion workmen following a split with both the SPA and NBOP, the Universal's Charles J. Kirk[74] turned to casting lower quality wares and two other non-SPA shops followed.[75] Kirk proudly proclaimed casting's success in 1913. His "unskilled workmen" produced vitreous china in molds which survived over one thousand casts. Kirk's pressers were "not practical workmen in the pottery business. They are Italians and people we pick up around town," men excluded from journeymen positions by NBOP operatives. Each man made nine water closets daily, 125 percent above the pressers' four-closet stint, at 30-44 percent pressing rates; some could almost earn a pressers' wage, assuming all their work emerged from the kiln in good condition--an unusual occurrence in most cases. His men wanted to make more, Kirk said, "but they would be apt not to finish [the work] as well as we require."[76] Scientific management techniques, including a Tayloresque bonus system, further enhanced Kirk's control over his shop by 1914. Still, technical control, or as sociologist Richard Edwards suggests, control "based on a technology that paces and directs the labor process," did not arrive in the pressing shops. Indeed, Kirk himself later acknowledged that, despite his sanguine assertions, casting took a very long time to come into its own.[77]

Kirk shook the trade again in 1915 by introducing a 245-foot, gas-fired continuous Dressler tunnel kiln from England. This kiln reduced the need for skilled kilnmen, cut kilncrew size, and lowered fuel costs per piece. He estimated 90 percent reductions in costs with steady use, but savings depended on high, sustained demand for standardized products, i.e., increased throughput, and he acknowledged that "we have never been able to make enough ware at our place to keep it going, to run it up to its full capacity." This kiln was expensive to operate.[78]

Tunnel kilns and casting were crucial to the shift from labor-intensive batch production to bulk, standardized, and increasingly capital-intensive work requiring fewer skilled workers. But casters still hand-finished ware cast in several molds and may well have been less productive in its early years than he suggested. Skilled pressers held their own in the face of its competition at first. And to say the least, continuous production did not arrive with the tunnel kiln. Nonetheless, the new techniques promised both improved throughput and the chance of eliminating the pressers and the team-conscious, militant kilnmen should conditions change.

Whatever their implications for the long run, SPA shops were slow to adopt these innovations. Archibald Maddock, for one, bought English casting equipment but chose to keep pressing his special vitreous clay body and preserve control of the market for better ware. SPA firms also delayed casting until they could use one-piece molds rather than rely on casters to join several cast pieces.[79] Finally, a commitment to batch production inhibited mechanization, since many specialty items were ill-suited to casting runs, and even shops with staple lines waited until one-piece casting permitted them to displace their pressers. Market control allowed them to defer innovations which would have destabilized price and wage agreements.

Erratic demand from 1900 through World War I also induced caution over tunnel kilns. Bust followed boom, and the war years were especially slow. Housing starts declined from 437,000 in 1916 to 118,000 in 1918, and federal rules limited the shops to only half their pre-1917 kiln fuel.[80] Firms were loath to increase fixed costs for a kiln which required full utilization to yield unit cost reductions. Few potters were, after all, risk-takers.[81]

Even localization inhibited innovation. Unlike the Universal, Trentonians lacked access to cheap land. Nor could they just pick up and move, since they depended on skilled urban workers who lived near potteries. Small shops could ill-afford tunnel kilns in any event.

Finally, cartel members avoided battle with both their pressers and kilnmen. Despite craft particularism, Trenton's skilled sanitary workers usually supported one anothers' aims. Premature mechanization in one major craft might have provoked resistance from the other, so SPA firms moved cautiously before installing a new production system.

The SPA warned workers about casting as early as 1910, when Campbell observed that the SPA-NBOP had to "control and handle it and get the benefit of it ourselves," or things would move "beyond our control." Two years later he insisted that the SPA had to cast at a profit to compete with outside firms.[82] Vice President Hutchins concurred, and the NBOP accepted casting for pressers at half the pressing price with the proviso that men earning under $3.50 could shift to day payments commensurate with their standing as skilled workers.[83] But while most casters earned the base rate, few garnered pressers' wages, and defective goods that brought no compensation further reduced earnings. Few pressers therefore took to the casting bench.[84]

Observant workers called for organizing casting to "control the labor market,"[85] but others hoped it would just disappear. Reports trumpeting casting's failures perpetuated this dream,[86] and the union bolstered it by reassuring pressers that they had little to fear because of casting's "many drawbacks."[87] Manufacturers thus filled casting benches with nonpressers.

And whatever the technical problems, nonunion shops had an advantage over pressing shops. Their focus on the market's bottom end and a limited product mix restricted sales somewhat, but low-cost fabrication let them charge below list for comparable goods and cut prices without sacrificing profits when prices fell.

### Conjuncture and Transformation

The war and postwar years saw intense conflict over the nation's direction as labor and capital struggled for power in shops and communities throughout the land. In the end, postwar political reaction undermined labor and enhanced capital's might.[88] But this business triumph was not unconditional. As Morton Keller suggests, formal price fixing became even less acceptable after the war as the Justice Department prosecuted trade association price rigging. Though Supreme Court rulings allowed information exchanges, enforced lists became taboo. Proscribed activity promoted the expansion of integrated, oligopolistic corporations by undermining one of the small manufacturers' key weapons. Court action accelerated shifts begun by market and technological forces.[89]

Pottery operatives saw their income and community standing fall as output shrank and inflation and downtime rose during the war.[90] Twelve and one-half percent rate increases in 1916 helped,[91] but not when trade slowed in 1917. Association officials complained of competition from nonunion shops and the impact of higher wages on general prices. They also noted that teachers and government workers earned less than potters. Still, 7.5 percent increases effective in August 1917 evoked fury from workmen demanding 25 percent. To the operatives, bureaucrats and women educators were not peers, and the sanitary trade hardly determined building cycles or the cost of living in any event.[92] The SPA then offered another 2.5 percent, effective January 1918, and NBOP negotiators led by Hutchins accepted these terms despite local opposition.[93] Even with another 15 percent "plussage," or increase on the prewar rate, in 1918, the potters lagged behind inflation.[94]

SPA members met in Pittsburgh in December 1918 to plan for the "chaos" they anticipated would follow on the armistice. Prices had to fall, and, accordingly, they adopted new, reduced lists for staples. Several shops initially resisted these changes, but 81-94 percent of ware listed at SPA prices and discounts between December 1918 and July 1920.[95] Though some firms violated their own rates and sold off-list to keep their shops working, most apparently honored the compact.[96]

While sanitary prices fell, trade and inflation increased as Americans spent their wartime earnings in a postwar frenzy. After two sluggish years, nonfarm residential building accelerated in 1919.[97] As profits fell with lower prices and increased competition, operatives facing spiraling inflation demanded a 40 percent rate increase.[98] The 5-10 percent raises granted by employers merely stoked worker anger and further compromised the NBOP leaders' standing with rank-and-filers.[99] Another 5 at 1920 contract time (as opposed to the 50 percent sought by the operatives) ratcheted tempers up another notch.[100] And conditions worsened as the 1920 monetary contraction slowed building and provoked uncoordinated price cuts by manufacturers. List observance fell to 70 percent as firms tried to stimulate trade and keep customers from turning to nonunion casters or cheap imports.[101] Mechanization continued in outside shops, and the SPA's market share fell to 82 percent by late 1921.[102]

The SPA demanded a renegotiation of the 1920 contract in early 1921. Ignoring the fact that the wartime raises they were essentially forced to provide lagged far behind inflation, the manufacturers pleaded in vain with the NBOP for voluntary rate reductions, time clocks, and an end to output restrictions. Despite Hutchins' cajoling, rank and file leaders testily reiterated their refusal as trade rebounded in late 1921. The operatives, said union delegates, needed higher rates to make up for wartime losses.[103]

The situation changed again as contract negotiations approached in September 1922. Housing starts skyrocketed from 449,000 in 1921 to 716,000 in 1922 with no peak in sight. SPA shops shifted to casting, and the number of casters in union firms rose from 190 in 1921 to 450. Nonunion companies also grew, and their unit costs remained roughly 20 percent below SPA firms.[104] Four nonunion shops even existed in Trenton.[105]

Two further developments shook the trade. Tepeco solidified its ties to the Crane Company, a large plumbing supply house, and together they built a casting-tunnel kiln pottery that doubled Trenton's largest pottery company's capacity in 1921. Ever cautious, these potters also hedged their bets by building nine periodic ovens along with the tunnel.[106] Clearly, Tepeco had turned to Crane anticipating a future merger, and their cooperation signified increased outside involvement in the trade. The new housing and renovation boom during the 1920s promoted such mergers by allowing ironmongers to cut transaction costs and develop full, standardized lines produced more easily with casting and tunnel kilns. In so doing, the shift to casting replicated standardization occurring throughout industry.[107]

A U.S. Justice Department investigation into New York City's housing industry begun in October 1921 proved to be equally important. Wartime housing prices had outraged the public, and with inflation and then recession, notes Robert Himmelberg, "hostility toward associationism was too intense safely to ignore." Hearings begun under the Wilson administration carried over into Harding's administration. Presidential advisor *cum* Attorney General Harry Daugherty pursued cases against housing related associationism over Secretary of Commerce Herbert

Hoover's objections and, in the potters' case, despite the manufacturers' important role in New Jersey's Republican Party.[108]

Agents seized SPA records during Spring 1922. Although Federal officers were indifferent about an indictment as a Brooklyn, New York, grand jury heard the case that summer, SPA Secretary Dyer's perjurous testimony clinched the outcome. Indictments against the firms and their owners and managers for price fixing and restrictions on sales followed that August.[109]

Indicted SPA leaders met NBOP delegates just one month later to hammer out a new contract for an industry in upheaval. Expanding markets, technology, and federal intervention had transformed the trade, and SPA leaders understood this. Indictment meant an end to restrictive covenants, and larger firms were now committed to casting and tunnel kilns. One large house even withdrew from the SPA on the eve of negotiations.[110] The cartel's ordered world was collapsing.

Angry SPA leaders insisted on large wage cuts in all crafts, an end to limits on output, and a shift from payment by kiln volume to direct piece rates to allow for competition with nonunion shops and tunnel kilns.[111] Yet for all their   bitterness, SPA firms offered to accept another contract and were furious when unionists rejected these demands. The union side viewed these changes as violations of trade custom and unwarranted given flush markets.[112] More importantly, the NBOP-men misinterpreted the indictment as a sign of the association's continuing market control.[113]

Intervention by SPA founder John Campbell and the recently retired Hutchins brought both sides back to the bargaining table in October. With the new Crane-Tepeco plant on line, Campbell had a great deal at stake in continued production, and both he and Hutchins feared that a strike would destroy the agreements they had built over twenty years. By force of personality--and his place as president of the industry's largest firm-- Campbell persuaded the SPA to accept a one-year contract featuring 10 percent reductions in pressing along with other stringent adjustments. The union leadership, on the other hand, accepted these wage cuts for the pressers, deeper reductions for the kilnmen, along with changes in kiln payment systems. These changes might not allow profit levels associated with nonunion shops, all agreed, but they would permit production during the housing boom, promote innovation over time, and enable union members to control new clay and kiln jobs.[114]

NBOP Executive Board members begged the sanitary operatives to accept the offer: nonunion competition was real, casting was destroying pressing, and the tunnel kilns threatened the kilncrafts. A strike would only displace skilled union men; hope lay in maintaining contracts.[115] Although never mentioned, the Board undoubtedly feared that a sanitary strike during an ongoing walkout by seven thousand generalware workers might compromise the latter. The union's renowned defense fund was shrinking fast.[116]

Despite these warnings, the sanitary workers voted 2,018 to 252 to strike. A way of life was on the line, and Trenton, a bastion of traditional work practices and recent English migrants who had fled casting abroad, backed the walkout wholeheartedly. Most believed the employers were bluffing and doubted the firms' willingness to forego profits during flush times, a determination the compromise offer probably encouraged. They still doubted casting's viability. The technique's long-delayed arrival had fostered a false sense of security and indispensability.[117]

Finally, few had memories of the dark days of the 1890s, and Frank Hutchins' 1921 retirement left less powerful and influential figures in command. These men proved unable to defuse the operatives' anger and distrust of the cozy relationship between NBOP and SPA leaders. The workers' rejection of the contract, the first voted on since 1908, thus also signified their disapproval of the union's traditional leadership style. Members followed militants who had correctly criticized the union leadership's accomodationism from 1915-1921 and, like skilled workers in many industries throughout the nation, called for a strike.[118]

Twenty-five hundred NBOP members struck on November 1, 1922, and another thousand workers fell idle with them. Within weeks, however, the workers realized they were in trouble and agreed to accept their bosses' offer only to find the manufacturers set on open shops. The failed negotiations had soured the employers on the NBOP. Only 300 of 2,000 strikers regained positions by August 1923, and they worked for 20-40 percent lower wages. Eight small shops signed union contracts during the strike, but NBOP power collapsed when most firms hired nonunion casters. The strike ended one year later with sanitary an open shop trade.[119]

The transformation accelerated when the antitrust suit eliminated SPA controls. The association argued that it simply shared information, that members' prices varied, and that they were not profiteers. After a one-month trial, however, the jury took only twenty-five minutes to convict 20 individuals and 23 firms of violating the Sherman Act. Seven, including Archibald Maddock, received prison sentences of six to ten months and fines of five thousand dollars.[120]

The defendants appealed but faced a dilemma: should they reorganize within the act's limits? Their refusal acknowledged the new order geared to mechanization and competition. Takeovers by vertically integrated plumbing supply houses were coming as large corporations sought to capitalize on the boom market. Selling and new production methods mattered more than price controls in this environment.[121]

Integration would have shattered the SPA eventually, but the 1923 decisions accelerated the process, especially after the strike left large manufacturers with heightened control of their shops using less-skilled workers and the casting-tunnel kiln system producing standardized, bulk products. As Archibald Maddock noted in 1962, "it was the Association's labor relations which necessitated getting together to talk over labor problems with the union that had the effect of keeping the organization going." This underestimates SPA market manipulation, but it was partly true. The organization dissolved "because the manufacturers had broken with the union and no longer entered into collective agreements with them."[122] Mechanization, market control, and class conflict were inseparable.

The defendants won their appeal in the Circuit Court, but the Supreme Court reinstated their conviction in 1926 with a five-three decision.[123] No manufacturer ever went to jail; they served their time on probation. The potters' case, however, demarcated the boundary of reason under Sherman: price fixing was illegal even if firms abstained from profiteering.[124] In so doing, the case also supported increased vertical incorporation over trade association controls and cartelization. By 1930, Trenton's largest independent firms (Tepeco, Maddock, Cochran-Drugan) belonged to vertically organized metalworking firms (Crane, American Standard, and Kohler, respectively). Casting and tunnel kilns slowly replaced pressing and periodic kilns, and the NBOP lost its membership as firms competed with one another within a "free market" dominated by large, oligopolistic plumbing supply houses.[125]

## *Conclusion*

Unlike industrialization in the large, "core," mechanized, and vertically-integrated industries discussed by Chandler and McCraw, the pottery industry in general, and the sanitary pottery industry in particular, grew during both the nineteenth and early twentieth centuries by capitalizing on the workers' skills. Skilled journeymen hand workers, not machines staffed by unskilled workers, pressed and fired America's bathroom products. Economies of scale were few and far between; the industry grew by starting new firms that achieved roughly the same scale while relying on hand workers who made a wide range of products in relatively small batches. Even the trade's one large, merged firm, the Trenton Potteries Co., had several plants, none of which were larger than those of the independents. But creative cartelization by the Sanitary Potters' Association and agreements with the National Brotherhood of Operative Potters brought market stability and labor peace that endured for two decades during which many other important American industries experienced devastating strikes and lockouts.

Localized in Trenton, New Jersey, the industry retained this pattern until the 1920s, when increased technical control of the production process and standardized, bulk production geared to slip casting and tunnel kilns facilitated the entry of large plumbing supply houses into the trade. Their involvement reflected the shift away from specialty production and towards fewer models produced for their increasingly standardized plumbing systems. Small firms played a diminishing role in trade affairs. Similarly, Trenton's strength declined as decisions were made by corporate directors in New York City, Chicago, or Pittsburgh. These innovations were introduced in relation to market forces; they entered the shops once the housing boom of the 1920s guaranteed their viability. This pattern confirms Chandler and McCraw's central thesis regarding the role of technological and market integration in encouraging absorption into vertically-integrated corporations. These changes were underway in response to changes in the market and technological innovations before the antitrust suit occurred, but they were clearly accelerated by that latter event.

In contrast to Chandler and McCraw's scenario, however, this inspection of the sanitary trade suggests the importance of using a broad-based factor matrix to examine the evolution of American capitalism and the industrialization process. In particular, this study underscores the importance of labor relations in industrial analysis. Market and shop controls were inextricably linked in this industry; several "visible hands" were at work in forming and directing industrial development. Indeed, one cannot understand the manufacturers' attempts at market controls without simultaneously considering the industrywide wage and shop controls that sustained them. To include them in the analysis, however, underscores the bilateral nature of power in the work place. The decisions made by the workmen in the 1920s reflected their role as active subjects rather than passive objects in the industrial process. They stemmed from labor's historic centrality in production that, along with intra-union conflicts, generated a profound blindness, an inability to perceive the arrival of new technological and market systems. Labor's importance in this tale is undoubtedly extreme and resulted from the remarkably low level of mechanization prior to the 1920s. But its role suggests that historians who ignore issues of labor relations do so at their peril. As the work of such labor historians as David Brody, James R. Barrett, and Stephen Meyer suggest, these same issues weighed in with profound effect in the oligopolized core as well as the periphery.[126]

Finally, this brief look at the sanitary porcelain industry also supports Scranton's call for paying more attention to bulk and batch manufacture in twentieth-century America. While the sanitary potteries finally belonged to Chandler and McCraw's vertically-integrated, "core" plumbing suppliers, associationism among mostly small, single-function firms dominated the trade well into the twentieth century. Yet in contrast to McCraw's characterization of "peripheral" industries tormented by perpetual competition and price wars and inherently doomed by antitrust restrictions, the potters' SPA (along with the USPA in generalware) proved themselves able to control prices and market relations in the industry for two decades without a serious price war. Although antitrust activity eventually undid the SPA's more explicit price arrangements, the potters were, not without reason, convinced that their "reasonable" prices placed their system within the "rule of reason." The Circuit Court's willingness to overturn the SPA's conviction testifies that the potters were hardly alone in that belief. Federal support for their system was palpable during World War I, and the system of middlemen and price sheets was hardly news to the Department of Commerce, where Hooverian associationism ruled the roost.  For twenty years it provided one of the many possible "paths" to industrial success and stability, until the market, technology, and the state overrode their institutional agreements.

1. I would like to thank Phil Scranton, Catherine Lugar, Bronwen Heuer, and Thomas Beal for their helpful comments on this essay.

2. Alfred D. Chandler, Jr., *The Visible Hand: The Managerial Revolution in American Business*, (Cambridge, 1977). On the issue of "throughput," see 241.

3. Thomas K. McCraw, "Rethinking the Trust Question," in *Regulation in Perspective*, ed. Thomas K. McCraw, (Cambridge, 1981), 18-19.

4. Philip Scranton, *Proprietary Capitalism: The Textile Manufacture at Philadelphia, 1800-1885*, (New York, 1983), 4-5; idem, "Diversity in Diversity: Flexible Production and American Industrialization, 1880-1930," *Business History Review*, 65 (Spring, 1991): 27-90; idem, *Figured Tapestry: Production, Markets and Power in Philadelphia Textiles, 1885-1941*, (New York, 1989). David Brody, "Labor and Small-Scale Enterprise During Industrialization," *Small Business in American Life*, ed. Stuart Bruchey, (New York, 1980), 264, notes that most American workers labored in shops with under 250 workers. The U.S. government terms under 20 workers very small; 20-99, small; 100-499, medium; and over 500, large. Mansel G. Blackford, "Small Business in America: A Historiographic Survey," *Business History Review*, 65 (Spring 1991): 3. On productive flexibility, see Michael J. Piore and Charles F. Sabel, *The Second Industrial Divide: Possibilities for Prosperity*, (New York, 1984). Daniel Nelson, *Workers and Managers: Origins of the New Factory System in the United States*, (Madison, 1975), 6-10, shows 1,000+ worker shops at batch work.

5. Scranton,"Diversity in Diversity," 30-33. Some bulk trades, e.g., nail, flour and turpentine, employed few skilled laborers.

6. Chandler, *Visible Hand*, 325.

7. "Potter" usually referred to owners and ware formers.

8. U.S., Census Office, *Compendium of the Eleventh Census: 1890*, pt.2, (Washington, 1894), 1010-11; U.S. Census of Manufactures, 1870, manuscript, Trenton, New Jersey. Population census samples suggest that the English and their children controlled over two-fifths of skilled places as late as 1900.

9. Men "played-off" new pieces by making as few as possible so that rates ran high. For technology and social relations see Marc J. Stern, "The Potters of Trenton, New Jersey, 1850-1902: A Study in the Industrialization of Skilled Trades," (Ph.D. Dissertation, SUNY-Stony Brook, 1986), 184-256, 286-400. For rate setting, see David A. McCabe, *The Standard Rate in American Trade Unions*, (Baltimore, 1912). In 1880, over 34 percent of the value of pottery, as opposed to 22 percent of total value in iron work lay in wages. Average capital per worker was $1,399 for Trenton iron and $663 in pottery. U.S., *Tenth Census of the*

*United States, 1880*, v.18, pt.1, (Washington, 1886), 731.

10. *Crockery and Glass Journal* (*CGJ*), 25 January, 20 May, 13 August 1880, 19 July 1883. Some dealers bought or invested in potteries, but most ceramic factories remained independent, see Stern, "Potters of Trenton," 177.

11. Stern, "Potters of Trenton," 121, 161-62.

12. Their resistance let workers organize unions. In 1885, the operatives built Knights of Labor assemblies which standardized rates and eventually claimed closed shops, apprenticeship rules, dues checkoff, unemployment benefits, and output limits at high wages. Stern, "The Potters of Trenton," 401-570.

13. See Stern, "The Potters of Trenton," 164-65. MPA President John Moses called for a national association in 1874 to counter competition and threatened tariff cuts. Unlike the New England Cotton Manufacturers' Association, which included "every cotton mill in the Northeast, large and small" by 1900, the USPA claimed few shops outside the main centers. Trentonians dominated the early USPA. Louis Galambos, *Competition & Cooperation: The Emergence of A National Trade Association*, (Baltimore, 1966), 21.

14Stern, "The Potters of Trenton," 143-145, 151-52, 354, 366-72; U.S. Commissioner of Labor, Eleventh Special Report, *Regulation and Restriction of Output*, H.R. Misc. Doc. 176, 51st Cong., 1st sess., 1904; U.S., Congress, House, Committee on Ways and Means, *Tariff Hearings Before the Committee on Ways and Means*, H.R. Misc. Doc. 43, 53rd Cong., 1st sess., (1893), Brunt, 85.

15. Stern, "The Potters of Trenton," 727-67. Trenton's two schemeware plants remained viable. *Daily State Gazette* (*DSG*), 12 February 1898. MPA refusal to allow lists for some, but not all, skilled workers allowed firms to pay low rates to most craftspeople.

16. David A. McCabe, *National Collective Bargaining in the Pottery Industry*, (Baltimore, 1932), 20-21, 38; U.S., *Regulation and Restriction*, 673-75; USPA, *Proceedings, 1901*, 46-49; NBOP, *Proceedings, 1901*, 8; Thomas J. Duffy, *History of the National Brotherhood of Operative Potters from 1890 to 1901* (Pittsburgh, 1901), 33-34.

17. NBOP, *Proceedings, 1904*, 20; *Trades Union Advocate* (*TUA*), 4 November 1904. Kiln and jiggermen rejoined the NBOP in 1902-3. See Stern, "Potters of Trenton," 761-67.

18. USPA, *Proceedings, 1903*, 16; *1905*, 11; Andrew McGeorge Lamb, "A History of the American Pottery Industry: Industrial Growth, Technical and Technological Change and Diffusion in the Generalware Branch 1872-1914," (Ph.D. dissertation, London School of Economics, 1984), 65-66.

19. Hotel china vied for institutional and government contracts.

20. Archibald M. Maddock, II, *The Polished Earth; A History of the Pottery Plumbing Fixture Industry in the United States*, (Trenton, 1962), 147-56, 209. Four English firms controlled the American trade before Maddock. Industrial goods included druggists' porcelain, door furniture, and electrical insulators.

21. *Trenton Times (TT)*, 24 January 1891. Most also made generalware.

22. They belonged to the MPA and USPA and negotiated with their workers from 1885-1891. *CGJ*, 15 December 1887, 3 May 1888.

23. *CGJ*, 14 December 1893. American-made enameled ironware remained competitive.

24. See Stern, "The Potters of Trenton," 251-53, 341-51; interview with an old potter, Bert Power, Trenton, April 1982.

25. Stern, "Potters of Trenton," 253-55.

26. The 1922 strike by 2,500 unionists idled 1,000 support workers. McCabe, *National Collective Bargaining*, 387-88; Donald A. Shotliff, "The History of the Labor Movement in the American Pottery Industry: The National Brotherhood of Operative Potters-International Brotherhood of Operative Potters, 1890-1970," (Ph.D. dissertation, Kent State University, 1977), 183-84.

27. Stern, 570-99, 609-612; U.S., *Regulation and Restriction of Output*, 704; *DSG*, 3 October 1895. Sanitary workers were only paid for work which survived the kiln (good-from-kiln).

28. Stern, 599-609; *CGJ*, 25 September 1893; *Trenton Sunday Advertiser (TSA)*, 11 December 1895. Housing starts fell from 381,000 in 1892 to 267,000 in 1893. U.S. Bureau of the Census, *Historical Statistics of the United States, Colonial Times to 1970*, pt.2, (Washington, 1975), 640. Competitors included Tepeco associates barred from starting firms by the original agreement. On mergers, see Chandler, *Visible Hand*, 315-344; Ralph Nelson, *Merger Movements in American Industry*, 1895-1956, (Princeton, 1959); Naomi R. Lamoreaux, *The Great Merger Movement in American Business, 1895-1904*, (New York, 1985); and Martin J. Sklar, *The Corporate Reconstruction of American Capitalism, 1890-1916: The Market, The Law, and Politics*, (New York, 1988).

29. *TT*, 22 June 1895; Stern, "Potters of Trenton," 715-24.

30. *CGJ*, 3 December 1896; SPNU, "Minutes," 7 April 1896, Trenton Free Public Library.

31. Stern, 767-71; NBOP, *Proceedings, 1902*, 11. NBOP committees sought to enforce rates and daily stints by talking and strikes. See LU 45, "Minutes," box 122, v.1, NBOP-IBOP Papers, Kent State University Archives.

32. Maddock, *Polished Earth*, 186; SPA-NBOP "Negotiations," 18 September 1906, Campbell, 358; *DSG*, 21 December 1896.

33. Trenton's share of national sanitary output fell from 67 (1909) to 57 percent (1912) as outside firms grew. Figures calculated from U.S. Geological Survey, *Mineral Resources of the United States, 1909*, pt.2, 478-79; *1912*, pt.2, 550-51; *1916*, pt.2, 538-39; Maddock, *Polished Earth*, 279, 282-94. Its nine sanitary firms employed 1,793 workers, or two-fifths of all Trenton pottery operatives in 1901. Directories found 2,435 sanitary workers in 1912, 3,068--two-thirds of the pottery labor force--in 1915, and 2,712 during the 1918 slump. Calculated from New Jersey, Bureau of Industrial Statistics, *Industrial Directory of New Jersey, 1901; 1912; 1915;* and *1918;* U.S. *Census of Manufactures, 1914*, v.1, (1918), 450-51. Trenton potteries employed 4,500-5,000 people during these years. See U.S. Census, *1900: Manufactures, States and Territories*, v.8 (1902), 572-573; and U.S. Census, *1920* , v.9 (1923), 598.

34. Standard Sanitary bought the Great Western Plant in Kokomo, Indiana. Mott moved to Trenton between 1902 and 1905 and made metal and clay sanitary ware. Maddock, *Polished Earth*, 197-200.

35. Three employed more, and Tepeco claimed 850 workers in five shops, New Jersey, *Industrial Directory of New Jersey, 1915*, 518-21.

36. M.E. Cooke, "The Establishment of Technical Training Schools for Artist-Craftsmen in Connection with Industrial Plants," *Fourteenth Transactions of the American Ceramics Society, 1912 (TACS)*, 549.

37. Tepeco stock was worth $3,000,000 by 1921. John Moody, *Moody's Analysis of Investments and Securities*, Pt.II, Industrial Investments, (New York, 1921), 1370. Campbell was an archetypal corporate liberal. Born in 1856, he entered the trade with Princeton College chum William Burgess in 1879 and soon diversified hnto banking, railroads, and insurance. He was active in civic affairs, and promoted commission government in 1911. *CGJ*, 12 July 1879; *Trenton Banking Company*, (Trenton, 1907), 108-109; John Cumbler, *The Social History of Economic Decline*, (New Brunswick, 1989), 63; Dennis Starr, "The Nature and Uses of Economic, Political and Social Power in Trenton, New Jersey, 1890-1917," (Ph.D. dissertation, unpublished, Rutgers University, 1979), 300.

38. Brief For Defendant-in-Error to the U.S. Circuit Court of Appeals, No.219, RG 60, box 2240, file 60-82-2, 3, 17, U.S. v. Trenton Potteries, et.al., National Archives (hereafter US v. Tepeco).

39. U.S. Brief, Circuit Court, 3, 17; McCabe, *National Collective Bargaining*, 382; U.S., *Industrial Relations Commission, 1914*, Campbell, 2989; SPA-NBOP

"Negotiations," 1922, Maddock, 162-63. According to U.S., *Regulation and Restriction of Output*, 701, the industry had 40 percent excess capacity in 1904.

40. McCabe, *National Collective Bargaining*, 382; U.S. Brief, Circuit Court, 3.

41. Maddock, *Polished Earth*, 187, 189, 193, 272-4; NBOP, *President's Report, 1907*, 4; SPA-NBOP, "Negotiations," 18 September 1906, Campbell, 349. In 1903, the SPA coordinated sales through a Potteries' Selling Company which purchased at cost and distributed proceeds based on each firm's kilnspace. This quickly collapsed. Boston's Dececo Company sued Tepeco in 1903 for infringing on their siphonic action patent. Every company used the system, so all were liable. Dececo's victory allowed it royalties, and Campbell negotiated an agreement to license SPA companies until the patent expired in 1906. The treaty, he noted, allowed the SPA to "control the selling price."

42. U.S., *Regulation and Restriction of Output*, 700-1; SPA-NBOP "Negotiations," 18 September 1906, Campbell, 358; Maddock, *Polished Earth*, 186.

43. SPA-NBOP "Negotiations," Campbell, 18 September 1906, 349; U.S. Brief, Circuit Court.

44. Maddock, *Polished Earth*, 190-92, 308; U.S. Brief, Circuit Court, 5-11.

45. Maddock, *Polished Earth*, 193; U.S. Brief, Circuit Court, 11-13, 17. Only 60 percent of kilns reported by 1919.

46. Sklar, *Corporate Reconstruction*, 153, 166-68. Arthur Eddy argued that open pricing was reasonable since the information would come out anyway. By 1918, 10-15 percent of trade associations, including many construction suppliers, used this system. Arthur Jerome Eddy, *The New Competition*, (Chicago, 1916) 4th ed., 18; Thomas C. Cochran, *The American Business System: A Historical Perspective, 1900-1955*, (Cambridge, Mass., 1957), 62. See also H.R. Tosdal, "Open Price Associations," *American Economic Review*, v.7, no.2, (1917): 331-352; Milton N. Nelson, "The Effect of Open Price Association Activities on Competition and Prices," *American Economic Review*, v.13, no.2, (1923): 258-275; Robert Wiebe, *Businessmen and Reform: A Study of the Progressive Movement*, (Cambridge, 1962), 41; Robert F. Himmelberg, *The Origins of the National Recovery Administration: Business, Government and the Trade Association Issue, 1921-1933*, (New York, 1976), 1-25.

47. Maddock, *Polished Earth*, 193; U.S. Brief, Circuit Court, 35-38; Thomas Maddock's Sons Co, *Catalogue G 1916*, (1916), n.p.

48. U.S. Brief, Circuit Court, 21-28; Maddock, *Polished Earth*, 193, says 20 of 23 SPA members violated this agreement, but prosecutors noted that violations

were infrequent.

49. SPA-NBOP "Negotiations," Campbell, 1912, 18-19; U.S. Brief, Circuit Court, 61; U.S. Supreme Court, *Records and Briefs in United States Cases*, Brief of the Respondant, October 1926, 273 US 392 Briefs 1926 No. 27. Trenton shop sizes suggests relative equality of economies of scale in medium size firms, i.e., shops from 200-450 workers. See New Jersey, *Industrial Directory, 1901, 1912, 1915*. The SPA's impact on profits is suggestive. Returns to capital in Trenton's potteries rose from 8.4 percent in 1899 to 9.2 percent in 1909 and 12.1 percent by 1914. These include non-sanitary shops, but suggest the SPA discouraged price wars. Calculated from U.S. census materials, 1899, 1909, 1914.

50. SPA-NBOP "Negotiations," 18 September 1906, Campbell, 349-50, 352; 12 September 1906, J. Maddock, 30; 1912, Campbell, 45; Maddock, *Polished Earth*, 185-86; NBOP, *President's Report, 1906*, 16-17.

51. Firms deviated from lists 12-30 percent of the time. U.S. Brief, Circuit Court, 6, 13.

52. Labor costs in pottery formed 55 percent of value added in manufacturing and 40 percent of total value of product in 1919 as compared to 40 and 17 percent for all manufactures. Wages equaled 28 percent all raw materials costs, but pottery wages were *143 percent* of pottery material. U.S., *Fourteenth Census, 1920*, v.8, Manufactures, 160, 167.

53. *Potters' Herald (PH)*, 7 January 1915.

54. See James Weinstein, *The Corporate Ideal and the Liberal State, 1900-1918*, (Boston, 1968), 14-16; James R. Green, *The World of the Worker*, (New York, 1980), 60-61; Scranton, "Diversity in Diversity," 47-48.

55. New Jersey, *Annual Report of the Bureau of Statistics of Labor and Industries, 1904*, 564-65; letter William Haywood to Harry Daugherty, 24 July 1922, file 60-82-2, US v. Tepeco.

56. U.S., *Revision of the Final Report and Testimony Submitted To Congress by the Commission on Industrial Relations*, v.3, (Washington, 1916), Senate doc. 415, 64th Congress, 1st sess., Campbell, 2992; McCabe, *National Collective Bargaining*, 381; U.S., *Regulation and Restriction of Output*, 700-1.

57. NBOP, *Proceedings, 1902*, 11; *1903*, 18; *1904*, 61; *TUA*, 13, 27 June 1902, 21, 28 August 1903.

58. Maddock, *Polished Earth*, 185-86, 197-200. Standard Sanitary purchased a sanitary porcelain pottery in 1913.

59. U.S., *Industrial Relations Commission, 1914*, Campbell, 2985; NBOP, *Executive Board, 1919*, 31-34.

60. LU 45 Minutes, v.1, 24 March, 1903; NBOP, *Proceedings, 1903*, 8-9; see McCabe, *National Collective Bargaining*, 95, 139.

61. One year agreements became normal in 1906. NBOP, *President's Report, 1909*, 6; McCabe, *National Collective Bargaining*, 384.

62. U.S., *Industrial Relations Commission, 1914*, Campbell, 2986-87, Hutchins, 2997; NBOP, *First Vice President's Report, 1914*, 26; SPA-NBOP "Negotiations," 18 September 1906, Duffy, 385; 1914, Campbell, 1370, 1373. NBOP convention delegates voted on labor's demands, while SPA members collectively developed proposals. NBOP Vice President Frank Hutchins sought moderate goals, but he was often disappointed. See letter Hutchins to Menge, 16 August 1913, box 19, folder 3, IBOP Collection.

63. Either side could bring a dispute. See SPA-NBOP "Negotiations," August 1903, 43-47, 225-31; SPA-NBOP, *Wage Scale, 1920*, 3.

64. SPA-NBOP, *Wage Scale, 1920*, 3; U.S., *Industrial Commission, 1914*, Campbell, 2985-87, 2991.

65. SPA-NBOP "Negotiations," 22 August 1903, Campbell, 230; and *Wage Scale, 1920*, 3; U.S., *Industrial Commission, 1914*, Campbell, 2985-87, 2991, see also Hutchins, 2996, 2998; NBOP, *President's Report, 1907*, 7, *First Vice President's Report, 1909*, 18; *1913*, 15; *1916*, 23; *PH*, 5 December 1912.

66. U.S., *Industrial Commission, 1914*, Campbell, 2985-87, 2991, see also Hutchins, 2996, 2998; SPA-NBOP, *Wage Scale, 1920*, 3. In 1914, John Maddock complained that the shop committee had become "a perfect farce," unwilling to rule honestly on almost anything, SPA-NBOP "Negotiations," 1914, 1312.

67. Maddock Family Papers, Book 2, 16; NBOP, *First Vice President's Report, 1908*, 18; *1910*, 22; *1913*, 15; *1916*, 23; McCabe, *National Collective Bargaining*, 430.

68. See *PH*, 10 October, 11, 24 November, 22 December 1910. Until retiring in 1921, Hutchins moderated rank-and-file demands. His tenure reflected his popularity among conservative NBOP leaders and western members, not the love of most local sanitary workers.

69. NBOP, *President's Report, 1907*, 6; U.S., *Industrial Commission, 1914*, Campbell, 2987, Hutchins, 2998.

70. SPA-NBOP "Negotiations," 30 September 1910, Hutchins, 18.

71. SPA-NBOP "Negotiations," 29 September 1910, Campbell, 19; 30 September 1910, 16-17; 1914, 1052-3; U.S., *Industrial Relations Commission, 1914*, Campbell, 2994.

72. Sanitary potters experimented with one-fire glazes, new saggermaking

machines to make clay boxes for the kilns, and oil fired kilns. NBOP, *Executive Board Report, 1919*, 31-34; *PH*, 22 September 1910, 26 January, 21 September 1911.

73. For casting techniques and their difficulties see Maddock, *Polished Earth*, 123-124; U.S., Department of the Interior, Bureau of Mines, Technical Paper 126, Taine G. McDougal, *The Casting of Clay Wares*, (Washington, 1916); C. J. Kirk, "Use of the Casting Process for Large Clay Wares," *TACS*, v.15, 1913: 573-84.

74. The Universal left the SPA over the SPA-NBOP contract in 1905. Most replacement workers left by 1907. Maddock, *Polished Earth*, 123-124; NBOP, *President's Report, 1908*, 15. Maddock called Kirk "a genius in many ways," responsible for "blazing the trail that was followed by others to their great benefit." He made colored ware and sold to mail-order houses but was "not the money-making type." He attempted "some other scheme that would offset the advantages enjoyed from the former." Ibid., 279-80.

75. The Abbington, Illinois pottery was staffed, the union newspaper reported, by "dagoes imported from New Castle, Pa." who made seven closets at $.50, half the pressing price. Pressers made 4-5 pieces. Another casting shop soon opened in California. *PH*, 11 February, 3 June, 19 August 1909, 29 September 1910.

76. C.J. Kirk, "Use of the Casting Process for Large Clay Wares," *TACS*, v.15, (1913): 573-84.

77. C.J. Kirk, "Scientific Management and the Bonus System as Applied to Pottery Manufacture," *TACS*, v.16 (1914): 270; Richard Edwards, *Contested Terrain* (New York, 1979), 113; U.S. Supreme Court, *Records and Briefs in United States Cases, October Term, 1926*, no.27, (1927), 471. For scientific management see Harry Braverman, *Labor and Monopoly Capital* (New York, 1974); Daniel Nelson, *Frederick W. Taylor and the Rise of Scientific Management* (Madison, 1980); David Montgomery, *Workers' Control in America* (New York, 1979); Idem, *The Fall of the House of Labor* (New York, 1987), 216-56; David F. Noble, *America By Design: Science, Technology, and the Rise of Corporate Capitalism* (New York, 1977); Dan Clawson, *Bureaucracy and the Labor Process: The Transformation of U.S. Industry, 1860-1920* (New York, 1980).

78. George Brain, "The Dressler Tunnel Kiln For Firing Sanitary Ware," *Journal of the American Ceramic Society (JACS)*, v.3, (1921): 709; C.J. Kirk, "Results Obtained in Firing Sanitary Earthenware in the Dressler Tunnel Kiln," *TACS*, v.18, (1916): 532-543; Lawrence E. Barringer, "A Continuously Operated Tunnel Kiln For High-Grade Clay Ware," *TACS*, v.18, (1916): 106-123; Maddock,

*Polished Earth*, 130-132; Carl B. Harrop, "The Continuous Tunnel Kiln," *JACS*, v.3 (1921): 697-700. Using natural gas allowed the Universal to save thousands of dollars on clay boxes for firing ware. See Brain, 709. None of the articles cited list capital cost figures, but all speak to operating cost savings.

79. Maddock Family Papers, 15; McDougal, *Casting*.

80. U.S., *Historical Statistics*, 640; U.S., *Mineral Resources*, 1918, pt.2, 859-60.

81. One declared "while I approve of all practical labor-saving devices, I do not consider any mechanical device a good investment that will not save its cost in one year." Arthur S. Watts, "Construction and Equipment of a White Ware Pottery," *TACS*, v.5 (1903): 347.

82. SPA-NBOP, "Negotiations," 28 September 1910, Duffy, 7, 29; September 1910, Campbell, 4: 1912, Campbell, 50-51.

83. *PH*, 10 October 1912; NBOP, *First Vice President's Report, 1913*, 14-15; SPA-NBOP "Negotiations," 1914, 1275.

84. NBOP, *First Vice President's Report, 1913*, 14-15. Operatives argued that casting was experimental and that the men should not be responsible. SPA-NBOP "Negotiations," 1914, Hutchins, 1075, 1080, McDevitt, 1093-1094.

85. *PH*, 7 January 1915; NBOP, *Executive Board Report, 1918*, 26-27. A 1917 call to unionize casting shops yielded little when Executive Board members decided that non-union casters sought to earn as much as they could and return to Italy. Organizing stopped with these findings and fragile war-induced trade.

86. *PH*, 5 February 1914, 22 March 1915.

87. NBOP, *Executive Board Report, 1918*, 26-27.

88. Montgomery, *Fall of the House of Labor*, 370-464; and *Worker's Control*, 91-138; David Brody, *Steelworkers in America: The Nonunion Era*, (Cambridge, 1960), 180-278.

89. Morton Keller, *Regulating a New Economy: Public Policy and Economic Change in America, 1900-1933*, (Cambridge, 1990). See also McCraw, *Regulation in Perspective*.

90. Wholesale prices doubled and consumer prices rose by three-fourths between 1915 and 1919, while average urban wages rose over 150 percent. Donald R. Adams, Jr., "Prices and Wages," *Encyclopedia of American Economic History: Studies in the Principal Movements and Ideas*, v.1, Glenn Porter, ed., (New York, 1980), 234, 241. Most workers earnings rose more than the potters. Only 7 of 25 trades selected for comparison by New Jersey's Bureau of Labor and Statistics averaged higher earnings than the potters in 1915. By 1916, 11 of 25 averaged

higher earnings and 10 surpassed them by over 5 percent. New Jersey, Bureau of Industrial Statistics, *Annual Report, 1916*, 23; 1917, 22. See also, U.S., Department of Labor, Bureau of Labor Statistics, Survey of Household Earnings and the Utilization of Income, September 1918, National Archives.

91. NBOP, *Executive Board Report, 1917*, 27; *1918*, 19; LU 45, "Minutes," v.4, 15 May 1917; v.5, 31 July 1917. Rate increases were tacked onto 1914 rates and did not compound.

92. NBOP, *Executive Board Report, 1917*, 27-28.

93. LU 45, Minutes, v.5, 2 August 1917; NBOP, *Executive Board Report, 1918*, 18-20.

94. NBOP, *Executive Board Report, 1918*, 21-25; LU 45, Minutes, v.5, 14 May 1918.

95. Maddock, *Polished Earth*, 314-15; U.S., Brief, Circuit Court, 6. The Universal rejoined the SPA to market its cast porcelain in 1919.

96. U.S. Supreme Court, *Records and Briefs*, 645-46.

97. U.S., *Historical Statistics*, 623; consumer prices rose by one-third from 1918 to 1920. Adams, "Wages and Prices," 234.

98. NBOP, *Executive Board Report, 1919*, 27-31.

99. NBOP, *Executive Board Report, 1920*, 30-32. Hutchins "purposely refrained from voicing any of the radical sentiment entertained by our members" and only requested 25 percent.

100. NBOP, *Executive Board Report, 1921*, 52-63.

101. Milton Friedman and Anna Jacobson Schwartz, *A Monetary History of the United States, 1857-1960*, (Princeton, 1963), 231-239; U.S., Brief, Circuit Court, 6; SPA-NBOP, Conference of Wage Committees of Sanitary Potters' Association and National Brotherhood of Operative Potters, 25-26 October 1921.

102. U.S., Brief, Circuit Court, 3.

103. Shotliff, "History of the Labor Movement," 106-107; SPA-NBOP, "Negotiations, Manufacturers' Statement Read at the Opening Session of Sanitary Conference," 12 September 1922, 4; Maddock, *Polished Earth*, 96-97; McCabe, *National Collective Bargaining*, 410-15; NBOP, *Executive Board Report, 1921*, 52-56. See debate and resolution on cuts by LU 45, Minutes, 8 February 1921, v.5. Housing starts rose from 247,000 to 449,000 between 1920 and 1921, U.S., *Historical Statistics*, 640.

104. U.S., *Historical Statistics*, 640. Casters worked in 16 SPA shops and made 11,400 pieces a week in 1921 and in 22 shops making 26,000 pieces by 1922. The 125 non-union casters made 7,500 weekly. NBOP, *Statement of the Executive*

*Board Regarding Conditions of the Sanitary Trade, Together with Propositions to be Submitted to a Referendum of the Trade,* 9 October 1922, 4-5.

105. SPA-NBOP "Negotiations," September 1922, 167-68.

106. *Trenton,* 10 (June 1934): 17; Maddock, *Polished Earth,* 323, 200-201, notes that Crane purchased the former Canadian Tepeco shop in 1920, although Tepeco had sold this plant in 1915. One tunnel kiln equaled from 9-20 periodic kilns. See William Gates, Jr., *City of Hills and Kilns: Life and Work in East Liverpool, Ohio,* (East Liverpool, 1984), 264-66.

107. See C. W. McCullough, "Reduction of Varieties in Manufactured Products," *JACS,* 5, (1922): 221-226; Himmelberg, *Origins of the NRA,* 10.

108. Himmelberg, *Origins of the NRA,* 10,; "MEMORANDUM FOR COL. GOFF.," from C.R. Keep [name unclear], 11 January 1921, file 60-82-2 [this date is undoubtedly an error and should be 1922]. Edward Stokes, banker, ex-governor, and a leading Republican, called the pottery bosses "good friends of yours" and "high class men" done in by disgruntled "Hebrew salesmen." See E. Stokes to Harry Daugherty, 22 December 1921, file 60-82-2; and letters from Sen. Jos. Frelinghuysen, file 60-82-2-1x, and Congressmen Joseph Begg, file 60-82-2-6, US v. Tepeco.

109. Maddock, *Polished Earth,* 189-90; letter from Wm. Hayward to Harry Daugherty, 23 July 1922, file 60-82-2, US v. Tepeco.

110. Standard Sanitary Manufacturing Co.'s withdrawal shocked everyone. Maddock, *Polished Earth,* 102; "Manufacturers' Statement," 131-32.

111. The "Manufacturers' Statement" presents their views. The negotiations were very hostile. SPA-NBOP "Negotiations," September 1922, 49. SPA negotiators insisted on 20-25 percent cuts and casting at 50 percent the pressing rate.

112. SPA-NBOP "Negotiations," September 1922, 24-5, 87, 99, 149-50. They defended the stint as crucial for older workers.

113. SPA-NBOP "Negotiations," September 1922, 154-63.

114. See NBOP, *Statement Regarding the Sanitary Trade,* 10; McCabe, National Collective Bargaining, 386-87; Shotliff, "History of the Labor Movement," 182-83. These negotiations were more conciliatory.

115. NBOP, *Statement of the Executive Board,* 15.

116. See NBOP, *Statement Regarding the Sanitary Trade*; NBOP, *Executive Board Report, 1923,* 11-57, 92; Shotliff, "History of the Labor Movement," 406. The fund stood at stood at over $724,000 in 1921.

117. NBOP, *Executive Board Report, 1923,* 11-57, 92; SPA - NBOP

"Negotiations," October 1922, Cartlidge, 40; see McCabe, *National Collective Bargaining*, 386-89, 428-30; Shotliff, "History of the Labor Movement," 182-85. Only two small locals voted against striking. Trenton's pressers voted down the contract 750-88. One newspaper noted after the strike began, ". . . the expert pressers do not feel that the expensive pieces can be made with any degree of success" by casting. *Daily State Gazette*, 3 November 1922. Bert Power recalled that younger and American men resisted the walkout. He remembered one radical English potter playing with a stack of gold coins and insisting the men could outlast their employers. A sample of the 1915 state census manuscripts suggests that English migration increased after 1910.

118. McCabe, *National Collective Bargaining*, 386-89, 428-430; Shotliff, "History of the Labor Movement," 182-85. For an inversion of this phenomenon of institutional miscommunication see Michael Schwartz, *Radical Protest and Social Structure: The Southern Farmers' Alliance,* (New York, 1976).

119. Letter from Executive Board to Officers and Members, 2 August 1923, box 40, folder 8, IBOP Collection; NBOP, *Executive Board Report, 1923,* 93-94, 1924, 33-49; McCabe, *National Collective Bargaining,* 387-88; Shotliff, "History of the Labor Movement," 183-84; Maddock, *Polished Earth,* 103-4.

120. Letter from William Hayward to Harry Daugherty, 16 February 1924; see telegrams from William Hayward to A. T. Seymour, Acting Attorney General, 11, 20 April 1923, box 2240, US v. Tepeco; Maddock, *Polished Earth,* 193.

121. Michael Fligstein, *The Transformation of Corporate Control,* (Cambridge, 1990), 123-24.

122. Maddock, *Polished Earth,* 188.

123. Brandeis recused himself because his daughter, Susan Brandeis, helped prosecute. SPA attorney, former Chief Justice Charles Evans Hughes, asked that the sentences be suspended, and the court agreed. No one convicted in the case ever went to jail. Ibid., 194-95.

124. Justice Stone's opinion said the Sherman Act's fundamental view is that "the public interest is best protected from the evils of monopoly and price controls by the maintenance of competition. . . . Whether the prices actually agreed upon were reasonable or unreasonable was immaterial. . ." U.S., *United States Reports*, v.273, "Cases Adjudged in the Supreme Court at October Term 1926," (Washington, 1927), 397. See also Keller, *Regulating a New Economy,* 39.

125. Maddock, *Polished Earth,* 194-202; Shotliff, "History of the Labor Movement," 185. Crane took control of Tepeco in April 1924. Moody's Analysis of Investments and Securities, 1924, Pt.II, 1600.

126. Brody, *Steelworkers in America*; James R. Barrett, *Work and Community in the Jungle: Chicago's Packinghouse Workers, 1894-1922*, (Urbana: University of Illinois Press, 1987); Stephen Meyer, III, *The Five Dollar Day: Labor Management and Social Control in the Ford Motor Co.*, (Albany, N.Y.: SUNY Press, 1981).

# Part Two

*Market Making:
Communications and
Structures of Business*

*Chapter 4*

Adam Smith's monumental *Inquiry into the Nature and Causes of the Wealth of Nations* appeared in 1776, the year in which 13 of Great Britain's 32 North American colonies declared their political independence, less than a twelve month after James Watt had achieved the first practical application of his "improved fire engine" (patented as recently as 1769). Smith's readers, however, would have found nothing in this work resembling, even foreshadowing, the late-Victorian understanding of the "industrial revolution," nor any reference to his sometime neighbor James Watt, instrument maker to the University of Glasgow, with whom he had likely discussed the possibilities of mechanical power. The topics of colonies and commerce received a far more intensive treatment from Smith than manufactures (division of labor and "secrets"), let alone steam engines or machinery. Expansion of markets at home and overseas had fostered division of labor and augmented industry and trade, almost in spite of the perverse commercial policies pursued by many European governments at the behest of special interests (such as "towns corporate" or royal exchequers). For Adam Smith, "the discovery of America and that of a passage to the East Indies by the Cape of Good Hope" were "the two greatest and most important events recorded in the history of mankind." Well, Clio was meretricious even before she took up with metrics.

Western Europeans in succession--following the Portuguese penetration of the ocean winds' secrets--had gained a foothold in the more commercially-developed markets of Asia and access to the material resource potentials of the Americas. Unfortunately, concluded Smith, the mutual benefits expected from such intercourse had *not* been realized. While their attempts to "engross as much as possible the commerce" of the trading-post empires of the African and Asian littorals, or to plant settlements in the Americas, had doubtless enriched many of their subjects, European states had failed to maximize either the wealth of their nations' commercial and manufacturing interests or the net revenues of their royal exchequers which would have occurred, Smith insisted, under a system of free and unfettered markets open to all. To be sure, the Scottish moralist was confusing "political economy" with history, as well as indulging his pet peeve, the monopoly of the East India Company, yet his complaint about the "opportunity costs," so to speak, of coercive economic policies and the narrow "corporation spirit" animating cities and nations, as well as joint-stock companies, were moderate compared with his condemnation of the cruelty and injustice visited on so much of the globe by the expansion of Europe. Sooner or later "superiority of force" enabled the invaders "to commit with impunity every sort of injustice in those remote countries" beyond the seas. The matter had never been more succinctly stated, except perhaps by Lemuel Gulliver at the end of *Travels* published in 1726. He had been there; but he sought "to vex the world rather than divert it."

In Chapter 4, "Merchants and Planters: The Developing Market Structure of the Colonial Chesapeake Reconsidered," Jacob M. Price reviews some of the longer term consequences of English encroachments on one of those remote and improbable countries. He carries the story down to roughly the time when Smith's *Wealth* was written. This particular country which he calls Chesapeake was expropriated by "authority" of letters patent issued to the Society of Adventurers (investors) by a Scot wearing the English Crown in 1606. The Virginia Company of London, the larger of two ventures sponsored by the Society, was the 18th out of 34 enterprises, mostly joint-stock, chartered by the Crown between 1553 (Muscovy Co.) and 1630 (Providence Island Co.) as essentially trading ventures into exotic parts. The first to capitalize England's pretension to North America (based on Caboto's voyage of 1497, sponsored by Bristol merchants), it was also the first to plant an enduring settlement of English outside the confines of the British Isles. Prior to 1607 English interests in the Americas had centered on the international fisheries off Newfoundland or bases for plundering forays to the Caribbean and Spanish Main. Whatever the actual (mixed) motives of adventurers and planters in the Virginia Company, its announced corporate intent was simply "propagating of the Christian Religion" among "Infidels and Savages living in those parts." Failing all else, and after two more reorganizations--to strengthen its capital, attract labor, and incorporate the Bermudas in its domain (1612)- -the Company devoted its principal missionary enthusiasm from c. 1615 to the cultivation, curing, and marketing of tobacco.

The tobacco culture furnished the enduring commercial base for English settlement in Virginia, if not for the London Company. Its exclusive charter was vacated by the Court of King's Bench in 1624 after an inquiry reported mismanagement, near insolvency, and negligence of life in pursuit of private gain. Of 7,549 people known to have entered the Company's mainland settlements since 1607 (mostly since 1618), only 1,095 remained alive in 1624 (most probably died from deficiency diseases, not massacres). Neither interest nor principal on the Company's enormous investment, exceeding £200,000, was ever repaid. A number of survivors got their tobacco-pickin' hands on greater or lesser share grants and headrights in land.

The oppressive work discipline and social degradation imposed on servants by former officers and larger land holders with magisterial backing thereafter in the briefly booming colony reduced the Crown's possession, in the words of one historian, "to a charnel house." Such conditions were worse than any voluntary servitude known in England and were an ominous portent of the fate awaiting enslaved Africans, present under various devices since the 20 "Christian Servants" of 1619 but not becoming numerous before the last quarter of the century when their proportion rose from c. 6 percent to nearly I 0 percent of the general population. By that time, the white "yeomanry" of former indentured servants retained little sympathy with their black brethren who remained permanently in bondage. At the close of the century tobacco accounted for nearly 78 per cent--Jacob Price's estimate--of the value of English imports from her mainland colonies. Only sugar, which--fortunately for the Chesapeake-- had rapidly displaced tobacco and much of white settlement in England's West Indian islands after mid-century, furnished a larger share of official import values from the Americas.

This vast wealth from tobacco cultivation was essentially created by the organization of demand and the extension of credit. Without effective demand at fairly stable, if low, prices, all the acres of Chesapeake land in Virginia and the Maryland proprietary and hours of burdensome labor by slaves, servants, small and large proprietors would have been in vain. Price uses the writings of earlier historians of Chesapeake society to focus his own analysis of the organization of supply: the changing commercial practices and marketing structures which carried a rising tide of tobacco exports to the British Isles and beyond.

Price seeks answers to questions concerning the contributions of different sized producers to the export, and the respective shares of different institutional arrangements--consignments, direct trade through resident factors, merchants, etc.--in accomplishing export transactions. Small and middling planters seem to have sustained a major role at all times in terms of numbers and market shares, with marketing effected principally by factors of English and Scottish firms, augmented by local merchants and store keepers, Consignments on commission from larger planters and merchants (some small operators, too) remained important, especially for those receiving substantial imports of manufactures and other "accoutrements of gentlemanly status" in return.

Adam Smith may have decried the heavy visible hand of customs and naval regulators in perverting "the natural courses" of profitable commerce on behalf of favored interests, but Price certainly makes expert use of their extant paperwork as sources for his quantitative answers. At different times English ports from London and Bristol to uttermost Whitehaven were involved in tobacco but, during the second quarter of the 18th century, Adam Smith's Glasgow--a part of the "British" empire since the Act of Union, 1707--was the rising star. Price estimates about 40 percent of all tobacco imports were shipped to Glasgow by 1765, most of which was re-exported. Regulations help give towns wealth as do reexports of goods produced elsewhere, Smith complained, but he probably did not have Glasgow in mind. The experience of living in growing Glasgow, and discussions with the city's "tobacco lords" almost certainly affected Smith's views on transoceanic commerce, particularly the difficulties many merchants had in collecting payments for goods--two to three years, he thought--shipped on the basis of credit advanced through resident factors in competition with each other for tobacco freights. The Glasgow district had an old manufacturing base dating from before the Union but, to meet the demands of Chesapeake colonials as payment for their weed, a dozen or more diverse manufactures located around the city between 1725 and 1763, including textiles, although none can be said exactly to presage "industrial revolution".

## Chapter 5

Political separation of Great Britain from the lucky 13 American colonies after 1783 was more the outcome of problems in imperial public finance - sharing some of the costs of a "down-sized" military and civil establishment in America after the French defeat in 1763--than of onerous burdens imposed on colonial economies by un-American acts of trade and navigation. The liberated commerce of the United States did not surge outward, notwithstanding some fast boats to China, nor thrust forward to "industrial revolution." Indeed, only after Britain and her continental allies went to war against the French Revolution and Napoleon after 1792 did business and shipping interests in the United States begin to enjoy the modest, albeit fragile, prosperity of the "neutral years" supplying both sides with colonial-type goods and services--until the ponderous weight of Jefferson's "embargo" came down on exports and re-exports alike at the end of 1807. The country drifted into campaigns to free wrongfully "impressed" seamen and liberate the land of nascent Canada from the imperialist yoke.

There were no great alternative markets yearning for American tobacco, which never recovered its colonial peak in quantitative terms, and had fallen below the upstart raw cotton by 1810. The cotton was mostly exported to--yes, Virginia!--THE FORMER MOTHER COUNTRY, since the mid-1790s. It was the cotton culture powered by the transoceanic "industrial evolution" in Britain that drove agriculture *and* slavery across the deep southern states to the lower Mississippi Valley.

In Chapter 5, "The Twilight of the 'Nabobs': Civil War Losses and the End of Natchez, Mississippi as an Investment Center," Morton Rothstein treats the effects of the political breakdown of the United States after mid-century upon the lives and fortunes of some wealthy planter families in the area of Natchez, Mississippi. Founded by French invaders as Fort Rosalie in 1716, Natchez claimed to be the "oldest city on the Mississippi River" and had once been the home of the largest and most unified indigenous culture in the lower Mississippi Valley: from whence came its proud name. With an 1850 population of 4,434, including slaves, Natchez was the largest city and port in Mississippi, 309 miles up river from the great port of New Orleans, whose export values had briefly surpassed those of New York City in the trade recovery of the early '40s. Immense cargoes of cotton and other commodities poured into New Orleans annually - on a thousand flat boats and 3,000 steamboats from Natchez and other places along Ole Man River and his tributaries as well as by Lake Pontchartrain and the New Canal. "When its railroads to the north are completed," opined one *New and Complete Statistical Gazetteer* hopefully in 1853, "much of the import trade now having its course from the northern Atlantic coast will certainly make New Orleans its entrepôt." Meanwhile, the longest railway then ran about six miles to Carrollton; a magnetic telegraph stretched 90 miles to the delta at Balize, the principal ship channel to and from the Gulf of Mexico.

More recently wired "lightning lines" also linked the Crescent City via Charleston, S.C. to New York, to boom town Cincinnati and on to Lake Erie at Cleveland. Commodity price movements, which had lagged up to three or four months behind the seaboard as recently as 1839, were known within minutes, according to Thomas S. Berry, in New Orleans or Cincinnati by "the Panic of '57." Wholesale price differentials in major cities had converged to within half-a-dozen percentage points. Average incomes from commodity production and commerce in the lower Mississippi Valley centering on New Orleans were high above the national average (regardless of whether slave heads are included in the denominator), surpassing even average incomes in the industrial urbanizing states of the northeast. From such income flows had so accumulated what Rothstein calls "one of the highest concentrations of wealth," embodied in slaves, lands, and in the cases of elite Natchez families at least, many diversified investments and other assets outside Cotton's kingdom. The resident population of old "feudal" Natchez had climbed to 7, 1 00 in 1860. As the American system of interacting regional markets slowly, irresistibly, evolved toward a more unified national economy after 1840, the older more perfect political Union was irrepressibly disintegrating well before the fateful election of 1860.

Civil Wars are likely to be among the more degrading and self destructive conflicts when the practised impostures of everyday politics are finally paid for on both sides in blood. The "whiggish" nabobs, tied by kinship, friendship, schooling, private sentiment and vested interest to the wider Union, as well as bound to the customs, institutions, and encumbering properties of provincial Natchez, became understandably ambivalent to a point, as Rothstein affirms, "verging on schizophrenia." If their estates and felt-obligations to their heirs immobilized them with a hope that the North might "let us part in peace", they were soon moved to accommodate the secessionist folly, accept preemptive strikes against fancied slave revolts, and abide the requisitioning of their sons, Then, after Vicksburg's fall in July, 1863, they must withstand the liberating embrace of cotton speculating officers from General Grant's army, under the reproachful eyes and pointed snubs of their Natchez neighbors. Most difficult, as trying to the nabob trimmers as to dejected secessionists, was the adjustment to "the new labor system" emerging under the Union occupation, aggravated in 1864 with the seizure of livestock and the reenslavement of "freedmen" crimped by Confederate raiders. Rothstein's elite planters and their heirs could never put it all together again.

## Chapter 6

New Orleans itself did not recover the export/import volumes of the antebellum years before the 1880s. The population of Natchez had by that time settled back to its prewar levels with roughly equal numbers of blacks and whites. For the first time in 1890 it exceeded 10,000 residents, when others were beginning to capitalize the area's rich resources of timber (and later of oil). The earlier expectation of New Orleans' boosters to capture "much of the import trade... from the northern Atlantic coast" had not materialized. The thrust of settlement in the re-United States had passed westward beyond the Mississippi Valley and the era of "transcontinental" development had begun.

During the 1850s seven railroad connections had been cobbled together--another built in Canada by a division of Tom Brassey's "industrial army--to link "the tidewater and the great interior basins of the country." Lines from Lakes Erie and Michigan struck the Ohio at eight places, the Mississippi at ten (from Memphis north), tieing together "the two great hydrographic systems of the West," Such a network "assisted by the Erie Canal," declared Joseph C. G. Kennedy, Superintendent of the 8th U.S. Census, affords "ample means" to move all "produce seeking eastern markets, and could, without being overtaxed, transport the entire surplus products of the interior." For the first time the full resource potential of the global land masses was being brought – independently of the primary river flows – into the channels of international exchange. Rail transit, nevertheless, was adduced by one New Orleans observer as "operating to impede the city's growth." His litany of grievance listed the rise of the Great Lakes carrying trade, the fractious delta, the scourge of yellow fever, and the earlier blight of black slavery (avoidance by "free labor"). Yet New Orleans did grow: in trade and population, if not as fast as some of the others (339,075 by 1910.) In fifth rank behind the nation's New York/ Brooklyn metropolis in 1860, it fell away to 11th rank in 1900. Between 1860 and 1910 eight major cities overtook New Orleans in size; nine, if the twin-cities of St.Paul-Minneapolis at the upper end of the Mississippi are included, 516,152 in 1910. St. Paul was there first (see Chapter 9); it became the HQ for the Great Northern R.R. after 1878, the focus of this chapter, although its transfluvial sibling soon set the pace in point of growth.

The transcontinental era had been signalled in October 1861, six months after the Confederate attack on Fort Sumter, when the Pacific Telegraph Company's line via Salt Lake City linked San Francisco and Omaha--a recently incorporated river and prairie freighting point on the Missouri, some 1,400 miles west of New York. This technological feat was accomplished scarcely 18 months after the organizational triumph of "the Pony Express" when, under the direction of the Central Overland California & Pike's Peak Express Co, its first mail carrier rode into Sacramento, completing a 1,950 mile relay from St. Joseph, Missouri in eight days. In 1861 also, the Wells, Fargo Co. (1851), which had operated a mail service to San Francisco via the Isthmus of Panama, took over the Overland Mail Co., which itself had been formed as recently as 1857.

Things were moving in the saddle, sure enough, but it was still a long time to wait for a Greyhound Bus. With the settlement of the Oregon boundary dispute in 1846 and the concurrent assault on Mexican lands (ceded in 1848), U.S. territory finally faced on the Pacific Ocean. The immediate lure of gold in 1849 had manifestly destined a greater migration to Alta California--despite the hazards and human costs of every available route--than could ever have been drawn by merchants and missionaries combined in pursuit of the old "China Market" mirage. Eventually a steam train did come along.

The first railway to California was not to be completed for another twenty years. Without benefit of Cliometrics, naive people at the time thought a federal subsidy was necessary, although both California and Kansas issued state charters to eager private enterprisers. Sectional deadlock in the Congress meanwhile had delayed government interference until after secession when land grants and loans were conditionally authorized by the rump Union Congress in 1862. The Union and Central Pacifics building respectively from Omaha and San Francisco finally met near Ogden, Utah, in the heart of Mormon country in 1869, with much of the 1,848 mile span then running through "unsettled" territory. Between 1881 and 1893 four other "transcontinentals" were completed, but the one true *trans*continental in North America, perhaps, was the Canadian Pacific

Railway built in fits and starts between 1872 and 1885, tying Montreal on the tidal St. Lawrence across 2,906 miles to Vancouver (founded by the CPR in 1877) on the Pacific Strait of Georgia, to secure British Columbia for the Dominion of 1867. The last of the U.S. "transcontinentals" was the Great Northern, a "streak of rust running through a desert," from St. Paul to Seattle on Puget Sound and New Westminster on the Fraser River in British Columbia. The G.N. was built by a Canadian-born store clerk, James J. Hill, and his associates between 1878 and 1893, with none of the chicanery found elsewhere in railroad construction on both sides of the border. Hill's genius turned "the desert" into an agricultural empire, promoting immigration and community settlements, finally establishing steamship connections from Seattle to the Orient, pioneering on the Pacific rim. It is fitting that in Chapter 6, "Market Coordination, Cooperation, or Competition: The Great Northern Railway and Bus Transportation in the 1920s," Margaret Walsh introduces Ralph Budd, a worthy heir to Hill as President of G.N. and, in his own way, a commendably farsighted builder.

The huge investment of funds and human effort into thrusting rail corridors from the Mississippi Valley over the Rockies to the coast (including satellite and feeder lines) did not set off an explosive growth of western cities. Some measure of urbanization, to be sure, occurred in every frontier state and territory but, with the exception of San Francisco, an empire apart, expanding for two decades *before* the first transcontinental, no city in the newly-developing resource regions beyond St. Louis had netted even 50,000 residents before Kansas City, Missouri, in the late '70s and Denver, Colorado, more than half a decade later. In fact, the urbanization tide ran eastward from the Mississippi Valley along the southern shores of the Great Lakes and in the Ohio Valley cresting in half a dozen great cities. Among them all, the most phenomenal was Chicago where the Great Lakes touch the Mississippi system, offering competitive waterways and rail linkages to the markets of the east coast. Since the pre-railroad 1830s, Chicago's population increase had undergone "such a continuous 'boom' no other American city had ever known": 8.6 per cent compounded annually. It was already the nation's second city in 1890, when net migration and annexation boosted its agglomerative total to more than 1, 100,000 inhabitants. It was *the* railroad city; by the early 1900s, 14 percent of global railway mileage centered on it. It was "the second largest Bohemian City of the world, the third Swedish, the fourth

Norwegian, the fifth Polish, the fifth German," New York being the fourth. Brooklyn, N.Y.--never a railroad city--was the only center east of the Appalachians to have grown like a "Mid-western" city; mushrooming from 97,000 (already rank 7) in 1850 to 838,547 (3) in 1890, and to 1,166,582 in 1900 and growing so fast that New York-Manhattan had joined it and other adjacent territory to make sure Gotham West was still No. 1.

The physiognomy of American capitalism was changed for ever over the latter half of the 19th century; and the face lifting was performed by Dr. Transportation. Unprecedented volumes of savings were mobilized at home and abroad for ventures in the construction, operation, and consolidation of railroads, with multiplier effects on land values, iron and steel, lumber and coal production. Every other branch of business was dwarfed by comparison excepting that of the Union itself in fighting and financing the Civil War. The country's capital markets pyramiding up to New York were transformed and, following the railroad model in its early resort to limited liability, *corporate* enterprise came to displace proprietaries and partnerships as legal cover for carving out continental markets. It was no coincidence, partly under the weight of railway financing across the ocean, that discussions leading to the Companies Act of 1862--assimilating English and Scottish mercantile law--had recommended a warning flag "limited" be attached to the title of all companies that sought to limit their liability "in order to prevent the obvious danger to persons trading with them in ignorance of their limitation..."

The historian Alfred D. Chandler, Jr., has characterized railroading as "the nation's first big business," while Henry Adams, at the time, spoke of "a generation mortgaged to the railroads." The question of by how much railroad transport services actually advanced the U.S. social economy *net* over possibly available water carrier services seems curiously scholastic in nature! Suffice, perhaps, that this vast space-time contraction allowed the railroad magnates in 1883 to one-up Caesar by dividing the conquered country *in partes quattuor*--standard time zones--where previously 50-odd local time belts had obtained: a celestial longitudinal coup by management not ratified by the very terrestrial, duly elected, representatives of the people in Washington D.C. before 1919.

The future of capital was at stake. As building activity had moved beyond the local resource capacities required for short eastern seaboard lines, the entire process--driven at once by fear of competition and inordinate greed--became more manic and turbulent. Contemptuous of public sentiment, ruthless in relation to their bondholders as well as their employees, debauching even of political entities never known for their probity, the magnates, who built up their overcapitalized and under performing assets--with critical aid from the likes of private bankers J.P. Morgan--into more stable and financially-solvent "systems," were abominations to "the people" in general and freight shippers in particular. By the early 20th century some 17 consolidated "systems" controlled 77 percent of railroads' 228,000 mileage and a larger share of revenues.

Consolidation was the outcome of "wasteful" competition among American railroad corporations that had shocked even Mr. Herbert Spencer. Competition was the bane of railroad leaders' existence: the unappreciated mother of technological and organizational invention. There was never "a level playing field" throughout the Golden West. "Survival of the Fittest" among railroads--with up to 60 percent of their stake tied up in "overhead"--necessitated either "responsible" collusion among corporate leaders or "sympathetic understanding" by public regulatory bodies. The industry had weathered the I.C.C.'s whistle-blowing threat in the late 1880s, and had continued to tie in competing lines and equipment manufacturers by lease, minority or majority stock ownership, and outright purchase, as well as through interlocking directorates and other "communities of interest" into the early 1900s. More difficult to cope with were technical changes *outside* the industry which at almost any moment might upset the organizational applecart. Such a threat--a speck on the horizon--was already there in 1893 when the Great Northern opened up from St. Paul to Seattle. By that time, the first American wagons powered by internal combustion engines guzzling petroleum-derived gasoline, were being demonstrated to a largely indifferent, yawning, public--increasingly turned on by "the bicycle craze."

A more immediate threat was posed by electric traction. From small beginnings on the streets of the old Confederate capital, Richmond, Virginia in 1887, overhead electric trolleys were soon displacing horsecar lines on city streets across the nation and, in spite of the depression of 1893-97, spreading into suburban districts and, in more populated parts, into interurban networks in direct competition with steam. No vector of scientific and technological progress was socially more significant than electricity: essentially a conversion and transmission of energy, generated by friction, induction, or chemical change. Communications, illumination, machinery, traction: there seemed no limit to its capitalizable applications. Electricity offered finance capital protean power.

The railroads' short-distance passenger traffic and small freight business was placed in immediate jeopardy by generally more economical electric lines. Affected railroads--as with Margaret Walsh's Great Northern in the 1920s--were obliged to reduce fares and provide more accommodating service. Some railroads bought into electric traction companies (as part of the huge corporate merger movement throughout U.S. industry, 1898-1902), just as subversive motor buses bought out interurban and electric streetcar lines in the brave new consumer world of the '20s. As early as 1895 the Baltimore and Ohio R.R. adapted heavy electric motors to pulling trains through its one-and-a-half mile tunnel under the city (to solve ventilation problems) and later extended the electrified track to eight miles. The New York Central did much the same thing out of Grand Central Terminal in 1906-07 and by 1908 the N.Y., New Haven & Hartford was electrified to Stamford. After another financial panic in 1907 and the ensuing liquidity "crisis" among commercial banks, investments in steam and electric railroads faltered, although that first decade had witnessed a quarter net increase in mileage nationwide. U.S. railroad mileage peaked around 1916, but thereafter more track was abandoned than built.

Chastened railroad operations emerged from the brief ordeal under wartime "federal control" (1917-18), and the struggle to deflect postwar nationalization, into the comparatively tranquil environment proffered by the compromises of the 1920 Transportation Act, only to be confronted by another technological menace: vehicles on public roads with motors powered by gasoline (essentially a former waste by-product of kerosine distillation.) In Chapter 6 Margaret Walsh treats the reactions of railroad leaders to this latest challenge and, following decisions of the Great Northern's management in 1925, traces the intricacies of what she has elsewhere called "the Minnesota roots of the Greyhound Bus Corporation."

By the early'20s it was clear in the market place that motor transport constituted a greater threat to capital vested in railroads than had electrification thirty years before. The "play thing of the idle rich" c. 1892 had, thanks to innovations in state financing of highway improvements, become the quintessential American people's chariot by 1922; for this the shot was heard around the world! Federal aid for "rural roads" dates from

1916; but the new "horseless carriage" did not depend on the old "Iron Horse." The quintessential American mechanic, Henry "Third Time Lucky" Ford, had created a mass market potential for the automobile with his low priced, standardized Model T back in 1909. Doubtless, a proliferating second hand car market would have done much the same thing but the Model T meanwhile had become the conspicuous substance and consummate symbol of the first emergent "consumer society." It promised the physical enlargement of capitalizable "social space" and, more important for the long term, the de-limiting of capitalizable "personal space": the unfathomable psychological realm of immediate gratification and "empowerment."

The Great Northern's management was among the first to recognize that, as Walsh indicates, it was "impossible to halt the private individual's purchase of automobiles and their spread." By 1925, when G.N. bought into the Northland Transportation Corporation, there was already one car for every five Minnesotans. Capital had long since mobilized in serried array--machine tools, steel, copper, petroleum, rubber, leather upholstery, lacquers and varnishes, plate glass, real estate, construction, advertising, sales finance and, of course, electricity--a preeminently Schumpeterian "cluster" to satisfy Americans' deep longing to go nowhere in particular, whenever. How did we do it? asked Lehmann Brothers banker for consumption, Paul Mazur, rhetorically, in his bully book, *American Prosperity*, a year before the Wall Street Crash. We did it by "forceful advertising and selling methods" which had "imposed upon each American family the buying standards of its neighbors." As for selling automobiles, the jewel in the consumer sovereign's crown, and other durables, it had been accomplished by "the sugar coated pills of partial payments." It was first called "instalment selling" rather than "instalment buying" but, if the price in right, says the economist, it's no big deal! On April 8. 1916, a two-page spread had appeared in the *Saturday Evening Post* announcing "Time Payments: The First National Service to Help Dealers Sell Automobiles." The advertisement was placed by Guaranty Securities Corporation, newly removed from Toledo, Ohio, to New York City (later absorbed by Commercial Credit Corporation), and specified 21 U.S. makes of car, by no means all from Detroit.

The old lake port and railroad hub--on its river linking Lakes Erie and Huron *via* the St. Clair lake and river--was already on its way to becoming "the automobile manufacturing capital of the world." Detroit had burgeoned as a manufacturing center before the automobile drove into town (I 899-1903): carriage works, ship building, railroad equipment, marine engines; but over the first three decades of the century its population rocketed more than fivefold to 1,568,662, and its municipal area likewise spread fivefold by annexation to 142 square miles in 1930 (with wide swaths of jerry-built housing for automobile workers). The twenties were roaring with millions of motor engines--over 17 million by 1925. Resistance by railroads was futile.

Great Northern's alertness to competitive early warning signals from motor buses was not, of course, unique. The closely linked New Haven and Boston & Maine R.Rs., for instance, had also caught on in the very different "urbanized" market setting of New England. In some of G.N.'s western regions, Walsh suggests there was yet little competition for a smaller short haul business but in Minnesota the railroad was aware of growing numbers of not-so-middle class folks taking to the roads in jitneys and buses, as well as private cars, since well before the war. In the Northern Iron Range district "cut throat" competition among scores of small-time hopefuls had enforced consolidation into seven larger companies when, in 1925, G.N. offered a cooperative and coordinating hand. The state government laid the foundations by undertaking the supervision and regulation of all commercial vehicles, buses, and trucks as common carriers. G.N.'s management now believed it could "influence and even control the number and shape of commercial motor companies."

While railroads in southern Minnesota chose to fight the inevitable with both positive and negative tactics, the G.N. President, Ralph Budd, with a business acumen worthy of the founder, James J. Hill, bought into a major bus consolidation, the Northland Transportation Corporation, as his supportive bus line subsidiary. With access to railroad capital, Budd went on with Northland's general manager, Eric Wickman, to launch a sequence of acquisitions, initiatives, and deals that emerged in February 1930, while the economy slipped into depression, as the *independent* renamed Greyhound Corporation destined, with other independents and railroad affiliates, to form into a transcontinental chain. This was the Greyhound Bus that in the grim decade of the 1930s became familiar around the world in drive-on parts wherever Hollywood's black and white depression movies could be shown.

## Chapter 7

Railroads were the "first big business" long before the business of America was big business. They were, moreover as H. Thomas Johnson indicates in Chapter 7, "the first business in the world in which there was a hierarchy of managers who managed other salaried managers," resembling the style, if not the motives, of an army or church. Managements had to derive "information" in the form of cost-reporting systems to appraise "the efficiency of their far-flung and diverse operations." Accurate cost information for systems like the Pennsylvania or Erie railroads costs per ton-mile, operating margins and so forth--not only allowed the top managers to evaluate the conversion of "intermediate inputs into transportation services," but likewise to assess "the performance of subordinate managers." In his essay "Accounting and the Rise of Remote-Control Management: Holding Firm by Losing Touch," Johnson confronts the mystique of American management and, from an historical perspective of accounting practice, finds it wanting for much of this century, especially in the decades since World War 11.

Johnson reminds the reader that, over the centuries business people have learned the hard way. There were accountants of sorts in ancient Sumer and, since Renaissance Venice, double-entry bookkeeping and "professionals" from the *Collegio dei Raxonati* (1581), but it was mostly by trial and error that merchants found how to become less misinformed concerning "relations between inputs and outputs, about selling conditions, and about competitive threats." Such information--even basic knowledge of prices and price tendencies--was never a *free good* and without "access to pertinent knowledge" many aspiring producers of the 18th and 19th centuries remained outside the market's enticing loop. Customary commercial usages and business relations were rapidly eroded as the more potent "market forces" of the 19th century prevailed over those of smaller, localized exchanges. Modern accounting emerged in England and Scotland over the late 18th and early 19th centuries with the growth of larger business organizations, but the proprietors of such firms in Britain or the U.S. did not find much *managerial* expertise among professional accountants however good they might be as auditors. Irrespective of their legal form or scale of operations the more capitalized and competitive enterprises--some of the Boston-based integrated cotton manufacturers, for example, Lyman Mills of Holyoke, MA.--began to develop more rational and abstract rules of conduct, founded upon their understandings of what today would be called "management information systems."

Such information--essentially a signal system--was necessary, Johnson affirms i) to direct workers' tasks within firms, ii) to direct subunit activity (if any), and iii) to plan overall scale and financing of the enterprise. As a rule, financial information based on bookkeeping or accounting records was used almost exclusively in regard to the third item in this managerial trinity. It was not a public matter and followed no generally accepted reporting rules. The *first two*, operational, items--even in cases of large manufacturing organizations ran by the likes of Andrew Carnegie, Gustavus Swift, or Cyrus H. McCormick--still involved mostly non-accounting information, which the chief and a couple of close associates knew from first hand, practical, experience of their production processes and customer demands. The kind of realistic cost and margin information (even when financial in nature) employed in making *internal* decisions at worker or organizational subunit level "was almost never derived from accounting information used to portray overall financial results." In this "hands on" approach to running the operations of an organization, albeit from "top down," a practical art of management grew up within firms without benefit of the scientific theory for controlling workers in shop situations which F.W. Taylor introduced on the basis of what enthusiasts for "efficiency" described as "hearty cooperation between management and men."

To be sure, territorially-dispersed and internally-complex organizations, such as emerged in vertically-integrated, multi-divisional corporations around the turn of the century had to evolve more complicated cost reporting (including price simulation) than was necessary even for early manufacturing giants. Johnson traces a succession coming forward from General Superintendent Albert Fink of the post-Civil War Louisville & Nashville Railroad, through later examples of costing *internally managed* transactions with simulated prices, such as the huge urban retailer, Marshall Field, or the catalogue mail-order distributor Sears Roebuck. The latter measured their profits on volume of inventory turnover (similar to railroad operating ratios), unlike the traditional markup-on-cost method.

The transfer of economic exchanges from actual, external, *market* settings to internally-managed business settings weakened the effect of price signals without which the profit consequences of decisions could not be effectively gauged. By 1910 the DuPont Powder Company--"the company that virtually invented modern management"--had integrated its production units' costs in manufacturing explosives with its marketing units' information on gross margins and turnover.

DuPont went on to contrive a formula for combining margin and turnover information into a overall rate of return on capital investment (ROI), which plainly "imitated" the market place for capital. It was able to check the ROI for each department of its expanding wartime output, while leaving production plant managers to devote their attention to the half-a-dozen or more tasks which together determined the company's competitiveness. The ROI planning budgets, Johnson avers, implied that DuPont's management could allocate capital among its highly diversified, multifunctional, postwar chemical lines *more* efficiently than the capital markets, and could likewise simulate information formerly furnished by the capital market alone. The closely associated General Motors Corporation followed a similar reorganizational structure and ROI analysis in controlling its own corporate divisions between 1921 and 1923.

Corporations had begun to disclose accounting information to outsiders in unaccustomed volume as they turned increasingly to the capital market for funding. Representatives of private bankers sat on corporate boards. Such "public" financial information tended to follow conventions established by *independent* auditors / accountants and public agencies such as IRS, SEC, and other regulatory bodies. The generally accepted principles of the accounting profession (GAAP) by the later 1930s furnished a convenient standard for financial accounting rule: the balance sheet (assets, liabilities, and net worth) and the income statement (profit and loss), and their interrelations which, argues Johnson, egregiously *mislocated* costs at functional locations in the corporation's organization chart "where accounting transactions occur, not with locations where activities occur that cause costs" in the first place. The latter are far more relevant than transaction-based cost information for making production decisions. GAAP also misattributed certain costs for unsold or unfinished goods inventories at the close of the reporting period -notably indirect or production overhead costs. The latter are conventionally and conveniently i.e. arbitrarily allocated by prorating them "over the direct labor hours expended on each product."

Over the past four decades these financial accounting figments have been used not only to impress outside third parties, friendly and unfriendly alike, with bottom-line "results", but, insists Johnson, also in-house "to drive operating activities" in manufactures (and some telecommunications activity).

U.S. industry grew historically behind high tariff walls in increasingly oligopolistic array to meet the growing demands of vast internal markets. Only rapid technological change outside an industry or unexpected (unfair?) foreign competition could rock the boat in the hegemonic years after World War II. The possible consequences for the competitiveness of U.S. manufactures (even some services) in international markets of using "irrelevant" management accounting information to enhance bottomline *efficiency,* as those talismanic words are comfortably used in business schools and the financial press, are dire indeed.

Hayes and Abernathy have suggested that managers were drawn increasingly from the financial and legal sides of business (where the newsworthy action is?) and less from the technical and marketing sides. Institutional investors, like pension funds and their expert advisors, regard the company as just "a 'portfolio' of income-producing assets" in the near term; the idea is often to make money, not goods. Can the vaunted lowcost U.S. micro-chip technology emerging in recent decades yet allow activity-based costing (ABC) to oust financial accounting misinformation from the operations' driving seat of planning and decision-support information? Johnson speculates on the philosophical implications of the Robert S. McNamara mindset. "I dream't I saw James J. Hill last night..."

# 4

# Merchants and Planters:
## the Market Structure of the
## Colonial Chesapeake Reconsidered

### Jacob Price

The economic and social life of the Thirteen Colonies, it has long been understood, revolved to a great degree around the prosperity of the staple products they sold to markets all over the Atlantic trading world. Foremost among these products was tobacco which, in 1697-1705, accounted for 83 percent of English imports from the mainland North American colonies. Its importance was not as pronounced when one takes into account colonial exports to the West Indies and Southern Europe and the progressive diversification of the colonies' economies in the eighteenth century. Nevertheless, on the eve of the Revolution, tobacco was still the most important colonial export, accounting in 1768-1772 for 25.4 percent of exports to all overseas destinations from the continental colonies and 72.2 percent of exports from Virginia and Maryland.[1]

When one attempts to analyze how markets worked, one must inevitably start with demand and supply. The growth of the economies of the Chesapeake in the seventeenth and eighteenth centuries rested in good part on the growth of European demand for tobacco, with American leaf finding its principal markets in the British Isles, France, the Low Countries, Germany and the Baltic, with less significant quantities wending their way to Russia and the Mediterranean countries. In this paper, however, I wish to focus not on demand but on supply. What kind of economy and society produced the tens of millions of pounds of tobacco carried to

Europe each year in the century preceding the American Revolution? What kind of commercial arrangements were utilized to get the leaf to the market from the planter's "tobacco house" (drying shed)?

Now, your average intelligent member of the American Automobile Association probably doesn't think that there is any problem about the social character of eighteenth century Virginia. He has driven his family to Mount Vernon and Williamsburg and, if interested in history or architecture, has taken them on a bus tour of the James River mansions. He *knows* that eighteenth century Chesapeake society was presided over by great slave-owning planters living in splendid mansions which the George Washington television series a few years ago made clear were decorated and furnished in impeccable *House Beautiful* taste.

Long before the advent of television, the automobile, and the bus tour, this "great house" image of colonial Virginia was deeply impressed on the mind and imagination of reading America by popular novels. William Taylor has explored the literary tradition going back to the 1820's in which the great plantation, if often a decayed plantation, was the embodiment of all that was quintessentially the old Virginia.[2]

However, in the contemporary world of would-be social scientists, the committed professional historian is not content to leave our image of the past to novelists, television script writers or tour guides. It should not be too controversial to expect that serious historians, not afraid of the archives, will break us loose from such literary conventions or cultural myths and show us who made how much of what. In this paper I shall not offer a bibliographic survey of historical writings on the colonial Chesapeake. I should, however, like to call to mind the work of a few published scholars, not all celebrated today, whose work suggests alternative ways in which professional historians could look at the economic life of the colonial Chesapeake, the society that produced all that tobacco.

## The Emergence of a Lifelike Picture

When I was starting out in research, the grand old man of Chesapeake studies was Thomas Jefferson Wertenbaker (1879-1966), a recently retired professor at Princeton. In his work we can see interesting indications of the evolution of university studies on the Chesapeake in the early decades of this century. His first book was *Patrician and Plebeian in Virginia, or the Origin and Development of the Social Classes of the Old Dominion* (1910). One need not take too seriously the reference to classes in the title; there is no Marx here. The book, concerned primarily with seventeenth century Virginia, is divided into two sections: part I, "The Aristocracy" occupies about two-thirds of the text; part II, the remaining third, is devoted to "the Middle Class", a catch-all rubric that includes almost everyone else. The book's chief iconoclastic feature and the basis of much of its reputation was its denial that the seventeenth century leading planter houses, "the first families of Virginia", were to any significant degree descended from gentle cavaliers fleeing the English civil war or from any other armigerous English families. They were rather distinctly bourgeois in origin, usually founded by successful merchants. The rest of Wertenbaker's picture was less shocking, with the familiar great house and its attractive rural style of living. From the standpoint of the modern graduate student, at least of my generation, a startling thing about this work, presumably his tenure book, was that it was based entirely on printed material, particularly earlier histories, travellers' accounts and published correspondence.

However, in the ten or so years following the publication of his first book, Professor Wertenbaker found the archives, both of Richmond and of London. In them he discovered a quite different range of materials, including quit-rent rolls, tithable lists, other tax assessments and post mortem inventories, all grist for the mill of the modern social historian. This new material was the basis of his succeeding work, *The Planters of Colonial Virginia* (1922). In it, implicitly if not explicitly, he confessed that this first book had been in error in its polarization of seventeenth century Virginia between the "aristocracy" and the "middle class", and in the exaggerated emphasis it gave to the former. From the evidence of the quit-rent rolls, his new work established that the most important class in seventeenth century Virginia was what he now called the "yeomanry", small proprietors of English origin, who owned no slaves but worked their own fields with the labor of themselves, their families and perhaps one or two indentured servants. At the end of their service, indentured servants found it relatively easy to become small proprietors themselves, making later Stuart Virginia a true land of opportunity for the poor. This populist paradise was ultimately lost, undone first by the falling price of tobacco, and then by the introduction of African slaves, a noticeable element in the colony's population by the end of the seventeenth century and of increasing importance in the eighteenth.

The increasing slave population, in Wertenbaker's analysis, led to the complete transformation of Virginia society in the eighteenth century, but not necessarily to the unqualified triumph of his now rejected "aristocracy". The slave plantations, he argued, were sufficiently efficient to prosper even with much lower tobacco prices; many of the small "yeoman" holdings were not. Some of the former yeomanry gave up the struggle and migrated to North Carolina or Pennsylvania or other frontier areas where they need not depend on tobacco. Others stayed in Virginia, but sank into the disreputable class of the "poor whites". But still others calculated that "if you can't beat 'em, join 'em", and strove to acquire slaves themselves. With credit available, this opportunity was open to a substantial fraction of the former smallholders. Thus Virginia in the eighteenth century came to be characterized by a broad class of slave owners, ranging from the small man with one or two (but striving for more) to the grandees with over 100 African bondsmen. (In many counties, 75 percent or more of property owners were also slave owners.) At no point on the scale between one and "King" Carter's 300 was there any clear break. Pre-Revolutionary and Revolutionary Virginia were thus dominated not by a few grandees but by a much broader class of slave owners, large and small, whose common interests were jealously guarded by the House of Burgesses.

Wertenbaker the pioneer left many parts of the forest unexplored. He did not really explain how the greater and lesser slave owners were able to work together in politics comfortably and effectively. Nor did he place this broad slave-owning class in a market context. How did they obtain their slaves? How did they market their produce and obtain needed supplies? In his first book, he had a few sentences on the consignment system of the bigger planters. What relevance did this institution have to his new picture of the seventeenth century Virginia of the small yeomanry or the eighteenth century Virginia dominated by a highly variegated but all encompassing class of slave owning plantation operators?

My reading would suggest that the general picture created by Wertenbaker's second book had a major impact, direct or indirect, on subsequent workers in colonial Chesapeake history, whether or not they acknowledged it. However, historians with different interests tended to focus on different parts of Wertenbaker's picture. Those interested primarily in political history were impressed by his picture of a broad slave-owning class the members of which, whether large or small, shared common interests for which the House of Burgesses was so solicitous. On the other hand, economic and social historians were more impressed by his exposition of the great variety in size and wealth among the slaveowners large and small; they wanted know more about how the slave plantation worked and how the slave population increased so dramatically in the eighteenth century. Without attempting a bibliographic survey, I should like to comment on a few of the varied scholarly interests stimulated by Wertenbaker's suggestions.

Wertenbaker's happy picture of the seventeenth century Virginia "yeoman" has been most seriously challenged by the important work of Edmund Morgan.[3] To be sure, Morgan points out, there was a relatively large population of ex-indentured servants (who appear in the tax rolls as single tithables) in late seventeenth century Virginia, but few of them had by the 1670's become proprietors and many did not on attaining their freedom even settle down as tenants. Instead this more footloose element became the floaters, drifters and frontier squatters of the colony. For such men Virginia's per capita tax or tithing system was a harsh burden -- a burden made all the more intolerable when they saw a relatively few wealthy men -- the councillors, their allies and their kin -- monopolize all the the more remunerative public offices. Such plutocrats also tended through grants, purchase or marriage to obtain title to much of the best accessible land in the settled areas, making it more difficult for ex-indentured servants to obtain smallholdings without going to the frontier where they were more exposed to Indian attacks. Morgan sees this class conflict and hostility towards the affluent leadership by the frontier squatters and other ex-servants as an indispensable element in understanding Bacon's Rebellion of 1676. In emphasizing the social extremes, however, he tends to neglect the middling elements in society. Even so, no one today can think about seventeenth century Virginia without pondering Morgan's picture. When, though, we turn to the period after 1689, years of reduced servant importation and expanding slavery, Morgan's picture has more in common with that of Wertenbaker. Both see the growth of African slavery creating bonds of common interest between the larger and smaller slave-owning planters. Social tensions, Morgan points out, were also reduced by the lower rates of direct (tithe assessed) taxes, with more of the tax burden shifted to indirect taxes. However, the relative productive or market importance of large and smaller planters remained for others to essay.

While the greatest significance of Morgan's work lay in encouraging historians to reconceptualize their picture of seventeenth century Virginia, other scholars have encouraged rethinking about the eighteenth century. Some forty years after Wertenbaker's second book, some of the implications of his picture of the wide diffusion of slave ownership in eighteenth century Virginia were explored in the very controversial 1964 book by Robert and Katherine Brown, *Virginia 1705-1786: Democracy or Aristocracy?*[4] According to Jack Greene, "One can say unreservedly that this volume is the most important and most substantial work ever published on the history of 18th-century Virginia." Greene felt that the Browns' great research fully supported most of their key findings: "There was wide economic opportunity and great social mobility through the 18th century; the great bulk of Virginians were small landowners, and there were few families without property in either land or slaves. Class distinctions were not sharp and there was little class consciousness or class antagonism. The social and economic structure of Tidewater and Piedmont were essentially the same. Property qualifications for voting were not very formidable, there was a wide electorate ... consisting mostly of men from the middle and lower classes. Voters usually chose men of above average social and economic status to represent them; [but] such representatives had to have the support of men of all classes to gain election." Greene felt, however, that the Browns did less than full justice to their valuable research by forcing all their data into the modern rubrics of "aristocracy" versus "democracy".[5] This criticism of anachronistic categories was more fully developed by other reviewers who, in general, found Virginia politics in the eighteenth century more deferential and less democratic than did the Browns. They also suggested that the Browns were inclined to misrepresent some of the work of those who had gone before in order to emphasize the novelty of their own findings. However, mo matter how critical they were of the Browns' literary method or interpretation of political life in eighteenth century Virginia, none of the reviewers challenged the Browns' picture of Virginia economy and society.[6]

For the historian of the Chesapeake tobacco market, the relevance of the Browns' work lies not in its interpretation of Virginia politics but rather in its suggestion of the possible distribution of capacity among Virginia's tobacco producers. In the counties analyzed by the Browns, the percentage of family heads who were slave owners ranged from 42 percent for Norfolk in 1751 to 77 percent  for tidewater Lancaster in 1775 and piedmont Amelia in 1778. However, as shown in Table 4.1, from 64 to 91 percent of the slave owners held five or fewer slaves. The overall picture is consistent with Wertenbaker's 1922 view of a Virginia dominated by small and middling proprietors owning only a relatively few slaves.

Since the Browns' work appeared in the early 1960's, a whole new generation of scholars publishing on the colonial Chesapeake has emerged to whom many of the disputes of the 1950's and 1960's are only marginally relevant. Many of them, including most of the "Maryland School", are only tangentially interested in the primarily political approach of the Browns or Charles Sydnor.[7] Instead they are much more concerned with the changing demographic and social profile of the region, with particular attention to the implications of slavery. Their new approach and new methods do not, however, necessarily mean that their findings would startle Wertenbaker or the Browns. For a very good example, Richard Beeman's study of "backcountry" Lunenburg county from 1746 shows the percentage of households owning slaves in this frontier area rising from 22.8 percent 1750 to 53.3 percent in 1769  with the percentages of slaves in the total population rising from 22.5 percent in 1750 to 44.8 percent in 1769 and reaching fifty percent in 1795.[8] The 1769 percentage was actually significantly higher than the estimated 40 percent black share of the total population in Virginia ca. 1770 and suggests how rapidly a newly settled area could accumulate a slave labor force.[9] Although Beeman does not attempt to calculate or estimate the percentage of tobacco (or any other commodity) production coming from different size plantations, he does show a society in which slaveholding  was widely diffused but characteristically small scale. In 1769, 82 percent of his slaveowning households held five or fewer slaves. In this general sense, his overall picture of a newly settled area is consistent with the social characteristics of Virginia suggested by Wertenbaker and the Browns.[10]

A more ambitious synoptic view of the whole Chesapeake has been attempted in the important book of Allan Kulikoff. The great interest of

Table 4.1
Slave Ownership in Three Virginia Counties, 1751-1778

| County | Year | % of Slaveownership Among All Family Heads | % of Slaveowners Holding Five or Fewer Slaves |
|---|---|---|---|
| Norfolk | 1751 | 42.3 | 91.0 |
| Norfolk | 1771 | 45.6 | 81.4 |
| Lancaster | 1745 | 68.1 | 80.2 |
| Lancaster | 1775 | 77.5 | 63.6 |
| Amelia | 1768 | 70.5 | 65.6 |
| Amelia | 1778 | 77.3 | 67.2 |

*Source:* Robert E. and B. Katherine Brown, *Virginia 1705-1786: Democracy or Aristocracy?* (East Lansing, MI, 1964) 75. *The records used for Lancaster (both years) and Amelia (1768) were incomplete.*

his book arises from both its emphasis on the demographic and its bringing together data from a large number of counties in both Virginia and Maryland over the whole of the eighteenth century. For him the main, indeed almost the only, theme in the social history of the Chesapeake is the increasing proportion of slaves in the ever-growing population and the increasing importance of the larger plantation as a social and economic unit. He is throughout sensitive not only to differences between regions (even the controversial tidewater/piedmont distinction) but also changes over time. Thus, he can show how median slave ownership of three slave per owner in several counties of Virginia and Maryland before the Revolution was transformed after independence into a figure of 5-6 per median owner.[11] More important, he makes clear that no median figure is going to tell one much about how the average slave lived nor about the productive capacity of different sized plantations. On the first point, his work suggests most revealingly how something approaching normal family life for slaves was much more likely on a large than on a small plantation. On the second point, he shows that despite the low median size of slave holdings throughout the eighteenth century, from 50 to 75 percent of slaves belonged to planters owning 11 or more slave and that in the extreme case of his Prince George's County in 1771-1779, 55 percent belonged to owners of 21 or more slaves.[12]

Now, if tobacco was produced only by slaves, Kulikoff's data would suggest a preponderant role in production for plantations with over 10 slaves or even over 20. However, his valuable tables do seem to neglect -- at least relatively -- the productive capacity of the white population. This is a theme to which this paper will return later.

I came to the study of the Chesapeake economy by a path quite different from that of such worthy scholars as Allan Kulikoff and Edmund Morgan[13] who appear to have been primarily interested in social structure. As an economic historian, I was was interested in international trade and in commodity markets. Tobacco, like coffee and tea and dyestuffs, was a commodity that passed through many markets before it reached its ultimate consumer. At the end of the seventeenth century about 65 percent of Chesapeake tobacco imported into England was re-exported, primarily but not exclusively to northern Europe. By the eve of the American Revolution, British tobacco re-exports, were around 85 percent of imports.[14] I was thereore interested in all the principal re-export markets for British colonial tobacco in Europe. But I was also obliged to be interested in the first market, the exchange by which the leaf's producers first vended their staple. When I started working on this topic in 1949, a respected American social historian advised that tobacco "had been done" and that I'd be wiser to choose another commodity. He was, of course, thinking of the survey of tobacco production and trade which had appeared in L. C. Gray's *History of Agriculture in the Southern United States* (1933), then the bible of the field.[15] Gray's work was staggeringly ambitious in scope. In the colonial section, he was able to consult almost everything in print and a sprinkling of manuscripts, usually correspondence, but could not make any systematic use of archives. (In that sense, his work was methodologically akin to Wertenbaker's first book, even if more quantitative.) His treatment of the purely agricultural side of the tobacco economy adds much to Wertenbaker, even if he offered no alternative macro-picture. On commerce and credit, however, he was bound by the limits of the available literature (and sources) and tended to concentrate almost entirely on the planter consignment mode with only a few paragraphs on the direct trade of the seventeenth century and the Scots stores on the eve of the Revolution. Glasgow, the most important tobacco port in Britain at that time, does not appear in his index.

When I started my own work, one of the first things I did was to construct a time series of British tobacco imports in the century or so before the Revolution.[16] The most striking message conveyed by that time series was the rising importance of Scotland in the Chesapeake economy from the Union of 1707, particularly striking after 1740. As late as 1738, Scotland had accounted for only 10 percent of British tobacco imports. But the growth in the Scottish share thereafter was rapid: 20 percent was first reached in 1744; 30 percent in 1758 and 40 percent in 1765. Imports at Scottish ports reached their greatest relative importance in 1768-1770 when their share of the British total hovered around fifty percent. In the following years, Scottish traders were hurt more than English by the financial panic of 1772 and, in the years of glut imports, 1771-1775, Scotland's imports did not grow as rapidly as Chesapeake exports so that the northern kingdom's share fell from 50 to a still impressive 45 percent. From 1758 onwards, Glasgow ranked ahead of London as the first tobacco import center in the country.[17] An investigation of the detailed postwar claims filed by many of the Glasgow firms ( for debts rendered uncollectable by the war[18] and American independence) showed that the business of the large Glasgow firms was carried on through scores of stores scattered over Piedmont Virginia and North Carolina, with some presence also in southern Maryland. The claims of such firms showed that they had extended small retail credit (usually for less than £10 per customer) to thousands of small men who undertook to repay in tobacco. These long lists of the names of small men naturally evoked Wertenbaker's picture of the Virginia of the small slaveowner.

In subsequent years, our knowledge of the Scottish stores in the Chesapeake has been expanded by the work of Thomas Devine, Robert Thomson, James Soltow in particular.[19] Yet others have been reluctant to accept either Glasgow's centrality in the history of Virginia's tobacco economy in the half century preceding the Revolution, or, conversely, the necessary lesser importance of the planter consignment system. It has been suggested that the Scottish store system was only important after 1740 or later and that earlier the planter consignment system had reigned supreme; or that the store system was only important for Scotland while the planter consignment system continued to characterize the Chesapeake's trade with England. There is no available evidence to support either hypothesis.

A brief sketch might be helpful here of my understanding of the institutional evolution of tobacco marketing in the Chesapeake. The unpublished thesis of Susan Hillier on the earliest years, 1607-1660, shows that trade to the Chesapeake from England was generally in the hands of ad hoc syndicates or "adventures" of several merchants not necessarily partners. A single outbound vessel could carry the goods of one or more "adventures". Responsibility for the actual trading or bartering of these goods was divided between the ship's captain and one or more supercargoes. In the Bay, the ship, its boats and hired craft moved about to reach and traffic with the scattered planters. This system, however, proved inefficient because it necessitated keeping the English merchants' vessel too long in the Bay running up heavy charges for sailors' wages and other operating expenses (or for demurrage on chartered vessels). Thus by mid-century, most "adventures" were entrusted to a "factor" temporarily or permanently resident in the colony. He was expected to have return cargoes substantially procured or arranged before the arrival of his employers' next ship, thus reducing turn around time and operating costs.[20] Such factors could be on salary or commission. Those on commission in particular frequently found ways to conduct private trade of their own on the side, usually to the West Indies, and thereby became a significant component of the growing independent merchant class in the Chesapeake. The most substantial of these, the great "merchant planters" Byrd, Carter, Hill, Randolph, had by the end of the century acquired extensive landed estates and even places on the council. Of such plutocrats, William Byrd II, who was in a position to know, wrote at the turn of the century, "On every River of the Province, there are Men in Number from ten to thirty, who by Trade and Industry have got very compleat Estates. The Gentlemen take Care to supply the poorer sort with Goods and Necessaries, and are sure to keep them always in their Debt, and consequently dependant on them. Out of this Number are chosen her Majesty's Council, the Assembly, the Justices and Officers of the Government."[21]

Most of the "yeoman" planters of late seventeenth century Virginia were too poor  and too debt-prone to escape their dependence on these great merchant-planter oligarchs or on the English factors, but a significant number of "mere planters" tried to escape by following the example of the local merchants and themselves consigning their tobacco for sale to merchants in England from whom they could also get their needed supplies. In a broadside of 1661, the merchant John Blande referred to consignment as a system then known but much less important than direct trade.[22] Most other references to planter consignment in the following half century treat it as a secondary system in both Virginia and Maryland. However, it was increasing, if only because the steady fall of prices in the Bay made the more substantial among the mere planters inclined to experiment.[23] The rise in European prices during the wars of 1689-1713 apparently made even more of them willing to chance the enhanced risks of the sea.

After 1685 English merchants for their part became much more interested in receiving consignments as "factors". Their 2½ per cent commission was calculated on the gross value of the transaction handled, including freight, all other expenses and duties paid or bonded, even though such customs duties were for the most part refunded and the bonds cancelled when tobacco was re-exported. To meet the rising revenue needs of the state, particularly in wartime, the net effective duty on bonded tobacco rose from 1.6 pence per lb. at the beginning of 1685 to 5.28 pence per lb. by 1704. As the peace-time price of tobacco in England "at the mast" (i.e., before duty) in the eighteenth century was normally in the range of 2-3 pence per lb.,[24] it can readily be seen that handling the duty and bonds accounted for the major part of the tobacco factor's commission earnings.

With both merchant and larger planter now finding tobacco consignments in their interest, there was a not unexpected increase in the practice during the war years 1689-1713. Ca. 1700, William Byrd II estimated "that [in Virginia] there is at least 400 or 500 of the Inhabitants that trade to England [i.e., consign tobacco there] and have Goods & Merchandizes hence."[25] Such an estimate, of course, would still leave several thousand other planters not consigning.

Despite the gradual increase in consignments from both planters and merchants in the Chesapeake, from an English standpoint direct trade remained the norm. In 1717, "several Virginia Merchants" of London (including William Byrd II, then in the capital) informed the Board of Trade that "the trade to Virginia is usually carryed on by sending Factors with their goods from Brittain, who had been brought up [in the trade] and understood the different nature of Tobacco: by which means they made returns in Exchange for their goods in such sort of Tobacco as was proper for that Market, for which it was designed....."[26]

The golden age of the planter consignment mode probably fell between 1713 and 1725, a period of both peace (for the most part) and relatively high European prices. Acute strain returned with the fall of European prices starting in the late 1720's. The tobacco inspection laws of Virginia (1730) and Maryland (1747) were more successful in protecting quality than in reducing production and thus had only a minimal effect on prices. The discontent of the consigning planters manifested itself in plant-cutting riots and in bitter charges against consignment merchants in the *Maryland Gazette*. More seriously, in Virginia it made the planter dominated council and House of Burgesses ready to cooperate with the British Treasury reformers by endorsing and petitioning for Sir Robert Walpole's excise scheme of 1732-1733. To read many of the charges emanating from Virginia at this time, one might assume that almost all the tobacco moving from the Chesapeake to Britain was shipped on planter consignment. However, in a most informative anti-excise pamphlet published in 1733, the merchants of London stated that "More than one half of the Importation of Tobacco from *Virginia* is on the proper Account of the Merchants of *Great Britain* trading to that Colony."[27] If we assume that "more than one half" meant something near sixty percent, then the remaining forty or so percent would have to cover consignments from both planters and merchants in Virginia. With the development of the Scottish store network after 1740, this forty percent is more likely to have shrunk than expanded. The low European prices characteristic of the years 1726-1756 would also have tended to discourage consignments.

Much of this nutshell sketch is based on contentious writings (memorials to the government, broadsides, etc.). However, the development of serious Chesapeake studies in the past thirty years has made most of us uncomfortable with generalizations drawn from a few sentences in such publications or in contemporary correspondence. We now prefer to ask tough questions that require hard data to answer. I should like to pose two questions inherent in the previous discussion that must be pondered if we are to understand how the tobacco market worked in the eighteenth century Chesapeake: (1) what was the contribution of different-sized producers to the total supply of tobacco coming onto the market? and (2) what were the respective shares of the different institutional arrangements (sketched above) in the marketing of tobacco? Though my suggested answers to these questions must in part be only tentative, I shall in conclusion attempt to suggest a relationship between the answers to the two main questions.

### The Problem of Market Share

Insofar as they have pondered the question of the market share of different sized producers, most previous writers have with considerable common sense considered it an obvious and simple reflection of the labor force available to different-size producers. But how does one measure labor force? If one just counts slaves, one misses the productive capacity of white farmers, their families and servants, and freed slaves. Counting "tithables" catches the white "yeoman" and his sons and male servants 16 years and over, but still omits the possible contribution of boys under 16 and of white women, both likely to have been significant, at least on the smallest units. More seriously, a calculation of tobacco production

based on tithables assumes that all taxed units applied an equal proportion
of their available labor to tobacco. That this was not so for the eighteenth
century is obvious, particularly when we consider the geographic
distribution of the mounting wheat exports then from the two "tobacco
colonies", as well as increasing reference to house slaves.

Nevertheless, for all their inadequacies, the surviving tithable records
provide a useful (*faute de mieux*) and not too crude measurement of labor
distribution in an agricultural economy. In fact, a county-by-county survey
conducted by the colony's government in 1724 showed that 91 percent of
Virginia's tithables (39904 out of 43877) were in some recognizable way
employed in the production of tobacco.[28] One must of course remember
that tithables lists report only productive capacity and not production itself.

Surviving tithable lists for the late seventeenth and eighteenth
centuries show individuals (overwhelmingly male) recorded as heads of
households containing anything from one to one hundred or more tithables.
For clarity, this paper will classify such heads of household according to
the number of tithables for whom they were taxed:

| | |
|---|---|
| one | husbandman or "dirt farmer" |
| 2-5 | small planter |
| 6-10 | middling planter |
| 11-20 | moderately large planter |
| 21-50 | large planter |
| 51-100 | very large planter |
| 101+ | magnate |

I have deliberately avoided using Wertenbaker's term "yeoman" for the
smallest heads of household because it is imprecise and in England often
carried the connotation of proprietor (freeholder or copyholder) whereas
in the Chesapeake many of the smallest heads of household were tenants.
The English term "husbandman" conveyed no such hints of ownership.

The use of such tax lists to measure the agricultural labor force has
two obvious drawbacks. The larger proprietors very likely had some of
their tithables, males and black females, employed outside of agriculture.
This was probably most evident in females employed primarily in the
home. Thus, the tithable lists may exaggerate somewhat the productive
capacity of the largest units. At the other extreme, this same measure

may underestimate the productive capacity of the small husbandman or
"dirt farmer". Paul Clemens has pointed out instances in which the
surviving records seems to suggest that the wives of small operators were
employed in the field.[29] Probably of greater importance in tobacco
production was the labor of non-tithable white males below the age of
sixteen, whether sons, other male relatives, or even servants. We get very
specific evidence of the significance of juvenile labor in the record of the
enforcement of Virginia legislation of the 1720's attempting to impose a
"stint" or limit on the production of tobacco. An act of 1723 tried to limit
cultivation to 6000 plants per tithable but allowed a single tithable to
cultivate up to 10,000 plants in his own name plus 3,000 for each boy
between 10 and 16 on his holding.[30] A surviving 1724 production census
for part of Stafford County (on the Potomac) shows a few such single
tithed "dirt farmers" assisted by two boys cultivating the maximum 16,000
plants (ca. 2670 lb.) each. In the whole district reported, Overwharton
Parish (lying between Aquia and Quantico Creeks and comprising the
greater part of Stafford County), we find 545 persons reported as "allowed
to tend tobacco". Of these roughly 75 percent were white (302 adult men;
6 adult women; and 100 boys between 10 and 16). The remaining 25
percent were black (137 adult tithables, male and female, and 14 boys).
The data on the plants cultivated also show that white labor was responsible
for approximately 75 percent of the tobacco tended. This is in rather
marked contrast to contemporary Norfolk County in the southern
tidewater, an older area of settlement, where a 1731 tax list shows that
male and female "negroes", aged 16 and over, constituted almost 55
percent of tithables. The remainder -- i.e., white males sixteen and over -
- consisted of: heads of households (25%), their sons and brothers (11.7%)
and servants (8.7%). It is obvious that Stafford had not gone as far as
Norfolk in the evolution of the larger slave plantation and still depended
somewhat more on white servants.[31] It is therefore dangerous to generalize
from the experience of any single county at any point in time. Recognizing
both their utility and their limitations, we must look at a fair number of
Virginia tithe reports scattered in time and space to get a reasonable sense
of the character and distribution of the labor force available for tobacco
production. In this search, we shall not be looking primarily at the
important black/white dichotomy just mentioned and emphasized by most
writers on Virginia, but rather on the size distribution of the productive

units which we must attempt to determine in order to understand the market mechanisms of the colony's tobacco economy.

Surviving lists of tithables are very rare for the seventeenth century but Edmund Morgan found such for six tobacco producing counties in 1677-1679.[32] They were geographically dispersed (two on the Eastern Shore) and range socially from Surry on the south bank of the James, with many smallholders, to Lancaster on the Rappahannock, with more larger proprietors. If we convert Morgan's size distribution data into shares of total labor pool reported, we find that households with only one tithable accounted for only 16.7 percent of the reported productive capacity of the six counties, while units with over five tithables accounted for 29.5 percent. That leaves "small planters" with 2-5 tithables to account for 53.8 percent of productive capacity. Morgan also reports data for his two extreme counties (Surry and Lancaster) in 1699. The previously noted distinctive character of each remains but there have been meaningful developments in each since 1679. In Surry of the smallholders, the share of productive capacity ascribable to units with 2-5 tithables has gone up from 50 to 60 percent, while in Lancaster the share of units with more than five tithables has risen from 36 to 41 percent. (Cf. Table 4.2.) The more detailed data given by Morgan for 1699 show that in both counties there were by then some plantations with 11-20 tithables and in Lancaster three with over 20. His data thus suggest that in late seventeenth century Virginia, the theoretical capacity for tobacco production lay overwhelmingly in units of from two to ten tithables, with larger units still of only modest importance. Farms with one tithable retained significant productive potential in 1699 but were a declining force.

For the eighteenth century, tithable lists, published and unpublished, have survived for scattered Virginia counties and isolated years. Data from some of the more usable of these have been assembled in Table 4.2. In order to show change over time, only counties with lists for two or more years have been included. The first three shown on the table (Surry, Lancaster and Norfolk) are in Tidewater, while the remainder (Amelia, Orange, Goochland, Lunenburg and Loudoun) are in Piedmont Virginia. This diversity permits comparisons in both space and time.

Counties settled at different times still went through comparable stages in their social evolution. At any given time, different counties in Virginia could give evidence of different stages of common patterns of evolution.

Table 4.2

Percentage Distribution of Tithables Among Different Sized Plantations/Farms in Six or Eight Virginia Counties, 1699-1774

| County | Year | One | 2-5 | 6-10 | 2-10 | 11-20 | 21-50 | 51+ | 11+ |
|---|---|---|---|---|---|---|---|---|---|
| Surry | 1699 | 24.8 | 60.0 | 9.6 | 69.9 | 5.5 | 0 | 0 | 5.5 |
| Lancaster | 1699 | 10.7 | 48.4 | 23.2 | 71.6 | 9.0 | 8.7 | 0 | 17.7 |
| Lancaster | 1720 | 12.8 | 38.2 | 20.4 | 58.6 | 14.6 | 4.1 | 9.9 | 28.6 |
| Norfolk | 1731 | 291. | 40.1 | 18.8 | 58.8 | 12.1 | 0 | 0 | 12.1 |
| Norfolk | 1751 | 16.7 | 48.1 | 22.5 | 70.5 | 8.8 | 3.9 | 0 | 12.7 |
| Norfolk | 1771 | 15.6 | 42.4 | 21.5 | 63.9 | 16.8 | 3.7 | 0 | 20.5 |
| Amelia | 1737 | 23.4 | 48.0 | 16.4 | 64.5 | 12.1 | 0 | 0 | 12.1 |
| Amelia | 1756 | 8.1 | 39.7 | 26.7 | 66.4 | 18.4 | 4.9 | 2.2 | 25.5 |
| Amelia | 1770 | 4.2 | 27.0 | 25.7 | 52.7 | 28.2 | 5.8 | 9.0 | 43.0 |
| Orange | 1739 | 12.9 | 46.9 | 27.6 | 74.5 | 12.5 | 0 | 0 | 12.5 |
| Orange | 1756 | 9.5 | 33.1 | 32.4 | 65.5 | 16.5 | 5.1 | 3.4 | 25.0 |
| Orange | 1769 | 7.3 | 30.9 | 33.0 | 63.9 | 18.9 | 9.9 | 0 | 28.8 |
| Goochland* | 1748 | 10.7 | 43.1 | 22.5 | 65.6 | 12.6 | 11.1 | 0 | 23.7 |
| Goochland* | 1754 | 9.3 | 43.8 | 24.7 | 68.5 | 13.5 | 8.7 | 0 | 22.2 |
| Goochland* | 1770 | 8.3 | 28.2 | 26.5 | 54.7 | 17.9 | 12.0 | 7.2 | 37.1 |
| Lunenburg | 1748 | 32.8 | 46.6 | 15.8 | 62.4 | 4.9 | 0 | 0 | 4.9 |
| Lunenburg | 1774 | 8.9 | 37.9 | 35.5 | 73.4 | 16.7 | 1.1 | 0 | 17.8 |
| Loudoun | 1761 | 29.2 | 43.0 | 18.4 | 61.3 | 9.4 | 0 | 0 | 9.4 |
| Loudoun | 1775 | 23.6 | 40.9 | 19.3 | 60.2 | 11.5 | 4.7 | 0 | 16.2 |

* Goochland was reduced in size in 1749; Lunenburg in 1764.

Source: Morgan, *American Slavery*, 419; Barbara Vines, *Orange County, Virginia, Tithables 1734-1782*, Part I (Orange VA, 1988); Landon C. Bell, *Sunlight on the Southside: Lists of Tithes: Lunenburg County, Virginia, 1748-1783* (Baltimore, 1974); Elizabeth B. Wingo and W. Bruce Wingo, *Norfolk County, Virginia Tithables*, 3 vol. (Norfolk, 1979-1895); A. Jean Lurvey, *Goochland Co. Virginia Tithe Lists*, 2 vol. (Springfield, MO, 1979) for 1748 only (incomplete). The later Goochland and Lancaster lists and those for Amelia and Loudoun are in the Virginia State Library. The Norfolk figures for 1771 do not include Norfolk borough, then a separate jurisdiction.

Table 4.2 permits comparison of the distribution of tithables among different sized units in three old seventeenth century counties (Surry, Norfolk and Lancaster) and five created in the eighteenth century: Loudoun, far up the Potomac; Orange, north of Charlottesville; Goochland on the north bank of the James; and Amelia and Lunenburg on the "South Side", the former about 30 and the latter about 60 miles southwest of Richmond. In all eight counties the greater part (52-73 percent) of productive capacity lay not with the smallest (single tithable) or larger (11 or more tithables) units but rather in between with the small and middling plantations (2-10 tithables). But, beyond this easy generalization, significant differences will be noted as well as interesting shifts over time. At the two geographic extremes of the colony, Loudoun in the north and Norfolk in the south were less involved in the tobacco export economy than the other counties noted. For Loudoun, far up the Potomac, wheat was a more central concern.[33] For Norfolk county, under the influence of the maritime and commercial activity in the Norfolk-Portsmouth area, other opportunities presented themselves to smaller men in shipwright's work, victualling and tar exports.[34] Such nontobacco activities suggest possible reasons why smaller householders (single tithables) were relatively more important in these counties and larger planters (eleven or more tithables) less important than elsewhere. Just the opposite appears to have been true of Amelia (on the Appomatox) and Goochland (on the James) where suitable soil and easy access to navigable water (less common on Piedmont than in Tidewater) would appear to have attracted would-be tobacco grandees and help explain why in the 1770's these two counties show quite low proportions of single tithables but the highest proportion of larger undertakings (both 11+ and 51+).

The remaining counties had their individualities but appear to have been moving in the same direction. Orange in 1739 had a tithable distribution similar to the 1699 configuration of Lancaster, already a county of relatively large holdings. Over the succeeding years the share of Orange's tithables on the large units (over ten heads) rose from 12.5 percent in 1739 to 28.8 percent in 1769. Newer Lunenburg in 1748 had a configuration closer to 1699 Surry, noted for its smallholdings. However, Lunenburg did not retain this character and in 1774, much reduced in size, had a configuration much closer to Lancaster in 1699 or Orange in 1739. However, these last four counties present much the same picture by 1775: their productive potential lay not in "dirt farmers" (single tithables) or in very large proprietors but most noticeably in the small and middling planters (2-5 and 6-10 tithables respectively), though the labor resources of larger (11-20 tithables) and very large (over 20) units were becoming more significant.

If the history of Virginia's archives is a tale of woe, Chesapeake studies can at least take consolation in the excellent probate records of Maryland centralized at Annapolis. These include both inventories made shortly after the passing of the deceased and administrators' accounts submitted a few years later showing exactly how the estate of the deceased was realized and allocated. A quarter of a century ago, Aubrey C. Land called researchers' attention to the fact that in several counties of southern Maryland, including inmportant tobacco counties, those preparing the administrators' accounts reported a fairly precise figure for tobacco left by the deceased, whether in the drying houses or still growing in the fields. Both were part of the estate and had to be accounted for by the executors or administrators.[35] Surveying all the *post mortem* accounts of 1750-1759 that have survived for deceased tobacco producers in four counties (St. Mary's, Charles, Calvert, Prince George's), Land could report that:

| | | |
|---|---|---|
| 40 percent | produced | 1- 2,000 lb. each |
| 40 percent | produced | 2- 5,000 lb. " |
| 18 percent | produced | 5-10,000 lb. " |
| 2 percent | produced | above 10,000 lb. each |

Land's data are very important for social historians of the Chesapeake, yielding a picture of the preponderance in Maryland of small producers consistent with the Virginia pictures of Wertenbaker and the Browns discussed above. However, for the student of the market, Land's work leaves unresolved the question of exactly who was selling how much tobacco, for, of course, a few big planters (in his over 10,000 lb. class) could produced ten or twenty or thirty times as much as the average planters in his bottom two groups (under 5,000 lb.)

To attempt to come to grips with this problem, I have in **Table III** recalculated the data from the administrators' accounts of three of Land's counties: Charles, Prince George's and St. Mary's. For bench marks I have chosen 3,000 lb. and 10,000 lb. Though the Virginia detailed survey data for 1724 shows an average tithable producing less than 1000 lb. p.a.,[36] other evidence suggests that a healthy, full-time field hand could produce 2,000 lb. Paul Clemens even reports the case of a single tithable (presumably with the aid of his wife or other non-tithable members of his family) producing 4000 lb.[37] This figure is probably too exceptional to be useful. However, the Stafford County (Virginia) 1724 report mentioned above contains several examples of a single tithable assisted by two non-tithable boys tending 16,000 plants.[38] As this was a year of stint, it would not be unreasonable to assume that the same family was likely to have tended 18,000 plants in an uncontrolled year. At 6:1, this would yield 3000 lb. of dried marketable tobacco leaf. I have therefore used 3000 as one bench mark, denoting the upper limit of the production of the servantless nuclear family without sons over 16 -- even though some units producing under 3000 lb. may have had a servant or slave. Ten thousand pounds represents the production of five full-time healthy field hands or of ten averge tithables, a convenient limit for the middling planter category. We can here consider those producing 10-30,000 lb. larger planters and those producing over 30,000 lb. very large planters. In the Maryland counties studied, we do not run into any grandees producing over 100,000 lb.[39], though a few such existed in Virginia.

When we compare the data in Table 4.3 with that reported from Land, we note at least one significant contrast. While Land showed 80 percent of cultivators producing 5000 lb. or less, Table 4.3 shows that our most modest category, those producing 3000 lb. or less, were of declining productive importance in all three counties and remained significant only in St. Mary's. In Charles County, where our data are fullest, from 1716 onward the major part of production came from the small and middling planters producing 3-10,000 lb. p.a. (and presumably employing the equivalent of up to five full-time field hands). Their share of production was regularly over 50 percent during 1716-1774. The Charles County data also show a steady rise of share for the larger planters producing 10-30,000 lb. This stratum was of even great importance in the more recently settled Prince George's.

Some problems remain in using these data. No consensus has yet emerged among scholars in the field as to the presence or absence of systematic bias in the preparation of the administrators' figures.[40] I am

Table 4.3
Crop Size of Decedents: Share of Total Production Provided by Different Sized Plantations

| Years | Nbr | -3000 lb. | 3-10,000 | 10-30,000 | over 30,000 lb. |
|---|---|---|---|---|---|
| | | | Charles County, Maryland, 1706-1774 | | |
| 1706-1715 | 69 | 22.1% | 32.7% | 9.9% | 35.3% |
| 1716-1725 | 91 | 27.9% | 53.4% | 18.6% | ------- |
| 1726-1735 | 109 | 26.1% | 55.3% | 18.7% | ------- |
| 1736-1745 | 105 | 22.0% | 53.7% | 24.3% | ------- |
| 1746-1755 | 123 | 13.2% | 59.6% | 27.3% | ------- |
| 1756-1765 | 104 | 14.5% | 57.6% | 27.9% | ------- |
| 1766-1774 | 191 | 18.3% | 55.6% | 26.9% | ------- |
| | | | St. Mary's County, Maryland, 1740-1779 | | |
| 1740-1749 | 79 | 40.2% | 48.4% | 11.4% | ------- |
| 1750-1759 | 94 | 42.8% | 51.2% | 6.0% | ------- |
| 1770-1779 | 62 | 28.6% | 30.5% | 15.0% | 25.9% |
| | | | Prince George's County, Maryland, 1703-1775 | | |
| 1703-1726 | 55 | 22.0% | 41.9% | 36.0% | ------- |
| 1749-1757 | 71 | 20.2% | 55.4% | 24.4% | ------- |
| 1758-1775 | 54 | 12.0% | 44.3% | 43.7% | ------- |

*Source:* The Charles and Prince George's data are from county level administrators' accounts in the Maryland Hall of Records. The St. Mary's data are from similar accounts there in the records of the provincial Prerogative Court and were kindly made available by Dr. Lois Green Carr.

also puzzled by the erratic appearance of very large producers (those over 30,000 lb.). For Charles County, the estates of two such very large producers accounted for 35.3 percent of reported crops in 1706-1715 but the over 30,000 class disappears thereafter in that county.[41] It was also absent from St. Mary's County until the 1770's, when two producers over 30,000 lb. suddenly accounted for 25.9 percent of production. If the disappearance of the very large producers in Charles can be readily explained by the expected effects of soil exhaustion in a long settled county, how do we explain the reappearance of such producers in equally old St. Mary's? Could there have been some erratic quality in the handling and filing of accounts of estates divided between two or more counties?[42] If not, Maryland, in its low number of very large planters, was significantly different from Virginia. This remains a problem worth further work and reflection.

In the meantime, the St. Mary's and Charles County data in particular show indisputably the continued importance of small and middling planters in Maryland both in terms of absolute numbers and in terms of share of total production. This is consistent with Wertenbaker's and the Browns' picture of eighteenth century Virginia planters and the evidence of the Virginia tithable lists. The preponderance of small and middling planters must be kept in mind as we return to the question of the structure of the market. They were natural customers for British-owned stores (whether English or Scottish) as well as for the businesses of indigenous merchants and country traders. Some, however, we shall see, chose to consign. Measuring the share of these different commercial institutions is our second big question.

## Measuring the Tobacco Trade's Market Mechanisms

We sketched above (from mostly non-quantitative evidence) our sense of the evolution of the shares of the differing marketing mechanisms for Chesapeake tobacco. Being quantitatively precise about them is a more daunting task. Fortunately, we do have one important piece of evidence: the official record of all the ship manifests of tobacco exported from the Upper District of James River during 1773-1775.[43] From the late seventeenth century, the naval officers in the several ports of British America had been responsible for sending to London quarterly reports of ships entering and clearing their respective jurisdictions. Since the naval officer was primarily an inspector of navigation, his reports were quite explicit about shipping, giving details of ownership, registration, tonnage, crew size, armament, port of origin and destination of each vessel but usually only summary data on cargo. However, the legal situation had been changed significantly by the Tobacco Act of 1751. After the failure of Walpole's excise scheme of 1733, the British Treasury remained dissatisfied with the yields of the tobacco duties. Tobacco, as a vegetable product, could lose weight when stored for several months in the close, unventilated and hot holds of transatlantic vessels, but could recover some of this lost weight when placed, after customs entry, in damp cellars along the Clyde, Mersey or Thames. These variations in weight created semi-legal and illegal opportunities prejudicial to the king's revenue. To check such possible losses, the 1751 act[44] created within customs the office of the Registrar-General of Tobacco responsible for a detailed and complicated program of keeping track of every hogshead of tobacco imported till re-exported or broken up for manufacture. Except for a few summary reports, no records of this office have survived in Britain. (Its central records must have been destroyed when the London customs house burned in 1814.) However, the new procedures mandated by the act started in America where the captain of every vessel carrying tobacco was before departure to receive from the local customs collector a manifest "with the number of hogsheads, casks, chests and other packages containing ... [tobacco], and the quantity of tobacco contained in each particular hogshead, cask, chest and other package, together with the marks and number set on each...." The master was to deliver the manifest to the customs officers at his British port of delivery, while the American customs officer was to send a duplicate to London. The volume in question, the only surviving evidence of the operation of the 1751 act in America, is reported to have been prepared by Lewis Burwell, the naval officer of the Upper James district.[45] By the letter of the act, it ought to have been kept by the customs collector of that district, the officer responsible under the 1751 act. If it was in fact kept by Burwell as naval officer, he must simply have copied or had copied the manifests prepared by the customs collector. The Upper District of James River began at Lyons Creek near Williamsburg and included a most important tobacco producing area along the James and Appomattox rivers, particularly the dynamic "South Side" and its major tobacco shipping center of Petersburg. Between 1768 and 1773, this district's share of total Virginia tobacco exports appears to have risen from 37 to 44 percent.[46] All this adds immensely to the interest and value of this volume.

In a 1961 article, Robert Polk Thomson called attention to this manifest book and summarized and tabulated its data.[47] I have re-processed the data contained in the volume *ab origine* using slightly different categories but restricting myself to the year 1 June 1773-31 May 1774. This was a more or less normal year. However, once the Continental Congress began discussing non-exportation in 1774, there was an immediate flurry of speculative tobacco purchases, bringing into the market people who had not previously been active in it. It seemed best therefore to omit the atypical later 1774 and 1775 from my analysis (Table 4.4). Whenever there was any reason even to suspect that a shipper was a planter, I have so classified him and have included in this category the few women on the list. There still remained a few total "unknowns" who could have been mariners or factors but whom I have thrown in with the Virginia non-merchants in the tenth line of the table.

Table 4.4 analyzes the character of the persons entering tobacco at customs for export from the Upper James River district. The largest category, expected but perhaps surprisingly large, was that of Scots factors, accounting for over 55 percent of exports. Less familiar are the English factors, working mainly for firms in Whitehaven which operated on something similar to, though not identical with, the Scots pattern. Some of the Whitehaven factors in Virginia were partners in their home firms. Others appear to have operated as independent merchants in the West India trade but as factors in the Whitehaven tobacco trade. No one would voluntarily have sent 80-100 percent of his tobacco to as out of the way place as Whitehaven unless he had some binding obligation to do so. One big London merchant, Sir Lionel Lyde, Bart., also maintained a factor in the district (Richard Hanson) who sent him 2047 hogsheads.[48] The English and Scots factors together thus accounted for over 71 percent of exports. More important than at least the English factors were the indigenous merchants of Virginia. They were a numerous and continuous element in Virginia society from the seventeenth century. They varied greatly in size, some being little more than country storekeepers who occasionally took a flier on a small consignment. Others operated on a much grander

Table 4.4

Exporters of Tobacco from Upper James River District, Virginia
1 June 1773 – 31 May 1774

|  | Hogsheads | Percent |
|---|---|---|
| Scots Factors to Scotland | 16,606 | 55.1 |
| Scots Factors to England | 129 | 0.4 |
| English Factors to England | 4,821 | 16.0 |
| Total Factors | 21,556 | 71.5 |
| Mariners to England | 32 | 0.1 |
| Virginia Merchants to England | 6,001 | 19.9 |
| Virginia Planters to England | 2,234 | 7.4 |
| Va. Professionals and Officials to England | 252 | 0.8 |
| Unknown to England | 42 | 0.1 |
| (Total Va. Planters, Professionals, officials and unknown to England | 2,518 | 8.3) |
| Grand Total | 30,117 | 100.0 |

Totals by Destination

|  | | |
|---|---|---|
| to Scotland | 16,606 | 55.1 |
| to England | 13,511 | 44.9 |
| to Great Britain | 30,117 | 100.0 |

Source: Virginia State Library, Auditor of Public Accounts #301,
Upper James River District Manifest Book, 1773-1775

scale, a single individual holding shares in several significant firms. Most impressive were the exports of the network of businesses in the district tied to Alexander and Peterfield Trent of Richmond:

| | |
|---|---|
| Carter & Trent | 368 hogsheads |
| Trent, Crump & Bates[49] (Henrico co.) | 349 " |
| Trent & Trent (Henrico co.) | 321 " |
| Trents & Calloway[50] (Henrico co.) | 263 " |
| Prosser & Trent | 162 " |
| Alexander & Peterfield Trent (Henrico) | 97 " |
| Trent & Mosely | 17 " |
| Trent & Prosser | 14 " |
| Total | 1591 " |

A similar pattern could be found in the firms in which John Tabb of Petersburg was a senior partner:[51]

| | | |
|---|---|---|
| William Watkins & Co. | (Petersburg) | 325 hogsheads |
| Richard Booker & Co. | (Petersburg) | 293 " |
| Richard Hill & Co. | (Sussex co.) | 32 " |
| Moss Armistead & Co. | (Petersburg) | 28 " |
| Total | | 678 " |

It is clear that among the minnows there were some big native fish feeding along James River.

All the above activity leaves only 7.4 percent for planter consignments, a figure which might possibly be reduced by further research. Even if we stretch our categories and add the shipments by professionals (mostly clergymen, lawyers and physicians) and "unknowns" to those by planters, we get only 8.3 percent of exports for all non-merchant Virginians.

How can we go from these very detailed figures for the Upper District of James River to all of Virginia and Maryland? Can we argue that the district was representative of the entire Chesapeake? In fact we cannot. Table 4.4 also shows that in the year covered (1773-1774) about 55 percent of exports from the district went to Scotland and barely 45 percent to England. However, British data show tobacco imports during 1773 and

1774 coming only 43.4 percent through Scottish but 56.6 percent through English ports.[52] Even if -- to obtain an estimate for the whole Chesapeake -- one were to adjust the Upper James River figures to make them approximate the general England/Scotland breakdown at that time, one would be adding only 25 percent to the shipments to England and thus raising the Virginia planter/professional/unknown element from 8.3 percent to about 10.4 percent -- hardly a change that alters the general picture conveyed by Table 4.4.

In conclusion, how can we link up the two panels of our market picture: supply coming mainly from small and middling planters; and marketing effected principally by the factors of British firms and local merchants. It is easy enough to hypothesize that the small and middling planters were the natural customers of the stores of both factors and local merchants, while the relatively few large planters could enjoy the luxury of the limited consignment system to get their silks, watches, books, coaches and other accoutrements of gentlemanly status. Like all useful hypotheses, this one is only partly true. First of all, although the stores dealt primarily with small and middling planters, they also dealt with a sprinkling of greater figures, including William Byrd III. Secondly, for whatever reason, mixed in with the great consignments are a flock of much smaller shipments. When we look at the planter consignments in the Upper District of James River for 1773-1774, we find them widely distributed by size of shipment:

| | | |
|---|---|---|
| 52 planter/consigners | shipped | 1-5 hogsheads each |
| 43 planter/consigners | shipped | 6-20 " " |
| 14 planter/consigners | shipped | 21-50 " " |
| 11 planter/consigners | shipped | over 50 " " |

By the 1770's almost all the consigners must also have given some of their patronage to local stores, though a significant number of them may have preferred shipping all their tobacco and paying for local purchases with bills of exchange.

However, consignment was not an option for all planters. As Virginia expanded inland in the eighteenth century, many planters found themselves in locations where consignment, if not impossible, was very inconvenient. Of the twenty principal landowners in "backcountry" Lunenburg County in 1769 listed by Richard Beeman, only one appears as an exporter in the Upper James district in 1773-1774 -- and that one (John Bannister) was a nonresident.[53] Tobacco could be carted overland for considerable distances. Some from North Carolina reached Petersburg by road. Most Lunenburg planters, however, appear to have felt that such transportation work had best be left to professional traders. Conversely, planters living close to navigable waters should have been more easily tempted to consign. In fact, five of the seven largest proprietors in Goochland County (on the James) in 1770 appear as consigners in 1773-1774.[54] Then there was also the matter of quality. It was only common sense for a planter to use his poorest tobacco to pay taxes and miscellaneous debts expressed in tobacco, and save the better for sale or consignment. Those considering consignment knew that there always was a good market in Britain for the best York River tobacco and the like. Those, however, who raised other grades had to be more realistic in their expectations. Beeman reports that his Lunenburg non-consigners raised only mediocre tobacco.[55] Many others raising comparable leaf must have come to a similar decision about the pointlessness of consigning.

Consignment, however, was a more important institution than its small planter volume would suggest. Virginia merchants, of course, were also consigners. By the 1770's, commission houses at London and Bristol in particular would appear to have been getting more consignments from merchants in the Chesapeake than from planters. As their planter consignments declined, such English firms exerted themselves, particularly through the "cargo trade", to get more commission business from merchant correspondents in the Bay. Merchants in the tobacco colonies had more pressing reasons than planters to maintain good credit records. This being so, merchants in London and Bristol were prepared to buy manufactures and other export goods for their American correspondents on credits of twelve months or more, trusting to such correspondents to remit tobacco or bills within the year to clear the debts when due. This "cargo trade" was a relatively new but very large part of the consignment business in the generation preceding the Revolution.[56]

Credit lay at the heart of the Virginia merchants' "cargo trade". Few planters could get comparable facilities, for English merchants knew that credit to planters could be unacceptably risky. Some of the best could get substantial advances, though even a Byrd or a Randolph could cause trouble for his British creditors. If a planter needed credit urgently, for example for slave purchases, he might have to give a bond.[57] As much as anything, it was desire for credit that propelled small and middling tobacco planters towards local stores, whether run by British factors or indigenous traders.

In conclusion, I should like to make two very general points. The first is methodological. It was useful to go all the way back to Wertenbaker if only to consider the changes in his research method between his two books. As noted above, the research for his first, heavily dependent on travellers' accounts, correspondence and other more or less literary material, led him to construct a picture in which the large planters, his "aristocrats", loomed large. When, for his second book, he turned his attention to tax records, he produced his much better known picture of the seventeenth century Virginia of the "yeomanry" and his still interesting analysis of the slow but cumulative significance of the changes wrought by the expansion of slaveholding in eighteenth century Virginia. His illuminating research experience eighty or ninety years ago is not without some relevance today -- both for graduate students and their mentors.

The second concluding point is that for anything more than bare subsistence Virginia agriculture operated in a market economy. To survive in a world market, colonial Virginia's planters and farmers in choosing crops and deciding when and how to sell, needed a basically commercial, market-oriented element in their makeup. Only a few have left written traces of such a *mentalité*; for the rest the traces are in the records of their actions. We know that tens of thousands of businesses go bankrupt each year in the contemporary United States and we need not be surpised to find that many in the colonial Chesapeake demonstrated a weak understanding of what a market orientation required. But, for the significant fraction who got ahead in that world, such a market orientation existed.

1. James F. Shepherd and Gary M. Walton, *Shipping, Maritime Trade, and the Economic Development of Colonial North America* (Cambridge, 1972) 38; John S. McCusker and Russell R. Menard, *The Economy of British America, 1607-1789* (Chapel Hill and London, 1985) 130, 132. The period 1697-1705 includes several years of war. If one prefers to use the peace years 1699-1701, tobacco's percentage of total English imports from the same colonies comes to 77.8 percent. R. Davis, "English Foreign Trade, 1660-1700", *Economic History Review*, 2d ser., VII (1954) 164-165; U. S. Bureau of the Census, *Historical Statistics of the United States, Colonial Times to 1970* (Washington, D.C., 1975) II, 1177.

2. William Robert Taylor, *Cavalier and Yankee: The Old South and American National Character* (New York, 1961), especially 148-161, 240-243.

3. Edmund S. Morgan, *American Slavery, American Freedom: The Ordeal of Colonial Virginia* (New York, 1975).

4. Robert E. and B. Katherine Brown, *Virginia 1705-1786: Democracy or Aristocracy?* (East Lansing, Michigan, 1964).

5. Review by Jack P. Greene in *New York Historical Society Quarterly*, XLIX (1965) 108-111.

6. For some other significant review of the Browns' work, see Carl Bridenbaugh in *American Historical Review*, LXX (1965) 472-473; Emory Evans in *Virginia Magazine of History and Biography*, LXXIII (1965) 356-358; Richard L. Morton in the *Journal of American History*, LI (1965) 700-702; Stephen Saunders Webb in *Wisconsin Magazine of History*, XLVIII (1964) 63-64; David Alan Williams in the *William and Mary Quarterly*, 3d ser., XXIII (1965) 149-152; and Chilton Williamson in *Journal of Southern History*, XXXI (1965) 98-99.

7. Charles S. Sydnor, *Gentlemen Freeholders: Political Practices in Washington's Virginia* (Chapel Hill, NC, 1952).

8. Richard R. Beeman, *The Evolution of the Southern Backcountry: A Case Study of Lunenburg County, Virginia 1746-1832* (Philadelphia, PA, 1984) 165.

9. *Historical Statistics of the United States*, II, 1168. Cf. also Brown and Brown, *Virginia*, 72-73 and following tables.

10. Beeman, *Southern Backcountry*, 65.

11. Allan Kulikoff, *Tobacco and Slaves: the Development of Southern Cultures in the Chesapeake, 1680-1800* (Chapel Hill, NC, 1986) 137, 154.

12. *Ibid.*, 331, 338.

13. Morgan, *American Slavery*.

14. *Historical Statistics of the United States*, II, 1190-1191.

15. Lewis Cecil Gray, *History of Agriculture in the Southern United States To*

*1860*, (Carnegie Institution of Washington, Publication No. 430) 2 vol. (Washington, DC, 1933; New York, 1941), esp. chapters X, XI, XII, XVII.

16. This was later published (in part) in *Historical Statistics of the United States*, II, 1189-1191; and in Jacob M. Price, *France and the Chesapeake: A History of the French Tobacco Monopoly 1674-1791, and of Its Relationship to the British and American Tobacco Trades*, 2 vol. (Ann Arbor, MI, 1973) II, 843-851.

17. Jacob M. Price, "The Rise of Glasgow in the Chesapeake Tobacco Trade, 1707-1775", *William and Mary Quarterly*, 3rd ser., XI (1954) 179-181.

18. Class T.79 in the Public Record Office (PRO), London. The debt phenomenon is discussed in Jacob M. Price, *Capital and Credit in British Overseas Trade: The View from the Chesapeake, 1700-1776* (Cambridge, MA, 1980).

19. Thomas M. Devine, *The Tobacco Lords: A Study of the Tobacco Merchants of Glasgow and their Trading Activities, c. 1740-90* (Edinburgh, 1975); *idem*, ed., *A Scottish Firm in Virginia 1767-1777 W. Cuninghame and Co.* (Scottish History Society, Fourth Series, vol. 20) (Edinburgh, 1984); James H. Soltow, "Scottish Traders in Virginia, 1750-1775", *Economic History Review*, 2nd ser., XII (1959) 83-98; Robert Polk Thomson, "The Tobacco Export of the Upper James River Naval District, 1773-1775", *William and Mary Quarterly*, 3d ser., XVIII (1961) 393-401.

20. Susan E. Hillier, "The Trade of the Virginia Colony, 1606-1660" (Ph.D. thesis, University of Liverpool, 1971).

21. [John Oldmixon], *The British Empire in America*, 2 vol. (London, 1708) I, 322-323; 2nd ed. (London, 1741) I, x-xi, 453-454.

22. John Blande, *To the Kings most Excellent Majesty, The humble Remonstrance of John Blande of London Merchant, on behalf of the Inhabitants and Planters in Virginia and Mariland* (s.l., [1661]). Reprinted in the *Virginia Magazine of History and Biography*, I (1893-4) 141-155 with the date 1660.

23. His letterbook indicates that William Fitzhugh, lawyer and planter, started consigning in 1681, a period of falling prices, but continued making large sales in the country. Richard Beale Davis, ed., *William Fitzhugh and his Chesapeake World 1676-1701* (Virginia Historical Documents, vol. 3) (Chapel Hill, NC, 1963) 86-7, 125, 137, 139, 143, 160, 166, 180, 196 et passim.

24. Jacob M. Price, "The Tobacco Trade and the Treasury, 1685-1733" (Ph.D. thesis, Harvard, 1954) I, 2.

25. William Byrd, *History of the Dividing Line and Others Tracts*, ed. Thomas H. Wynne, 2 vol. ( Historical Documents from the Old Dominion, II, III )

(Richmond, VA, 1866) II, 163. For European prices during the wars, see Price, *France and the Chesapeake*, II, 852. For American prices and conditions, see Russell R. Menard, "The Tobacco Industry in the Chesapeake Colonies 1617-1730: An Interpretation", *Research in Economic History*, V (1980) 109-177, esp. 159-160; and John M. Hemphill, *Virginia and the English Commercial System, 1689-1733* (New York and London, 1985) 311-314.

26. PRO C.O.5/1318/2.

27. *Considerations Relating to the Tobacco Trade at London, so far as it relates to the Merchants who are Factors* (s.l., [1733]).

28. PRO C.O.5/1319 fo. 220.

29. See Paul G. E. Clemens, "Economy and Society on Maryland's Eastern Shore, 1689-1733", in Aubrey C. Land, Lois Green Carr and Edward C. Papenfuse, eds., *Law, Society and Politics in Early Maryland* (Baltimore and London, 1977) 156-157. See also discussion in Gloria L. Main, *Tobacco Colony: Life in Early Maryland 1650-1720* (Princeton, NJ, 1983) 38-40.

30. For the Act of 1723, see C. G. Chamberlayne, ed., "The Tobacco Acts of 1723 and 1729", *Virginia Magazine of History and Biography*, XX (1912) 158-167; Hemphill, *Virginia and the English Commercial Ssytem*, 66; Kulikoff, *Tobacco and Slaves*, 108; PRO C.O.5/1321 ff. 74-75 Gooch to Board of trade, 9 Aug. 1728. For contemporary similar Maryland legislation, see Vertrees Judson Wyckoff, *Tobacco Regulation in Colonial Maryland* (Baltimore, MD, 1936) 140-154.

31. "A List of the Tithables Allowd to Tend Tobacco and Quantity of Plants in the Precincts Between Aquia and Quantico [Creeks]", in John Vogt and T. William Kethley, Jr., comps., *Stafford County Virginia Tithables: Quit Rents, Personal Property Taxes and Related Lists and Petitions, 1723-1790*, 2 vol. (Athens, GA, 1990) I, 19-42; Elizabeth B. Wingo and W. Bruce Wingo, *Norfolk County, Virginia Tithables*, 3 vol. (Norfolk, VA, 1979-1985) I. For the employment of white and black boys (and a few girls) aged 12-16 in tobacco cultivation in contemporary Maryland, see Maryland Hall of Record, Somerset county tax lists, 1730. It is not easy to state with certainty the number of plants cultivated needed to make one pound of dried tobacco leaf. Morgan (*American Slavery*, 109) quotes an "old planter" of the 1620's to the effect that four plants made one pound of tobacco. This may have included inferior lower leaves that later would have been discarded. The detailed report of 1724 (PRO C.O.5/1319 fo. 220) used an 8:1 ratio to convert number of plants into pounds of merchantable dried leaf. But those preparing the report most likely had a motive to underestimate production and thus enhance the

apparent effectiveness of the 1723 act. At the suggestion of Lois Carr and Lorena Walsh, I have used an intermediate 6:1 ratio for my conversions.

32. Morgan, *American Slavery*, 228.

33. For some indication of the centrality of wheat on the Potomac above Alexandria, see Kate Rowland Mason, ed., "Merchants and Mills", *William and Mary Quarterly*, 1st ser., XI (1902-3) 245-6.

34. On Norfolk, cf. Thomas Jefferson Wertenbaker, *Norfolk, historic southern port* (Durham, NC, 1931 and 1962).

35. Aubrey C. Land, "Economic Behavior in a Planting Society: The Eighteenth Century Chesapeake", *Journal of Southern History*, XXXIII (1967) 469-485, esp. 473n. Cf. also his "Economic Base and Social Structure: the Northern Chesapeake in the Eighteenth Century", *Journal of Economic History*, XXV (1965) 639-654.

36. PRO C.O.5/1319 fo. 220.

37. Clemens, *loc. cit.*, 156-157..

38. See n. 31.

39. For the highest crop figures appearing in the Maryland counties checked, see n. 41 and Table III.

40. Main, *Tobacco Colony*, 38-40.

41. The two large producers in Charles County in the first decade shown were William Dent (74,263 lb.), lawyer, planter and merchant; and Col. John Courts (47,072 lb.), planter and merchant. Although they had other interests, the administrators' accounts in both cases describe the tobacco as "crop". Both had enough slaves to grow that much tobacco on their own land. See Maryland State Archives, Charles County, Register of Wills A.E.6 (with accounts) pp. 194-196; Register of Wills (Admin. Accounts) 1708-1738 pp. 47-49. I am indebted to Lois Carr for help on this point.

42. When the decedent had estates in two or more counties, the normal procedure appears to have been for the executors or administrators to file separate inventories of movables in each county where such goods were discovered, but to file the final estate accounts in the provincial prerogative court with copies only sent to the counties. Cf. Maryland Hall of Records, Prerogative Court, vol. 21, p. 126. It isn't clear that copies always reached the appropriate county courts. Cf. also vol. 12 p. 418 for an example of a decedent with property in five counties.

43. Virginia State Library: Auditor of Public Accounts no. 301.

44. 24 Geo. II c. 41 in Danby Pickering, ed., *The Statutes at Large* (Cambridge, 1763) XX, 251-271, esp. section I.

45. Thomson, "Tobacco Export", *loc. cit.*, 393-4.

46. Price, *France and the Chesapeake*, I, 670; *Virginia Gazette* (Purdie and Dixon), (11 Nov. 1773) 2. For the bounds of the district, see Thomas C. Barrow, *Trade and Empire: The British Customs Service in Colonial America 1660-1775* (Cambridge, MA, 1967) 271.

47. See n. 19.

48. For Hanson as "Loyds Factor" see Frances Norton Mason, ed., *John Norton and Sons: Merchants of London and Virginia* (Richmond, 1937; Newton Abbot, Devon, 1968) 381. Lionel Lyde & Co. were the third largest importers of tobacco at London in 1775 and the largest specializing in Virginia. See Jacob M. Price, ed., *Joshua Johnson's Letterbook, 1771-1774* (London Record Society, 15) (London, 1979) 161-162.

49. The partners were Alexander Trent, Peterfield Trent, Richard Crump and Daniel Bates. Virginia State Library, U.S. Circuit Court (Virginia District) Ended Cases, box 7.

50. The partners were the two Trents plus James Calloway. Ibid., box 10.

51. Ibid., box 11.

52. PRO Customs 17/1-4; *Historical Statistics of the United States*, II, 1190.

53. Beeman, *Southern Backcountry*, 232.

54. The five were Thomas Mann Randolph (88 tithables; 88 hogsheads consigned); John Wayles (67 tithables; 144 hogsheads consigned by his estate); Thomas Bolling (41 tithables; 30 hogsheads consigned); Col. Lewis Burwell (40 tithables; 18 hogsheads consigned); and Thomas Randolph (27 tithables; 10 hogsheads consigned). T. M. Randolph would appear to have consigned close to his whole production, while Bolling, Burwell and T. Randolph obviously consigned considerably less than their full crops. John Wayles was a lawyer and a slave trader and part of his consignment obviously came from outside the production of his own land. For 1770, see Goochland tithe lists in the Virginia State Library, II, ff. 215-30.

55. *Ibid.*, 35-37.

56. The cargo trade is discussed in several of my works including *Capital and Credit*, 127-136, 139, 141, 156-157; for its credit implications, see "The Last Phase of the Virginia-London Consignment Trade: James Buchanan & Co., 1758-1768", *William and Mary Quarterly*, 3d ser., XLIII (1980) 64-98.

57. For credit in slave purchases, see my article "Credit in the slave trade and plantation economies", in Barbara L. Solow, ed., *Slavery and the Rise of the Atlantic System* (Cambridge, 1991) 293-339.

# 5

# The Twilight of the "Nabobs":
## Civil War Losses and the end of Natchez, Mississippi, as an Investment Center

### Morton Rothstein

S ome settlers in the Natchez District during the first decade of the nineteenth century dubbed their more affluent and successful planter neighbors "nabobs," a derisive term then used in Britain to mock the *nouveaux riches* who had returned from India with great wealth.[1] It was a tag that survived into the 1850's, for this small river town and its environs was still widely known for the extent of its unusual private banking activities than for its functions as a market or manufacturing center. General Thomas Kilby Smith, assigned in July, 1863, to take charge of the town's military occupation, described his new post as

> "... a beautiful little city of about 7,000 or 8,000 inhabitants, a place for many years past of no great business significance but rather a congregation of wealthy planters & retired merchants & professional men, who have built magnificent villas along the bluffs of the river & in the rear covering for the city a large space of ground. Wealth & taste, a most genial climate & kindly soil have enabled them to adorn these, in such a manner as almost to give the Northerner his realization of a fairy tale." [2]

That picture was wrong in one major respect, however, for the planter-merchant-bankers who headed the wealthiest and most prestigious families in the town were very much involved in business throughout the locality and for more than fifty miles both up and down the Mississippi River. They not only ran several large-scale plantations, but also made many private loans to both newer and older families in the area. In addition, several of the more sophisticated and acquisitive members of the town's business elite invested capital well beyond the boundaries of the South. The small river port, once notorious (erroneously) for debauchery and violence in the taverns on its waterfront "Under the Hill" at the river bank, had by the eve of the Civil War one of the largest concentrations of wealth in the antebellum United States. Lee Soltow, one of our best analysts of changes over time in the distribution of American wealth and income, has largely substantiated the long-standing claim of natives that the town and its District had more millionaires per capita than any other community in the United States in the 1850's, except for some neighborhoods in New York City.[3] The town was, in short, a major center of investment activities.

There are several layers of myths about Natchez, some that grew during the ante-bellum period, some invented during and after the upheaval of the Civil War, and many over the last century. But it is clear that this urban enclave's inhabitants were passionately divided over secession and support for the Confederacy. Many leading citizens had vacillating, often ambivalent loyalties, especially those with the most to lose from war. The evidence shows that the river port's economy was damaged more by the financial losses of its wealthiest inhabitants than by the hazards of wartime battles and occupation.[4] The ante-bellum Natchez "District," however defined, had several dozen families with accumulated assets of more than one million dollars in 1860, a few of them several times as much. They maintained homes in or near Natchez largely as convenient bases for reaching scattered land holdings, for rapid access to market news that steamboats and later the telegraph brought them, for banking and market services in New Orleans, for schooling their younger children, and for social reasons. This range of interests among the top of the upper crust, most of whom opposed secession, contributed to sharp divisions between them and other District residents and also made them more vulnerable to losses from encounters with military forces on both sides.

One major circle, or network, of families and friends, connected by marriages and long-standing friendships, dominated many of the main business enterprises in Natchez by the 1830's. With some major exceptions, such as John Quitman and James C. Wilkins, most members of this group were then staunch Whigs and champions of Henry Clay.

But they lost much of their political influence in the state's Jacksonian realignment during that decade. Instead of political activity, they concentrated on their interests into banking, shipping, and myriad other enterprises. Their actions and beliefs show complex, highly variable patterns, more than easy generalizations have led us to believe. To be sure, there is much in common between them and elites in other parts of the South. In Natchez, as elsewhere, the bonds of friendship and kinship were often disrupted during the war and only partly healed afterwards. In addition to seeking maximum returns on their investments, and their touchiness about pride and honor, stand out among motives that influenced their behavior, as revealed candidly in numerous letters. The ties of family, which included the usual bourgeois commitment to preserve property for the next generation, were perhaps the most powerful force. Their sense of serving as trustees and guardians of inheritances pervades their records and correspondence, as in the records of lawyers who served as agents for those planters who by the 1840's spent more and more time away from the South.[5]

The central figure in a largely Unionist network was Dr. Stephen Duncan, who came to Natchez in 1807 from Carlisle, Pennsylvania at age twenty one with a medical degree earned under Benjamin Rush and very little money in his pocket. But his uncle in Natchez, Samuel Postlethwaite, was of the town's leading merchants and had recently married Ann Dunbar, daughter of the redoubtable "Sir" William, a leading early planter with a scientific bent, large land grants, and pretensions to titles, who settled a few miles outside of Natchez during the English period. The connections he made through his uncle brought Duncan a medical practice and entree into the town's frontier elite. Within a few years he married Margaret Ellis, of the pioneering Butler-Ellis-Farrar extended family, abandoned his medical practice, and began planting on lands acquired through his marriage. Years later William J. Minor, son of the well-known "Don" Stephen Minor and married to a Duncan niece, defended the former doctor from criticism about his allegedly elitist tendencies. Minor described the energetic, hard-driving Duncan as a generous man who had personally stirred the muck in the great vats of indigo (soon to be abandoned) then on many of the plantations near the town, and who later took charge of keeping the newly introduced cotton gins on his place in good repair. Margaret's death in 1816 left Duncan with two young children and an inclination to return to the North, where his mother and two sisters still lived and where people had "steadier habits." He abandoned such thoughts when he weathered the price collapse of 1819 and cotton prospects improved. A second marriage, this time to Adam Bingaman's sister, Charlotte, gave him connections to the Surget family and to James C. Wilkins, who was then perhaps the town's leading merchant and banker, despite an unquenchable thirst for bottled spirits and involvement in Jacksonian politics.[6]

By then, Duncan's friendship with Dr. William Newton Mercer had also ripened. Mercer was a Navy doctor, from Maryland, about ten years younger than Duncan and stationed at New Orleans. He met Anna Farrar at Bay St. Louis, Mississippi, a nearby resort, and was smitten while treating her and her family there during the 1820 yellow fever epidemic. Much of her immediate family perished, and Anna inherited an Ellis family plantation, which she brought to her marriage to Mercer. He managed it so well, that the family asked him to take charge of two adjoining places. He regarded himself primarily as custodian of lands that would eventually be divided among his wife's heirs. But he was soon able to acquire in his own name other real estate and shares in Natchez-area enterprises.

In the late 1820's Duncan succeeded his uncle as President of the Bank of Mississippi, had acquired additional lands across the Mississippi in Louisiana's Tensas and Concordia parishes and in the developing sugar country on the Bayou Teche. He also had brought his younger sister and her husband, the Gustine family, and two cousins, Duncan and Robert J. Walker (who would serve in the U.S. Senate and as Secretary of Treasury in the 1840's), from Carlisle to help them gain access to the District's opportunities. The Gustines had four marriageable daughters. By the end of the decade the oldest had married a minister from Port Gibson (about twenty miles north of Natchez), and two had married two brothers from New York City, Charles and Henry Leverich, who were expanding their business as merchants and bankers and establishing mutually beneficial relations with many of Duncan's friends and relations. Such reliance on distant agents was due in part to changes in banking laws in Mississippi that in effect canceled the Bank of the State of Mississippi's tacit monopoly, and forced its leaders to rely on business connections in New Orleans, Philadelphia, and New York for banking services. The fruits of the state's "bank war" soon led to the repudiation of bonds the state issued to obtain funds for the new unrestrained banks, which led to speculation and an inevitable crash. Afterward, it also gave the wealthier planters more chances to make profitable, selective private loans to planters who needed them.[7]

Another connection for Duncan and his circle within the first generation of American settlers in Natchez was in the marriage of the fourth Gustine daughter, Rebecca Ann, to William J. Minor, whose father had been a planter and Spanish official before 1803. In the 1840's William was investing in three sugar plantations near Houma, Louisiana, 150 miles southwest of Natchez. In 1860 he estimated that his holdings were worth about $1,000,000, but that his expenses for several years in the 1850's had exceeded his income, in part because of his passionate involvement with horse-racing. His widowed mother, Katherine, presided over Concord, the family mansion in Natchez, and ran the plantation there, but William had to turn to Duncan for financial help in expanding and improving his holdings. By the 1861 election, he owed Duncan over $180,000. Of all members in the "network" he perhaps comes closest to the stereotype of Southern planters as profligate and debt-ridden. But during most of the 1850's he did not go North to the watering holes at Saratoga or Newport with his wife's relatives. Instead, he worked through the steamy summers managing his sugar production to reduce his obligations. Through it all he remained firm and unyielding in his Unionist loyalties.

Meanwhile, Duncan's involvement in business beyond his plantations and his banking interests, particularly his growing role as a trustee and executor of estates, became so demanding that he rented an office near the bank buildings in the town's center. He rode the several miles to it on horse-back daily from his home at Auburn, a showplace residence he had bought in 1820. Mercer, too, distraught after the deaths of his wife in 1843 and of his daughter, an only child, a decade later, kept his large house in the town's business district as an office more than as a residence. Increasingly, however, Mercer spent his time in New Orleans, managing his investments there in banks, real estate, and local enterprises. He also engaged in philanthropy on a scale that by the 1850's earned him the designation of the "Judah Truro of the Protestants." From the 1820's to the Civil War, Mercer acted as agent and companion for Eliza Young, the orphaned, unmarried and sickly daughter of a former business associate, as Duncan did for Mary Linton, whose father had been a partner with James Wilkins in a Natchez-New Orleans merchant firm. In addition, Duncan took care of investments he placed in the District for his twice-widowed mother, Emily Postlethwaite Blaine, who lived in a Chestnut Street house in Philadelphia until her death in 1849, then for his sister Emily, who moved from Philadelphia to New York to live with a widowed sister. He placed most of these and other family funds in private loans to planters in the District, including those in Concordia and Tensas Parishes, and kept strict, separate accounts of them with the Leverich firm in New York, which handled most of his affairs there. Duncan got much better returns from the loans to planters — a standard eight per cent per annum during the 1840's and '50's — than he could get safely from most investments in the North. Both Duncan and Mercer also handled similar loans as executors of numerous estates for other close friends and relatives. This type of private banking was neither novel nor anachronistic. Recent studies show that it was a major but often over-looked factor in the financial world of the United Kingdom, the Netherlands, and France from at least the 16th century to modern times. Moreover, studies in the 1950's have shown that as much as 90 percent of loans to farmers in the American Midwest then were from retired farmers who knew their debtors well.[8]

Another of Duncan's and Minor's neighbors and friends in Natchez, Levin R. Marshall, took a similar route to wealth, first accumulating a modest estate from his banking connections and knowledge, then from his experience as a merchant. He invested in--or foreclosed on-various slave-holdings. His first marriage, to Marie Chotard, gave him a connection to the Ellises and Minors. Marie died in the 1830's, when Marshall was busily absorbed with his first job in the District, running the Woodville branch of the Second Bank of the United States. A few years later he married Charlotte Hunt, a wealthy widow, and started a new family. By the 1850's he owned more than six large cotton plantations in Louisiana and Mississippi, and was bringing several others into production in Arkansas.[9] Like Duncan and Mercer, Marshall also had a portfolio of investments in Northern securities and was spending more time each year at his New York City house on Madison Avenue and his mansion at Pelham, in the Bronx. Between those residences he had only a little time during summers to join the Duncans, Mercer, and Leveriches at Newport, Rhode Island.

One other person in this network of Deep South slaveholders at Newport in the 1850 summers was Mrs. Mary Porter, who may never have visited Natchez but became close friends of the elite group. In the mid-1850's, as the recent widow of Judge Alexander Porter's brother and heir, she became the custodian for her young son and two daughters of two sugar plantations on the Bayou Teche in Louisiana, adjoining some of Duncan's holdings there. She had property in her own name in her native Tennessee, yet felt responsible primarily for retaining her husband's estate for her children. She relied on Duncan and Mercer for advice in managing her estate and marketing her crops, and through them on the Leverich brothers for much of her banking and factorage services. Like most other women plantation owners, Mary Porter quickly learned that it was essential to keep her costs down, to preserve her capital and credit (which also meant caring for the well-being of her slaves), and to seek prices that would yield a profit. She sent a stream of detailed letters through the Leveriches to her overseers with that objective. In 1859 she considered selling her holdings in Louisiana, organized into single plantation called "Oaklawn," because she calculated that since the lowering of the tariff on sugar in 1857 she had gotten only a two per cent return on her capital. Such liquidation of assets at an acceptable price was difficult in that depression period, then impossible after Lincoln's election, so she rented the Newport house that had been her main residence for several years, put her teen-age daughters in a New York City boarding school, where they could be watched and guided by the Leveriches. In January, 1861, she was in New Orleans looking for a new overseer and working for "compromise" candidates to the state's secession convention, writing bitter letters to the Leveriches and to Mercer about the folly of the coming conflict. In May, 1861 she returned to St. Mary's Parish to spend most of the war on her property and was the "only white person" there. The state's Civil War Tax returns show that she had a higher assessment than most of her neighbors, although she had mortgaged her northern property to the Leverich firm to secure her outstanding debts to them, to pay for her children's expenses, and to provide herself with $300 a month to run the plantation, still listed on the tax rolls as the "Estate of James Porter," with title fully secure.[10]

Both Porter and Mercer, like most of the circle, vacillated between despair and hope as events brought war closer. Appalled by what he regarded as fraud and intimidation in the election of Louisiana's secession convention, Mercer still hoped for reconciliation between the sections in early 1861. Concerned after the firing on Fort Sumter over whether he would find hostility among Northerners if he made his usual trek in May to Newport, Saratoga, and Niagara Falls, he asked whether "a man of my age and character" (he was then in his late 60's) would suffer gratuitous insults. He solved the problem by arranging for lodgings at Niagara Falls in the Clifton Hotel, on the Canadian side.[11] After the first bloody battle at Bull Run, he abandoned hope for peace and returned to New Orleans, fearful that otherwise his property there and in the Natchez District might be confiscated by the Confederates.. With premonitions about a future "devoid of reason," he discovered that the Bank of Louisiana, in which he was a major shareholder and director, had been required by rebel officials to ship most of its large holdings of specie into the deep

South. He agreed to take over the presidency of the bank, and when the city fell to Union forces a year later his reputation as a staunch Unionist was such that General Ben Butler appointed him to serve on a three man committee to investigate the city's banks. [12]

In a war rapidly becoming a revolution, a tough confrontation with "Stormy Ben" Butler was inevitable, and it drove the old man into exile. Mercer had weathered investigations of his own behavior, of his bank's affairs, and cooperated with Union authorities in many ways, but he then balked when told he must take a newly required oath of allegiance or face forfeiture of all his property. He refused to comply, on the grounds that he had taken such an oath when serving in the Navy in the War of 1812, had never renounced it, and had remained "neutral" by refusing to take a Confederate oath. He also believed his vigorous opposition to secession was enough testimony to his loyalty. Mercer sent a long version of his explanation to his friend August Belmont, who was impressed enough to find a way to show it to Lincoln as an example of the support for a peaceful solution to the conflict that was being lost by requiring the oath.[13] He then conformed meticulously to Order No. 76 by drawing up a list of his properties in New Orleans, including the home on Canal Street that has since become the Boston Club (the only building left in the downtown part of that thoroughfare originally a private dwelling), and more than $60,000 in "personal notes" that he held. His assets totaled more than $500,000. He informed Butler that he was ready to be stripped of all his property and rendered penniless, except for about $3,000 he needed for travel expenses. He did not mention the property he held outside New Orleans, including 7,000 pounds in British Consols held by his old friend Washington Jackson, in London, or the several thousand acres of prime Illinois prairie land in almost half of Macoupin County, that was even then being sold to settlers by his agent in Springfield. [14]

The confrontation was never directly resolved. General Butler left New Orleans soon after sequestering Mercer's property in the city. Mercer left the country, spending some time in Cuba that winter, then to the New York City house on 14th Street that belonged to his friend, Dr. James Metcalf, another Natchez area planter. When the war was reaching a military climax at Vicksburg and Gettysburg, Mercer was again in Newport, writing a will (the first of many) and appointing executors, switching investments in search of greater liquidity and security, and getting lawyers in both New Orleans and Washington to work for restoration of his Louisiana property. They succeeded. The full value of his estate is barely indicated by his federal income tax payment in 1865 of $8,000. That autumn he closed his place in Newport, sent ahead a stock of fine wines, and returned to his Canal Street house, principles and assets intact.[15] Just before Christmas, 1865 he went up river to Laurel Hill, his plantation just a few miles south of Natchez and under the supervision of Wilmer Shields, a relative of his deceased wife. He had trouble accepting the new relationship with his former slaves, and with customary imperious paternalism told them he would expel "all who misbehaved," and that any who left without permission would not be allowed to return. He left Shields with funds, arranged for him to draw more cash for advances on wages, food, and clothing, and returned to New Orleans after a single night. There is no evidence that the aging banker-planter ever went near Natchez again.

Meanwhile, Levin Marshall faced similar, if less serious, dilemmas. Early in 1861 he sent his wife and two youngest children to New York, at least partly out of fear of Federal confiscation of his houses. Yet he was also concerned about how a "Southern lady" would be treated in that city, and brought them back to Natchez as soon as the danger of confiscation seemed to subside. Some of his Arkansas and Louisiana lands were virtually wiped out by flooding during the first two years of the war, due to breaks in the levees he had built, and he was the target of growing threats from Confederate sympathizers. When Yankee forces reached Natchez two weeks after the fall of Vicksburg, Marshall was ready to leave the town and all his southern holdings, even though by then he, like his friend William J. Minor, had sons in the Confederate Army.[16] Like Marshall, Minor tried to scatter his family to protect their property by occupying it. He left his wife, Rebecca Ann, at Concord with his mother. Several years before the war came, he had given his oldest son, John, a family holding across the river near Vidalia as a wedding gift, but according to one witness John had gone to Harvard University and was thus ruined for business. John's young wife, the former Catherine Surget, managed the place.

She later submitted one of the largest claims for damages ever to the Southern Claims Commission, and collected much of it. William stayed for most of the war at his two sugar plantations in Terrebonne Parish, where he was well known for his opposition to secession, and co-operated with Union officers as soon as they appeared. His wife Rebecca entertained Union officials at Natchez when they occupied the town in July 1863, and received many snubs from local residents who had been old friends. She had a lonely time thereafter, as did other women with Unionist sympathies. The Minors worried about their two younger sons, who had enlisted against their parents wishes in the Confederate Army. One died in camp, the other endured a long imprisonment, though slightly aborted through their special pleading. Meanwhile, Minor lost much expensive equipment and livestock, and found the new labor system that was evolving under Union occupation as trying as did any of his secessionist neighbors.[17]

In the 1850's Stephen Duncan had begun putting his assets in order so he could transfer them to his five children and the estate of his dead daughter from his first marriage. His objective was to provide each heir with the equivalent of roughly $600,000 in land, slaves, promissory notes, or mortgages. He had long since sold most of his slave-holdings in the Natchez District, or counted as part of their inheritance the land for a residence given at time of marriage, as was the case with his daughter Maria and her husband Samuel M. Davis (brother of Alfred Vidal Davis), who lived in "Sunnyside," a residence next to "Auburn." More substantial was his investment early in the decade in land and levees at the Yazoo delta, an area near Skipwith's Landing in Issaquena County from which he carved roughly equivalent adjoining plantations, with a slave force for each to work the rich alluvial soil. He had supervised the improvements, including building quarters and levees, on regular trips up the river from Natchez while he reached and passed his 70th birthday. Each son and son-in-law was to receive full title to these enterprises after demonstrating their ability to run them well. One daughter had married the aristocratic John Julius Pringle of the famous South Carolina family. Pringle joined Davis and the three Duncan brothers each autumn at the Issaquena plantations. Another South Carolina planter, the well-known Wade Hampton, whose father had established plantations south of Natchez in the early part of the century and had been called the "richest planter in the South," was himself eager to follow the Natchez planter's lead in exploiting the newly opened lands of the Yazoo delta. Duncan lent him and his sons over $400,000 for that purpose. In the 1850's, Duncan's age, failing health, and dread of the growing sectional crisis, moved him to speed the transfer of his assets to his heirs, including the signing over of title to many of the loans he had made. He planned to set aside most of his northern properties, which included more than $500,000 in Northern railroad and related securities, and the valuable mansion he bought and renovated in the early 1850's at No.12 Washington Square, where he could live during part of summer, and conduct business more conveniently than in hotels, as was his habit, en route to the summer haunts of the group. After 1863 it became his only residence.[18]

Duncan was in his mid-'70's in January, 1861 when he completed his bequests to his children. He then calculated that he still was worth over $1,300,000. He also still hoped in May, 1861 that the North would "let us depart in peace." But his growing conviction that slavery would end without compensation, that his real estate was declining in value, and that he would not be able to collect payments on loans he had made in Mississippi and Louisiana, led him to pessimistic calculations. In 1863 he complained bitterly that he "would gladly accept an offer of *one twentieth*" of the amount he had loaned. He had foreseen this outcome, and his letters early in the war to his sisters and friends in Carlisle and New York were filled with fulminations about the wickedness of the effort by the North to force the South back into the Union, and about the ruin that he believed the war would bring to the entire nation. Still, from the beginning of fighting until July 1863, he stayed at Auburn and induced his sons and his son-in-law to remain for long periods at their Yazoo delta plantations to protect as much of their holdings as possible, though their wives and children lived in the North or in Paris and London. Meanwhile, he sent a stream of letters to his attorney, the highly respected Josiah Winchester, urging more rapid collection or re-negotiation of the loans he made, especially to planters in Tensas Parish. One of the debtors there reported to Winchester that Duncan's loans to planters involved virtually all of that parish's improved acreage.[19]

Duncan's efforts to minimize his losses by nominally identifying with the Confederate cause soon wore thin. His sons and son-in-law, whose ages ranged from mid-thirties to mid-fifties, neighbors noticed, showed no interest in fighting for the Rebel cause. Duncan did buy substantial amounts of cotton from several friends in the District, including some who were either neutral or loyal to the Stars and Bars, such as John T. McMurran, Frederick Stanton, Gustavus Colhoun, and Alexander K. Farrar. The last named had helped Duncan to acquire the land in the "Reach," a section in Issaquena County along the Mississippi delta from which he had carved five plantations. Farrar, a "cooperationist" in the state's secession convention, then cast his lot with the Confederacy and served as Provost-Marshall of Natchez during the next two years.[20]

By the end of 1862 Duncan had closed his "business" office and became a virtual recluse, to avoid the taunts of numerous rebel sympathizers.[21] Natchez and its hinterland had a high proportion of its white males serving in the military of the "Lost cause," including two generals and an admiral, and resentment against Duncan, Marshall, and other cooperationists grew stronger. Duncan still hoped for some reconciliation of the sections as late as March 1863, but three months later showed a bitterness that would die hard. "My mind is made up to quit this country, and quit it forever," he wrote Mercer, adding with his usual hyperbole that he "would rather live, in...hell itself, than around secessionists ... for I hate them, one and all." He would later lace his business letters to Farrar with jeremiads, denouncing him and the secessionists he served for ruining the country. It was with great relief that Duncan, Marshall, the Surgets, and the Minors greeted the Union forces when they first occupied Natchez in late July 1863, and opened the escape routes by river. They had no qualms about taking loyalty oaths, and some were known to Grant and several of his high officers through contacts at plantations north of Vicksburg. The Duncans and the Marshalls were also lucky to have Lorenzo Thomas, the federal Adjutant General who had known them socially since the 1840's, passing through the area on a special mission for Lincoln. Thomas helped arrange for a naval gunboat to take members of the two families to Memphis, where they booked steamboat passage for voyages to their Northern homes. [22]

The Duncans stopped en route at Carlisle to visit surviving relatives, then went straight to Washington Square, where the disconsolate Stephen Duncan, convinced that the southern property he tried so hard to save was largely worthless after all his efforts to collect from his debtors failed, died at the age of eighty in 1867. His sons were left with the task of liquidating the many loans still on the books, with disappointing results. Meanwhile, Marshall spent his remaining days until his death in 1870 at Pelham. Stephen Duncan, Jr. kept his ties to the area longest, invested in a few local enterprises, but also began spending more time in Europe and the North. He was still trying to collect the Hampton's debts to the family into the 1880's. As the heir to "Auburn," he was in the position to donate the house and surrounding land to the city of Natchez as a park near the turn of the century. The two older Duncan sons retreated to their comfortable homes in Philadelphia, as did Samuel and Maria Davis. The Pringles sent their children to school in France, and at least one of the Surgets to an ancestral home near Bordeaux. An archivist reported in the 1980's that she had just attended a wedding in Jackson with many descendants of these families.

The long, gradual dissolution after the Civil War of the "nabob" estates is finished. Several of the descendants and of a new generation of entrepreneurial families now have houses in or near Natchez, recovered and restored in the prosperity brought by a booming oil industry and the revived agriculture of the post-World War II economy. Memories of slavery days and the segregation era have not dimmed, but along with the mixture of emotions they bring, they should not divert attention from the record, still to be properly assessed, of the functions provided by a group of entrepreneurs who once made the town and its environs a special place for business, one that could match almost any town of its size, such as those in upstate New York or Ohio, as an investment center. Considering the disparity between the political power in the state they had lost, and their economic position in both the lower Mississippi Valley and the emerging world economy, it is not surprising that the "District" and the town still carry their imprint.

1. On the use of the term in England, see James M. Holzman, *The Nabobs in England. A Study of the returned Anglo-Indian* (New York: p.p., 1926). The earliest use I have seen is in an anonymous document in the holdings of the American Philosophical Society, Philadelphia, with the title 'A List of Gentlemen Little Nabobs of Second Creek.' On continuous use of the term, see D. Clayton James, *Ante-bellum Natchez* (Louisiana University Press, 1968) 136-161.

2. Thomas Kilby Smith, Natchez, to "My Dear Wife," Yellow Springs, Ohio, July 19, 1863, T.K. Smith papers, Huntington Library. The census of 1860 reported a population of 6,612. It is likely an in flux of "contraband" freedmen and their families increased the population significantly. The censuses of 1870 to 1900 showed small increases of the white population and larger increases for blacks for both the town and the county. On the other hand, Natchez had a low rate of population growth when compared with other river towns in either the South or North both before and after the Civil War.   See *James, Ante-bellum Natchez,* 61-62; Timothy R. Mahoney, *River towns in the Great West, The Structure of Provincial Urbanization in the American Midwest, 1820-1870* (Cambridge University Press, 1990); Michael Allen, *Western Rivermen, 1763 - 1861: Ohio and Mississippi Western River Transportation: The Era of Early Internal Development, 1910-1860* (Johns Hopkins University Press, 1 975).

3. Lee Soltow, *Men and Wealth in the United States, 1850-1870* (Yale University Press, 1975). On the concentration of wealth among Southern planters, see James Oakes, *The Ruling Race: A History of American Slave-holders* (New York: A.A. Knopf, 1982) 37-68; Claudia Goldin, *Urban Slavery in the American South, 1820-1860: A Quantitative History* (University of Chicago Press, 1976); Gavin Wright, 'Economic Democracy' and the Concentration of Agricultural Wealth in the Cotton South, 1850-1860. *Agricultural History* XLIV (Jan. 1970) 63-85 and his *The Political Economy of the Cotton South: Households, Markets, and Wealth in the Nineteenth Century* (New York: W.W. Norton, 1978). William K. Scarborough has identified forty-seven of the fifty "nabobs" he estimates lived in the Natchez District during the 1850's, of whom Francis Surget was the wealthiest. Scarborough is now working on a full-length comparison with the wealthiest planters in South Carolina. See his "Lords or Capitalists? The Natchez Nabobs in Comparative Perspective," *Journal of Mississippi History* vol. 55 (Aug. 1992) 239-267.

4. On Natchez during the Civil War, see John K. Bettersworth, *Confederate Mississippi: The People and Politics of a Cotton State in Wartime* (Baton Rouge: Louisiana State University Press, 1943); William L. Coker, "Cotton and Faith: A Social and Political View of Mississippi Wartime Finance, 1861-1865," (unpublished dissertation, University of Oklahoma, 1973). On the effect of the war and of Reconstruction, see Ronald F. Davis, *Good and Faithful Labor. From Slavery to Sharecropping in the Natchez District,1860-1880* (Westport, CT.: Greenwood Press, 1982); Michael Wayne, *The Reshaping of Plantation Society: The Natchez District, 1860-1880* (Louisiana State University Press, 1983).   On the town's post-war stagnation, see David L. Cohn, "Natchez was a Lady," *The*

*Atlantic Monthly* vol. 165 (Jan. 1940) 13-19, and William C. Harris, *Presidential Reconstruction in Mississippi* (Louisiana State University Press, 1967).

5. One of the richest troves of such letters is in the recently opened papers of Josiah and George Winchester (and their predecessor firms) that is part of the Natchez Trace Collection at the University of Texas, Austin. On concerns about honor as more a Southern than Northern characteristic, see Bertram Wyatt-Brown, *Honor and Violence in the Old South* (Oxford University Press, 1986) an abridged version of his longer *Southern Honor. Ethics and Behavior in the Old South* (1 982).

6. For a more detailed description of Duncan's ante-bellum career, see my "The Natchez 'Nabobs': Kinship and Friendship in an Economic Elite," in Hans L. Trefousse, ed., *Toward a New View of America: Essays in Honor of Arthur C. Cole* (New York: Burt Franklin & Co., 1977) and "The Changing Social Networks and Investment Behavior of a Slave-holding Elite in the Ante-bellum South: Some Natchez 'Nabobs,'1800-1860," in Sidney M. Greenfield, Arnold Strickon, and Robert T. Aubey, eds., *Entrepreneurs in Cultural Context* (Albuquerque, NM: University of New Mexico Press, 1979) 65-88. A copy of Minor's letter is in his letterpress copy book for the late 1850's, Minor family papers, L.S.U.

7. One example of Duncan's investments in non-agricultural enterprises is shown in John Hebron Moore, *Andrew Brown & Cypress Lumbering in the Old Southwest* (Louisiana State University Press, 1967), a business in which for a time Duncan was a silent partner. On the critical role of central figures such as Duncan and Mercer in social networks, and their use of position and power, see Karen S. Cook, "The Exchange Perspective," in Peter Marsden and Nan Lin, eds., *Social Structure and Network Analysis* (London: 1982) 177-191. There is a three page sketch of "Dr. William Newton Mercer" in *Jewell's Crescent City Illustrated* (New Orleans, 1872); on his philanthropic work, see Hodding Carter and Betty Werlein Carter, *So Great A Good. A History of the Episcopal Church in Louisiana and of Christ Church Cathedral, 1805-1955* (Sewanee, TN : 1956) 130-133, 178, and *New Orleans Time Picayune,* May 7, 1955.

8. Mercer's papers are largely confined to a collection at Tulane University Library and a larger collection, including accounts, memoranda books, etc. at Louisiana State University's Hill Memorial Library. Other letters from him are in the Leverich family papers, New York Historical Society. Among his investments in New Orleans were holdings in real estates, the local railroads, gas company, and warehouses. Duncan's letters to his sisters and mother are in the Pennsylvania Historical Society, Philadelphia. For a fuller discussion of the various family connections in Pennsylvania see Nicholas B. Wainwright, *The Irvine Story* (Historical Society of Pennsylvania, 1964). On private banking in the United Kingdom and the Netherlands see Larry Neal, *The Rise of Financial Capitalism* (Cambridge University Press, 1990).; for France, see Jean-Laurent Rosenthal, "Credit Markets and Economic Change in Southeastern France, 1630-1788," E*xplorations in Economic History* XXX (April, 1993) 129-158. On farm credit in the United States, see Allan G. Bogue, "Land Credit For Northern Farmers," *Agricultural History* 59 (April, 1976) 68-100. For a recent study of

the banking crisis of the 1830's, and its effects throughout the South, see Larry Schweikart, *Banking in the American South from the Age of Jackson to Reconstruction* (Louisiana State University Press, 1987). See also Robert Weems, "The Bank of Mississippi: A Pioneer Bank of the Old Southwest," (unpublished doctoral dissertation, Columbia University,. 1952), and Marvin Bentley, 'The State Bank of Mississippi: Monopoly Bank on the Frontier (1809-1830)," *Journal of Mississippi History* vol. 41 (Aug. 1978) 297-318.

9. On Marshall's early career, see Theodora B. Marshall and Gladys C. Evans, eds. , "Plantation Report from the Papers of Levin R. Marshall , of 'Richmond,' Natchez, Mississippi," *Journal of Mississippi III* (Jan. 1941) 45-55 and their compendium, *They Found it in Natchez* (n.d., pp. ) 82-130. On his holdings in Mississippi and Louisiana, see Joseph K. Menn, "The Large Slaveholders of the Deep South, 1860," (unpublished doctoral dissertation, University of Texas, 1964) 223-224. On his Arkansas plantations, which were not counted in those two studies, see Marshall's letters in James Sheppard papers, Duke University, from the 1850's. Menn's study is confined to four states and includes a chapter on "Pluralists and Giants," which identifies planters with holdings across state lines and includes most of the "nabobs." A different measure of top slaveholders is Ralph A. Wooster, "Wealthy Southerners on the Eve of the Civil War," in Gary A. Gallagher, ed. *Essays on Southern History Written in Honor of Barnes A. Lathrop* (University of Texas Press, 1980) 133-159. The only Natchez area planter to make the list in that study, limited to those with estates valued at more than one million dollars, was David Hunt, one of whose daughters was married to one of Marshall's sons. Haller Nutt, the builder of "Longwood," asserted that he had *lost* $1,500,000 by the time that federal forces occupied the town. See *New York Herald* dispatches , Oct. 16, 1863, in Nutt family papers, Huntington Library.

10. There is a rich recent literature on plantation women, but few efforts to count those who actually held places in their own name, reflecting legal barriers then in force, as discussed in Carole Shammas, Marylynn Salmon, and Michel Dahlin, *Inheritance in America: From Colonial Times to the Present* (Rutgers University Press, 1987). Menn, who confined his study of the 1860 census materials to four states and to holdings of more than 50 slaves, found that roughly ten per cent of owners were women, but that among the owners of larger slaveholdings (over 200 slaves each) they were mostly concentrated in Louisiana, reflecting the different legal environment there. At least one letter from a British firm's agent to a planter in the hinterland of New Orleans in the 1830's indicated that the firm 'specialized' in handling the crops of women planters. See *Miscellaneous Louisiana Records,* New York Historical Society. On the changing roles of Southern women during the 1860's, see George C. Rable, *Civil Wars: Women and the Crisis of Southern Nationalism* (University of Illinois Press, 1989). For an earlier example of a widow who held on to the family plantation, see Avery 0. Craven, *Rachel of Old Louisiana* (Louisiana State University Press, 1975). For a broad study of women of both races see Elizabeth Fox-Genovese, *Within the Plantation Household: Black and White Women of the Old South* (University of North Carolina Press, 1988).

11. On the probability that Mercer was correct in believing that secessionists did represent a majority of the electorate in that convention, see Charles B. Dew, "Who Won the Secession Election in Louisiana?" *Journal of Southern History* XXXVI (Feb. 1970) 18-32; on the larger context of the elections in other states see Peyton McCrary, Clark Miller, and Dale Baum, "Class and Party in the Secession Crisis: Voting Behavior in the Deep South, 1856-1861," *Journal of Interdisciplinary History* VIII:3 (Winter 1978) 429-457.

12. Mercer accepted the appointment in spite of fears of reprisal by Confederate sympathizers in New Orleans, as shown in his behavior in receiving an old friend from Philadelphia, a Union officer, soon after the occupation began. See Peyton McCrary, *Abraham Lincoln and Reconstruction: The Louisiana Experiment* (Princeton University Press, 1978) 79-80.

13. Jessie Ames Marshall, ed., *Private and Official Correspondence of General Benjamin F. Butler*, 5 vols. (p.p.1917) 1 : 480-482; II: 278-279, 332-333, 437. On Belmont's reaction, see Irving Katz, *August Belmont. A Political Biography* (Columbia University Press, 1968) 110-111. The letter of explanation and responses are in the Mercer papers, Louisiana State University Library.

14. Mercer's agent in Springfield was William J. Conkling, a lawyer who knew and had a high opinion of Abraham Lincoln. Mercer Papers, Louisiana State University Library. Box 3, Folder 27.

15. On Metcalf's connections with New York and Morristown, New Jersey, families such as the Colles, Wetmore, and related kin, see Emily Johnston De Forest, *James Colles, 1788-1883* (p.p.; New York, 1926), and James, *Ante-bellum Natchez*, 212, 249, 263.

16. Marshall asked Charles Leverich for guidance on whether "our property in New York, would be confiscated to indemnify or retaliate" if the Confederates confiscated northern property. He then added, "I should hope not, for I mean, *if I can,* to occupy mine. I cannot leave here in the present excited feeling without rendering myself obnoxious and laying myself open to serious injury." Marshall to Leverich, May 1, 1861. For an excellent study of the Acts and their limits as well as their objectives, see John Syrett, "The Confiscation Acts: Efforts at Reconstruction During the Civil War," (unpublished doctoral dissertation, University of Wisconsin, 1971. On the dangers of flooding along the Mississippi, see Arthell Kelly, "Levee Building and the Settlement of the Yazoo Basin," *The Southern Quarterly* I (July 1963) 285-300. On the service of George M. Marshall in the Natchez Southrons, see *Natchez Daily Courier*, March 27, 1863.

17. J. Carlyle Sitterson, "The William J. Minor Plantations: A Study in Ante-Bellum Absentee Ownership," The *Journal of Southern History* IX (Feb. 1943) 57-74 and his "The Transition from Slave to Free Economy on the William J.'Minor Plantations," *Agricultural History IX* (Oct. 1943) 57-74 tell about major developments on the sugar plantations. Charles L. Wingfield, "The Sugar Plantations of William J. Minor, 1830-1860," (unpublished M.A. thesis, Louisiana State University, 1950) provides more on the family. On the planter's obsession with horse-racing, see Mark A. Keller, "Horse Racing Madness in the Old South:

the Sporting Epistles of William J. Minor of Natchez, (1837-1860) ,"*Journal of Mississippi History* XLVII (Aug. 1985) 165-185. On Minors' wartime problems and losses, see Charles P. Roland, *Louisiana Sugar Plantations during the American Civil War* (Leiden, Netherlands: 1957) 80-81, 124-128, and Frank W. Klingberg, The *Southern Claims Commission* (University of California Publications in History, 1955) 110-112, 222-225, and his "The Case of the Minors: A Unionist Family within the Confederacy," *Journal of Southern History* XIII (Feb. 1947) 27-45. On the standing of John and Catherine Minor, and his "fast life," see the testimony of Julia Nutt, in Minor Claims, File 7960, Adams County, Mississippi, RG217, National Archives.

18.  By the 1850's Duncan's reputation as an entrepreneur was legendary. William Henry Sparks, in his *The Memories of Fifty Years* (Philadelphia, pp, 1870) 345-346, referred to Duncan as "one of the best business-men in the Union... a man of rare sagacity and wonderful energy." Reports on Duncan in the Dun & Co. credit books, Baker Library, Harvard University, for March 1857 describe him as 'well known' in Wall Street and one who deals largely in "both domestic & Sterling Exchange for his shipments of cotton and for a few friends." The July 1859 entry described him as "shrewd, economical & given to bus. like a poor man. Yet a Prince in generosity." On the Hampton connection, see Virginia G. Meynard, *The Venturers: The Hampton, Harrison, and Earle Families of Virginia, South Carolina and Texas* (Charleston, 1981) 184-186; Charles E. Cauthen, *Family Letters of the Three Wade Hamptons, 1782-1901.* For an effort to make a broad calculation of losses with the end of slavery for planters as a whole, see Louis A. Rose, 'Capital Losses of Southern Slaveholders Due to Emancipation,' *Western Economic Journal* v.3-4 (1966) 39-51.

19. After his father's death, Stephen Duncan, Jr. carried on the correspondence with Winchester about collecting the debts owned in Tensas Parish, and persisted in that effort into the 1870's.

20.  Coker, *Cotton and Faith* 165-167, inferred that Duncan shipped all the cotton he bought at high prices, but there is little evidence of this. Farrar was confronted with allegations of plans for a slave revolt in the District in 1861, and presided over the large, outdoor "trial," of those charged, an event discussed briefly in Armistead L. Robinson, "Day of Jubilo: The Civil War and the Demise of Slavery in the Mississippi Valley, 1861-65," (unpublished dissertation, University of Rochester, 1977) 37-38, and at length in Winthrop D. Jordan, Tumult and Silence at Second Creek: *An Inquiry into a Civil War Slave Conspiracy* (Louisiana State University Press, 1993).

21.  Duncan actually straddled the issue of loyalty at the outbreak of the war, and was one of the largest subscribers to a fund to purchase arms for a local volunteer company of Confederates. He also renegotiated terms of many of his loans to secessionist planters to make repayment easier, actions he later regretted.

22. John Simon, ed. *The Papers of Ulysses S. Grant,* vol.9 (1982) 24-27, 216-217, 320; Lawrence N. Powell, *New Masters: Northern Planters During the Civil War and Reconstruction* (Yale University Press, 1980) 20, 45-49, 136-39, 146-

148; James A. Green, Commander, U.S.S. "Burton," Sept. 12, 1863 to Dr. Duncan, Duncan papers, Louisiana State University Library. For a thoughtful discussion of Natchez and other planters after Appomatx in a different context, see Dan T. Carter, *When the War Was Over: The Failure of Self-Reconstruction in the South, 1865-1867* (Louisiana State University Press, 1985).

# 6

# Coordination, Cooperation Or Competition:
## The Great Northern Railway and Bus Transportation in the 1920s

### Margaret Walsh

"What are the railroads going to do about the bus?" asked Edward F. Loomis, Secretary of the Motor Truck Committee of the National Automobile Chamber of Commerce in an article in the trade journal *Bus Transportation* in October 1925.[1] It was a question which Ralph Budd, President of the Great Northern Railway (GN), had been considering for several years and to which he would address himself with some vigor for the rest of the decade. Unlike many of his counterparts heading major steam railroads he decided not to engage in a competitive rate warfare. He early concluded that the motor coach should be regarded as an asset rather than a threat. The substitution of the cheaper mode of highway transportation for the expensive train, particularly in rural areas or for local service, could effect considerable savings for hard-pressed rail companies. Ideally the railroads should go into the bus business through establishing subsidiary companies, but they could also cooperate with independent bus companies provided that government legislation ensured fair regulatory structure of both modes of transport.[2] Budd, however, had not taken sufficient cognizance of either the development of the bus industry in its own right or of the ambitions of its entrepreneurs. The relationship between the GN and the bus industry in the critical decade of the 1920s thus fluctuated as managers tried to work out a constructive approach to the competition developing in passenger transportation in the United States in the early twentieth century.[3]

What then were the alternative ways in which Americans could travel as the nation emerged from World War I and the railroad industry adjusted to the Transportation Act of 1920? The steam railroads were still the only viable form of long-distance transport. The electric railways offered primarily interurban and reasonable short-distance intercity travel in certain parts of the country. The automobile, now being mass-produced, was becoming more popular, with over eight million vehicles registered and a distribution of one car per 13 persons. But the technology of automobiles and poor road surfaces still meant that these vehicles were mainly used in fair weather and for short-distances. Buses, which were little more than stretched-out automobiles or touring cars, were offering local services on an increasingly regular basis and were becoming popular because they offered flexibility and convenience. Railroads then were dominant in the field of passenger movement, but they were about to feel the competitive winds as their own operating costs rose and as automobile registration doubled and bus companies expanded and gained in stability.[4]

The spread of motor vehicles in the early 1920s was indeed rapid. In 1925 sales of passenger cars reached 3,735,171, and by then 17,481,001 automobiles were registered. With prices of popular vehicles like the Model T dropping and mechanical innovations like the self-starter, four wheel hydraulic brakes, low-pressure 'balloon' tires and the shift to the closed car making vehicles easier to drive and more comfortable, then the average American family took to the road. Indeed by the end of 1925 there was one car for every 6.6 persons.[5] For those who could not afford a car or who preferred not to use their vehicle for all their mobility requirements increasing numbers of buses ran on the highways. By the end of 1925 there were 69,425 buses in operation, 54 percent of which were classified as being common carriers. Of these commercial operators the independent companies were growing in strength and confidence.[6] They had emerged from the cut-throat competition of the jitney days and had greater knowledge of operating costs and good management practices. Responding to this increase in private and commercial motor transport, including trucks as well as buses in the latter category, state governments, financed in large part by new gasoline taxes, took greater responsibility for maintaining and improving local roads and primary highways. Furthermore, in 1921 the federal government committed itself more substantially, albeit still somewhat tentatively, to supporting a program of better roads.[7] 'Motormobility' was definitely coming into its own. No longer were Americans content to be tied to the routes, schedules and charges of the railroads, whether steam or electric; nor would they be confined to the slow pace of the carriage, buggy, bicycle or their own feet.

Minnesota, through whose northern portions the GN provided a main artery of passenger transportation, mirrored developments in the western parts of the nation, if not the nation at large. Motor vehicle registration had already reached 351,212 in the three year period 1918-1920 and by 1925 was recorded as standing at 526,405. Then there was approximately one automobile for every five residents of Minnesota. Motor buses, originating in the Northern Iron Range district in the middle years of the second decade of the century, numbered 205 by 1925 and the seven companies operating there were offering a variety of attractive services. This growth in motor transport had stimulated increased expenditure for improved roads. Rising from $2,466,347 in 1908, it had reached $23,628,674 in 1920. Financed by gasoline taxes as well as by licence fees, total expenditure by state and local governments fluctuated between $23 million and $28 million in the early 1920s. By 1925 investment by the State of Minnesota and its residents in automobility was reckoned to total $440,434,055, an amount similar to the then total valuation of the railroad system in Minnesota.[8] Motoring had come of age in a state where the conditions of driving, especially the weather and the distances between communities, were not ideal.

GN management was well aware of the nature and extent of these developments. As early as 1921 William P. Kenney, Vice President of Traffic warned Ralph Budd that motor transportation in Minnesota, Montana and the Pacific Northwest was having a serious impact on the health of the railroad's passenger business.[9] Short-distance rail travel in particular was being badly affected by the increase in automobiles and buses. As 80 percent of the GN's passenger revenues originated from local journeys then its officials needed to quickly adopt some remedial strategies. The situation in Minnesota demanded priority attention because about half of the railroad's 2,100 miles of track in the state consisted of short branch lines. A survey of ticket sales at 26 railway stations in Minnesota showed an average drop of 64.6 percent between 1920 and

1924. Commenting on such alarming figures Edgar Zelle, President of the Jefferson Highway Transportation Company (JTC), noted at the Interstate Commerce Commission (ICC) hearings in 1926 that 'the people of the State of Minnesota have local transportation, and have shown a desire to travel by other means than the facilities offered by steam carriers'. As the GN not only operated a quarter of the rail miles in Minnesota but had about twice as many miles as its nearest contender in Minnesota, then it was not surprising that its officials were anxious to take some action.[10]

What could or should management do? To meet the challenge of the new competition GN officials, like those of other steam railroads facing financial stringencies, might and did look to internal improvements in services. Tighter schedules and concessionary fares were attractive incentives in retaining passengers. It was also possible to reduce running costs by discontinuing some passenger services, by substituting less expensive means of locomotion like gas-electric motors on some services or by occasionally pooling services with other rail companies. But a more effective way of dealing with the new road competition was to take some incursive action. It was impossible to halt the private individual's purchase of automobiles and their spread, but it was possible to influence or even control the number and shape of commercial motor companies. Negatively railroads might seek to destroy some of these rivals by a temporary campaign of rate-cutting or by agitation for strict motor regulation and taxation. Positively they might decide to work with buses by using them as adjuncts to or in lieu of some of their trains. GN officials, led by Ralph Budd, early saw the benefits of taking the positive approach at the same time as supporting moves for a fair regulation of motor vehicles.[11]

While the bus business in Minnesota was still in an unstable or chaotic condition, GN management was content to seek out information on local bus companies running on highways parallel to the railroad and to consider alternative strategies. It was of no avail to become involved with motor passenger transport if it was unregulated and consisted of very diverse operations, some of which were very small, others being poorly financed and operated and most being involved in an internecine rate-cutting war.[12] When in April 1925 the Minnesota State government at last passed legislation providing for the supervision and regulation of commercial motor vehicles, GN decided to move.[13]   Other railroads in Minnesota had already refused to become involved in any cooperative scheme to run bus companies so GN felt free to 'go it alone'. Initially management formed two new subsidiary companies capitalised at $2,000,000, the GN Transit Company and the Minnesota Transportation Company, to carry passengers and freight. These companies were still awaiting government permission to operate when the management abandoned them in favor of buying into existing bus operations.  This policy offered several  advantages;   the railroad would  acquire  expertise  of  bus practices;  it would eliminate the competition between independent and railroad-owned bus companies and it would  secure the  franchises  of  some  independent  firms  at  a reasonable price before their market value rose.[14]

The Northland Transportation Company (NTC) headed by Eric Wickman was the vehicle through which GN chose to enter the bus business.  The Northland had originated in the Iron Range country of Northern Minnesota in 1913 when Carl Eric Wickman set up a jitney service, acquired two partners, expanded and then merged with another bus operator to form the Hibbing Transportation Company. With increased business they established a new corporation, the Mesaba Transportation Company, in 1915.  In two years theirs was the largest bus concern in the region having a fleet of 14 buses, and they were already attracting considerable attention. Further growth followed and in 1922 Wickman sold out his interest in the Mesaba Transportation Company and moved to Duluth where he bought the White Bus Lines. This operation running on the north shore of Lake Superior, in the eastern range country and to Minneapolis proved to be a profitable venture.  In December 1924 Wickman and other entrepreneurs sold the properties of the White Company to the NTC and incorporated this new company which was poised to expand.  By this time GN officials, especially Ralph Budd and Alex Janes, Assistant to General Counsel, were well aware of Wickman's skills and determination in building up the bus business.  When they decided to abandon their own motor vehicle companies in favor of one based on existing bus lines, they were quick to approach him as a potential ally.[15]

After lengthy negotiations Wickman decided to sell NTC to the GN for $378,000. He himself thought that consolidation of bus lines with the railroads offered great possibilities and by this time, mid May 1925, he did not envisage any problems in obtaining franchises from the Minnesota Railroad and Warehouse Commission for both the Northland and the Range Rapid Transit Lines which he had recently purchased. He was anxious to retain a financial share in any new company and was prepared to offer his services as manager. GN officials welcomed both propositions, allowing Wickman a 10 percent interest in what would be a substantially reorganised NTC and appointing him President and General Manager. Armed with railroad capital it was then possible to buy other lines, obtain their franchises and form a large bus consolidation.[16]

The Interstate Transportation Company, all of whose lines were in competition with GN lines, was acquired in May and June of 1925. The Boulevard Transportation Company with some routes parallelling the GN and the Motor Truck Service Company whose operation were in competition with both GN and the Northern Pacific Railway Company (NP), were also purchased in June 1925. But perhaps the most significant acquisition of routes came in an agreement with the JHTC in July 1925. This company operated lines in southern as well as central and northern Minnesota and had recently been acquired by another outstanding bus entrepreneur, Edgar F. Zelle. GN officials were quite clear that they were not interested in operating buses outside their catchment area. A deal was thus made with Edgar Zelle to sell the NTC the operating rights of the JHTC to all the routes north of St Paul. Zelle thereby acquired the finance to retain the Jefferson's southern routes and to remain an independent bus operator. By the end of 1925 the GN, through its subsidiary the NTC, was the largest bus company in Minnesota.[17]

When news about the restructured NTC became public the bus, railroad and local press spent much column space discussing developments in Minnesota and the precedents being set for the future relationship of road and rail transportation. For Minnesotans generally the ABC of the $2,500,000 merger was part of the official recognition of the burgeoning bus industry. With GN as the owner of the Northland properties, railroad capital had been used to sanction and strengthen the comparatively new means of transport which had already demonstrated its viability in terms of economy and flexibility. By coordinating with trains buses were given respectability as an adjunct or auxiliary. This was one way forward in the changing patterns of early twentieth century transportation. Whether it would be a positive way for both modes remained to be seen, but at least the residents of Northern Minnesota did not face the discordance witnessed by their counterparts in the southern portions of the State. Here Gophers were party to the 'hottest transportation fight in the state's history' as several major steam railroads with routes in Minnesota sharply contested the right of independent bus companies to operate. They found, however, that they could not run the companies off the highways simply because they parallelled their rail lines. The Minnesota Railroad and Warehouse Commission, as licencing authority, was concerned about the public's broader transportation needs rather than the railroad's narrower survival interests. This was a lesson which many railroads throughout the nation had to learn and in doing so they too came to operate bus subsidiaries. The GN like two other major steam railroads, the New York, New Haven and Hartford (NYNH&H) and the Boston and Maine (B&M) pioneered a defensive path to retaining passengers.[18]

This path, however, was neither smooth nor long-lasting. The NTC faced teething troubles in its process of restructuring and modernization as well as competition from both other bus and train companies. The railroad subsidiary had scarcely resolved these difficulties when its managers, who were clearly bus entrepreneurs as distinct from rail operators, spread their wings and ventured into a national bus organization. They thus challenged the railroads in an area in which the latter considered themselves to be unchallengeable, namely long-distance passenger traffic. A new relationship then needed to be forged in which Northland buses were to have equal if not higher status than GN passenger trains. The railroad had not succeeded in funnelling highway passengers back towards the trains either directly or indirectly.

In its first year of business the GN subsidiary encountered many difficulties not least of which was opposition from other railroad and bus companies. It was important to deal quickly with the objections of other railroad companies to the bus routes which the Northland operated both within and beyond the GN territory before the railroad was accused of treachery to members of the rail fraternity. When purchasing the independent bus companies which formed the Northland GN officials had rationalized that

"If the Northland Transportation Company had not continued the operation of mileage not competitive with the Great Northern Railway Company, such operation would have been carried on by other common carrier companies for the reason that the Railroad and Warehouse Commission of this state had found that public convenience and necessity required such operation.[19]

But this type of argument was not conducive to good will if railroads strongly objected to bus companies let alone rail subsidiaries.

In Northern Minnesota within the GN catchment area railroad opposition to the operations of the Northland was muted. The NP only contended that if routes were franchised then certain of its train services would be discontinued. The Duluth, Winnipeg and Pacific Railway Company only objected to the operation of buses between Virginia and International Falls, a route which the Northland then dropped. But opposition from other railroads in Southern Minnesota to the routes beyond the GN territory was stronger and more vociferous. Here the Northland proposed disposing of its bus routes and if outraged railroads like the Chicago, Milwaukee St Paul Pacific failed to buy the franchises and then set up their own subsidiaries, they at least could not accuse the GN of directly undermining the livelihood of another railroad.[20]

As for relations with independent bus companies, the Northland was primarily concerned about lines in Northern Minnesota. Here the only large operation was the Mesaba Transportation Company run since 1922 by two of Eric Wickman's former partners, Andrew Anderson and Ralph Bogan. The Northland already had its own routes into the Iron Range country and was also running buses between Hibbing and Duluth for the Eagle Transportation Company pending a decision to buy this franchise. Anxious to avoid duplication of service the managers of the Northland and the Mesaba eventually agreed to reduce the number of their daily trips. Nevertheless competition on this important route to Duluth remained strong. For the Northland the solution lay in a buy-out. After lengthy negotiations the rail subsidiary in 1928 acquired all the Mesaba routes other than the local North and South Hibbing line which continued to be run by Andrew Anderson. It was then able to continue integrating and building up its bus services and coordinating its buses with GN trains.[21]

The reorganized Northland had quickly taken steps to become an efficient bus company working closely in alliance with the railroad. One of the advantages of being a rail subsidiary was an injection of working capital, while another was managerial advice from men with long experience of working in transportation. Both were used to good effect. Finance was needed for new equipment and improved facilities. The acquisition of independent bus companies in 1925 and 1926 had brought with it poor quality equipment. New buses of the parlor type, having individual well-cushioned chairs, luxurious fittings and luggage compartments were ordered and 33 of these vehicles were added to the existing fleet in the first six months of 1926. Between 35 and 40 new buses per annum were the target if the company remained at a similar size of 150 buses. Attempts were made to use four cylinder buses on the shorter runs where the roads were paved while six cylinder motors were preferred for the more frequent long-haul routes. Models of buses were also standardized within a given area and particular vehicles were assigned to a specific driver thereby raising morale and encouraging company loyalty. To house and service these buses garages were located at Hibbing, Duluth and Minneapolis. The new showpiece garage at Minneapolis, capable of maintaining 100 buses was designed to cut down the losses in both time and money which had resulted from having three separate garages in the same city. In the state more than 100 depots, often at hotels, drug stores or restaurants, were established. Northland was setting an example which other bus companies could follow.[22]

It, in turn, was following the example of the GN. The bus industry was a comparatively new service being some 10 years old at best. Bus entrepreneurs could thus usefully learn some transport economics and managerial skills from rail operations which had been in existence for half a century. With rail men as officers of Northland, namely C.O. Jenks as Vice President, W.P. Kenney also as Vice President, F.L. Paetzold as Secretary and Treasurer and G.H. Jess, Jr. as Comptroller, bus operations were systematically divided into three divisions, Duluth, Northwest and Southwest. Each division had regular daily schedules and drivers assigned to each. Strict accounting procedures were followed as state law now demanded and attempts were made to systematize rates so that they would be lower than those of an equivalent automobile journey. More attention was also paid to advertising so as to attract not only regular business but also the seasonal and tourist trade. Soon the Northland was recognized as the leading bus company in the Northwest. Whereas in 1926 it had operated 22,000 bus miles daily over 3,000 miles of highway carrying 2,500,000 passengers that year, with a gross revenue of $1,734,367, in

1928 its 134 modern buses had travelled 8,425,844 miles carrying 3,163,801 passengers.[23]

Yet the Northland was not only a prominent bus company; it was also one of the nation's leading rail subsidiaries. As early as spring 1926 *Railway Age* was proclaiming to its readers that the Northland was the largest railway-owned bus line in the United States. By the end of that year *Bus Facts* noted that it operated the second largest number of buses among the rail subsidiaries while *Bus Transportation* recorded that its route mileage more than doubled that of its two rival pioneers, the New England Transportation Company and the Boston and Maine Transportation Company together.[24] With the Northland's route mileage generally parallelling the 2,100 miles of GN rail track in Minnesota Ralph Budd had envisaged the birth of a new pattern of efficient and economical transportation. He commented in April 1926:

> The buses of the Northland Transportation Company operate in such a way as to coordinate with the train service of the Great Northern and supplement it. In this way for a given expenditure we feel that we can furnish more and better transportation to the public than if the same expenditure were made partly by the Railway Company on its right of way and partly by independent bus companies on parallel highways.[25]

Since it cost five times as much money to operate a steam train as it did to run a bus, the GN soon applied to the Minnesota Railroad and Warehouse Commission for permission to reduce some of its train services. Such requests were granted provided there was an adequate bus service. If such a service was not available then GN could pay the Northland the cost plus 2 cents a mile to guarantee this. Already by August 1926 the discontinuance of two trains between the Twin Cities and Willmar resulted in a net savings of $50,000 annually while the discontinuance of train service between Minneapolis and Lake Minnetonka points brought a net annual savings of $35,000. By 1928 GN had made a savings of some $700,000 over its 1924 passenger mile costs through cooperation with its rail subsidiary. As a bonus passengers seemed to approve of the more efficient, flexible and frequent bus-rail or bus service.[26]

The message was not lost on other steam railroads. Already by 1928 great strides had been made in the effective use of buses for 60 companies were running buses directly or through subsidiaries. Though the number of railroads with buses did not increase significantly in the next two years there was a remarkable upsurge of large railroad subsidiaries such that seven companies had over 100 buses each. With such railroads as the Union Pacific system (UP), the Missouri Pacific Company (MP), the Southern Pacific Company (SP), and the Pennsylvania Railroad (PR), joining the pioneering NYNH&H, B&M and the GN and being the subject for discussion in the major rail and bus trade journals, there was a greater push for railroads to take a positive attitude to the bus as an adjunct. Furthermore in 1928 the ICC report on 'Motor Bus and Motor Truck Operation' concluded that the transportation of passengers and property on the public highway was a well-established and useful factor in the nation's transportation system and suggested that railroads should be authorized to participate in such service. Official sanction was thus given to coordination and cooperation. Railroad companies might differ in how they used buses; to replace branchline trains, eliminate train stops, supplement rail service, provide a feeder service, set up new routes independent of the train service or establish a recreational tour facility, but they should certainly not fail to use them.[27] Gone were the experimental days. The motor coach had proved to be 'an efficient transportation medium and a worth while servant of the railways'.[28]

Many bus operators, however, did not wish to be handmaidens to the paternalistic railroads. They wanted liberation and a separate path. By 1929 they had vehicles and experience which pointed them firmly to their independence. The motor coach was now a much improved and more reliable vehicle displaying adaptability for urban transit, local and long-distance intercity service, school service and recreational use. There was ample scope for entrepreneurs to take different paths within the emerging bus industry without being rail subsidiaries. Though the statistics showed that both steam and electric railroads had only a toe-hold in bus operations in that they owned 3.6 percent and 28.5 percent of buses and controlled 5.8 percent and 7.0 percent of bus route miles, motor carrier operators feared that rail auxiliaries were a means whereby the railroads would retain their much vaunted dominance of the nation's transportation network. Bus men wanted their industry to be a separate entity which made good use of the highways. Pursuing this goal they not only formed consolidations capable fo offering regional service but they were making plans to inaugurate a transcontinental bus route and challenge the railroads in an area in which they considered themselves to be rock solid--namely long-distance passenger transport.[29]

Among the notable entrepreneurs active in forming such bus amalgamations in the late 1920s was Eric Wickman, President of the Northland. He managed to straddle the contradictory position of running a rail subsidiary at the same time as directing a major independent bus corporation, the Motor Transit Corporation (MTC). Furthermore he apparently accomplished this feat without alienating either the management of GN, other railroad officials or his bus company colleagues and financial backers. As early as 1925 Wickman had become involved in independent bus business in Indiana in the shape of the Southland Transportation Company. Then in September 1926 in conjunction with some of his ex-Iron Range partners who were now scattered in the Middle West, Duluth bankers and businessmen and a Minneapolis investment firm, he established the MTC, a Delaware corporation with business offices in Chicago and Minneapolis. For the next three years until his resignation as President of the Northland in August 1929, he divided his time between running the rail subsidiary and building the MTC into one of the most important bus lines in the United States. An almost breathless expansion, mainly by acquiring existing bus operations which started to use the Greyhound name, gave the MTC a dominant position in the Middle West and the Eastern United States. When in 1929 Wickman and his directors looked further west to hook up with the regional companies developing there in order to form a transcontinental system, it was time to leave the well-established shelter of the Northland for the riskier and larger venture of independence.[30]

What course should GN follow now that MTC was poised to enter the long-distance passenger market and the Northland was about to lose its dynamic bus-oriented President? It might not be disastrous to replace Eric Wickman despite his outstanding reputation. He had, after all, been giving considerable attention to Motor Transit affairs since mid-1927 and there were now a range of managers with experience of running motor coach operations for railroads.[31] But the broader decision to cooperate, coordinate or compete with the emerging national bus industry was of much more lasting significance not only for GN or even for other railroad corporations, but also for the country's transportation network.

Railroad and national bus companies might develop a variety of relationships. Already Ralph Budd as President of a transcontinental railroad had publicly recognised that what was good for one section of the GN route would not work for another section. Buses were well suited to rural travel needs in Minnesota, but in Montana where the traffic was light and the distance between settlements was longer GN had not ventured into the motor vehicle business. Or in the Pacific Northwest Budd had failed to achieve the needed cooperation between the GN, UP and NP in running road transportation between Portland and Seattle. Beyond his own territory Budd was also aware that different conditions like heavily populated areas were accommodated by other variants like those worked out by the NYNH&H, the B&M or the PR. Some flexibility was desirable. The only consideration which was strictly unadvisable was the reduction of rates which caused both the railroad and the bus industry to operate below labor costs without bringing the desired gains in passenger business.[32]

Among the flexible schemes was rail cooperation with the MTC. About the same time as the GN needed to alter its relationship with the bus industry other major railroads were reorganizing their transportation policies. In the mid-1920s the PR had experimented with substituting a small number of buses for some trains on local routes and having made financial savings it established a subsidiary company, the Pennsylvania General Transit Company, to run bus routes in Pennsylvania. Not content with this course of action, in 1927 it cooperated in the formation of the People's Rapid Transit Company, a company running interstate routes between New York, Washington, Baltimore, Philadelphia and Atlantic City. Two years later in 1929 it purchased this company. By now the PR had become even more involved in, if not committed to the bus industry. In September 1928, following a thorough investigation of MTC, it bought $343,000 worth of the company's stock. It then increased its investments in 1929 and 1930 to a total of $1,200,000 and with the status of principal stockholder it nominated two PR rail men as directors of the Board of the newly renamed Greyhound Corporation. The PR, poised to take advantage of any new development in long-distance surface transportation, then formed a holding company with the GC in April 1930, the Pennsylvania Greyhound Lines (PennGL), to take over their companies operating buses in the territory of the railroad. Each parent company took a 50 percent investment in the new company which was to be run by

Swan R. Sundstrom, another Iron Range bus pioneer and now regional superintendent of Greyhound Lines of Indiana. After a slow beginning the PR had become fully committed to the buses.[33]

The PR was not alone among the major railroads. In the Far West the SP also became involved with the MTC in its merger and consolidation moves in the years 1928-30. Having experimented with a small number of buses in 1926 the SP entered the motor coach business proper through its subsidiary the Southern Pacific Motor Transport Company (SPMTC) in the following year. By this time long-established large independent bus companies like California Transit, soon to become Pioneer Yelloway, and Pickwick Stages, and smaller bus companies like Pacific Northwest and Oregon Stages Incorporated held most of the bus operating franchises on the region's major highways. SP thus found difficulties in establishing itself and though there was close coordination between the train and the new bus services the subsidiary ran at a loss. To strengthen this weak position in the bus business SP management in December 1928 decided to buy three operating companies in the northwest, Oregon Stages Incorporated, Pacific Stages Incorporated and the Coast Auto Lines. By this time, however, bus mergers with national implications were being discussed by the major Midwestern and Californian companies who wanted to avoid cut-throat competition in the long-distance trade.[34]

MTC of Chicago had acquired the operating properties of the Pioneer Yelloway system and was negotiating for the purchase of the Pickwick Stages system. Not wishing to be left in a vulnerable position in the passenger transportation services of the Far West and having been impressed by the recommendations of GN managers about MTC entrepreneurs, SP management decided to invest in the emerging bus consolidation. The railroad obtained one-third interest in the Pacific Transportation Securities Incorporated (PTSI) alongside MTC and Pickwick and in the fall of 1929 the merger was showing effective economies in operations. In the following spring of 1930 the name PTSI was changed to Pacific Greyhound Corporation (PGC). The new operating company, PGC was to be run by Thomas B. Wilson, formerly Vice-President and General Manager of the SPMTC. Yet another railroad had affiliated with the emerging GC through holding minority status in the new Pacific coast organization.[35]

The management of GN was well aware of the moves to affiliate railroads to the bus industry in 1928 and 1929 because of their personal acquaintance with both MTC officers and financiers and with other railroad company officers. They themselves, however, proceeded cautiously in moving into a new relationship with the rapidly expanding bus company. They already enjoyed a sound working arrangement with the Northland where they owned the controlling interest, albeit the company operated independently. Northland was run well and efficiently; it had reduced unremunerative rail passenger service and GN actually made a profit out of bus operations.[36]

But a new era was emerging in the bus industry towards the end of the 1920s and Ralph Budd was increasingly aware that the bus business was taking on national dimensions and was becoming an entity in its own right. It might thus be more appropriate for the 1930s if he worked out an alliance with the MTC for the Northwest which was similar to that being worked out by the SP and the PR. If the Northland was to change ownership and become an affiliated bus company, it would gain important advantages from being part of an integrated system. If it remained under railway ownership it would be isolated and might encounter strong competition from new bus companies associated with MTC. If GN were to retain a substantial financial interest in any new affiliate and if it was adequately represented on its Board of Directors then the railway could still benefit from bus passenger business in its territory and ensure that the policies of the affiliate were consistent with its own goals.[37]

The management of MTC was eager to draw the Northland into its emerging corporate fold because it was a well-run, low-cost operation which could form a solid link in its national chain. But to make this link more important existing Northland routes needed to be expanded from Minneapolis-St Paul to the bus center of Chicago. A new and larger Northland bus line was needed and this MTC put together in stages in the second half of 1929. On 15 August they incorporated a holding company, Northland Greyhound Lines Incorporated (Delaware) which shortly thereafter acquired the Northland. The GN took a 30 percent interest in the common stock of this Delaware company as part payment of the purchase, MTC acquired 30 percent, Automotive Investments, a Minneapolis investment trust specializing in bus lines and related enterprises, bought 15 percent and the rest was sold to the public and to the management. Much later in the year, on 31 December, NGL Inc. (Del.)

bought the Royal Rapid Corporation, subsequently renamed Northland Greyhound Lines of Illinois (NGL, Ill.), an Illinois Corporation which had two bus routes between Chicago and the Twin Cities. The Northland now had direct access to Chicago and despite worsening economic conditions in the nation which resulted in a decline in operating revenues in the early 1930s, the company was regarded as a sound and well-run operation.[38]

GN's pioneering rail subsidiary was now part of an emerging national bus corporation. Indeed it had made a major contribution to the establishment of GC and the bus industry as a respectable business at a time when they were still regarded as being somewhat 'fly-by-night'. Affiliated bus companies like NGL, PGL and Penn GL had not only brought money-making bus operations into the bus industry, but they had also provided much needed capital, managerial and operational facilities as well as a substantial injection of confidence, prestige and stability. The GC, as the leading bus consolidation, was in no doubt that a policy of cooperation with the railroads in different sections of the United States had been advantageous to their development. Furthermore they anticipated that the ongoing substitution of buses for local passenger trains would constitute an important part of their future business and profit.[39]

If Greyhound directors were pleased about their relatively harmonious relationship with some of the nation's major railroads as the decade of the 1920s closed, the attitudes of railroad managers to the bus industry were much more ambivalent. Though all rail men had moved well beyond their initial scepticism about motor coaches, they differed about the merits of competing, cooperating or coordinating with them. Many still thought that railroads were the backbone of the country's transportation network and that improving their train services and cutting rates provided a sound means of competing with the newer mode of transport. Others, including GN, had decided that an alliance with the buses made economic sense because buses could provide a cheaper and more flexible local passenger service than trains. An increasing number of railroads thus established bus subsidiaries. Nevertheless, in 1930 the total route mileage of these subsidiaries including the Greyhound affiliates was only 8.3 percent of total intercity bus mileage. Railroads were still uncertain about which direction to move as the depression started to take hold.[40]

GN under the presidency of Ralph Budd had experienced a strong challenge for passenger service from motor coaches, especially in Minnesota where the bus industry was strong, but the railroad had never sought to dominate its rival. Budd was essentially a transportation man rather than a railroad-at-all-costs man and thus he was interested in general as well as particular transport interests. Investment in the Northland seemed a rational step and it helped to eliminate unprofitable passenger trains. Yet the success of the rail subsidiary did not mean that the sole or major use of motor coaches should be as an adjunct to the railroads. With the maturing of the bus industry and moves towards consolidation Budd accepted that the two modes of transportation were sufficiently different to be operated separately. Perhaps his attitudes were influenced by personal knowledge of leading bus managers and financiers as well as by his long experiences in railroading. But he was satisfied that cooperation with the major bus company through minority stockholding would restrain crippling competition and was a promising step forward into the next decade.[41]

Whether the relationship of the railroad industry in general and of GN in particular would follow a cooperative path depended on much more than the influence and leadership of one railroad president. Bus operators, many of whom now had more than a decade of experience working in the transportation sector, were much more confident about their business and its viability as an independent system. Railroad managers who had delayed entering the motor bus field found increasing difficulties in acquiring licences to operate subsidiaries in the 1930s and often continued to compete with independent motor carriers whether large or small. The severe economic depression of the 1930s and new federal government regulations altered both patterns of passenger behavior and rules of business conduct. The uneasy relationship which had developed between the major railroads and buses in the third decade of the twentieth century thus became only the first stage in a continuing struggle. GN management had opted for one solution about what to do about the buses, but within the space of five years had followed a different course of action. It would review the relationship again in the 1930s making more adjustments to meet growing bus competition. Generating passenger traffic was an up-hill task for railroads in the early days of the highway age. There was considerable room for maneuver among the options of meeting the challenge of commercial motor vehicle passenger service, but the railroads would never find themselves in as strong a position as they were in the 1920s.[42]

1.  *Bus Transportation* (hereafter cited as *BT*) 4 (October 1925): 482.

2.  W.P. Kenney (Vice President, Traffic) to R. Budd (President) August 12, 1921, A.L. Janes (Assistant General Counsel) to Attorneys of 11 Railroad Companies, January 12, 1923 both in President's Subject File 10190 in Great Northern Railway Company Records, Minnesota Historical Society (MHS) (hereafter cited as GNR); R. Budd to C. McCormick (Director of International Harvester) June 18, 1928, GNR President's Subject File 11532. Ralph Budd's speeches on the relationship of rail and road transportation are very numerous. Two of the most noteworthy are R. Budd "The Relation of Highway Transportation to the Railway", American Society of Civil Engineers, Paper 1663, *Transactions* 92 (1928): 394-433, (being a paper presented at the spring meeting, Kansas City, Missouri, April 14, 1926), Presidents Subject File 11864 and R. Budd, "The Present Trend in Passenger Travel", *BT* 7 (March 1928): 151-153.

3.  For the brief history of the Great Northern Railway (GN) see R.W. Hidy *et al.*, *The Great Northern Railway* (Boston: Harvard Business School Press, 1988). The long and thoroughly documented two volume history of GN, 'Great Northern Railway Manuscript' (hereafter cited as 'GNRM') is only available in manuscript format at specific research libraries. It is well worth consulting and can be found, along with other relevant manuscript materials, in the 'Ralph and Muriel Hidy Papers', James J. Hill Library, St Paul, Minnesota. For information on the bus industry in Minnesota in this period see M. Walsh, 'Tracing the Hound. The Minnesota Roots of the Greyhound Bus Corporation', *Minnesota History* 49/8 (Winter 1985): 310-321 and M. Walsh, 'Minnesota's "Mr Bus"': Edgar F. Zelle and the Jefferson Highway Transportation Company', *Minnesota History* 52/8 (Winter 1991): 307-322.

4.  For historical surveys of individual modes of transport and for comments on the state of the highways see J.B. Rae, *The Road and the Car in American Life* (Cambridge, Mass.: M.I.T. Press, 1971); B.B. Crandall, *The Growth of the Intercity Bus Industry* (Syracuse, N.Y.: Syracuse University, 1954); G.B. Hilton and J.F. Due, *The Electric Interurban Railways in America* (Stanford, Cal.: Stanford University Press, 1960); J.F. Stover, *American Railroads* (Chicago: University of Chicago Press, 1961) and C.L. Dearing *American Highway Policy* (Washington, D.C.: The Brookings Institution, 1941).

5.  For longer discussions on the coming of age of the automobile see J.B. Rae, *The American Automobile* (Chicago: University of Chicago Press, 1965), 87-104; J.J. Flink, *The Automobile Age* (Cambridge, Mass.: M.I.T. Press, 1988, pb ed. 1990), 112-187 and A. D. Chandler Jr., *Giant Enterprise. Ford, General*

*Motors and the Automobile Industry* (New York: Harcourt, Brace & World Inc., 1964), 95-175.

6. Early statistics on the bus industry were compiled by the trade journal *Bus Transportation* and were reported in both the journal itself and in *Bus Facts,* a collection of facts and figures, published initially by the Bus Division of the American Automobile Association and then by the National Association of Motor Bus Operators (hereafter cited as NAMBO). Common carriers include motor carriers, electric railways and their subsidiaries and steam railways and their subsidiaries. Non-common carriers include school buses, hotel buses, sightseeing and tour companies, industrial use and miscellaneous (including railroad terminal and transfer buses). For the early history of the bus industry see Crandall, *The Growth of the Intercity Bus Industry,* 1-154; A.E. Meier and J.P. Hoschek, *Over the Road. A History of Intercity Bus Transportation in the United States* (Upper Montclair, N.J.: Motor Bus Society, 1975), 1-25 and M. Walsh 'The Early Growth of Long-Distance Bus Transport in the United States' in *The Economic and Social Effects of the Spread of Motor Vehicles,* ed. T.C. Barker (London: Macmillan, 1987), 81-96.

7. For a discussion of roads see Dearing, *American Highway Policy* and B.E. Seely, *Building the American Highway System. Engineers as Policy Makers* (Philadelphia: Temple University Press, 1987), 67-135.

8. This paragraph is based on the testimony of Edgar F. Zelle, President of the Jefferson Highway Transportation Company and President of the Minnesota Bus Association, to the hearings of the Interstate Commerce Commission (hereafter cited as ICC) 'Motor Bus and Truck Operation' held in St Paul, July 30, 1926. These hearings, held in several cities, were part of a nationwide investigation into motor truck and bus operations to which over 400 witnesses, including railroad officials, provided over 5,000 pages of testimony. Zelle made a point of collecting transportation statistics which he was able to use in giving testimony here and elsewhere and in writing his many speeches and press releases. ICC, 'Motor Bus and Truck Investigation', Docket 18300, Testimony and Exhibits, Vol. 5, St Paul, Minn., July 30, 31, 1926, pp.827-834, 838-840 (ICC Archives, Washington DC); ICC 'Motor Bus and Motor Truck Operation', Docket 18300, *Reports* 140 (1928), 698; Walsh, 'Tracing the Hound', 312-316, 318. It is difficult to obtain accurate statistical data on the number of motor passenger carriers and their vehicles in Minnesota in the early 1920s. When the regulatory commission held hearings to grant licences to operate in 1925 it approved 35 applications and refused four. In 1926, after amalgamation and consolidations, there were 17 passenger carriers

with 283 buses and 8 city lines with 119 buses. Minnesota Railroad and Warehouse Commission (MRWC), Auto Transportation Company Division, *Biennial Report* 1926, 3, 164-167.

9. Kenny to Budd, August 12, 1921.

10. 'GNRM', II: Ch. 7, 2, 10; M. Hidy interview with R. Budd, August 2, 1954, 6-7 (R. & M. Hidy Papers); Zelle 'Testimony', July 30, 1926, 847; Budd to McCormick, June 18 1928; Budd, 'The Relation of Highway Transportation', 401-402.

11. 'GNRM', II: Ch. 7, 1-10; Janes to Attorneys of 11 Railroad Companies, January 12, 1923; L.A. Rossman (Editor, *Grand Rapids Herald Review*) to R. Budd, June 21, 1926, GNR President's Subject File 11532; L.A. Rossman, *A Romance of Transportation* (Grand Rapids, Minn., 1940) 10, L.A. Rossman Collection, Grand Rapids Minn. (hereafter cited as LARC. Rossman was also an informal bus consultant to the Greyhound Corporation and the bus industry); *Railway Age* 72-81 (1921 - 1925) (hereafter cited as *RA*) contains discussion of the attitudes of particular railroads to bus transportation.

12. G.H. Hess, (Comptroller) to G.R. Martin (Vice President, Executive Office), June 30, 1924, GNR President's Subject File 10190; 'GNRM' II: Ch.7, 10; Hidy interview with Budd, 7.

13. Minnesota was by no means the first state to regulate motor carriers. Eleven states passed legislation prior to 1920; 15 more followed between 1921 and 1924. Minnesota was one of 10 states legislating in 1925. See ICC, 'Coordination of Motor Transportation', Docket 23400, *Reports* 182 (1932) appendix F, 410-413. Earlier efforts to pass legislation in Minnesota had failed and in 1925 considerable opposition was expressed in the hearings of the Senate and House committees and in public forums; *Minneapolis Journal* January 13, pp.1, 2, February 15, p.8, February 18, p.1, March 4, p.1, March 6, p.1, March 19, pp.17, 21, April 9, p.1, April 10l, p.18 all 1925; (unsigned) to G.W. Lupton (Assistant to Vice President Atchison, Topeka & Santa Fe Railroad) May 14, 1926, GNR Vice President Operating-General Manager, Subject File 227-06.

14. R. Budd to E.H. Harman (Assistant to the General Manager, Terminal Railroad Association, St Louis) September 8, 1925, R. Budd to S.O. Dunn (Editor, *Railway Age*), December 2, 1925, both in GNR President's Subject File 11532; C.O. Jenks (Vice President Operations) to W.H. Edmonds (General Manager, Denver & Interurban Railroad Company) April 12, 1926, GNR Vice President Operating General Manager Subject Files 227-06); M. Hidy interview with A.L. Janes, August 5, 1954 (R. & M. Hidy Papers), p.3; 'GNRM' II: Ch. 7, 11; *RA*

80: May 22, 1926, p.1401; *Bus Age* 5: (July 1925): 17; *Minneapolis Journal* May 21, p.1, June 15, p.1 both 1925; *Commercial West* November 7, 1925, p.17.

15. 'Statement of Mr Wickman in connection with his operation of the Northland Bus Company and predecessors of the Northland Bus Company', May 15, 1925, GNR Northland Greyhound Lines INC. (Delaware); Hidy interview with Budd, pp.7,8; Hidy interview with Janes, pp.3,4; Northland Transportation Company (NTC) (Minnesota) Circular for Equipment Mortgage, 6% Gold Notes, January 1, 1925, 'Carl Eric Wickman', Biography, p.5, both in Greyhound Corporation Records, Collection 3191, American Heritage Center, University of Wyoming, Laramie, Wyoming (hereafter cited as CGR); Walsh, 'Tracing the Hound', pp.312-317.

16. 'Statement of Mr Wickman'; 'Memorandum from G.H. Hess Jr., (re GN Railway Company's ownership in various bus companies), December 19, 1925, GNR President's Subject File 11532; Application of NTC for a Certificate of Public Convenience and Necessity, October 8, 1925, GNR President's Subject File 11933; Hidy interview with Budd, pp.7-8; Hidy interview with Janes, p.4.

17. Statement covering operation of NTC showing routes operated, August 1, 1926, GNR President's Subject File 11933; A.L. Janes to R. Budd, June 9, 20, 1925, R. Budd to H.E. Byram (Receiver, Chicago, Milwaukee & St Paul Railway) August 1, 1925, R. Budd to L.E. Gettle, June 21, 1928, all in GNR President's Subject File 11532; Agreement between E. F. Zelle and NTC for the purchase of 'certain property, busses and rights of the Jefferson Highway Transportation Company', July 11, 1925, E.F. Zelle Papers, Jefferson Lines Inc. Minneapolis (Hereafter cited as EFZP); MRWC, Auto Transportation Division Company, *Biennial Report* (1926), pp.164, 165; Walsh, 'Minnesota's Mr Bus', p.311.

18. *Minneapolis Journal* offers both factual evidence and commentary on the rail/road controversy in the state as it unfolded in 1925. See February 13, p.14, May 19, p.17, May 21, p.1, June 11, p.2, June 15, p.1, June 19, pp.1 and 33, July 16, p.13, July 31, pp.1 and 8, August 2, pp. 1 & 4, August 4, p.1, August 5, p.9, September 5, p.1, September 20, pp.1 & 6, October 8, pp. 1 & 6, October 22, p. 1 & 4, November 1, pp.1 & 4, November 22, pp. 1 & 4, all 1925; local newspapers give 'in depth' coverage of the disputes in their area, Newspaper Clippings File, Folder for 1925, (EFZP); *Commercial West* September 5, p.42, September 19, p.11, November 7, p.17 all in 1925, February 13, 1926, p.10. For specific pieces on GN and NTC see *BT* 4 (June 1925): 303, (July 1925): 357, (September 1925): 462-462, (December 1925): 634-635, 5 (January 1926): 48, (June 1926): 313-315, 341-342; *RA* 80: May 22, 1926, pp.1401-1404; *Bus Facts for 1927*,

pp.7 & 9.

19. 'Statement covering operation of NTC', p.2.

20. Statement covering operation of NTC; Budd to Byram, August 1, 1925; Memorandum from Hess, December 29, 1925, unsigned to Lupton, May 14, 1926; A.L. Janes to R. Budd, August 2, 1926, GNR President's Subject File 11933; G.R. Martin, to F.N. McGray, April 19, 1927, GNR President's Subject File 11532; MRWC, Auto Transportation Company Division, *Biennial Report* (1926); *Minneapolis Journal* July 15, p.15, July 16, p.13, August 16, p.1, September 20, pp.1 & 6, October 4, pp.1 & 8, October 8, pp.1 & 6, October 22, pp. 1 & 4, November 22, pp.1 & 4 all in 1925.

21. Northland Greyhound Lines Inc., 'Association of Routes by Purchase', GNR, Northland Greyhound Lines Inc. (Delaware); A.L. Janes to R. Budd, June 9, 1926, R. Budd to C.O. Jenks, January 4, 1928, C.O. Jenks to R. Budd, January 6, 1928 all in GNR President's Subject File 11532; *Hibbing* (Minnesota) *Daily Tribune*, February 1, p.8, February 6, p.5, February 10, p.4 all 1928; *Minneapolis Journal* May 11, 1926, p.19, January 29, 1928, p.1; NTC *Travel By Bus*, April 1928, inside front cover; H.V. Anderson, 'A History of the Beginnings of the Bus Industry with Grass Roots in St Louis County, C.1954, pp.5-11 (copy in MHS); Walsh 'Tracing the Hound', p.319.

22. R. Budd to W.P. Kenney and C.O. Jenks, December 1, 1926, and Memorandum prepared by C.E. Wickman (President, Northland Transportation Company) to D.J. Kerr (Assistant to Vice President, St Paul), August 27, 1926 both in GNR President's Subject File 11532; 'GNRM' II: Ch.7, 12-13; NTC *Travel By Bus*, December 1927, outside front cover, April, 1928, inside back cover; *Minneapolis Journal* June 19, p.33, July 30, p.1, October 8, p.1, all 1925, March 1, 1926, p.15, February 5, p.7, November 16, p.1, both 1927; *BT* 5 (June 1926): 313-315, (October 1926): 548-549, 6 (March 1927): 176, 7 (March 1928): 174; *RA* 80: May 22, 1926, pp.1401-1403, 81: September 25, 1926, pp.605-608.

23. W.R. Mills to J.A. Lengby, April 27, 1926, Budd to Kenney and Jenks, December 1, 1926; W.P. Kenney to R. Budd, December 21, 1926, C.E. Wickman to C.O. Jenks, September 7, 1928, R. Budd to C.O. Jenks, September 13, 1928 all in GNR President's Subject File 11532; R. Budd to F.I. Plechner, December 4, 1926, GNR Vice President Operating, General Manager, Subject File 227-06; Statement of Stock Issue, Northland Greyhound Lines, August 5, 1929 (GCR); 'GNRM' II: Ch.7, 12-13; *Travel By Bus* 1926-1928 contains descriptions of Northland's activities as well as bus schedules and acted as a form of advertising

as well as a source of information; *BT* 5 (June 1926): 313-315; *RA* 80: May 22, 1926, pp.1401-1403.

24. *BT* 6 (February 1927): 95; *RA* 80: May 22, 1926, p.1401; *Bus Facts for 1927* p.7.

25. R. Budd to J. Chase (Directing Editor, *The Commercial Car Journal*), April 16, 1926, GNR President's Subject File 11532.

26. A.L. Janes to R. Budd, August 16, 1926, GNR President's File 11933; C.O. Jenks to R. Budd, September 23, 1926, GNR President's File 11532; Budd to McCormick, June 19, 1928; Budd, 'The Relation of Highway Transportation to the Railway', pp.397-98; Zelle Testimony, July 30, 1926, pp.860-862, 864; 'GNRM' II: Ch.7 pp.13-14; *BT* 5 (June 1926): 313-315; *RA* 80: May 22, 1926, pp.1401-1404.

27. *Bus Facts* for 1927, p.7, for 1928, p.13, for 1929, pp.15 & 16; *BT* 6 (February 1927): 84, 95-97, (July 1927): 379-81, 7 (February 1928): 66-67, (March 1928): 174, 9 (June 1930): 319-321; *RA* 84: April 28, 1928, pp.1007-1011; 85: July 28, 1928, p.190-193, October 27, 1928, pp.858-859, 86: April 27, 1929, p.998; ICC 'Motor Bus and Motor Truck Operation', *Report* 140 (1928), pp.745-756.

28. *R* 86: April 27, 1929, p.998.

29. *Bus Facts for 1929*, pp.5-7, 13-16; L.A. Rossman, 'Motor Bus Transportation' (typescript, February 26, 1930), pp.1-19, The Greyhound Lines, 'Motor Bus Transportation' (Chicago, n.d.), pp.12-13, both in LARC; Walsh 'The early growth of the long-distance bus industry', 86-87.

30. The detailed story of the origins and growth of the Motor Transit Company (hereafter cited as MTC) which changed its name to become the Greyhound Corporation (hereafter cited as GC) on February 3, 1930 has not yet been told. An accessible, though very general account is available in 'Jitney into Giant', *Fortune* 10: Pt 2 (August 1934): 42-43, 110-113. Much more detail is available in GCR, GNR and in Richard L. Griggs Papers, Northeast Minnesota Historical Center, University of Minnesota, Duluth (hereafter cited as RLGP). Yet even this material does not provide the full story on some of the main participants and subsidiary companies.

31. Budd to McCormick, June 18, 1928; R. Budd to C.R. Gray (President, Union Pacific System) May 17, 1929, C. McCormick to P. Shoup (President, Southern Pacific Company), Western Union Telegraph, July 11, 1929, Manuscripts of the History of Greyhound, C.H. Gohres, 'The Greyhound Corporation', 1948, pp.10-11, 'Southern Pacific Motor Transit Company', p.40,

all in GCR; 'GNRM' II: Ch. 7, 7-15.

32.  L.A. Rossman to R. Budd, March 10, 1928, W.P. Kenney to R. Budd, March 21, 1928, R. Budd to C. McCormick, April 18, 1928, Budd to McCormick, June 18, 1928, all in GNR President's Subject File 11532, GN Railway Company 'Return to Interstate Commerce Commission, Order No.1 18300, Questionnaire On Motor Bus and Motor Truck Operation' (decided April 10, 1028), GNR President's Subject File 11933; Budd to Gray, May 17, 1929; 'GNRM' II: Ch.7, 15; *BT* 7: (January 1928): 66-67; *RA* 84, April 28, 1928, pp.1025-27, 85: October 1928, pp.858-859, 87: August 24, 1929, pp.492-497, 95: October 21, 1933, pp.564-565.

33.  Supplementary Information for Salesmen, February 27, 1930, pp. 5-6 & 8,. The Greyhound Corporation, 'New Issue' (of Stock), February 28, 1930, Manuscripts of the History of Greyhound, 'Brief History of the Development of the Greyhound Lines', (1936), pp.2-3, Manuscripts of the History of the Greyhound, S.R. Sundstrom, 'The Story of Greyhound Lines', p.1, 'The Greyhound Corporation', pp.10-11, all in GCR; A.J. County (Vice President-Treasury, Accounting and Corporate Work) to W.W. Atterbury (President) October 13, 1925, Board Files B158/1, Pennsylvania Railroad (PR) 'Announcement to the Public' (re. coordination of rail and passenger service), January 21, 1929, Greyhound Correspondence Files, Pennsylvania Greyhound Lines (PennGL) Law Department No. 14, PennGL Inc., 'Stock Certificate', October 1, 1930, Board Files PennGL Roll 171, all in PR records, Accession 1807, Hagley Museum and Library, Wilmington, Del; W.P. Kenney to R. Budd, March 21, 1930, PR, 'For the Information of the Public', March 17, 1930, both in GNR President's Subject File 11532; *Bus Facts* for 1927, p.27, for 1928, p.13, for 1929, pp.15 & 16; *RA* 86: June 22, 1929, pp.1539-1540, 87: September 28, 1929, p.761, 88: June 21, 1930, p.1511, 95: October 21, 1933, pp.564-565; *Motor Coach Age* (hereafter cited as (*MCA*), June 1954 (n.v. given): 6, 11-12; 31 (September 1979): 4-14 (October 1979): 4-7.

34.  Manuscripts of the History of Greyhound, C.H. Gohres, 'History of Pacific Greyhound Lines', March 1949, pp.1-17, 'Pickwick Stages System', pp.1-27, 'The Greyhound Corporation', p.8, 'Southern Pacific Motor Transport Company', pp.28-31, for 1929, pp.15 & 16; *RA* 85: July 29, 1928, pp.190-193, 89: October 25, 1930, pp.82-83; *MCA* 12 no. 2 (Fall 1960): 4-10.

35.  American Motor Transit Corporation, 'Share Issue', April 10, 1929, American Motor Transit Corporation, 'Gold Certificate Note', April 15, 1929, MTC, Directors' Meeting 'Minutes', December 5, December 28, 1928, February

188     *Endnotes*

18, August 6, 1929 all in RLGP;  R.B. Wilson (Vice President and Manager, Southern Pacific Motor Transit Company) to P.  Shoup, July 6, 1;929, C. McCormick to P. Shoup, August 12, 1929, P. Shoup to F.L. McCaffery (Auditor, Southern Pacific Company), January 13, 1930, 'Supplementary Information for Salesmen', p.6, 'The Greyhound Corporation', pp.7-8, 'Southern Pacific Motor Transit Company', pp.28-40 all in GCR;  *BT* 8:  (March 1929):  168-169;  *RA* 86:  June 22, 1929, all in GCR;  *BT* 8:  (March 1929):  168-169;  *RA* 86:  June 22, 1929, pp.1503-1505, 89:  October 25, 1930, pp.882-886, 892.

36.  Budd to McCormick, June 18, 1928, R. Budd to F.E. Williamson (President, Chicago, Burlington & Quincy Railroad), March 25, 1929, Northland Greyhound Lines (hereafter cited as NGL) Stock Issue Notice, August 5, 1929, Press Release from H.M. Sims (Executive Assistant, GN) in Tuesday p.m. Papers, August 6, 1929, R. Budd, suggested reply to A.P. Russell, January 6, 1930, R. Budd to P.E. Crowley (President New York Central Lines), January 26, 1931, all in GNR President's Subject File 11532;  'GNRM' II:  Ch.7, 15.

37.  Budd to Williamson, March 25, 1929, NGL 'Stock Issue Notice', August 5, 1929, Press Release, August 6, 1929, Budd suggested reply to Russell, January 6, 1930;  'Memorandum' re. offer of MTC to purchase 55% or more of the stock of the NTC held by GN, from F.L. Paetzold (Secretary, GN) c. August 9, 1929, GNR Comptroller File 4899;  'The Greyhound Corporation', pp.7-9;  *BT* 8:  (September 1929):  509-10.

38.  MTC, Directors' Meeting, 'Minutes', August 6, 1929, G.W. Traer Jr (Traer & Company, Investment Brokers and Member of the Executive Committee of MTC) to S. Weinberg (Goldman Sachs Trading Co.), August 29, 1929 both in RLGP;  Private Memorandum from G.W. Traer Jr re. Sale of NTC, July 29, 1929, L.A. Rossman, 'The Northland Greyhound Lines. A Story of a Successful Motor Bus Operation' (c. July 1930), pp.8-15, G.H. Hess to W.P. Kenney, June 7, 1934 all in GNR President's Subject File 11532;  L.A. Rossman to J.L. Williams (Traffic Manager, NGL) April 25, 1931, GNR President's Subject File 12663;  NTC, 'Questions and Answers Form under Railroad Retirement Act, 1937', p.8, GNR Northland Transportation Co. (Minnesota), Histories and Corporate Records;  NGL Inc. of Illinois, 'Corporate History', GNR Northland Greyhound Lines, Inc. of Illinois;  NGL, *Annual Report* 1930-1936, GNR Northland Greyhound Lines, Inc., Delaware, Histories and Corporate Records;  Supplementary Information for Salesmen, p.7.

39.  Manuscripts of the History of Greyhound, F.H. Schultz, 'Greyhound the Greatest Name on the Highway', c.1952, pp.15-16, Supplementary Information

for Salesmen, p.8, both in GCR; Greyhound Corporation, *Annual Report* 1 (1929), n.p.; 'Coordination of Motor Transportation', Appendix D, pp.408-409.

40. Remarkably little attention has been given to the competition of buses and trains for passenger traffic. See for example Stover, pp.l212-213 or D.M. Itzkoff, *Off the Track. The Decline of the Intercity Passenger Train in the United States* (Westport, Conn., Greenwood Press, 1985), pp.29-30. More information is available in Crandall, pp.107-115, 126-131, 177-192 and M. Walsh, 'The Intercity Bus and Its Competitors in the United States in the Mid Twentieth Century', in *On the Move. Essays in Labour and Transport History in Honour of Philip Bagwell,* ed. C. Wrigley and J. Shepherd (London, Hambledon Press 1991), pp.231-251.

41. R. Budd to T.J. Ross Jr., June 16, 1931, GNR President's Subject File 10190; Ralph Budd was president of GN from 1919-1931 when he became President of the Burlington Railroad. He has been described as the best railroad officer of his generation. Certainly he was very influential among his peers. See R.C. Overton, 'Ralph Budd: Railroad Entrepreneur', *The Palimpsest* 36: (November 1955): 421-84; Hidy *et al.*, *The Great Northern Railway* and R.C. Overton, *Burlington Route. A History of the Burlington Lines* (Lincoln, University of Nebraska Press, 1965 ed.).

42. Walsh, 'The Intercity Bus and Its Competitors'. For a summary of GN's position in the 1930s see 'GNHM', II: Ch.14, 6-15.

### Acknowledgements

I would like to extend many thanks to the Nuffield Foundation without whose generous financial support the research for this paper could not have been undertaken.

# 7

# Accounting and the Rise of Remote-Control Management:
## Holding Firm by Losing Touch

## H. Thomas Johnson

Accurate information is deemed essential to the conduct of a business, regardless of the legal form of the enterprise or the scale of its operations. Nevertheless, not everyone agrees on a definition of information. Is it "bits" of data to be disseminated among decision makers who use them to make order out of disorder? Or, is it an underlying pattern that materializes through relationships among people in an organization? Until very recently, almost no one outside the realms of quantum physics or evolutionary biology discussed information in the latter sense--as the vital, dynamic essence giving rise to observable forms (Wheatley 1992, ch. 6). Indeed, virtually all business writers and practitioners view information in the former sense--as a separate thing that influences action from without, like a force that moves the proverbial Newtonian billiard ball. I will refer to information in the more conventional sense--as inert bits--until the final section of this paper, where I refer briefly to its "quantum" side.

As an object deemed necessary to decision making, information is not readily, let alone freely, available to enterprisers. Even price information--especially in relation to costs--is often incomplete, dated, or otherwise flawed. Yet, business people over the centuries have learned, often by costly trial and error, how to be informed about relations between inputs and outputs, about selling conditions, and about competitive threats.

Notwithstanding the great flowering of the North Atlantic market in the later eighteenth century, requisite information was often lacking and competition was not always strong enough to compel firms to adapt their operations in response to clear market signals. Pertinent information itself entailed costs, whether about production or potential sales, especially in interregional trade or innovative ventures. Choices need to be made about which variables to observe, how often to observe them, and how to combine them into summary measures. The route that information takes within the business enterprise needs to be specified, whether horizontally or vertically, generally available or privately held. And the reverse flow of information--feedback--can emphasize or exclude any or all of the information gathered or forwarded. Absent ready access to pertinent knowledge, many would-be producers remained outside the markets of the early nineteenth century.

During the nineteenth and early-twentieth centuries, businesses devised sophisticated management information systems to: i) direct workers within firms, ii) direct the activities of subordinate units (if any), and iii) plan the scale and financing of the enterprise as a whole. Financial information from the accounting records commonly guided decision makers for the third of these activities, but rarely for i) or ii) before about 1950. In the nineteenth and early twentieth centuries the management information needed to conduct operating activities (i and ii) usually came from practical knowledge of actual production processes and marketing conditions.

Late-nineteenth century examples of non-accounting management information used to control workers' activity (especially to reduce craft autonomy), to evaluate subunit production, and to facilitate coordination of large-scale organization are found in historical records of enterprises run by entrepreneurs such as Andrew Carnegie, John D. Rockefeller, Gustavus Swift, Pierre DuPont, and Cyrus McCormick. These individuals and their close associates knew the business and its major customers firsthand. They generally financed the bulk of their own activities, even after incorporation. Therefore, while they all kept books from which to periodically compile information about their companies' overall financial results, they kept such information close to their vests. The cost and margin information they used to manage decisions at the worker and the business unit levels was almost never derived from the accounting information used to portray overall financial results.

The twentieth century, especially since World War I, has seen the steady encroachment of financial accounting information into the realm of information used to manage operating activities. A subtle result has been for managers to substitute remote control by accounting numbers for direct understanding of actual operating conditions. Most observers of contemporary management practice see this substitution of abstract financial generalities for concreteness as a move giving managers firmer control over the financial performance of enterprises. In a sense, this conclusion reflects a widespread belief that cultural maturity in the modem world implies continually substituting abstract or conceptual understandings for direct or immediate perceptions (Lampard 1977, 27; Leonard 1972, ch. 3). Or, as expressed once by Eric Lampard, the belief that "we [apparently] amplify our grasp of the world by losing touch with it."

This paper explores and describes how businesses in the twentieth century have used accounting to progressively generalize and conceptualize the information that guides the "visible hand" of management. The discussion that follows is divided into four parts: the first part describes management information in American companies before financial reporting became important, during the century or so ending in the 1920s; the second part focuses on the development of cost information since the 1920s, after financial reporting became a commonplace fixture in the business world; the third part describes how companies have used cost accounting information to manage costs since the 1950s; finally, the fourth part examines reasons for and consequences of business migrating from pre-1920's management information practice to the post-1950's practice of using financial accounting abstractions to manage by remote control.

## I. Management Information in the Era before Financial Reporting

Although organizations had carried out trading activities for centuries, the idea of internalizing market activity and managing it inside a company was fairly new in the late 18th century. But the concept evolved rapidly, from simple manufacturing establishments that supplied small, local markets in northern Europe and North America around 1800 to complex multi-industry enterprises that served world markets by the early 1920s

(Chandler 1977).

Accompanying that evolution of managed business enterprise was the development of virtually all the management information tools used in modern times--costing systems for labor, material, and overhead; budgets for cash, income, and capital; flexible budgets, sales forecasts, standard costs, variance analysis, transfer prices, and divisional performance measures (Johnson and Kaplan 1987). Companies created and modified these tools as needs arose for information to plan and control their actions. In the era before financial reporting, however, top managers seemed comfortable with having accounting information to portray overall financial results and with not using that same information to set targets to drive the operating activities that produce those results. Managers in charge of 19th and early 20th century companies seemed to have understood the difference between viewing financial results through accounting abstractions and managing the concrete activities that cause cost, profit, or ROI. For the latter pursuit, most companies before the 1920s developed numerous and sophisticated non-accounting sources of information.

Perhaps the most novel aspect of this management information in late-nineteenth and early twentieth-century enterprises was the "cost" information they compiled to simulate the market prices that had disappeared when companies internalized and managed transactions involving workers and business units (levels i, and ii above). For example, reports showing the cost to convert raw materials into finished products arose as soon as businesses began to manage the work of individuals who had previously supplied output at spot prices in the market. Later, systems to forecast cash flows, to budget financial results, to track gross margins, inventory turnover, and return on investment appeared when companies began to manage "vertical" transactions between diverse production units that previously exchanged through the market (or not at all).

Management information tools developed from 1800 to the early 1920s largely in response to one force -- the transfer of economic exchange from market settings into managed business settings. Before the early 1800s, market prices in "arms-length" transactions between individuals guided virtually all economic exchange outside the household. Then around 1800 people began to "internalize" economic activity and manage it in a business. During the 19th and early 20th centuries, companies engaged in mining, manufacturing, transportation, and distribution decided to internalize numerous opportunities for exchange that went begging in the marketplace. Results of these decisions included, for example, managing workers' time to stabilize and increase output of textiles and metal goods; ownership by steelmaking companies of raw material sources; and ownership of distribution channels by producers of oil and processed beef.

As these businesses soon discovered, managing economic activity inside a company destroys price signals that people take for granted when they exchange in the marketplace. Without those signals, managers managers were at a loss to evaluate the profit consequences of choices in order to plan. Consequently, companies developed management information between the early 1800s and the early 1920s to *simulate* market price information and to judge whether their economic activity is conducted as profitably as it might be in another company or in the marketplace. These developments can be grouped roughly into two categories: first are the systems for cost information to control workers in operating activities; secondly are systems for information to plan and evaluate the profitability of organizational subunits.

## 1. Controlling Workers in Operating Activities

Some of the earliest examples of this management information discovered to date in manufacturing enterprises were in textile factories -- establishments where people found it more lucrative to conduct simple raw material conversion in a managed setting than through continual exchanges in the marketplace. Having substituted hired workers for subcontractors to process raw and intermediate materials, these enterprises lacked prices with which to evaluate comparatively their managed processes. To simulate these prices, they developed systems for compiling information about the cost of converting raw materials into finished output. These systems produced summary measures such as cost per hour or cost per pound produced for each process and for each worker. The chief goals of the systems were to identify different costs for the output of the company's internally-managed processes and to provide a benchmark to measure the efficiency of conversion processes.

Examples of these systems come from the records of American textile companies, many of which copied the Boston Manufacturing Company's innovative management methods. One such company was Lyman Mills Corporation, an integrated water-powered cotton textile establishment built during the 1840s in Holyoke, Massachusetts. From its inception, Lyman Mills used cost information to manage the processes by which they converted raw cotton into yarn and finished fabric (Johnson and Kaplan 1987, 30-31). Lyman Mills drew information from manufacturing cost statements to evaluate and control the one aspect of their operation not governed by market exchange prices, the conversion of raw materials into finished goods. The company did not need information systems to derive the market prices beyond their control, such as prices for finished goods, raw cotton, supplies, and workers' time. They used cost information to evaluate and control their main managed activity -- workers converting raw cotton into yarn and fabric. Such information included the labor and material cost per pound of output by department (e.g., picking, carding, spinning, weaving) for each worker.

Information from the Lyman Mills cost statements was also used to monitor employee performance. They compared productivity among workers in the same process at the same time. In addition, they compared productivity for one or more workers over several periods of time. This comparative information helped managers evaluate internal processes and perhaps encouraged workers to achieve company productivity goals.

The transportation industry provides other examples of 19th-century companies that developed management information to evaluate their internal activities. Railroads such as the Pennsylvania and the Erie invented systems to compile costs per ton-mile, operating margins, and other statistics to evaluate the efficacy of their far-flung and diverse operations. The railroads, like manufacturers, devised cost reporting systems to evaluate and control the internal processes by which they converted intermediate inputs into transportation services. Using the ton-mile as a basic unit of output, they created complex procedures to calculate the cost per ton-mile.

Perhaps the first railroad manager to use cost per ton-mile information was Albert Fink, general superintendent and senior vice president of the Louisville & Nashville in the late 1860s (Johnson and Kaplan 1987, 36-37; Chandler 1977, 116-120). Fink constructed sixty-eight sets of accounts grouped into four categories according to the different ways that costs varied with output. One category included maintenance and overhead costs that did not vary with the volume of traffic; another category included station personnel expenses that varied with the volume of freight, but not with the number of miles run; a third included fuel and other operating expenses that varied with the number of train-miles run; the fourth included fixed charges for interest. In the first three categories, Fink kept track of the operating expenses on a train-mile basis for each subunit of the railroad. With formulas he worked out to convert costs in each category to a ton-mile basis, Fink not only could monitor costs per ton-mile for the entire road and each of its subunits, but he also could pinpoint reasons for cost differences among the subunits.

The great complexity and geographic scale of a railroad suggest why managers such as Fink felt compelled to develop more elaborate cost reports than one finds in manufacturing concerns before the 1880s. The railroads did not simply appoint one person to manage the integration of several specialized processes in one physical location, as was the case with early textile factories. In railroads, the division of specialized tasks was carried out on such a vast and complex scale that there also had to be division of management tasks as well. American railroads were the first businesses in the world in which there was a hierarchy of managers who managed other salaried managers. Cost information in the railroads became, then, more than just a tool for evaluating internal conversion processes; in the hands of Fink and those who followed him, it also became a tool for assessing the performance of subordinate managers.

Still other examples of 19th-century businesses that developed cost reporting systems to control internal processes come from the distribution industry (Johnson and Kaplan 1987, 41). Like the cost management systems devised by manufacturers and railroads, the distributors' systems simulated market prices with which to evaluate the efficiency of internally-managed processes -- in this case, processes for reselling purchased goods. Giant urban and regional retailers such as Marshall Field and Sears compiled gross margin and turnover statistics to measure the effectiveness and efficiency of their purchasing, pricing, and selling activities.

Field's, for example, collected departmental information on both gross margins and inventory turnover. The information on gross margins (sales receipts minus cost of goods sold and departmental operating expenses) was analogous to the information railroads used to calculate operating ratios.  Gross margin information measured each department's performance and provided a means of comparing departments with each other and with the company's overall performance.  The information on turnover, however, was probably unique to mass distributors.  Inventory turnover (cost of sales divided by inventory) was for the mass distributor a crucial determinant of profitability.  Unlike the traditional merchant, who considered markup on cost as the determinant of profit margins, the new mass distributors were driven to make profit on volume.  Hence, they placed enormous importance on the rates at which departments turned over their stock each period.

## 2. *Planning and Evaluating the Profitability of Organizational Subunits*

These 19th-century financial management developments were largely independent of companies' financial accounting systems.  Almost all companies kept a transactions-based bookkeeping system that recorded receipts and expenditures and they often produced periodic financial statements for owners and creditors -- usually distributed privately, but sometimes publicly.  Before the 1920s, however, no rules or laws shaped the contents of those statements.  Management information systems and financial accounting systems could operate independently of each other, or they could be one and the same -- a company was free to decide for itself.

Top managers in most companies before World War II would have blanched at the idea of using financial accounting information to control operations (Johnson and Kaplan 1987, chs. 2 and 4-6).  They often used it to plan and evaluate results.  But financial plans and budgets were secret documents that top management usually kept under lock and key.  Their contents were not used to drive or control the actions of subordinates.  Managers below the top level were not made to think about conducting operations with an eye to overall profitability.  At most, plant and departmental managers were apprised of direct operating costs and were pressed to keep them under control.  But it went without saying that those cost-control efforts would not be at the expense of customer satisfaction, employee morale, or product quality.  Because they did not control indirectly through financial accounting targets, as if by remote control, top managers were not likely to be "gained" by opportunistic subordinates.

Indeed, 19th and early-20th-century top managers usually were intimately familiar with their companies' customers and technologies. They did not have to hide behind a facade of accounting information to converse with subordinates. They could use financial accounting information to plan and make decisions and at the same time use non-accounting information to control operations. A case in point is Andrew Carnegie. Carnegie was obsessed with production costs and output. He drove his plant superintendents to continuously improve their costs and their output (Wall 1970, 337). But he did not drive for high output in order to achieve low costs. He knew that low costs and high output were no guarantee of profits without satisfied customers. "Carnegie insisted that he be provided with a quality product to sell, for he knew that one adverse comment on his rails circulated by word of mouth among the railroad offices could offset a dozen testimonials in writing that he might distribute throughout the country. There was little chance that plant managers would achieve cost savings by cutting corners that might risk quality. Moreover, Carnegie could inform his plant people about customers' expectations because he knew his customers very, very well and understood what they expected. "There was not a railroad president or purchasing agent in the entire country with whom he was not personally acquainted and few with whom he had not had business in some capacity or other" (Wall 1970, 348). And he also knew the steel-and iron-making processes so well that he could evaluate his plant managers' cost-cutting efforts and, in turn, keep them apprised of new developments in the world. "The daily communiques [to his partners and superintendents], dealing with every detail of the manufacturing process from the amount of limestone to be used in the blast furnace charge to the relative merits of hammered versus rolled blooms for rails, left no doubt in their minds that Carnegie knew his product probably better than most of the workmen." (Wall 1970, 352). In short, a keen concern for his company's financial condition never led Carnegie to manage operations by remote control, by driving subordinate managers to achieve financial targets at any cost.

The same spirit was voiced many years later by Alfred Sloan, chairman of General Motors from the 1920s to the 1950s, when he said "the chairman's job is to control the purse strings, not guide the hands of the artisans" (Lee 1988, 90). Sloan, like Carnegie, obviously appreciated the value to top managers of having a broad financial view of a company's affairs. Like most of his contemporaries before World War II, however, Sloan also seemed reluctant to focus the attention of operating managers on the same financial targets. Three sets of cases, drawn from opposite ends of the time spectrum from the early 1800s to the early 1900s, indicate how companies in the era before financial reporting used financial accounting results to provide a window for top management, but used different information to provide marching orders for operating personnel.

The earliest example comes from the records of Lyman Mills, the Massachusetts cotton textile manufacturer discussed above (Johnson and Kaplan 1987, ch. 2). The company's top managers, located in the Boston home office, prepared fully articulated income statements for each of the mills located in Holyoke. However, top management does not appear to have shared the information in those statements with the mill managers in Holyoke. Only the Treasurer and his peers in Boston saw the mill revenue and net income figures. Correspondence between Home Office and the mill manager suggests that top managers focused the mill managers' attention on local mill operating costs, on meeting customer delivery schedules, the condition of cotton inventories, mill safety and housekeeping, the condition of workers, and mill productivity measured in terms such as output per worker and cost per pound (or yard). It seems the mills were not viewed as profit centers, nor even as cost centers.

As we noted previously, the cost information reported to mill managers at Lyman Mills focused almost entirely on the mill's consumption of cotton and labor time. The mill cost reports paid no attention to so-called fixed costs. Consequently, the mill manager had no incentive to produce output for output's sake, simply to minimize total costs per unit. He had no incentive to influence reported costs by building inventory. His main concern was to run the mill efficiently, not to use its capacity fully. Top management in Boston seems to have assumed responsibility for the impact of excess capacity on profitability.

Over seventy years later, around 1910, one finds similar differences between the financial information viewed by top management and the operating information used by subordinate managers in the company that virtually invented modern management, E. I. DuPont de Nemours Powder Company (Johnson and Kaplan 1987, ch. 4). A notable feature of the DuPont management information system was the way it used and transformed the cost information devised earlier in the 19th century by companies engaged in single functions. Thus, DuPont's manufacturing units compiled regular information with which to evaluate the costs of converting raw materials into gunpowder and dynamite. And their marketing units compiled information on gross margins and inventory turnover. But having integrated these functions into one company, DuPont pushed further and developed a unique formula that combined margin and turnover information into a global analysis of return on investment (ROI).

In effect, the information in DuPont's ROI system simulated market prices for capital in a complex company that had internalized the market for capital. To simulate market prices with which to evaluate a diverse internal market for capital, the DuPont Powder Company developed systems before World War I to plan and monitor ROI in every corner of their complex business. Vertically-integrated enterprises such as the DuPont Powder Company, having concluded that their top managers could allocate capital among diverse operating functions more efficiently than the marketplace, proceeded to design information systems that simulated information provided by the capital market itself.

However, DuPont seems not to have controlled operating managers with the financial information from its early ROI planning budgets. In the decade before 1920 top managers at DuPont had detailed monthly statistics on the net income and ROI of every operating unit in the company. But they seem never to have imposed net income or ROI targets on managers of their explosives manufacturing plants. Instead, plant managers followed targets dealing with direct operating costs, timeliness of delivery to customers, product quality, plant safety, customer training (to use a very dangerous product), and comparative physical (not dollar) consumption of labor, material, and power among plants. Secure in their knowledge that plant managers would look after those key determinants of competitiveness, top managers took responsibility for the company's financial performance.

Companies by 1925 put these ROI-based systems for monitoring capital allocation decisions to a new use -- evaluating managerial prowess in organizations that had, in effect, internalized the market for managers. In the early 1920s the DuPont ROI system was modified and used to evaluate and control a decentralized market for managers at both DuPont and General Motors. DuPont, for instance, faced the need after World

War I to administer a diverse array of new product lines created in large part by the company's efforts to use by-products of their wartime smokeless gunpowder production. By 1919 the company no longer made just explosives. Now they were on the way to producing paints, plastics, synthetic fibers, and gasoline additives. However, they found it too complicated and chaotic to manage such diverse technologies and product markets inside the explosive company's old departmentalized functional structure. So, they partitioned the organization into multiple multifunctional divisions, each defined by a distinct product line or technology (Chandler 1966, ch. 2). A similar reorganization, orchestrated largely by DuPont executives, occurred at General Motors between 1921 and 1923 (Chandler 1966, ch. 3; Johnson and Kaplan 1987, ch. 5).

In the new multi-divisional arrangement, managers of divisions performed the same role as top managers did earlier in the multifunctional vertically-integrated companies. The difference was that divisional managers did not answer to the capital market -- they reported to a still higher group of managers who answered, ultimately, to the capital market (Chandler and Redlich 1961). But top managers began using financial accounting information, especially ROI information, to monitor the performance of divisional managers. Here is the first time top managers unequivocally use financial accounting information to control the actions of subordinate managers. Managers of very large multifunctional enterprises -- corporate divisions -- were now hired, trained, and disciplined by other managers, not by the capital market or its representatives. To insure commitment and company-wide loyalty among divisional managers, top managers also created incentive devices, such as the Managers Security Company bonus plan at General Motors (Raff and Temin 1991, 16).5

## II. Cost Accounting for Financial Reporting After 1900

Companies in large numbers began to disclose financial information to third parties after 1900, when manufacturers turned to financial markets for capital almost for the first time. In disclosing financial information, companies ultimately followed reporting rules mandated by accountants, auditors, and by public agencies. In the United States these rules evolved in the 1920s and 1930s in somewhat different detail among various agencies (e.g., the SEC, the IRS, and numerous regulatory authorities); however, the auditing profession's generally accepted accounting principles (GAAP) provided the framework for most financial reporting rules by World War II.

Most GAAP-style financial reports contain at least two items: a statement of financial condition, popularly known as *the balance sheet*, and a statement of financial results, usually referred to as *the income statement*. A balance sheet lists the stock of assets and claims on those assets at one moment, usually the last day of an accounting period. An income statement reports the total flow of revenues and expenses over a period of time. Net income reported in the income statement usually equals the change in balance sheet net worth (assets minus claims) from beginning to end of the period.

GAAP affects cost information in two important ways. First, it requires costs to be classified in the income statement by functional areas of the business (e.g., purchasing, production, marketing, selling, administration, and finance). Those functional classifications usually conform to subdivisions in a company's organization chart. They do not reflect underlying categories of work, or activities, that cause costs. In other words, these classifications tend to identify costs with locations where accounting transactions occur, not with locations where activities occur that cause the costs. However, once companies began to sort costs by functional categories for financial accounting purposes, they began to use the same cost information for all purposes. As we shall see later, transaction-based cost information is not as relevant and reliable as activity-based cost information for making most management decisions.

The second major influence GAAP has on cost information results from two rules for preparing balance sheets and income statements. First, balance sheet assets must be valued at historical cost, not current market price (unless market price is lower than cost). Secondly, production expenses deducted from revenue in an income statement must relate specifically to (i.e., "match") revenues generated *in the period*. To fulfill the historical cost rule, accountants derive all cost information for financial reports from original transactions recorded in a company's double-entry accounts. To fulfill the matching rule, they attach those original transaction costs to manufactured products, using cost accounting systems they designed around 1900.

Accountants designed product costing systems in the early 1900s to divide manufacturers' production costs between goods sold -- an expense deducted on the income statement -- and goods still on hand -- an asset listed on the balance sheet as inventory. If expense deducted on the income statement includes outlays to produce goods sold in prior or later periods -- violating the matching rule -- then income for the period is misstated. The need to divide production costs between output sold and output still on hand does not arise in service organizations, where output is produced and sold at the same moment, or in a manufacturing establishment that never has any inventory of unfinished or unsold production at the end of an accounting period. In those cases all production expense incurred during a period are deducted from revenue as a cost of the period -- a simple matter requiring no special accounting system. Therefore, accountants did not develop product cost accounting systems for industries that do not manufacture products, such as service companies in banking, insurance, telecommunications, health care and so forth. Presumably they would not have developed product costing systems even for manufacturers, except that a manufacturers production in one period almost never equals the amount sold in the same accounting period.

To value unfinished and unsold inventories of manufactured products at their original (i.e., historical) transaction costs, accountants after 1900 devised product costing systems to attach direct and indirect production costs to products. Procedures for attaching direct costs are straightforward since each product's consumption of direct resources (e.g., raw materials, purchased components, and touch labor) is clearly visible. Indirect production costs (often referred to as production overhead), where the consumption of resources in production is not visibly connected with a specific product, are attached to products using various arbitrary -- but relatively inexpensive -- allocation procedures, the most common procedure being to prorate them over the direct labor hours expended on each product. For convenience, businesses often use a single plant-wide rate for allocating overhead to products, regardless of the diversity of their products and processes.

It is interesting to observe that manufacturers before the era of financial reporting concerned themselves very little with the subject of product costing, arguably the topic that contributes most to managerial accounting's fall from relevance after World War II. This inattention occurred simply because they did not feel compelled to "cost" products for financial reporting purposes. Indeed, to prepare in-house financial statements they were content to value unsold and unfinished inventories at market prices, a practice proscribed by generally accepted accounting rules after the 1920s.

### *III. Managing with Financial Accounting Information after 1950*

Businesses in the past 40 years have used financial accounting information not only to report results to outsiders, but also to manage activities inside the company. Thus, financial information intended primarily for reporting the results of business operations is used to shape decisions and actions that determine those results. This use of financial accounting information may not be surprising. Unlike non-accounting management information, which can be subjective and biased, financial accounting is objective and rules-oriented. Accounting experts therefore agree that financial accounting information provides "an aggregate test of the efficacy of the operational control systems in achieving their objectives" and financial accounting systems "provide the aggregation and summary necessary to reduce complex operations data to comprehensible scores of performance" (Armitage and Atkinson 1990, 141).

However, financial results do not "provide the basis for understanding what needs to be changed and how." They merely "provide a diagnostic of whether there has been a failure in the operations control systems that needs to be discovered and corrected" (Armitage and Atkinson, 141). Consequently, the practice in the past forty years of using accounting information to drive operating activities is problematic. As many believe, the practice may have impeded competitiveness and impaired profitability in recent years. For evidence to support this claim, consider two managerial tasks that have been particularly affected by the practice of controlling activities with remote accounting information: planning and decision support; and control of operations.

## 1. Planning and Decision Support

In running a business managers commonly seek information about the financial consequences of intended actions. As a guide for planning, and to choose among alternatives, managers compile profitability information. For this purpose they often place great importance on having reliable cost information. Cost information serves in many planning and decision support roles, such as estimating profit margins of products and product lines, evaluating decisions to make or buy components, preparing departmental cost budgets, and charging administrative services to production departments.

An important source of cost information in American business since the 1950s has been the financial cost accounting system. As we mentioned above, those costing systems were designed originally to attach production costs to manufactured goods in order to divide an accounting period's total production costs between products sold and products still unfinished or unsold at the end of the period. They were not intended to provide information about costs of individual products. Moreover, companies rarely used them to gauge individual product's costs before World War II. But companies everywhere used information from the financial cost accounts to evaluate costs of individual products after the 1950s.

An example can be drawn from the history of a regulated public utility. AT&T was a regulated monopoly for many years during which accounting techniques were designed to measure the overall rate of return of the company and, as time went on, to separate revenues and costs into interstate and intrastate categories. Competition was allowed into a small corner of AT&T's business in 1959. AT&T responded by cutting its prices for the affected services, and the new entrants complained to the regulators.

The regulators asked AT&T if the new prices covered AT&T's costs. The problem was that no one had ever calculated the cost of an individual service before. The question had not arisen in the previous 80 years of AT&T history. AT&T had been managed by a variety of specific indicators that did not involve the allocation of overhead to specific activities. There consequently were no rules or guidelines with which to allocate AT&T's huge fixed costs to individual services. The quest for a solution to this problem, still controversial today, would consume vast amounts of legal and regulatory time for the next 20 years (Temin 1990).

Financial accounting systems provide poor information to evaluate product costs in manufacturing as well as in regulated telecommunications companies (Johnson and Kaplan 1987, ch. 8; Cooper and Kaplan 1988). The manufacturing cost accountants' traditional approach to allocating overhead costs, in proportion to units of output (e.g., using direct labor hours as an allocator), systematically distorts the costs of individual products. Attaching overhead costs in proportion to volume of output is a convenient and economical way to insure that production costs are properly matched against revenues at a macro level in financial statements. But at the micro level of the individual product this allocation technique provides reliable cost information only if we assume most overhead costs are caused by or vary in proportion to units of output (Cooper 1990).

This assumption is probably never true, and certainly not in American manufacturing companies after the 1950s. Indeed, a steady -- some would say explosive -- growth in manufacturing overhead costs since the 1950s accompanied an equally steady drop in the usual overhead allocator -- manufacturing direct labor hours. Moreover, products that consume relatively large chunks of direct labor, established lines of commodity-type products that are mass-produced with older labor-intensive technologies, did not cause overhead to grow after the 1950s. Causing overhead to grow were less labor-intensive products that were custom-made with newer, less familiar, and more expensive materials and equipment; as well as rapidly-proliferating varieties of new products that demanded expensive design, scheduling, and rework time: all sources of overhead cost. By allocating overhead on direct labor hours, products that caused indirect costs to increase were systematically undercosted and products not responsible for the increase were systematically overcosted.

These distortions tend to cancel out at the macro level and therefore do not affect income and asset totals reported in financial statements. But they give a misleading picture of individual product's margins, as many American and European manufacturers discovered in the 1970s and 1980s when, using financial cost accounting information to measure product costs, they erroneously assumed they could improve their company's profitability by abandoning commodity-type product lines and by proliferating varieties of newer "high-tech" lines. In fact, that strategy usually depressed earnings and, in all too many cases, generated a "death spiral" that led companies to the edge of bankruptcy (e.g., see Cooper 1985).

Recognition of this problem grew during the 1970s and a solution to the problem, known today as activity-based costing (ABC), began to appear in the early 1980s (Cooper 1987; Johnson and Kaplan 1987, ch. 10). Advocates of ABC tell companies, in effect, to cost products differently for financial reporting information than for planning and decision support information. For strategic planning information, ABC costs the activities, or work, that cause overhead costs and then assigns overhead costs to products by adding up costs of activities that each product consumes. Simple in concept, ABC was a practical impossibility until the advent of low-cost microchip technologies in the 1970s made it economic to collect and compile activity-based cost information.

## 2. Controlling Operations

A major cause of management accounting's lost relevance after the 1950s is the habit companies developed of using accounting information to control operating activities. While companies always had used accounting information to view results of operations, accounting targets generally were not considered a tool for controlling operations until after World War II. By the 1950s, companies began to evaluate and motivate the performance of operating personnel at all levels with targets that were defined in terms of accounting results such as costs, net income, or return on investment (ROI).

An analogy that helps clarify the difference between using financial accounting information to "see" results and to "manage" results is the giant electronic display board controllers use to monitor activities in a modern oil refinery, chemical plant, or power generating station. If they followed the logic implicit in managing by the numbers, top managers of power generating stations or oil refineries would tell personnel in each department to come in from the plant and run things "by the lights" on their respective sections of the control board. Following those instructions, which people are likely to do if an incentive scheme links their compensation to the performance of lights on the board, people will forget what they must do to fulfill the plant's original purpose. Instead, they will take to conducting operations in the plant with an eye to manipulating their department's lights on the board. While that does not portray how electronic control boards are used in processing plants, the following two examples suggest it may accurately depict how companies used accounting information to control operating performance after the 1950s.

The first example shows how driving people with cost accounting targets often confounds efforts to manage the concrete actions that cause costs simply because accounting information shows only where money was spent, and how much, not why it was spent. A company's production department in Cleveland records costs in two separate lines for resin and maintenance incurred in running extrusion machinery. These cost accounts do not indicate, however, that resin and maintenance consumed in the production department reflect a policy, carried out by the company's purchasing department in Baltimore, to "buy in large quantities from vendors that quote the lowest price." A dumpster full of defective extrusions and extra maintenance to unclog gummed-up extrusion machines simply *show* up in the accounts as extra costs of production in Cleveland, not as the price paid for a Baltimore purchasing agent's efforts to win a bonus by acquiring raw material at the lowest cost. Attempts to drive workers in Cleveland to achieve cost targets will not affect purchasing policies executed in Baltimore. Instead, favorable price variances on raw material purchases will encourage more of the same policies, while unfavorable production cost variances will focus attention on "inefficiencies" in Cleveland, perhaps prompting a decision to reduce costs by outsourcing extrusion to a Third World country.

A second example of how "managing by remote control" caused harm after the 1950s is the use of standard cost variances to control the performance of operating personnel. Almost all American manufacturing companies for the past forty years have used cost targets from top-level planning budgets to set standards for operating personnel. These cost targets are seen as an important tool to control the operating performance of plant managers and department supervisors. Like the setting for desired room temperature on a thermostat, cost targets are a setting to compare against actual costs. Variances between actual and desired costs provide "feedback" that is supposed to prompt operating personnel to adjust what they are doing, as a furnace adjusts in response to feedback from the thermostat.

Standard cost variance systems monitor costs in each and every process of a company's production system.  For direct costs, labor and machine tracking schemes report direct costs per hour or per unit of output.  For overhead costs, reporting schemes track the percentage of overhead "covered" or "earned" by units produced.  The goal of these reporting schemes is to have all recorded direct labor or machine hours go toward production of standard output and thereby "absorb" or "cover" direct and overhead costs, a condition referred to as "efficient."

Department managers beat this system by scheduling workers and machines to produce output in long runs, so less time is charged to categories of indirect or "nonchargeable" time such as changeovers or setups.  Because output enables a department to "earn" the direct hours incurred each reporting period, supervisors keep workers and machines busy producing output.  Every unit produced -- including the equivalent of full units in partially finished work -- entitles the department to a standard allotment of machine or man hours.  If a department produces enough equivalent finished output to "earn" all the direct hours reported in the period it is declared "100 percent efficient." It doesn't matter if the output is not saleable.  In fact, hours spent on "allowable" rework are often considered to be "efficiently covered." With so flawed a system, people sometimes put in hours creating defects, just to build inventory and to create more rework.

Ironically, managers' efforts to achieve high standard cost efficiency ratings have tended over time to increase a company's total costs and to impair competitiveness (Johnson 1990; Kaplan 1985). Achieving standard direct cost efficiency targets leads to larger batches, longer production runs, more scrap, and rework -- especially if incentive compensation is geared to controlling standard-to-actual variances.  Pressure to minimize standard cost variances, by encouraging department supervisors to keep machines and people busy producing output, regardless of market demand, often causes unnecessary inventories of finished and in-process merchandise to accumulate, product lead times to increase, and dependability at keeping schedules to decrease.  Standard cost systems reward personnel for meeting abstract finance-driven targets, not for satisfying actual customers, internal and external.  Indeed, customers scarcely fit into the world of standard cost performance.  "The customer" is merely someone the company persuades to buy the output  managers are driven to produce, at prices which, it is hoped, exceed variable costs.

Managing costs with accounting information in standard cost systems impedes companies' competitiveness and long-term profitability primarily because it motivates people to sustain output in order to achieve cost targets. It encourages managers to achieve financial cost targets by producing output for its own sake, instead of encouraging them to focus on the one key to competitive operations and long-term profitability -- namely, empowering people to efficiently satisfy customer wants.

This impetus to produce output for its own sake, rather than to concentrate on the work needed to satisfy customers, also results from using net income or return on investment (ROI) targets to control operations -- another example of managing by remote control that appeared in the 1950s. Moreover, managing profit or ROI targets, just as managing cost targets, also motivates managers to produce output for its own sake because of GAAP "matching" rules that require accountants to attach production overhead costs to manufactured goods. Only overhead costs attached to products sold are deducted against revenue in the income statement. Therefore, the more units of output produced in a period and the more of those units that remain unsold (but marketable) at the end of a period, the less overhead cost is deducted from revenue in the period. Smart managers who need to temporarily boost income know what to do: go into overtime, rent temporary warehouse space, and get busy producing output.

Obviously this practice has a backlash. In the next period, unless selling prices rise, income is reduced by prior period's costs carried forward in inventory sold in the next period. But managers usually assume they can build inventory to boost income in one period and then spread the effect of the backlash over several future periods, meanwhile hoping no one notices the added inventory carried over from the first period.

Actions taken by operations managers who are driven by remote financial controls will impair company-wide competitiveness and long-term profitability, not just because GAAP rules drive them to produce output for its own sake. Other steps they take to manipulate financial performance that impair a company's long-term economic health include deferring discretionary expenditures for research and development, postponing maintenance programs, encouraging employee turnover as a way of holding down direct labor costs, cutting back employee benefit programs, purchasing materials and supplies only from vendors who bid the lowest prices, cutting employee training programs, postponing capital investments in expensive new technologies (i.e., scrape by as long as possible on old, fully depreciated assets), and much more.

The practices spawned by using accounting numbers to manage business operations culminated by the 1970s in people viewing a company as a "portfolio" of income producing assets. Strategists who adopted that view saw top managements' job as maximizing the value of a company by properly balancing the risks and returns of a company's asset portfolio. While appropriate for managing portfolios of marketable securities, such strategies are totally misapplied when used to manage a business. Managers of conglomerates who followed such strategies turned their attention completely away from internal operating activities and customer satisfaction and attempted to create value out of thin air by "acquiring stars," "milking cash cows," and "divesting dogs."

The consequences of managing operations with financial targets are revealed in the recently published history of a company swallowed up in the conglomeration boom of the 1970s. The company, Burgmaster, was the largest American machine-tool maker west of Chicago when it was bought out by a conglomerate in the mid-1960s. Fifteen years later the conglomerate became the nation's first large leveraged buy out. Burgmaster's history falls into two phases: twenty years of excellent growth and profitability in the hands of a brilliant, customer-focused engineer who founded the company, followed by twenty years of decline into bankruptcy in the hands of finance-driven, numbers-oriented professional managers. Burgmaster's demise, mirrored by countless other companies whose stories have yet to be documented, can be attributed in no small way to the lack of interest in people and customers associated with an obsessive push to manage operations with accounting numbers by remote control (Holland 1989).

## IV.  Management Accounting's Lost Relevance After 1950: Reasons and Consequences

Underlying modern management accounting -- and the cause of its lost relevance -- is the belief businesses can both *Plan* and *control* their affairs with abstract financial accounting information (Johnson 1988). This belief was not widespread before the 1950s. Indeed, before World

War II companies rarely viewed financial accounting information as anything other than a compilation of results (after-the-event information) or as data that could be used to project, or simulate, the financial consequences of proposals and plans (before-the-event information). Financial accounting information was almost never used to set targets for driving the work of operating personnel.

Businesses suffered when managers began to take accounting numbers seriously as an object to manage rather than considering them as passive measures of results. By the 1960s, for example, top managers had begun to impose ROI and net income targets on subordinates other than just divisional managers. They weren't content simply to budget and plan based on these financial targets. Instead, financial planning targets were used to control the actions of subordinate managers and operating personnel. Companies drove the profit center concept of responsibility lower and lower into organizations and thereby made it necessary to evaluate growing numbers of people with short-term financial measures like ROI. "Tight financial controls with a short-term emphasis" inevitably impairs long-term profitability because it will "bias choices toward the less innovative, less technologically aggressive alternatives" (Hayes and Abernathy 1980, 70 and 77).

Top managers after the 1950s took a fateful leap that their 19th and early 20th-century predecessors had resisted. They began to use accounting information for a purpose it was not intended to serve. They began using accounting information "to guide the artisans' hands." That practice, more than any other, defines management accounting's lost relevance in recent years. In effect, the decline into irrelevance of management accounting was a case of putting the cart before the horse. Abstract financial information about business results—the cart—became the prime object of managers' attention. Managers quickly lost sight of the horse, i.e., the concrete forces that produce financial results. The rest, as they say, is history. Financially-oriented managers were poorly equipped to lead companies through the competitive wars of the 1970s and 1980s.

What caused the change that we notice by the 1960s? Usually people blame either the accounting profession, for reporting rules that cause perverse consequences, or Wall Street, for pressuring top managers to achieve market-pleasing quarterly financial results. However, financial reporting information and Wall Street pressures may simply shoulder blame for a much deeper problem; namely, the gradual but relentless power of accounting abstractions to conquer and shape managers' attitudes. As we said before, accounting is more than just a neutral, technical tool that measures financial outcomes. It also influences the thinking that determines outcomes. Indeed, the history of management accounting in the last 50 years is the story of accounting information taking on a life of its own and shaping the way managers run businesses.

By the 1960s, the intrusion of financial accounting into management information systems was causing top managers to abdicate their strategic responsibilities. Instead of being broad-gauged integrators -- conversant in production, marketing, and finance -- American senior executives by 1970 were focused excessively on the financial dimension of business. They had adopted a "new managerial gospel" that encourages "a preference for (1) analytic detachment rather than the insight that comes from 'hands on' experience and (2) short-term cost reduction rather than long-term development of technological competitiveness" (Hayes and Abernathy 1980, 68).

Hayes and Abernathy, believing this new gospel "has played a major role in undermining the vigor of American industry," ask two very important questions: "(1) why should so many American managers have shifted so strongly to this new managerial orthodoxy? and (2) why are they not more deeply bothered by the ill effects of those principles on the long-term technological competitiveness of their companies?" (Hayes and Abernathy 1980, 74). To answer the first question they cite the significant change since the 1950s in the typical American manager's road to the top. "No longer does the typical career, threading sinuously up and through a corporation with stops in several functional areas, provide future top executives with intimate hands-on knowledge of the company's technologies, customers, and suppliers" (Hayes and Abernathy 1980, 74). Increasingly top managers come from financial and legal backgrounds, less and less from the technical and marketing sides. Their answer to the second question cites a growing pseudoprofessionalism that deprecates the value of industry experience and hands-on expertise as opposed to analytic-quantitative-finance training -- exactly the same tendency that EricLampard noted for modern cultures to substitute abstract understanding for concrete perceptions (1977, 27). This pseudoprofessionalism salves the conscience of today's managers by glorifying "an individual having no special expertise in any particular industry or technology who [supposedly] can step into an unfamiliar company and run it successfully through strict application of financial controls, portfolio concepts, and a market-driven strategy."

In trying to explain how the top managers in American industry migrated during the past century from the likes of Andrew Carnegie to the type of individual just described, one must place a great deal of emphasis on the growing influence accounting information has had on managers since World War II. The influence did not come all at once. Its proximate origins probably lie in the increased use of ROI information that accompanied the spread of the multi-divisional form of business after the 1920s. In multi-divisional companies, the "increased structural distance between those entrusted with exploiting actual competitive opportunities and those who must judge the quality of their work virtually guarantees reliance on objectively quantifiable short-term criteria" (Hayes and Abernathy 1980, 70). These diversified organizations were "nurseries" for top-level corporate managers' graduate training grounds, as it were, before there were many graduate business schools. Having been schooled in the virtues of managing through accounting systems, division managers took the same lesson with them when they rose to the top. Eventually, financial abstractions dominate managers' attention to the point where they no longer know, or care, about the production, technological, and marketing determinants of competitiveness.

The multi-divisional organization is not, of course, the only influence that reinforced and justified the practice of remote management through accounting systems. Another influence was business education itself. Following World War II American business schools adopted the economist's model of the firm as the paradigm for teaching business decision-making. Writers of management accounting textbooks also used the model to show how financial accounting information could be made "managerially relevant," largely by separating fixed from variable costs. This model was appropriate for studying price behavior in market settings, but it was not relevant to understanding the workings of a managed enterprise. Nevertheless, thousands of managers by the 1960s were trained to work with a version of economics that doesn't deal with concrete activities inside managed firms.

Teaching this economic theory to business students and using it to rationalize management by remote accounting controls tended to reinforce in managers' minds the virtues of the mass-production / mass-market mindset that had shaped the way companies organized their operations since early in the century. A mass-production/ mass-market mindset that took root in the last quarter of the 19th century was nourished and promoted after World War II by the new management accounting practices.

This mindset tends to be linked to a vertical-hierarchical approach to managing that focuses on the performance of individuals, not groups. It is the approach associated with the poor competitive performance and falling profitability of American manufacturers in the 1970s and 1980s (Aoki 1990). The approach is reinforced by, but not necessarily caused by, using financial accounting abstractions to control operating activities. An alternative horizontal / team-oriented approach is seen by most people today as more conducive to competitiveness and profitability in the global economy. It reaches for enhanced flexibility by building to smaller scale and encouraging people to move constraints, not optimize within them. This approach to management overcomes the real short-term bias, which is not simply thinking in terms of next period's income statement, but refusing to move constraints and believing that the best results are had by "optimizing" inside existing constraints.

To get from the vertical to the horizontal approach, companies must change the way they do business and change the way they organize operations. The lost market share, closed plants, and other ills that we associate with American manufacturing in the 1970s and 1980s were not caused by poor quality management accounting numbers as much as they were caused by an approach to management that was reinforced by the habit of controlling concrete operations with accounting abstractions (Johnson 1992).

## V. Wrap-Up

The underlying problem large American businesses faced in the 1970s and 1980s -- and most continue to face even today -- is the behavior that results when people in organizations are driven to pursue targets set by accounting abstractions. That behavior ultimately is destructive to the organization because it is so *un*natural: it violates so many patterns one perceives in life systems in nature. Remote-control management by numbers promotes behavior that encourages fragmentation, divisive competitiveness, and subordination of holistic goals to local self-interest. However, remote control management by numbers did not lead to such behavior only in the business world in the last half-century. In the following passage, George Leonard provides a compelling example of its influence in the Vietnam War:

> [Consider] the highly trained young abstractionists sitting at the controls of giant bombers, many miles removed in height and psychic distance from the consequences of their acts. They address themselves to grid coordinates which first were expressed abstractly on pieces of paper, then encoded in electronic-inertial devices. At a certain point in the sky, the abstractionists actuate the devices, which then release hundreds of tons of high explosives. Neither the abstractionists sitting in their orderly, antiseptic surroundings in the sky nor those on the ground who conceived the operation are motivated by personal malice. They are concerned only with clearing out specified rectangular areas of jungles. The planes wheel in the sky and fly away, and that's all there is to it. But the great bombs continue downward and murder is done, not only to every man, woman and child who happens to be in the rectangle marked out so neatly in grid coordinates, but also to all manner of living things that fly and walk and crawl and swim and burrow, and to strong trees and tender shoots and fruit and flowers and fungi and the rich humus of many seasons. And later there may be a small newspaper headline: BOMBS BUST JUNGLE.

Perhaps it is not coincidental that one of the chief architects of America's numbers oriented strategy in Vietnam during the 1960s and early 1970s had also served as one of the pioneering exemplars of remote-control management by numbers in big business in the 1950s: Robert McNamara. As McNamara's career suggests, in both modern warfare and modern business there is an underlying tendency to view circumstances in techno-oriented mechanistic terms rather than in life-oriented systemic terms. Indeed, this bias is evident in our customary tendency to view information as mechanistic bits, not as a life-forming essence. It is our seeing information as bits that has enabled it to serve the purposes of remote-control management. Seen as a pattern in nature that emerges only through empowered relationships among people, information may hopefully serve a far different purpose in the future.

Aoki, Masahiko. 1990. "Toward an Economic Model of the Japanese Firm," *Journal of Economic Literature* (March), 1-27.

Armatage, Howard M. and Anthony A. Atkinson. 1990. *The Choice of Production Measures in Organizations: A Field Study of Practice in Seven Canadian Firms* (Hamilton, Ontario: The Society of Management Accountants of Canada).

Chandler, Alfred D., Jr. 1966. *Strategy and Structure* (Garden City, N.Y.: Doubleday, reprint of 1962 ed.)

_____ 1977. *The Visible Hand: The Managerial Revolution in American Business* (Cambridge: Harvard University Press).

Chandler, Alfred D., Jr. and Fritz Redlich. 1961. "Recent Developments in American Business and Their Conceptualization," *Business History Review* (Spring), 1-27.

Cooper, Robin. 1985. "Schrader Bellows," Harvard Business School, Case number 6186-050.

_____ 1987. "The Two-Stage Procedure in Cost Accounting: Part One," *Journal of Cost Management* (Summer), 43-51.

_____ 1990. "Cost Classification in Unit-Based and Activity-Based Manufacturing Cost Systems," *Journal of Cost Management* (Fall), 4-14.

Cooper, Robin and Robert S. Kaplan. 1988. " Measure Costs Right: Make the Right Decisions," *Harvard Business Review* (Sept./Oct.), 96-103.

Hayes, Robert H. and William J. Abernathy. 1980. "Managing Our Way to Economic Decline," *Harvard Business Review* (July-August), 67-77.

Holland, Max. 1989, *When the Machine Stopped: A Cautionary Tale from Industrial America* (Boston: Harvard Business School Press).

Johnson, H. Thomas. 1987. "The Decline of Cost Management: A Reinterpretation of 20th-Century Cost Accounting History," *Journal of Cost Management* (Spring), 5-12.

—————————— 1988. "Let's Return the Controller To Relevance: A Historical Perspective," *Cost Accounting for the '90s: Responding to Technological Change* (Montvale, N.J.: National Association of Accountants), 195-202.

—————————— 1990. "Performance Measurement for Competitive Excellence," in *Measures for Manufacturing Excellence*, Robert S. Kaplan, ed., (Boston: Harvard Business School Press), 63 - 90.

—————————— 1991. "Managing by Remote Control: Recent Management Accounting Practice in Historical Perspective," in *Inside the Business Enterprise: Historical Perspectives on the Use of Information*, A National Bureau of Economic Research Conference Report, Peter Temin, ed., (Chicago: The University of Chicago Press), 41 - 66.

—————————— 1992. *Relevance Regained: From Top-Down Control to Bottom-Up Empowerment* (New York: The Free Press).

Johnson, H. Thomas and Robert S. Kaplan. 1987. *Relevance Lost: The Rise and Fall of Management Accounting* (Boston: Harvard Business School Press).

Kaplan, Robert S. 1985. "Accounting Lag: The Obsolescence of Cost Accounting Systems," in *The Uneasy Alliance: Managing the Productivity-Technology Dilemma*, Kim B. Clark, Robert H. Hayes and Christopher Lorenz, eds., (Boston: Harvard Business School Press), 195 - 226.

Lampard, Eric. 1977 "Figures in the Landscape: Some Historiographical Implications of Environmental Psychology," *Comparative Urban Research* (5), 20-32.

Lee, Albert. 1988. *Call Me Roger* (Chicago: Contemporary Books).

Leonard, George B. 1972. *The Transformation: A Guide to the Inevitable Changes in Humankind* (New York: Delacorte Press).

Raff, Daniel M.G. and Peter Temin. 1991. "Business History and Recent Economic Theory: Imperfect Information, Incentives, and the Internal Organization of Firms," in *Inside the Business Enterprise: Historical Perspectives on the Use of Information*, A National Bureau of Economic Research Conference Report, Peter Temin, ed., (Chicago: The University of Chicago Press), 7 - 35.

Temin, Peter. 1990. "Cross Subsidies in the Telephone Network after Divestiture." MIT Working Paper (January).

Wall, Joseph Frazier. 1970. *Andrew Carnegie* (New York: Oxford University Press).

Wheatley, Margaret J. 1992. *Leadership and the New Science: Learning about Organization from an Orderly Universe* (San Francisco: Berrett-Koehler Publishers).

# Part Three

*Human Adaptations to
Changing Industrial-Urban
Environments*

**Chapter 8**

In 1752 there were 25 houses in recently consolidated Jones-Town (Old Town) and Baltimore -- no more than 200 residents in all. To the Germans busily engaged in tapping resources beyond the Patapsco River, it was barely a *Dorf!* There were 26,000 inhabitants net by 1800 and more than double that number when British ships attacked the nation's third largest city during the War of 1812. It was actually 1814 when Francis Scott Key, detained on one of the enemy vessels investing Fort McHenry at the harbor's entrance, composed "The Star Spangled Banner" in honor of his country's flag proudly waving through the night glare over the city's embattled Fort: "...o'er the land of the free and the home of the brave."- For many residents of Baltimore, the first post-colonial boom town and the surrounding state of Maryland, it was "the land of the free," perhaps, but for others -- the black population of African ancestry or origin -- it was, irrespective of their valor, "the home of the slave."

In Chapter 8, "Barely a Part of the Equation: The Adjustment of Baltimore's Mid-Nineteenth Century Black Population in Perspective," Joseph Garonzik suggests that two-score and more years after "The Star Spangled Banner," Baltimore's large black population -- nearly 28,000, the largest of any city in the U.S. -- was still, despite its size, a highly unequal quantity in that city's equilibrium. Barely a part of the equation; yet the overwhelming majority of the Monument City's black population are referred to in the 8th U.S. Census in 1860 as "free colored" and no more than tenth as "negro slaves" (*sic*), quite the reverse of New Orleans' proportions. Jacob M. Price's other Chesapeake tobacco province, Maryland, by 1860 contained almost as many "free colored" as "Negro slaves" but it was indisputably a "slave state." Baltimore had to be placed under military rule after a mob attacked the Sixth Massachusetts regiment in 1861 marching through the city to preserve the Union: not to abolitionize the South. "Among the southern ports," Baltimore then ranked next to New Orleans with an immense inland trade "which will be greatly increased when the lines of communication are completed to a junction with those of Ohio and other western states." Baltimore still claimed to be "the greatest market for tobacco in the United States and the principal flour market in the world."

If there is almost always something "Orwellian" (Rousseauian?) about the designation "free," Garonzik is able to show that in the Baltimore context of "free colored" much was achieved despite the legal disabilities and discriminations affecting free "people of color" before the Civil War. Using the federal MS schedules, city directories, contemporary documents, and a rich secondary literature, Garonzik demonstrates that antebellum Baltimore did not develop a single black "ghetto" and that "it was not uncommon for black families to have immigrants for next-door or same building neighbors." This was true for all large bodies of foreign born in most cities after mid-century, especially for German and Irish elements (somehow the English don't count), but almost never for free blacks (usually fewer in number, as among Boston's plain people). As late as 1870 the patchwork of nationalities and establishments around Baltimore was such that "blacks scattered throughout the social quilt." Not before the "new" immigration towards the close of the century and the late emergence of heavy industry would Baltimore's neighborhoods lose their "integrated character," even though blacks increasingly "brought up the rear in jobs and wealth."

Despite the mounting pressure on their situation around the city, however, the free blacks -- old and new -- had been "able to develop racial and cultural consciousness." That awareness, in spite of the emerging socioeconomic divisions within the black population, the glut of unskilled labor, and the reinforcements of institutionalized and politicized (Democrat) racism by the majority white population, had strengthened their sense of black identity and fortified them in their long and stormy struggle for inclusion. Within the larger black community settings Garonzik can point to the stabilizing structure of the *patriarchal* family as the primary residential and household unit and to the pervasive role of black churches. The presence of the hierarchical churches -- 90 percent of membership and nearly 66 percent of the edifices in 1860 belonged to one or other of the three black Methodist denominations -- was crucial as the proving ground for civic leadership and voluntary organizations as well as for personal and spiritual strength. This was no "slave religion"!

Garonzik's retrospective on more recent black adjustments does not make for easy reading. It is especially ironic that as recently as the 1960's black rebellion that professorial pundits of "social mobility" studies and mainstream electronic and print journalists were still calling on black people to "shape up", that they were, in effect, only the latest in a long and proud tradition of "huddled masses" adjusting positively to the opportunity of the city as a social escalator!  Given the tendency of the majority population to add insult to injury, it is understandable why black Americans must always maintain a somewhat different perspective on  American history from James Town in 1619 to present-day Baltimore. They have barely been a part of the American celebration.

## Chapter 9

Many townsites were called during the long "deflowering" of America's virgin lands, but few were chosen.  At one time or another almost every crossroads hamlet, canoe portage, two-creak confluence, and every "Main Street on the Middle Border" aspired to become "the Queen City" of its region -- and was lucky indeed to settle for a county seat!  Among the great variety of human settlement patterns exhibited by different indigenous peoples before the European invasions, there were some substantial population concentrations serving some functional-cultural role as a "central place."  That of the Natchez people in the lower Mississippi Valley was one, but they were few and mostly far between, and otherwise bore little or no resemblance to the American concentrations that sooner or later displaced them.  "The Winnebago Urban System" discussed by Kathleen Neils Conzen in chapter 9 was certainly not any kind of indigenous "system of cities," but as the poet Whittier once saw: in the wake of the fur traders' canoe, new towns rose over old Indian graves.  Conzen's subtitle suggests how so called "Indian policy" could be adapted to the Anglo-American's need to engage in townsite promotion; more especially, to finance urban real estate speculations on the upper Mississippi by manipulation of federal annuity payments to persuade Winnebago people, in this instance, to go quietly into their sunset hunting ground.  It certainly helped when Indians were in debt to the licensed traders, who often worked hard to keep the settlers out of protected areas, while they prolonged the natives' peonage for their own advantage.

Federal treaty promises to indigenous peoples -- with or without dollars attached -- were more numerous and false even than the informal promises and legalized deceptions practiced on black people, not excluding the postbellum constitutional amendments. Indian removal to a new "reserve," like extinction of Indian title, was a precondition for legally platting out towns and other developmental activities, hence the  symbiosis between intending platters and their cronies serving as advisors to the Winnebago or other people in negotiating their treaties and annuity payments with federal officials. By 1846 Winnebago tribal numbers were down to fewer than 2,600 members but the tribe was "receiving $93,000 annually in services, supplies, and gold." Such people obviously needed "protection" from others and no less from themselves. Conzen suggests that the situation in the Minnesota Territory arose "from the peculiar combination of land hunger and conscience." Seven hundred towns were reported as platted in Minnesota alone in 1855 -- a cohort that went far beyond that of Henry Mower Rice five or six years earlier to make St. Paul "the centerpiece of his urban system." By 1855 several of the most persistent and successful townsite promoters, such as Rice, were turning from exploiting Indian removal "to now greener pastures of politics, pineries, and railroad promotion."

There were no happy endings to these authentic westerns. As late as 1860 there were fewer organized Winnebagos left in the State of Minnesota and traders were losing interest in them. Emphasis was shifting in the new 1859 treaty to financing individual farms "to give them an idea of individual property..." Oh!! Free marketplace -- what crimes are committed in thy name. Only 2,639 Indians were reported in the 8th U.S. Census (259 blacks) compared with 172,000 whites; but Minnesota was credited with the largest tribal (not enumerated) Indian population, nearly 18,000 wholly east of the Missouri and Arkansas River valleys. The remaining Winnebago remnant could take little part in the desperate Dakota revolt of 1862 in the Minnesota Valley, but they were just "injuns," and were swept along in the Dakota removal -- "Westward the jug of Empire [took] its way." To add insult to injury, perhaps, there were already three counties in 1860 called "Winnebago": in Illinois (Rockford), Wisconsin (Oshkosh), and Iowa, "surface undulating, and is mostly prairie and timber land. Set off since 1850." But in the morning light, and in the setting of the sun across the hard and clear windswept waters of Lake Winnebago, we remember their enduring presence.

White America has finally become more appreciative of indigenous needs and cultures, "the heritage," not with fine-tuned disbursements from the Indian [Land] Claims Commission, but since 1986 with new "licenses" for enterprise: casino gambling. Connecticut's Pequots grossed $600 million in 1994!

## Chapter 10

Adjustments made by the large "free black" population to Baltimore's rapid growth before and after emancipation, and the manipulation of Indian Removal to facilitate and finance town speculation on dwindling Winnebago lands, were alike observable aspects of industrial-urban development. But adjustments also go on inside peoples' heads and find outward expression in the public prints. In Chapter 10 Sam Bass Warner, Jr., provides an "Environmental Re-Reading" of Three Urban Novels, written respectively by Herman Melville (1849), William Dean Howells (1890), and John Dos Passos (1925). While the three authors wrote their novels to express their personal views on industrial-urbanization effected under market auspices, Warner re-reads them as "environmental fiction" representing "very different sets of urban technological environments": man-made environments as opposed to "natural systems" which "stand apart from human beings." Warner examines the divergent emphases of the novelists: on the speed of large city growth (Liverpool) and/or "sheer size" (New York City). For Dos Passos, of course, the city is itself a protagonist, not merely a stage or backdrop. Not surprisingly, urban environments do not do well when judged according to these authors' mainly pastoral predilections. But *pace* the wise poet, man made the country too! In the telling of these stories, with their authors' distinctive concerns, Warner concludes: "we meet the conflicts within our own environmentalism." Such mirrors held to life by art may sometimes tell more than the fine flummeries of social science.

## Chapter 11

In "Pictures from the Magazines," one of the chapters in Dyos and Wolff's monumental *The Victorian City: Images and Realities*, Michael Wolff and Celina Fox focus on the growth of the Victorian press, "much more rapid even than that of the Victorian city." It was perhaps "the first demonstration of the potential of the mass media and the closest verbal and graphic equivalent which we have of Victorian urbanism." Their special concern is with "evidence of attitudes toward the city" and its denizens as present in a dozen or so illustrated magazines over half a century of mostly London life. The contrast of *Illustrated London News* with its "always prosperous... always healthy" City and the short-lived *Pictorial Times* "digging deeper" to reveal "the inadequacies of the New Poor Law" is most instructive. The series, "The Crime of Poverty and Its Punishment" in the *Pictorial Times*, conclude the authors, portrayed "the city that the *Illustrated London News* never encountered and *Punch* so quickly forgot."

In Chapter 11, "On Urban Types Comic and Social: From Egan to Mayhew," Peter G. Buckley considers how recent critics of Victorian social investigators, almost regardless of personal political bias, have failed to appreciate the role of comic sketches, caricatures, and plays -- particularly of low life -- in preparing the way for social analysis in the Anglo American tradition of urban writing." Comic low-life sketches emphasize the "oddities of occupations" -- the tribal trades -- and their attendant behaviors, while the vogue for city "typing" is the route by which popular scribblers gain "careers," says Buckley, in a market which goes for "depictions of everyday life." By such narrative means both authors and the paying readers may descend into "the unknown metropolis of degradation and despair," viz: the Cruikshank brothers, aquatints for Pierce Egan's early *Life in London* (1821) which make "narrative ... subordinate to the illustrations." Apparently comic angles on high life, except for plebeian swells, did not sell as well. Buckley shows that by the 1820s "translations, or transpositions, also take place across the Atlantic," including the incredible "Bowery B'hoy" culminating iconographically at least in Benjamin Baker's *Life in New York in 1848*.

One of the emergent bigger guns, Walt Whitman, points the way. In his "editorial" in *New York Aurora* in 1842 he characterizes "the city," not as an inscrutable crowd but rather as "the realm of accident and idiosyncrasy, a crowd of different interests, occupations and appetites that amounted to a parody of Smith's division of labor," also, catering perhaps to the more specialized segmentation of the market for social analysis. Eventually, Buckley concludes, "society comes to predominate over story" -- Sam Warner's novelists almost put environment over story -- without altogether forgoing humor. No longer "reductive," to be sure, but not altogether divesting itself either of "oddity" or "the type." No sectarian or ethnic jokes, cartoons, or the like, today, please, but suggestive innuendo for a promiscuous age and nothing comically incorrect. Meanwhile, as the cockney barrow-boy might roar: "Knees up, Tina Brown ... ! "

*Chapter 12*

   Finally, in a highly personal postscript to the volume, Leo F. Schnore
provides "a personal note" on some sociological concepts in the historical
study of human ecology: "Cohorts and Communities." The notion of the
"cohort," (a *temporal* idea) is juxtaposed with that of the community (which
is almost always given a *spatial* reference. Schnore makes clear his
indebtedness to the works of historians in reshaping his own research
and writing on American cities. A recent count by an enthusiastic
accountant revealed Schnore to be the most-often cited sociologist in
U.S. urban historiography. Thus historians have returned the compliment,
not least because of Schnore's generous support for the work of graduate
students in urban history.

   In conclusion to this volume, it is specially fitting to note here the recent
   passing, (June 24, 1995) of PETER R. KNIGHTS, the most diligent and
   successful tracer of "missing persons" since radio's celebrated Mr.
   Keen. Peter should have been here with us, but his two great empirical
   studies of Boston's population in the 19th century form a unique memorial
   to his contributions in the field of urban history and urban migration.
   We shall not now see a third such volume nor, sadly, shall we ever see his
   like again. He is even now being introduced by a proud Clio to her sister
   Muses.

# 8

# Barely a Part of the Equation:
## The Adjustment of Baltimore's
## Mid-19th Century Black
## Population in Perspective

## Joseph Garonzik

By 1865, Baltimore was the only U.S. city of commercial-industrial significance to juxtapose blacks and immigrants in large numbers and proportions, and its black population--as early as 1850--was America's largest.  The situation of Baltimore's blacks among the demographic upheavals of the 1850s and 1860s created twin research goals: to measure the physical and demographic characteristics of "neighborhoods" in mid-nineteenth-century Baltimore *and* to obtain a fuller understanding of the city's black community and its institutions.

During the first century of its history, the city's foreign trade elevated Baltimore to national importance among American cities.[1]  By 1810 Baltimore's population of over 46,500 made it America's third largest municipality.  Its economic nexus was foreign commerce, especially its exports of tobacco, wheat, and flour.  This latter trade, largest among all American cities before 1827, sustained a host of other operations such as the import of Latin American sugar, coffee, and copper and the related industries of sugar and copper refining, as well as shipping.  This trade also nurtured the hopes of merchants and city boosters that Baltimore would expand its hinterland eventually to overtake New York and Philadelphia and become the largest and wealthiest American city.[2]

The next fifty years saw Baltimore grow not only in absolute terms, but also as a regional commercial center with limited manufacturing. The introduction of the railroad to American transportation by some of Baltimore's daring merchants protected and enlarged the city's mercantile position during the 1830s and 1840s. Reaching all the way to St. Louis in 1860, the Baltimore and Ohio Railroad contributed to a 450 percent increase in flour inspections and diversifications of domestic imports. Similarly, from 1810 to 1870 her population increased almost six-fold. But the railroad could not entirely compensate for New York's advantages of rail and water communications to the interior, closer proximity and regular shipping service to Europe, and greater population and business resources, or for Philadelphia's headstart as a manufacturing center. In 1860 Baltimore still trailed both cities and Boston in the number of patents per capita, the proportion of employees engaged in manufacturing, and the value added from manufacturing.[3]

This lagging industrialization and subsequent efforts to expand the city's western and northern trading territory confirmed Baltimore's regional significance in the national urban network. With the exception of a boom in textile production, Baltimore's economy neither changed nor diversified significantly from 1850 to 1870. Light industrial production performed in shops employing less than ten workers was the rule. The city achieved a five-fold expansion in flour exports during the 1850s, but these failed to support the expensive and ruinous efforts of the B & O to dominate the western trade and to destroy the Pennsylvania Railroad. After Appomattox, rate wars and parallel construction (implemented by John Garrett and his successors at the head of the line) ultimately tumbled the B&O into receivership. Meanwhile, more realistic merchants were looking to the South for a heretofore untapped consumer market. Although the jobbing trade to Norfolk, Petersburg, Richmond, and Charleston started earlier, it expanded markedly on the eve of the Civil War and afterward. What resulted was a growing exchange of western wheat, Baltimore clothing, and refined sugar for southern cotton and other raw materials. In fact, Baltimore's growing dependence upon southern consumption of her commerce was the material evidence of the city's political-economic character. Though it possessed in Hezekiah Niles and Daniel Raymond two of the nation's leading spokesmen for protective tariffs, the city's politics consistently favored slavery and low tariffs--both thought to be impediments to industrialization.[4]

Accompanying Baltimore's emergence as a regional commercial metropolis, the middle decades of the nineteenth century witnessed the city's greatest influx of immigrants to date. Almost entirely Northern and Central European in origin, and particularly German and Irish, this immigration changed drastically the ethnic make-up of both established cities of the eastern seaboard and the developing cities west of the Appalachians, and their neighboring regions. But the immigration did not represent the only demographic force changing the urban scene. Slavery, sectionalism, and the Civil War had caused some cities to become racially mixed; in others black and white rural Americans and foreign immigrants were discovering urban America simultaneously.[5]

Amid the helter-skelter of demographic changes in post bellum America, Baltimore takes on special significance. Over the period 1850-1870, thousands of Germans, and, to a lesser extent, Irish flooded into the city, giving to it an ethnic character more like cities of the midwest than east coast cities. The emancipation which followed the Civil War unloosed a large rural in-migration, increasing by 50% the already large Negro component in the city. In this way, Baltimore became the only city of commercial-industrial significance to juxtapose blacks and immigrants in large numbers and significant proportions. To be sure, by 1870 the city's absolute size and rate of population growth would fall behind those of Chicago and St. Louis. Baltimore's relative ethnic-racial mixture had become less diversified than Washington and New Orleans, and scarcely more varied than St. Louis. Baltimore was again becoming a provincial place, but until the process was complete, Baltimore was at the epicenter of the urbanization in America.

At this point it is useful to consider the city's configuration in space and its neighborhood makeup in response to the gross economic and demographic shifts outlined above.

By 1850 the city had already differentiated into a central industrial district and areas of specialized production. Ward 9 situated on the upper harbor, or Basin, housed more establishments than any other ward. However, wards 1 and 2--located on the lower harbor--and wards 10, 12, 13 and 14--north and northwest of Ward 9--exhibited considerable manufacturing. Light industry, on the other hand, exhibited both centralized and localized patterns.

Table 8.1
Population of Selected U.S. Cities by Race and State or National Origin, 1860

| City | Total Pop. | Native Whites | | | | Foreign Whites | | | | | Blacks | |
|---|---|---|---|---|---|---|---|---|---|---|---|---|
| | | Same State | New Eng. | Other North | Other South | Ger. | Ire. | Other Br. Is. | France | Other For. | Free Same St. | All Other |
| Boston | 177841 | 85666 | 21745 | 4260 | 456 | 3202 | 45991 | 5589 | 382 | 8288 | 897 | 1365 |
| New York | 813669 | 371166 | 20252 | 22788 | 3586 | 119977 | 203700 | 37153 | 8074 | 14399 | 7868 | 4706 |
| Philadelphia | 565529 | 334728 | 4369 | 31757 | 3323 | 43634 | 95523 | 23052 | 2616 | 4342 | 13724 | 8461 |
| Baltimore | 212418 | 119191 | 1400 | 7189 | 4325 | 32608 | 15511 | 2778 | 391 | 1127 | 25487 | 2411 |
| Washington D.C. | 61122 | ------ | ------ | ------ | ------ | *3254 | *7258 | *1316 | *160 | *223 | #9209 | #1774 |
| Richmond | 37910 | ------ | ------ | ------ | ------ | *6905 | *16501 | *6106 | *570 | *497 | #2576 | #11699 |
| Charleston | 40522 | ------ | ------ | ------ | ------ | *2947 | *4906 | *1271 | *219 | *643 | #3237 | #13909 |
| New Orleans | 168675 | 62866 | 1985 | 8044 | 7435 | 19752 | 24398 | 3849 | 10515 | 5757 | 9661 | 14413 |
| St. Louis | 190524 | 56782 | 2977 | 19988 | 8492 | 50510 | 29926 | 6745 | 3072 | 5830 | 852 | 5350 |
| Cincinnati | 161044 | 64576 | 2200 | 12307 | 4632 | 43931 | 19375 | 5144 | 1884 | 3269 | 1266 | 2460 |
| Chicago | 109260 | 27933 | 6563 | 18128 | 1095 | 22230 | 19889 | 6217 | 882 | 5368 | 160 | 795 |

* Figures refer to entire foreign population of state for city in question.
# Figures refer to entire urban free and slave black populations for cities in question without regard to nativity.
Source: U.S. Census Office. The Eighth Census (1860). Population of the United States in 1860 (Washington, 1864), 453, 525, 589, 608-615.

Population of Selected U.S. Cities by Race and State or National Origin, 1870

| City | Total Pop. | Native Whites | | | | Foreign Whites | | | | | Blacks | |
|---|---|---|---|---|---|---|---|---|---|---|---|---|
| | | State Same | New Eng. | Other North | Other South | Ger. | Ire. | Other Br. Is. | France | Other For. | Free Same St. | Free Other |
| Boston | 250526 | 126341 | 26898 | 5354 | 832 | 5606 | 56900 | 7877 | 615 | 16607 | 1276 | 2220 |
| New York | 942292 | 475354 | 14668 | 16204 | 4327 | 151203 | 201999 | 32558 | 8240 | 24824 | 8762 | 4317 |
| Philadelphia | 674022 | 416162 | 6149 | 41178 | 4961 | 50746 | 96698 | 26710 | 2471 | 7006 | 12008 | 9853 |
| Baltimore | 267354 | 151493 | 1636 | 9036 | 9267 | 35276 | 15223 | 2824 | 428 | 3612 | 35156 | 3402 |
| Washington D.C. | 109199 | 31930 | 2952 | 18526 | 6630 | 4131 | 6948 | 1552 | 191 | 884 | 10761 | 24694 |
| Richmond | 51038 | 21889 | 213 | 1411 | 643 | 1621 | 1239 | 460 | 144 | 308 | 22708 | 402 |
| Charleston | 48956 | 16513 | 247 | 627 | 530 | 1826 | 2180 | 355 | 97 | 408 | 25657 | 516 |
| New Orleans | 191418 | 78209 | 1234 | 1607 | 7519 | 15224 | 14693 | 2653 | 8806 | 6517 | 36477 | 13979 |
| St. Louis | 310864 | 121931 | 4953 | 38008 | 11648 | 59040 | 32239 | 6720 | 2788 | 11449 | 12281 | 9807 |
| Cincinnati | 216239 | 109148 | 2168 | 12932 | 6515 | 49446 | 18624 | 4821 | 2090 | 4505 | 1942 | 4048 |
| Chicago | 298977 | 87385 | 10395 | 49246 | 3832 | 52316 | 39988 | 14809 | 1417 | 35898 | 606 | 3085 |

Source: U.S. Census Office. The Ninth Census (1870). The Statistics of the Population of the United States (Washington, 1871), 380-391.

One outgrowth of this differentiation, which grew more pronounced over the next twenty years, was that wealthy persons decided to relocate and commute to work by foot, buggy, and eventually omnibus rather than continue to live in neighborhoods growing crowded with workers and their families. Most pronounced in wards 15, 2,4,5 and 10, this exodus had two effects: It left behind wards of more uniformly poor residents and made available lots for industrial expansion outward from the harbor, which were sought after by heavy industry and factories whose layers of outgrowth reflected their needs to remain as close as possible to waterborne raw materials and fuel, and to transshipment points.[6] Increasingly perplexed and suffocated by changes in older neighborhoods, persons of middle and modest incomes were lured by developers' promises and the new horsedrawn trolley. By 1870 employees in the garment district, lumber yards, piano factories, bakeries, newspapers, and cigar stores commuted to work from over 10,000 new structures built in peripheral wards 6, 7, 8, 18 and 19 since the Civil War.[7]

Despite the impetus behind centralization of the industrial district, the 1870 neighborhood was only a transitional, not a radical, departure from the original Baltimore Town. Obviously, not all residents who could afford to move to the fledgling suburbs had done so by 1870. Moreover newer and older neighborhoods retained or regenerated many businesses and services--merchants, doctors, dentists, hotels, churches, real estate brokers, and some lawyers. Some of these new neighborhoods were closer to bedroom suburbs while others housed both place of work and place of residence, but on the whole, they could still be thought of as replicas of the original urban village, rather than a bold departure. Most neighborhoods were finite in terms of the number of people they could house and employ, and most of them retained or regenerated the business and service facilities which afforded large measures of self sufficiency. Just as manufacturing and commerce were gradually clustering in the downtown area, some neighborhoods--mostly to the north and west-- acquired a residential specialization, and still others retained the traditional pattern of residential-employment proximity.[8]

By this time, the city's ethnic groups were still living in small clusters scattered throughout the residential area of the city. Thus, while Germans did concentrate in East Baltimore wards 1 and 2 and the Irish clustered in the northern ward 8, a plot of the virtual locations of all heads of households

Table 8.2
Baltimore City Wards

## Baltimore City Wards, 1850-1860

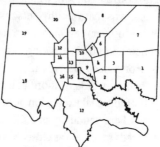

Source: R.J. Hatchett, *Hatchett's Baltimore Directory for 1849-50* (Baltimore, 1850), 42-45.

Conversion of 1850-1860 boundaries to 1870 ward boundaries:

| 1850-60 Ward | 1870 Equivalent |
|---|---|
| 1 | Ward 1 minus northern tip; eastern third of Ward 2 |
| 2 | Ward 2 minus eastern third; southern tips of 3 and 4 |
| 3 | ward 3 minus southern tip; southern half of Ward 6 |
| 4 | Ward 4 minus southern tip |
| 5 | Southwestern half of Ward 5 |
| 6 | Northeastern half of 5; northwestern corner of 7 |
| 7 | Ward 7 minus western third; northern half of 6; northern tip of Ward 1 |
| 8 | Ward 8; western third of Ward 7 |
| 9 | Southern half of Ward 9 |
| 10 | Middle third of Ward 9 |
| 11 | Northern tip of 9; Ward 11 minus western fourth; eastern fourth of Ward 12 |
| 12 | Southwestern corner of 11; northwestern corner of 10; southwestern corner of 20; eastern half of 13 |
| 13 | Ward 10 minus western third and northeast corner |
| 14 | Ward 14 minus western half; southwestern fourth of 10 |
| 15 | Ward 15 minus southern tip |
| 16 | Ward 16 minus western half and southeastern corner |
| 17 | Ward 17 plus southern tip of 15, southeastern corner of 16 and far southeastern corner of 18 |
| 18 | Ward 18 minus southereastern corner and northern tip; western half of 16; western half of 14; southern tip of 19 |
| 19 | Ward 19 minus southern tip; western half of Ward 13; western half of 20 |
| 20 | Ward 20 minus western half; northwestern corner of 11; Ward 12 minus eastern fourth |

## Baltimore City Wards, 1870

Source: John W. Woods, *Wood's Baltimore City Directory* (Baltimore, 1870), 907.

showed that persons of divergent origins lived next door to one another in the same building as well as nearby. While racial prejudice undoubtedly caused black households to concentrate the most on a block-by-block basis, it was not uncommon for black families to have immigrants for next-door or same-building neighbors.[9]

When it came to choosing a place to live, only if one of two things happened would the native, German, Irishman or black Baltimorean be likely to find himself surrounded by his compatriots: (1) if he possessed contacts and/or capital and/or a skill which enabled him to earn a good living, he could live more or less where he chose. And he usually chose to follow a trend set by his fellow countrymen--to live in small ethnic communities predicated upon the attainment of wealth. On the other hand, (2) should he find himself without money and skills, he would face a limited choice of residences in or around the manufacturing district or servant communities where he would find many of his countrymen and possibly other poor, unskilled ethnics. For the many living in between economic comfort and real desperation, neighborhoods consisting of mixed national and ethnic origins were a virtual certainty.[10]

By 1870, residence on the basis of wealth was resulting in a pattern of relative economic homogeneity within various quarters of the city. Wards 5, 6, and 7, heavily inhabited by Germans, generally embraced households of middle and upper middle-class wealth in 1870. The increasing Germanization along Harford Road and near what is today Johns Hopkins University Hospital would lead one to conclude that in the selection of residence, ethnicity followed wealth, which in turn depended upon one's occupation. Wards 9, 10, and 14, adjacent to the central business district, now housed diverse households. The southern wards 15, 16, and 17 had become poorer since 1860, though in ward 16 affluent German and Irish households proliferated on certain street near Ross Winans' locomotive works. Wards 11, 12, 19, and 20 drew increasing numbers of wealthy native-born households to the northwestern parts of the city. Yet far from being homogeneously wealthy or native, wards 11 and 12 still contained many black and Irish households at the other extreme. Thus by 1870, despite the formation of wealthy German suburbs to the northeast and even more lavish native white residences in Mount Vernon and Bolton Hill, the location of other minority groups who owned varying amounts of property within the interstices of these suburbs denied

Table 8.3

Heads of Household by Ethnic and National Origins and Wards,
Baltimore, 1850

| | National or Ethnic Origin | | | | | | | |
|---|---|---|---|---|---|---|---|---|
| | Native | German | Irish | British | French | OtherForeign | Black | Total |
| Ward | | | | | | | | |
| 1 | 753 | 638 | 232 | 84 | 7 | 34 | 168 | 1916 |
| 2 | 420 | 1021 | 180 | 51 | 10 | 31 | 168 | 1881 |
| 3 | 1122 | 301 | 130 | 67 | 8 | 16 | 335 | 1979 |
| 4 | 704 | 199 | 140 | 46 | 12 | 23 | 118 | 1242 |
| 5 | 430 | 131 | 126 | 52 | 6 | 15 | 225 | 985 |
| 6 | 820 | 233 | 154 | 58 | 5 | 12 | 466 | 1748 |
| 7 | 789 | 244 | 119 | 45 | 3 | 8 | 187 | 1395 |
| 8 | 714 | 348 | 309 | 72 | 5 | 6 | 118 | 1572 |
| 9 | 237 | 194 | 153 | 33 | 4 | 19 | 28 | 668 |
| 10 | 353 | 184 | 66 | 26 | 11 | 14 | 40 | 694 |
| 11 | 579 | 96 | 244 | 46 | 4 | 12 | 250 | 1231 |
| 12 | 727 | 167 | 90 | 16 | 5 | 7 | 461 | 1473 |
| 13 | 318 | 198 | 81 | 22 | 6 | 11 | 126 | 762 |
| 14 | 538 | 221 | 91 | 34 | 4 | 6 | 209 | 1103 |
| 15 | 810 | 314 | 137 | 54 | 6 | 9 | 498 | 1828 |
| 16 | 484 | 190 | 114 | 25 | 2 | 9 | 307 | 1131 |
| 17 | 749 | 440 | 87 | 39 | 8 | 9 | 396 | 1728 |
| 18 | 1328 | 249 | 210 | 67 | 6 | 16 | 152 | 2030 |
| 19 | 663 | 392 | 208 | 57 | 8 | 8 | 147 | 1483 |
| 20 | 589 | 317 | 147 | 37 | 3 | 11 | 235 | 1339 |
| Total | 13127 | 6077 | 3018 | 933 | 123 | 276 | 4634 | 28188 |

Source: U.S. Census (1850). Schedule I (Population), Baltimore City.

Table 8.4

Heads of Household by Ethnic and National Origins and Wards,
Baltimore, 1860

| | National or Ethnic Origin | | | | | | | |
|---|---|---|---|---|---|---|---|---|
| | Native | German | Irish | British | French | OtherForeign | Black | Total |
| Ward | | | | | | | | |
| 1 | 941 | 1653 | 328 | 79 | 13 | 55 | 83 | 3152 |
| 2 | 321 | 1254 | 238 | 40 | 12 | 55 | 120 | 2040 |
| 3 | 1230 | 914 | 198 | 56 | 7 | 20 | 335 | 2760 |
| 4 | 564 | 400 | 181 | 38 | 7 | 36 | 53 | 1279 |
| 5 | 382 | 163 | 134 | 32 | 1 | 23 | 189 | 924 |
| 6 | 782 | 443 | 180 | 57 | 7 | 18 | 403 | 1890 |
| 7 | 1131 | 661 | 175 | 63 | 8 | 18 | 264 | 2320 |
| 8 | 974 | 717 | 731 | 102 | 8 | 17 | 125 | 2674 |
| 9 | 130 | 197 | 152 | 13 | 6 | 13 | 14 | 525 |
| 10 | 209 | 270 | 61 | 13 | 6 | 15 | 57 | 631 |
| 11 | 775 | 160 | 312 | 34 | 12 | 13 | 343 | 1649 |
| 12 | 731 | 416 | 163 | 36 | 6 | 10 | 417 | 1779 |
| 13 | 253 | 233 | 56 | 25 | 8 | 8 | 90 | 673 |
| 14 | 475 | 282 | 93 | 18 | 2 | 6 | 181 | 1057 |
| 15 | 647 | 468 | 226 | 44 | 6 | 23 | 411 | 1825 |
| 16 | 647 | 471 | 133 | 34 | 3 | 6 | 314 | 1608 |
| 17 | 1039 | 1145 | 254 | 66 | 6 | 22 | 468 | 3000 |
| 18 | 2055 | 722 | 446 | 90 | 15 | 36 | 166 | 3530 |
| 19 | 1172 | 713 | 271 | 68 | 14 | 9 | 221 | 2468 |
| 20 | 1152 | 448 | 301 | 60 | 10 | 12 | 326 | 2309 |
| Total | 15610 | 11730 | 4633 | 968 | 157 | 415 | 4580 | 38093 |

Source: U.S. Census (1860). Schedule I (Population), Baltimore City.

Table 8.5

Heads of Household by Ethnic and National Origins and Wards, Baltimore, 1870

| | | | | National or Ethnic Origin | | | | | |
| Ward | All Native | 2nd. Gen. Native | German | Irish | British | French | Other Foreign | Black | Total |
|---|---|---|---|---|---|---|---|---|---|
| 1 | 1226 | 1045 | 1513 | 404 | 69 | 12 | 33 | 53 | 3310 |
| 2 | 567 | 390 | 1978 | 198 | 56 | 11 | 105 | 235 | 3150 |
| 3 | 1083 | 935 | 1025 | 181 | 44 | 4 | 30 | 432 | 2799 |
| 4 | 632 | 576 | 596 | 255 | 43 | 4 | 30 | 115 | 1675 |
| 5 | 830 | 768 | 621 | 240 | 66 | 5 | 29 | 746 | 2537 |
| 6 | 1362 | 1271 | 780 | 149 | 59 | 4 | 35 | 442 | 2831 |
| 7 | 1359 | 1044 | 1228 | 207 | 72 | 6 | 41 | 152 | 3065 |
| 8 | 771 | 644 | 279 | 803 | 60 | 6 | 10 | 133 | 2062 |
| 9 | 403 | 326 | 427 | 242 | 37 | 10 | 43 | 262 | 1426 |
| 10 | 589 | 583 | 553 | 132 | 34 | 18 | 27 | 365 | 1718 |
| 11 | 951 | 887 | 168 | 252 | 45 | 7 | 8 | 519 | 1950 |
| 12 | 1059 | 998 | 91 | 246 | 35 | 3 | 9 | 265 | 1708 |
| 13 | 884 | 798 | 465 | 142 | 30 | 7 | 13 | 301 | 1842 |
| 14 | 995 | 911 | 512 | 215 | 43 | 7 | 18 | 284 | 2024 |
| 15 | 851 | 769 | 679 | 239 | 29 | 10 | 23 | 651 | 2482 |
| 16 | 1303 | 1225 | 943 | 261 | 51 | 8 | 20 | 660 | 3241 |
| 17 | 957 | 794 | 745 | 277 | 43 | 5 | 13 | 55 | 2095 |
| 18 | 1468 | 1418 | 1030 | 431 | 57 | 10 | 18 | 556 | 3578 |
| 19 | 1292 | 1126 | 323 | 236 | 49 | 12 | 18 | 346 | 2278 |
| 20 | 1330 | 1175 | 668 | 208 | 49 | 17 | 23 | 513 | 2808 |
| Total | 19862 | 17683 | 14626 | 5318 | 971 | 166 | 546 | 7085 | 45879 |

Source: U.S. Census (1870). Schedule I (Population), Baltimore City.

Baltimore a residential homogeneity solely on the basis of wealth and/or ethnicity.[11]

In summary, Baltimore as late as 1870 was really a patchwork of nationalties and establishments stitched together by a complex thread of economic and demographic change. It consisted of white natives, Germans, Irish, other foreign groups, and blacks scattered throughout the social quilt. Some neighborhood clusters of one group appeared here and there, but heterogeneous mixtures of various ethnic origins were more common. Even the apparently similar clusters differed on the basis of wealth--one forced to work in the growing business center of the city, the other fortunate enough to escape it. Still others brewed their beer and liquors in the only parts of the city where they could conveniently find the necessary ingredients. Individuals of a given heritage were more likely to work at one job than another, but unless they had become financially comfortable or toiled for the lowest wages, no one could have predicted where they might live.

In the light of their ethnic and racial heterogeneity, these neighborhoods depended upon their institutional fixity and autonomy to create an operational basis for "community" in mid-nineteenth-century Baltimore. The spatial distribution of minority groups governed all persons' sense of community. For example, all whites may have profited psychologically by their proximity to impoverished, unskilled blacks. If this generation was migrating as rapidly as persons in Boston, Milwaukee, and other cities, the neighborhood's self-sufficiency may have provided an incubator against those currents and cross-currents. For no matter where a householder lived in Baltimore, he could expect to have access to all the markets, shops, and churches he might have needed. Not until the turn of the century arrival of Italians, Poles, Russians and the spread of heavy industry into east and south Baltimore would Baltimore's neighborhoods lose this integrated character.

Paradoxically this quality of neighborhood may help to account for the remarkable continuity of Baltimore's black community at this period. For of all the minority groups in Baltimore, the conditions of residence, occupation and wealth possessed greatest certitude for the blacks. Both before and after the immigration/migrations of 1850-70, they generally brought up the rear in jobs and wealth. Compared to other groups, given the small scale on which clustering existed--and discounting black

Table 8.6
Locations of All Black Denominations, Baltimore, 1850 & 1870

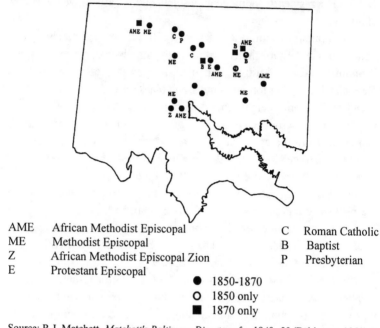

| | | | |
|---|---|---|---|
| AME | African Methodist Episcopal | C | Roman Catholic |
| ME | Methodist Episcopal | B | Baptist |
| Z | African Methodist Episcopal Zion | P | Presbyterian |
| E | Protestant Episcopal | | |

● 1850-1870
○ 1850 only
■ 1870 only

Source: R.J. Matchett, *Matchett's Baltimore Directory for 1849 -50* (Baltimore, 1850), 15-17; John W. Woods, *Wood's Baltimore City Directory* (Baltimore, 1870), 312-414.

Location of Local Markets, Baltimore, 1850 & 1870

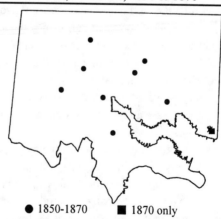

● 1850-1870    ■ 1870 only

Sources: R.J. Matchett, *Matchett's Baltimore Directory for 1849 -50* (Baltimore, 1850), Appendix; John W. Woods, *Wood's Baltimore City Directory* (Baltimore, 1870), Appendix.

domestics residing in white households--black alleyway concentrations were the most homogeneous in the city. This might point to the influence of a decentralized racial segregation practice on top of economic and occupational discrimination and deprivation. On the other hand, since blacks were, of all the ethnic groups, most likely to live next door to each other, they may have had greater opportunities to develop racial and cultural consciousness than the immigrants--in spite of their lowly economic status. In any case, these patterns clearly set them apart from the rest of the population.

The 1850s and 1860s worked stresses upon all blacks in Baltimore even as they underscored differences between elements of the black population. Urban slaves, who accounted for about one-tenth of the total black population, declined by 25 percent during the 1850s, yet far from demonstrating that urban slavery was relaxing its grip upon African-Americans, this diminishment of young male slaves and the declining fertility rate among females may point up the sale of Baltimore slaves to the lower South with severe attendant effects upon slave family ties.

Black domestics residing at the homes of their employers comprised a small (15-18%) but important minority among free blacks. Primarily a female institution, live-in domesticity siphoned off most of the city's surplus black women, who could find income, housing, and companionship in no other form. Persons who had learned early to fend for themselves--perhaps to send income back to families they seldom saw--their numbers were filled with very young maids and waiters, ancient nannies and butlers. Generally they were growing poorer, less literate or educated than, and, since many lived in the more affluent outskirts of the city, were separated in space from, the majority of Baltimore's Negroes, who lived in their own households.[12]

For the free black family (about 80% of all blacks), the twenty years under study worked hardships.[13] Black householders proportionately already comprised the mainstays of the city's unskilled and propertyless classes; yet two decades later they found their conditions had deteriorated still further. Although the German and Irish immigrants took away many of the remaining skilled jobs blacks had possessed--indeed by the 1870s foreigners of German birth were virtually equal in number per capita to native born residents among the city's middle class--Baltimore's African-Americans saw their overall resources grow slightly during the economic

Table 8.7
Black Male Heads of Household by Occupation Within Wards, 1850

| Wards | 1 | 2 | 3 | 4 | 5 | 6 | 7 | 8 | 9 | 10 | 11 | 12 | 13 | 14 | 15 | 16 | 17 | 18 | 19 | 20 | City | %City |
|---|---|---|---|---|---|---|---|---|---|---|---|---|---|---|---|---|---|---|---|---|---|---|
| NONE | 3 | 0 | 2 | 1 | 0 | 0 | 0 | 2 | 0 | 0 | 1 | 1 | 1 | 2 | 2 | 0 | 1 | 1 | 2 | 0 | 19 | 6.7 |
| 1LABOR | 0 | 0 | 1 | 2 | 3 | 10 | 6 | 3 | 1 | 0 | 0 | 1 | 3 | 3 | 10 | 10 | 9 | 3 | 3 | 4 | 74 | 26.1 |
| 1BRICK | 0 | 0 | 3 | 0 | 0 | 0 | 1 | 0 | 0 | 0 | 0 | 0 | 0 | 2 | 2 | 2 | 7 | 2 | 1 | 0 | 19 | 6.7 |
| 1STEVE | 0 | 1 | 0 | 0 | 0 | 1 | 1 | 0 | 0 | 0 | 1 | 2 | 0 | 0 | 0 | 2 | 0 | 0 | 1 | 2 | 13 | 4.6 |
| 1WWASH | 0 | 0 | 1 | 0 | 1 | 1 | 1 | 0 | 0 | 0 | 1 | 1 | 2 | 0 | 1 | 0 | 1 | 1 | 1 | 1 | 10 | 3.5 |
| 1SAWYR | 2 | 1 | 3 | 0 | 0 | 2 | 0 | 1 | 0 | 0 | 0 | 4 | 0 | 1 | 1 | 1 | 0 | 0 | 0 | 1 | 20 | 7.0 |
| 1OTHER | 0 | 1 | 3 | 0 | 0 | 0 | 0 | 1 | 0 | 0 | 0 | 1 | 0 | 0 | 0 | 0 | 0 | 0 | 0 | 0 | 5 | 1.8 |
| 2PORTR | 0 | 0 | 1 | 1 | 5 | 3 | 2 | 0 | 1 | 0 | 3 | 4 | 1 | 2 | 4 | 0 | 1 | 0 | 0 | 0 | 23 | 8.1 |
| 2DRAYM | 0 | 0 | 2 | 0 | 3 | 4 | 0 | 0 | 0 | 0 | 7 | 8 | 0 | 1 | 0 | 1 | 3 | 1 | 0 | 8 | 46 | 16.2 |
| 2DOMES | 0 | 0 | 0 | 0 | 0 | 0 | 0 | 0 | 0 | 1 | 0 | 0 | 0 | 0 | 0 | 1 | 0 | 0 | 0 | 0 | 1 | .4 |
| 2SEAMS | 0 | 0 | 0 | 0 | 0 | 0 | 0 | 0 | 0 | 0 | 0 | 0 | 0 | 0 | 0 | 0 | 0 | 0 | 0 | 0 | 0 | .0 |
| 2NURSE | 0 | 0 | 0 | 0 | 0 | 0 | 0 | 0 | 0 | 0 | 0 | 0 | 0 | 0 | 0 | 0 | 0 | 0 | 0 | 0 | 0 | .0 |
| 3MASON | 0 | 0 | 0 | 0 | 0 | 0 | 2 | 0 | 0 | 0 | 0 | 0 | 0 | 0 | 0 | 0 | 0 | 0 | 0 | 0 | 2 | .7 |
| 3CAULK | 7 | 0 | 3 | 0 | 0 | 1 | 0 | 0 | 0 | 0 | 0 | 2 | 0 | 0 | 1 | 0 | 1 | 0 | 0 | 0 | 12 | 4.2 |
| 3WOODN | 1 | 0 | 0 | 1 | 0 | 0 | 1 | 0 | 0 | 1 | 0 | 2 | 0 | 0 | 0 | 0 | 0 | 0 | 0 | 0 | 4 | 1.4 |
| 3PROVI | 0 | 1 | 0 | 1 | 0 | 1 | 0 | 0 | 0 | 0 | 0 | 1 | 0 | 0 | 0 | 0 | 0 | 0 | 1 | 1 | 7 | 2.5 |
| 3BARBM | 0 | 1 | 1 | 0 | 1 | 0 | 0 | 0 | 0 | 0 | 1 | 0 | 0 | 3 | 1 | 0 | 0 | 0 | 1 | 0 | 10 | 3.5 |
| 3PRINT | 0 | 0 | 0 | 0 | 0 | 0 | 0 | 0 | 0 | 0 | 0 | 0 | 0 | 0 | 0 | 0 | 0 | 0 | 0 | 0 | 0 | .0 |
| 3MUSIC | 0 | 0 | 1 | 0 | 0 | 0 | 0 | 0 | 0 | 0 | 0 | 0 | 0 | 0 | 0 | 0 | 0 | 0 | 0 | 0 | 1 | .4 |
| 3TEXTL | 0 | 0 | 0 | 0 | 1 | 2 | 0 | 0 | 0 | 0 | 0 | 1 | 0 | 0 | 0 | 0 | 0 | 0 | 0 | 0 | 5 | 1.8 |
| 4MARIN | 1 | 1 | 0 | 0 | 0 | 3 | 0 | 0 | 0 | 0 | 0 | 0 | 0 | 0 | 2 | 0 | 1 | 0 | 0 | 0 | 8 | 2.8 |
| 4CLERI | 0 | 0 | 0 | 0 | 0 | 0 | 0 | 0 | 0 | 0 | 0 | 0 | 0 | 0 | 0 | 0 | 0 | 0 | 0 | 0 | 0 | .0 |
| 4HUCKS | 0 | 2 | 0 | 0 | 1 | 0 | 0 | 0 | 0 | 0 | 0 | 0 | 0 | 0 | 0 | 0 | 0 | 0 | 0 | 0 | 3 | 1.1 |
| 4FOOD | 0 | 0 | 0 | 0 | 0 | 0 | 0 | 0 | 0 | 0 | 0 | 0 | 0 | 0 | 0 | 0 | 0 | 0 | 0 | 0 | 0 | .0 |
| 4OPROP | 0 | 0 | 0 | 0 | 0 | 1 | 0 | 0 | 0 | 0 | 0 | 0 | 0 | 0 | 0 | 0 | 0 | 0 | 0 | 0 | 0 | .0 |
| 4MINIS | 0 | 0 | 0 | 0 | 1 | 0 | 0 | 0 | 0 | 0 | 0 | 1 | 0 | 0 | 0 | 0 | 0 | 0 | 0 | 0 | 2 | .7 |
| 4PHYS | 0 | 0 | 0 | 0 | 0 | 0 | 0 | 0 | 0 | 0 | 0 | 0 | 0 | 0 | 0 | 0 | 0 | 0 | 0 | 0 | 0 | .0 |
| 4APOTH | 0 | 0 | 0 | 0 | 0 | 0 | 0 | 0 | 0 | 0 | 0 | 0 | 0 | 0 | 0 | 0 | 0 | 0 | 0 | 0 | 0 | .0 |
| 4TEACH | 0 | 0 | 0 | 0 | 0 | 0 | 0 | 0 | 0 | 0 | 0 | 0 | 0 | 0 | 0 | 0 | 0 | 0 | 0 | 0 | 0 | .0 |
| 4LAWYR | 0 | 0 | 0 | 0 | 0 | 0 | 0 | 0 | 0 | 0 | 0 | 0 | 0 | 0 | 0 | 0 | 0 | 0 | 0 | 0 | 0 | .0 |
| 4FINAN | 0 | 0 | 0 | 0 | 0 | 0 | 0 | 0 | 0 | 0 | 0 | 0 | 0 | 0 | 0 | 0 | 0 | 0 | 0 | 0 | 0 | .0 |
| MALE | 14 | 8 | 21 | 6 | 15 | 29 | 15 | 6 | 2 | 2 | 16 | 27 | 7 | 14 | 27 | 15 | 26 | 9 | 10 | 15 | 284 | 73.8 |

Source: Sample Data

Table 8.8
Black Male Heads of Household by Occupation Within Wards, 1860

| Wards | 1 | 2 | 3 | 4 | 5 | 6 | 7 | 8 | 9 | 10 | 11 | 12 | 13 | 14 | 15 | 16 | 17 | 18 | 19 | 20 | City | %City |
|---|---|---|---|---|---|---|---|---|---|---|---|---|---|---|---|---|---|---|---|---|---|---|
| NONE | 0 | 1 | 2 | 1 | 0 | 0 | 1 | 0 | 1 | 1 | 0 | 2 | 0 | 0 | 1 | 1 | 2 | 0 | 2 | 2 | 17 | 5.7 |
| 1LABOR | 2 | 2 | 6 | 1 | 6 | 8 | 10 | 2 | 0 | 0 | 0 | 7 | 1 | 5 | 5 | 3 | 1 | 6 | 5 | 3 | 71 | 23.8 |
| 1BRICK | 1 | 0 | 1 | 1 | 0 | 0 | 0 | 0 | 0 | 0 | 0 | 2 | 0 | 1 | 5 | 8 | 7 | 2 | 1 | 0 | 29 | 9.7 |
| 1STEVE | 0 | 0 | 1 | 0 | 0 | 1 | 0 | 0 | 0 | 0 | 0 | 0 | 0 | 0 | 1 | 0 | 1 | 2 | 0 | 0 | 8 | 2.7 |
| 1WWASH | 0 | 0 | 0 | 0 | 0 | 1 | 1 | 1 | 0 | 0 | 0 | 1 | 0 | 0 | 0 | 0 | 0 | 0 | 0 | 0 | 4 | 1.3 |
| 1SAWYR | 0 | 0 | 0 | 0 | 0 | 2 | 0 | 1 | 0 | 0 | 0 | 0 | 0 | 0 | 2 | 0 | 1 | 0 | 0 | 0 | 5 | 1.7 |
| 1OTHER | 0 | 0 | 0 | 1 | 1 | 3 | 0 | 1 | 0 | 1 | 1 | 6 | 3 | 3 | 2 | 0 | 3 | 0 | 0 | 1 | 8 | 2.7 |
| 2PORTR | 0 | 0 | 4 | 1 | 4 | 3 | 0 | 2 | 0 | 1 | 10 | 3 | 3 | 3 | 3 | 4 | 4 | 1 | 1 | 6 | 44 | 14.8 |
| 2DRAYM | 3 | 0 | 0 | 0 | 0 | 2 | 3 | 0 | 0 | 0 | 3 | 0 | 1 | 3 | 7 | 0 | 6 | 0 | 0 | 4 | 51 | 17.1 |
| 2DOMES | 0 | 0 | 0 | 0 | 0 | 0 | 1 | 0 | 0 | 0 | 0 | 0 | 0 | 0 | 0 | 0 | 0 | 0 | 0 | 0 | 1 | .3 |
| 2SEAMS | 0 | 0 | 0 | 0 | 0 | 0 | 0 | 0 | 0 | 0 | 0 | 0 | 0 | 0 | 0 | 0 | 0 | 0 | 0 | 0 | 0 | .0 |
| 2NURSE | 0 | 0 | 0 | 0 | 1 | 0 | 0 | 0 | 0 | 0 | 0 | 0 | 0 | 0 | 0 | 0 | 0 | 0 | 0 | 0 | 0 | .0 |
| 3MASON | 1 | 5 | 0 | 0 | 0 | 1 | 0 | 0 | 0 | 0 | 0 | 0 | 0 | 0 | 1 | 0 | 0 | 0 | 0 | 0 | 1 | .3 |
| 3CAULK | 0 | 0 | 1 | 0 | 0 | 0 | 0 | 0 | 0 | 0 | 0 | 0 | 0 | 0 | 0 | 0 | 0 | 0 | 0 | 0 | 9 | 3.0 |
| 3WOODN | 0 | 0 | 0 | 0 | 0 | 1 | 0 | 0 | 0 | 0 | 0 | 0 | 0 | 0 | 0 | 0 | 0 | 0 | 0 | 2 | 0 | .0 |
| 3PROVI | 0 | 0 | 1 | 0 | 1 | 1 | 0 | 0 | 0 | 0 | 2 | 1 | 0 | 0 | 1 | 0 | 1 | 0 | 1 | 0 | 8 | 1.7 |
| 3BARBM | 0 | 0 | 0 | 0 | 0 | 0 | 0 | 0 | 0 | 0 | 2 | 0 | 0 | 0 | 0 | 0 | 0 | 0 | 0 | 0 | 7 | 2.3 |
| 3PRINT | 0 | 0 | 0 | 0 | 0 | 0 | 0 | 0 | 0 | 0 | 0 | 0 | 0 | 0 | 1 | 0 | 0 | 0 | 1 | 0 | 1 | .3 |
| 3MUSIC | 0 | 0 | 0 | 0 | 1 | 0 | 0 | 0 | 1 | 0 | 0 | 1 | 1 | 0 | 0 | 1 | 0 | 0 | 0 | 0 | 1 | .3 |
| 3TEXTL | 0 | 0 | 0 | 0 | 0 | 0 | 0 | 1 | 0 | 0 | 0 | 0 | 0 | 0 | 0 | 0 | 0 | 0 | 0 | 0 | 4 | .1.3 |
| 4MARIN | 0 | 0 | 3 | 0 | 0 | 6 | 2 | 0 | 0 | 0 | 1 | 3 | 0 | 0 | 2 | 0 | 6 | 0 | 0 | 0 | 24 | 8.1 |
| 4CLERI | 0 | 0 | 0 | 0 | 0 | 0 | 0 | 1 | 0 | 0 | 0 | 0 | 0 | 0 | 0 | 0 | 0 | 1 | 0 | 1 | 1 | .3 |
| 4HUCKS | 0 | 0 | 0 | 0 | 0 | 0 | 0 | 0 | 0 | 1 | 0 | 0 | 0 | 0 | 0 | 0 | 0 | 0 | 0 | 0 | 3 | 1.0 |
| 4FOOD | 0 | 0 | 0 | 0 | 0 | 0 | 0 | 0 | 0 | 0 | 0 | 0 | 0 | 0 | 0 | 0 | 0 | 0 | 0 | 0 | 1 | .3 |
| 4OPROP | 0 | 1 | 0 | 0 | 1 | 0 | 0 | 0 | 0 | 0 | 1 | 0 | 1 | 0 | 0 | 0 | 0 | 0 | 0 | 0 | 1 | .3 |
| 4MINIS | 0 | 0 | 0 | 0 | 0 | 0 | 0 | 0 | 0 | 0 | 1 | 0 | 0 | 0 | 0 | 0 | 0 | 0 | 0 | 0 | 2 | .7 |
| 4PHYS | 0 | 0 | 0 | 0 | 0 | 0 | 0 | 0 | 0 | 0 | 0 | 0 | 0 | 0 | 0 | 0 | 0 | 0 | 0 | 0 | 0 | .0 |
| 4APOTH | 0 | 0 | 0 | 0 | 0 | 0 | 0 | 0 | 0 | 0 | 0 | 0 | 0 | 0 | 0 | 0 | 0 | 0 | 0 | 0 | 0 | .0 |
| 4TEACH | 0 | 0 | 0 | 0 | 0 | 0 | 0 | 0 | 0 | 0 | 0 | 0 | 0 | 0 | 0 | 0 | 0 | 0 | 0 | 0 | 0 | .0 |
| 4LAWYR | 0 | 0 | 0 | 0 | 0 | 0 | 0 | 0 | 0 | 0 | 0 | 0 | 0 | 0 | 0 | 0 | 0 | 0 | 0 | 0 | 0 | .0 |
| 4FINAN | 0 | 0 | 0 | 0 | 0 | 0 | 0 | 0 | 0 | 0 | 0 | 0 | 0 | 0 | 0 | 0 | 0 | 0 | 0 | 0 | 0 | .0 |
| MALE | 6 | 9 | 20 | 5 | 15 | 27 | 18 | 9 | 2 | 4 | 18 | 26 | 6 | 13 | 28 | 19 | 32 | 11 | 10 | 20 | 298 | 77.4 |

Source: Sample Data

Table 8.9
Black Male Heads of Household by Occupation Within Wards, 1870

| Wards | 1 | 2 | 3 | 4 | 5 | 6 | 7 | 8 | 9 | 10 | 11 | 12 | 13 | 14 | 15 | 16 | 17 | 18 | 19 | 20 | City | %City |
|---|---|---|---|---|---|---|---|---|---|---|---|---|---|---|---|---|---|---|---|---|---|---|
| NONE | 0 | 0 | 0 | 0 | 1 | 0 | 0 | 0 | 0 | 2 | 0 | 0 | 1 | 0 | 0 | 1 | 0 | 0 | 0 | 0 | 5 | 1.7 |
| 1LABOR | 1 | 4 | 7 | 3 | 11 | 0 | 0 | 0 | 1 | 2 | 3 | 8 | 1 | 8 | 7 | 10 | 0 | 10 | 3 | 5 | 84 | 28.5 |
| 1BRICK | 1 | 0 | 1 | 0 | 1 | 4 | 0 | 0 | 0 | 0 | 0 | 0 | 0 | 0 | 1 | 0 | 0 | 1 | 3 | 0 | 12 | 4.1 |
| 1STEVE | 0 | 0 | 2 | 0 | 0 | 1 | 0 | 1 | 1 | 0 | 1 | 0 | 3 | 0 | 1 | 2 | 0 | 0 | 5 | 1 | 18 | 6.1 |
| 1WWASH | 0 | 0 | 0 | 0 | 3 | 0 | 1 | 0 | 0 | 1 | 0 | 0 | 0 | 0 | 0 | 0 | 0 | 0 | 0 | 1 | 6 | 2.0 |
| 1SAWYR | 0 | 3 | 0 | 0 | 2 | 0 | 0 | 0 | 0 | 2 | 2 | 0 | 0 | 0 | 0 | 2 | 0 | 1 | 0 | 0 | 12 | 4.1 |
| 1OTHER | 0 | 0 | 0 | 0 | 3 | 0 | 0 | 1 | 0 | 1 | 1 | 0 | 0 | 0 | 0 | 0 | 1 | 3 | 1 | 0 | 11 | 3.7 |
| 2PORTR | 0 | 0 | 0 | 0 | 1 | 0 | 0 | 0 | 2 | 3 | 8 | 0 | 2 | 3 | 0 | 5 | 0 | 3 | 0 | 1 | 30 | 10.2 |
| 2DRAYM | 0 | 2 | 2 | 0 | 3 | 4 | 2 | 1 | 2 | 2 | 3 | 1 | 6 | 1 | 7 | 4 | 0 | 4 | 3 | 10 | 57 | 19.3 |
| 2DOMES | 0 | 0 | 0 | 0 | 0 | 0 | 0 | 0 | 0 | 0 | 0 | 0 | 0 | 0 | 0 | 0 | 0 | 0 | 0 | 0 | 0 | .0 |
| 2SEAMS | 0 | 0 | 0 | 0 | 0 | 0 | 0 | 0 | 0 | 0 | 0 | 0 | 0 | 0 | 0 | 0 | 0 | 0 | 0 | 0 | 0 | .0 |
| 2NURSE | 0 | 0 | 0 | 0 | 0 | 0 | 0 | 0 | 0 | 0 | 0 | 0 | 0 | 0 | 0 | 0 | 0 | 0 | 0 | 0 | 0 | .0 |
| 3MASON | 0 | 1 | 0 | 0 | 0 | 0 | 0 | 0 | 0 | 0 | 0 | 0 | 1 | 0 | 0 | 0 | 0 | 0 | 0 | 0 | 2 | .7 |
| 3CAULK | 1 | 0 | 3 | 0 | 0 | 2 | 0 | 0 | 0 | 0 | 0 | 0 | 0 | 0 | 0 | 1 | 0 | 0 | 0 | 0 | 7 | 2.4 |
| 3WOODN | 0 | 0 | 0 | 0 | 0 | 0 | 0 | 0 | 0 | 0 | 0 | 0 | 0 | 0 | 0 | 0 | 0 | 0 | 0 | 2 | 2 | .7 |
| 3PROVI | 0 | 0 | 0 | 0 | 0 | 0 | 0 | 0 | 0 | 0 | 2 | 0 | 1 | 1 | 1 | 0 | 0 | 0 | 0 | 2 | 7 | 2.4 |
| 3BARBM | 0 | 0 | 0 | 0 | 0 | 0 | 0 | 0 | 0 | 2 | 0 | 0 | 1 | 0 | 0 | 1 | 0 | 0 | 0 | 1 | 5 | 1.7 |
| 3PRINT | 0 | 0 | 0 | 0 | 0 | 0 | 0 | 0 | 0 | 1 | 0 | 0 | 0 | 0 | 0 | 1 | 0 | 0 | 0 | 0 | 2 | .7 |
| 3MUSIC | 0 | 0 | 0 | 0 | 0 | 0 | 0 | 0 | 1 | 0 | 0 | 0 | 0 | 0 | 0 | 0 | 0 | 1 | 0 | 0 | 2 | .7 |
| 3TEXTL | 0 | 0 | 1 | 0 | 0 | 0 | 0 | 0 | 1 | 0 | 0 | 0 | 0 | 0 | 2 | 0 | 0 | 0 | 0 | 1 | 5 | 1.7 |
| 4MARIN | 1 | 0 | 2 | 0 | 2 | 0 | 0 | 0 | 1 | 1 | 2 | 0 | 2 | 0 | 2 | 3 | 0 | 2 | 1 | 0 | 19 | 6.4 |
| 4CLERI | 0 | 0 | 0 | 0 | 0 | 0 | 0 | 0 | 0 | 0 | 0 | 0 | 0 | 0 | 0 | 2 | 0 | 0 | 0 | 0 | 2 | .7 |
| 4HUCKS | 0 | 0 | 0 | 0 | 0 | 0 | 0 | 0 | 1 | 0 | 1 | 0 | 0 | 0 | 0 | 0 | 0 | 0 | 0 | 0 | 2 | .7 |
| 4FOOD | 0 | 0 | 0 | 0 | 1 | 0 | 0 | 0 | 0 | 0 | 0 | 0 | 0 | 0 | 0 | 0 | 0 | 0 | 0 | 0 | 1 | .3 |
| 4OPROP | 0 | 0 | 0 | 0 | 0 | 0 | 0 | 0 | 1 | 0 | 0 | 0 | 0 | 0 | 0 | 0 | 0 | 0 | 0 | 0 | 1 | .3 |
| 4MINIS | 0 | 0 | 0 | 0 | 0 | 0 | 0 | 0 | 0 | 0 | 0 | 0 | 0 | 0 | 0 | 0 | 0 | 0 | 0 | 1 | 1 | .3 |
| 4PHYS | 0 | 0 | 0 | 0 | 0 | 0 | 0 | 0 | 0 | 0 | 0 | 0 | 0 | 0 | 0 | 0 | 0 | 0 | 0 | 0 | 0 | .0 |
| 4APOTH | 0 | 0 | 0 | 0 | 0 | 0 | 0 | 0 | 0 | 0 | 0 | 0 | 0 | 0 | 0 | 0 | 0 | 0 | 0 | 0 | 0 | .0 |
| 4TEACH | 0 | 0 | 0 | 0 | 1 | 0 | 0 | 0 | 0 | 0 | 1 | 0 | 0 | 0 | 1 | 0 | 0 | 0 | 0 | 0 | 3 | 1.0 |
| 4LAWYR | 0 | 0 | 0 | 0 | 0 | 0 | 0 | 0 | 0 | 0 | 0 | 0 | 0 | 0 | 0 | 0 | 0 | 0 | 0 | 0 | 0 | .0 |
| 4FINAN | 0 | 0 | 0 | 0 | 0 | 0 | 0 | 0 | 0 | 0 | 0 | 0 | 0 | 0 | 0 | 0 | 0 | 0 | 0 | 0 | 0 | .0 |
| MALE | 4 | 10 | 19 | 4 | 28 | 17 | 4 | 3 | 10 | 14 | 22 | 10 | 14 | 13 | 27 | 32 | 1 | 25 | 17 | 21 | 285 | 76.6 |

Source: Sample Data

boom of the 1850s. Following the war, however, the unprecedented numbers of rural ex-slaves glutted the unskilled job market and in many respects returned black society to its 1850 conditions. Between 1860 and 1870, the number of households increased by 55% and the density of the population increased from 1.3 to 1.5 households per dwelling. The percentage of men out of work declined but unskilled employment and a decrease in working wives filled the void. Even worse, by 1870 residential crowding was at its most dense level.

The in-migration of blacks during the 1860s exerted a harsher effect upon the African-American job market than did the influx of foreign born in the 50s. During the first decade, 81 percent of male heads were employed in unskilled jobs or unemployed. When they were employed, they were more likely to work as laborers in 1850; waiters or draymen in 1860. Black tradesmen had decreased by 36 percent by 1860; those employed in commerce, especially seamen, picked up the slack. Ten years hence, unemployment had dropped from six percent to two percent; trades had recovered from nine percent to 12 percent of black employees, and persons in commercial occupations slipped only slightly. Black men, however, were unskilled and their community grievously lacked persons with business and professional expertise. Their ranks may also have been depleted by service in the Civil War.[14]

In the first place, the apparent proletarianization of black employees was a hardening of economic class lines. As with jobs, the foreign immigration of the 1850s worked far less hardship upon black property owners--or upon the likelihood of property accumulation--than the black migration which followed the Civil War. While the increase in heads owning $100 or more during the 1850s is exaggerated because the 1850 census takers tallied real estate only, it is likely that their total earnings had not declined still further by 1860. During the following decade, the percentage of heads who owned no property increased from 83 to 87 percent; the size of the economic "elite," who owned $200 or more remained virtually the same--albeit tipped slightly to the more prosperous end of the scale. Apparently the competition for jobs within the black community blocked renewed prosperity for the group as a whole.[15]

Despite the shortage of unskilled tradesmen in the black community, they, as well as the few businessmen and professionals, saw their economic position improve considerably or at least keep pace with the wartime inflation. During the 1860s, property-owning caulkers, whose total numbers fell victim to the deterioration in ship building, jumped from 27 percent to 59 percent owning $1,000 or more. Barbers, always the mainstay of the 19th-century Negro middle class, jumped from 53 percent to 68 percent owning $1,000 or more. Wood tradesmen, mariners, clerks, and various businessmen and professionals all experienced similar jumps in status. In 1870 the wealthiest of all occupational groups were musicians, proprietors, and the ministry respectively. By contrast, African-American physicians and teachers were not nearly so affluent. Thus the black middle class of the 1860s became an increasingly closed society, based upon one's good fortune to have been included in it before the end of the Civil War. In this respect, black society proved to be less open than white society in Baltimore, where the German-born element was well on its way to prosperity as early as 1860. The black influx seems to have placed even more distance between a tiny, secure middle class and the Negro proletariat below.

These divisions within black society became more noticeable. More prosperous Negroes, especially those who had lived in Baltimore before 1865, began to move to the near northeast wards. In their wake, African-American south Baltimore (wards 15 & 16) became a rallying point for younger, poorer rural black migrants, many of them from Virginia. And the black social structure began to harden along economic lines, as well as geographical ones. Following the short-lived prosperity of the 1850s, African-American economic mobility came to a near-standstill. Only the remaining tradesmen and professionals who had amassed their fortunes before 1865 managed to hold on to their wealth--consolidating positions that set them apart in status as well as geography from the rest of the black population.

Despite the stress, the stable structure of this society appears to have survived, at least until 1870. Despite the hardships for families in slavery and the scarcity of men which compelled many women to seek work and a kind of companionship as live-in nannies in white households, the black patriarchal family remained the dominant living arrangement for African-Americans. In fact the number of families headed by men increased from 74 to 77 percent during the 1850s, falling by a mere 0.8 percent during the following decade. This stability was also reflected in a stable sex ratio for black households (between 54 and 56 percent female throughout the period).

We are left to speculate about the reasons behind these findings concerning the black family. Perhaps because more than ever before all blacks had to face pervasive conditions of hardship, the core of society was not touched: maybe parents were boosted by their children's new education opportunities opened up by the Freedman's Bureau.[16] In any case, the black patrifocal family survived this generation much as it had begun, the primary institutional unit of this urban black society.

For survive it did in the face of a quasi-Southern brand of racism, which, after all, played the preeminent role in constraining the opportunies for Baltimore's mid-nineteenth-century African-American residents.

As Maryland residents, blacks were limited by a host of legislated restrictions. From 1808 to 1870, no black male voted in the Free State. While the freedmen could own and dispose of property, in a number of other ways they saw their civil rights impaired. Freedmen could testify against whites in some cases, but they could not sit on juries nor pass before the bar. They were generally excluded from a host of licensed jobs, the police force, and fire department. An 1852 statute prevented blacks from becoming business partners with whites; in 1860, they were formally excluded from mechanics' trades. After 1831 the license became a pre-requisite for selling liquor or owning firearms.[17]

More threatening than these disbarments were curtailments upon movement and assembly and the city and state apprenticeship and labor contract laws. A city ordinance denied blacks the liberty to stay out after 11:00 p.m. Although they could wander in their alleyways at any hour, to be caught in hostile surroundings--with or without a certificate of freedom--was to risk kidnap or re-enslavement for vagrancy. From 1858 to 1860, 89 Maryland freedmen were sold back into slavery, including 24 by Baltimore city courts. An 1841 statute outlawed all secret societies among free African-Americans. Although this was amended the following year to enable the mayor to authorize meetings attended by a policeman, an 1846 law prohibited the incorporation of black lyceums, fire companies, masonic lodges and other forms of black assemblage except for benevolent societies and churches.[18]

Prior to 1865 the apprenticeship and contract labor laws of the nineteenth century established a fine line between freedmen and urban slaves. According to an 1818 statute, any white or black adolescent not working was liable to apprenticeship, though his parents could have a say in the choice of a master. Violations of apprenticeship were subject to imprisonment in the state penitentiary, or, if waived, by sale into slavery--a feature presumably only applied to blacks. Under the provisions of statutes enacted in 1854 and 1856, adult freedmen who deserted their labor contracts--even verbal contracts--risked enforced completion of the contract without pay for the time lost and the cost of the court's services or imprisonment. One historian has argued that, during the 1850s, confinement of apprenticeship and contract labor violators in the city jail testifies to the declining status of the Maryland freedman on the eve of the Civil War. One notable exception, of course, was the establishment of the Chesapeake Marine Railway and Dry Dock Company by a group of black caulkers led by Isaac Myers in response to the displacement of 1,000 black caulkers by striking white counterparts in 1865. Before very long, however, the black caulkers were destined to be permanently displaced because of the decline of the wooden shipbuilding industry in Baltimore.

The dominant white society's attitude towards its black citizenry alternated between outright repression and disavowal. Following the Nat Turner Insurrection, for example, the state legislated harsh freedom of movement statues in 1831 and 1832. Maryland was also a stronghold of the ante-bellum colonization to Africa movement and Baltimore was its state headquarters. Eastern Shore legislators, who represented the most pro-slavery region of the state, even endeavored to float a re-enslavement statute in 1860.

For its part, Baltimore's black community continued to strive for inclusion. For example, barely 1,200 Maryland blacks opted for emigration during the existence of the state colonization society from 1831 to 1857. On the other hand, blacks were enthusiastic participants in divided Maryland's support of the Union effort, first behind the lines building fortifications and, after October 26, 1863, as soldiers in the Union ranks. Nearly 9,000 Maryland troops, including the Fourth Colored Regiment from Baltimore, fought for the Union.[19]

In their pursuit of the freedom *after* 1865, blacks were continually frustrated by the political process. The return of the Democrats in Annapolis and at City Hall foreshadowed an era of non-reconstruction. The Democratic State Constitutional Convention of 1867 omitted a Negro suffrage clause only to have the suffrage forced upon the state by the ratification of the Fifteenth Amendment, an event celebrated in Baltimore on May 26, 1870, with Frederick Douglass in attendance. Over the remainder of the century the Democratic party became increasingly lily-white in its composition and race-baiting in its tactics. Then, on three occasions, between 1900 and 1912, the Jim Crow-oriented Democratic party sought to constitutionally disenfranchise the blacks of Maryland. Only because the proposed "grandfather" clauses contained in the Poe, Straus, and Digges Amendments would also have disenfranchised many recent immigrants did white and black voters, especially in Baltimore, combine to defeat the referenda.[20]

For its part, the Republican Party alternately grudgingly welcomed or openly discarded black membership. In 1873 there was only one black member on the Republican state committee, and in 1881, blacks held down only 24 of 1,311 federal jobs in Maryland  filled by President Garfield's appointees. Flirting with the "fusion principle" Baltimore blacks formed Negro Democratic Clubs in 1870, 1872, 1876, 1879, and 1893. On the whole and with the notable exception of the African-American Harry Scythe Cummings from the llth Ward, Baltimore blacks had to look outside the two-party system for substantive improvements in the quality of their lives.

Black civil rights organizations had greater success through the courts. Prior to 1870, blacks could ride only on the platforms of trolleys. An 1870 lawsuit forced the railway companies to provide at least separate carriers for black passengers. The economic disadvantages to the companies of such a ruling delayed segregation aboard public carriers until 1904, after which time Jim Crow practices would prevail throughout Maryland. In the interim, courtroom efforts by non-partisan reformist organizations like the Colored Equal Rights League founded by Dr. J.H. Brown and the United Brotherhood of Liberty, led by the charismatic Baptist minister Harvey Johnson, produced for blacks the right to serve on juries in state courts (1880), and the admission of blacks to the University of Maryland Law School and before the bar (1885). The Colored Advisory Committee (1879) and Maryland Progressive Assembly (1887) also protested against the unresponsiveness of the political system for blacks.[21]

Given the constraints imposed by white Baltimore, blacks would have experienced insupportable frustration had they predicated their expectations or aspirations upon entrance into the dominant white culture. One would have expected to find the usual signs of social deterioration borne out of such anxiety--family instability, crime, suicide, etc. Instead none of these is much in evidence in the immediate postwar era because black men and women responded to the harsh facts of everyday institutionalized racism by forming their own society rich in heritage and dignity.

Outside of the family the most important and continuous of these institutions was, of course, the black church. These churches performed a host of functions both spiritual and temporal. Pastors were able to promise ultimate salvation to their neighborhood flocks, if the latter would only find solace in the discipline of church ethics. Sermons animated by fire and brimstone elicited participation by the congregation, which in turn, took the edge off the week's frustrations. In the process, black aspirations took on a heavenly orientation and church folks came under a form of social control. Pastors effectively stressed temperance and other forms of abstinence. Both Bethel and Ebenezer African Methodist Episcopal Churches housed temperance societies during the 1840s. What's more, the church as an organization provided the black community with a structure that was denied them by the white community. Both the general hierarchial structure of some denominations, especially Methodism, and the local hierarchy of parishes--clergy, trustees and stewards-- reaffirmed their members' sense of commitment to a group and created a genuine status system--even if the penny donations to Bethel church in 1825 did not exceed $472. The church also represented the primary training area for black leaders. Thus, impoverished or not, Baltimore's African-American men and women acquired a sense and need for participation because the church offered a personalized answer to the problem of racial alienation at the level of the specific congregation/neighborhood it served.[22]

The vast majority of and the oldest black churches in Baltimore were Methodist: Methodist Episcopal, African Methodist Episcopal (AME), and African Methodist Episcopal Zion. By 1859 the combined membership of the Sharp Street and Wesley Chapel M.E. churches totalled 1,812 persons. Bethel AME, re-built in 1848 at a cost of $16,000, had 1,400 members. In fact, over 90 percent of all Black church members and two-thirds of the edifices were black Methodist in 1860.[23]

By 1870, however, in addition to Methodists, black churches also numbered important Protestant Episcopal, Baptist, and even Catholic congregations. Saint James African Protestant Episcopal Church, located to the northwest on Dolphin and Park, had a membership of 111 and a Sunday School enrollment of 70 persons by 1859. Baltimore's black Roman Catholic Congregation, St. Francis Xavier, whose origins went back to the Santo Domingo uprising of 1793 and subsequent founding by the Society of Saint Sulpice, also housed the first black religious order in the U.S., the Oblate Sisters of Providence. Finally, despite the large size of the Baptist denomination in contemporary Baltimore, only two black Baptist churches functioned in the city as late as 1870. A surge in Baptist membership commenced after the Civil War, however, and was centered in south Baltimore, yet another spin-off from the rural in-migration.[24]

The black church also led the way in providing educational facilities for its community. With the exception of church-affiliated schools, few examples of black educational facilities existed before 1868. The city of Baltimore excluded blacks altogether from the inception of its public school system in 1829 until 1868, providing schools thereafter only on a separate basis. Republican state and local administrations failed to establish public schools for blacks during the Civil War. So, despite the fact that Maryland had never seceded from the Union, the Freedman's Bureau was authorized to create the first state-wide system of public education for blacks. By 1867, thirty-seven schools had been opened in Baltimore and eighty-one throughout the state. Blacks cooperatively owned over half of these schools outright and nearly seventy percent of them in whole or part. They also donated over $23,000 to educational causes. Among the schools was Douglass Institute, which opened in September 1865, at a cost of $16,000. Probably the single largest source of black funding was a $7,000 inheritance from the will of the free black Nelson Wells. Although the schools were often makeshift--built from lumber which had housed an army barracks and hospital in Baltimore-- they served useful purposes until the first ten black public schools in Baltimore opened in 1868.[25]

During decades of white indifference, the black church had sought to fill the educational vacuum. The Methodist Episcopal Church took the lead in establishing Sunday Schools. In 1838, nine Sunday Schools were operating in Baltimore. Besides religious subjects, some of the schools taught Greek, Latin and other rudiments of the classical education. Daniel Payne of the AME Baltimore Conference, in particular, was most instrumental in promoting innovation in black church schools. By 1859, the combined Sunday School attendance of the various methodist churches in Baltimore totalled 2,086 students.

Nor did the church abandon its educational role after 1868, and for good reason. The first black public high school did not open until 1883. Most of the black public schools were old and dilapidated or at least repossessed structures. The 2,700 students in the system in 1871 were taught by white teachers, and the state allocated $2.31 per white student but only $1.65 per black pupil. When they could collect the resources, Baltimore African-Americans continued to display the kind of self-reliance exhibited by the black Methodist church, which in 1867 founded the Centenary Biblical Institute, the forerunner of Morgan State College.[26]

Just as they learned to improvise their own religious and educational institutions, Baltimore's blacks sought and devised social and recreational situations where they might do good works or simply relax among persons who could appreciate their good fellowship. The first black benevolent society had materialized in 1821. By 1833, thirty of these sickness and burial societies were working to provide money for the sick and widows and their children. These forerunners of the black insurance industry included the Friendship Society for Society Relief, the Star in the East Association, the Daughters of Jerusalem, and the Young Men's Mental Improvement Society. The benevolent societies usually met in local churches. Determined to provide their members with proper Christian burials, these church auxiliaries comprised the vanguard ushering in the Promised Land. By 1880, an estimated sixty benevolent societies had been created.[27]

More exclusive than the benevolent societies were the various black fraternities and brotherhoods. Usually organized around their members' occupations, like many of their white counterparts, these clubs or lodges sometimes functioned as sickness and burial societies, but they also provided opportunities for secular gatherings and recreation. As was the case with the first black fraternity in America, black masons formed the first fraternal organization in Baltimore in 1825. In 1845, Friendship Lodge #6 was joined by two additional lodges to form the First Colored

Grand Lodge of Baltimore. Before the end of the century its membership numbered 700. A few of the larger societies or ones whose members earned higher wages had buildings of their own.[28]

The occupationally-organized brotherhoods sometimes grew into trade unions. Although black trade unionism developed mainly after 1870, it was probably an outgrowth of the ethnic job competition created by the immigrations of the 1850s and 1860s. The Caulkers Fraternity owned a hall on Dallas Street in east Baltimore appraised at $1,500 in 1866. At its 1867 convention, the National Labor Union accepted as members--among nine black delegations--the Colored Engineers Association, represented by H.H. Butler, and the Colored Caulkers Trade Union Society, represented by Isaac Myers. The Caulkers later regrouped under the Knights of Labor and Myers--who led an organizing campaign on behalf of the National Colored Labor Union throughout the South in 1870--was still active at the time of the railroad strike of 1877.[29]

Good fellowship was no substitute, however, for the capital, expertise and luck needed for major business undertakings or social services. Between 1867 and 1890, over a dozen black newspapers failed because of insufficient advertising and dwindling readership. The Freedman's Bureau Bank, whose executive officer was the Reverend Harrison Holmes, failed in 1874. By 1892, the Negro Lexington Savings Bank, headed by Everett J. Waring, contained $57,000 in deposits; yet it too failed some years later. The same fate befell Myers' Marine and Railway Corporation, a venture aimed at providing tram service from disconnected railway terminals in the city.

Unlike the immigrants, who faced little discrimination in hiring or licensing, Baltimore's mid-nineteenth century blacks did not come by the material proof that mobility was possible in America. German and Irish tradesmen were able--and willing--to risk their savings in neighborhood ventures. Their groceries, dry goods stores, bakeries, butcher shops and taverns dotted the ethnically mixed landscape as they found within their own--and other--groups the makings of their American dreams. Ethnic retailers thus constituted dual economies parallel with their dual societies. In the long run much of their profits found its way into relatives' hands or added to the overall purchasing power of their "dual societies," until later generations of prosperity dissolved much that had been socially and economically dual.

So hopeless was the vision of the would-be black capitalist, however, that one searches the breadth of the sources in vain for black purveyors of "vice." Gamblers (i.e., "speculators"), liquor peddlers or bartenders existed but the ladies of "easy pleasure" were non-existent or anonymous, unlike the German or native prostitutes in southeast Baltimore. Community pressures had evidently curtailed intemperance or black customers shopped elsewhere or went without. All things considered, only the black cabinet maker-undertaker had a strong incentive to go into business.

The lowly status of the black community was reflected in their public health. Because blacks were excluded from all hospitals save the state insane asylum and Johns Hopkins Hospital, their fatality rates in the plague epidemics of 1819 and 1832 and the typhus epidemic of 1850 far exceeded their percentage in the total population. It was not until several black physicians rented a home on Orchard Street that adequate hospital care began. Happily, this home later became the black Provident Hospital, supported subsequently by the donations and time of black churchmen.[30]

These and other sufferings went unseen or unheeded by the white population. From 1850 to 1870, blacks were disproportionately present in the county almshouse by 29 percent to 18 percent respectively and, since the 1840s, in a segregated fashion. Not until 1872 did the state build a special school for black blind and deaf children. Whites seemed more concerned about the influx of blacks to the city after 1865, lest the newcomers get out-of-hand. A cursory survey of city jail records shows that the black proportion of inmates increased from 23 percent in 1850 to 51.2 percent in 1870, at a time when the capacity of the institution almost doubled. (Conversely, reported immigrant crime did not keep pace with the increase in the foreign component of the population.) White philanthropists grew concerned over an apparent increase in adolescent black anti-social behavior. Enoch Pratt and J.H.B. Latrobe promoted the construction of a House of Reformation and Institution for Colored Children (1870) to house delinquent boys. On the other hand, the executors of Johns Hopkins' estate refused to allocate funds that the late city father had authorized to build a 300-400 person capacity black orphanage. Perhaps the white society's specter of the emancipated black race was changing from docile to bestial a generation before the novels of Thomas Dixon.[31]

In the final analysis, 19th century black Baltimoreans preserved their identity and dignity in the face of these economic and racial constraints. The occasional protests raised by organizations like the Brotherhood of Liberty take on greatest significance not for their limited success but for the chances they gave to blacks to vent their frustrations. Otherwise black folks withdrew into their own proletarian culture. Although only a few middle class blacks benefitted from the new victories won in the 19th century courts, civil protest was also the highest expression of the black community's nationalist character--and of its determination to carry on.

## RETROSPECTIVE & CONCLUSION

From the perspective of today's greater Baltimore metropolis, the most important feature of mid-nineteenth-century Baltimore was that it forced its diverse inhabitants to live in close proximity, however great the social and economic barriers. Perhaps more important, all residents had a stake in the urban problems of the day at the neighborhood level. While the Baltimore of 1870 had problems with business cycles, public health epidemics, fires, drainage, foul waste and drinking water, the problems were, nonetheless, within the capacity of the neighborhood to address or resolve. This is a far cry from the spatial-ethnic realities in Baltimore of today.[32]

Although it is tempting to romanticize about the mid-nineteenth century city--a life that was immediate, close, and even pastoral--life was no picnic for Baltimore's African-Americans of that era. As we have seen they faced discrimination in jobs, licensing, schools, civil rights, assembly, and housing--a discrimination, I should hasten to add, that persisted until the last generation. Yet, in spite of these hardships, living in alleyways, attending their own churches, schools and societies, they persevered owing to their sense of a common struggle. Their neighborhoods were not unlike communities of rural sharecroppers who rallied around the parish church, the one enduring focus of their collective association. The church not only helped manage the internal affairs of the community but also, on occasion, managed to parlay community identification into a lever for civil protest. The black families of post bellum Baltimore--and I dare say all subsequent black communities in Baltimore until at least the 1930s[33]-- substantially averted the self-hate and self-destruction so commonplace in urban centers now.[34]

As subsequent history has shown, however, Baltimore's African-Americans were pawns in the urbanization process. Just as they had been needed to caulk vessels and build fortifications in the last century, their fortunes were greatest when they were employed in the canning and defense factories of East Baltimore in this one. As soon as new white laborers appeared on the scene, however--Germans and Irish from 1850 to 1870, Poles and Italians around the turn of the century, and Koreans in recent years--they again became expendable. With the end of slavery and the limited opportunities of post bellum southern agriculture, black peasants flocked to the Monumental City only to find scant opportunities there and no place else to venture[35]. Subsequently, overcrowding bred public health problems in the new, expanding black *ghetto* of south Baltimore and later west Baltimore but it was treated only as little more than an eyesore by the surrounding white society.

As the city grew, the plight of the vast majority of African-Americans became more and more desperate. The growth of the city and suburbs was spurred by the invention of the electric streetcar and then the automobile, such that today the radius of the metropolitan area is ten times greater than in 1870, reaching deep into Anne Arundel County to the South, Howard County to the west, Carroll County to the northwest, the Pennsylvania border to the north, and Harford County to the east.[36] At each stage of urban growth, a small group of upwardly mobile blacks were the beneficiaries of used housing which was, in any case, far superior to what they were vacating. Like the whites before them, they followed radial paths into the older and then the new western suburbs of Druid Hill Park, Mount Washington and Randallstown and, to a lesser extent, the eastern, more industrial suburbs of Patterson Park and Turner's Station. For these blacks, like whites, the move to the suburbs really meant greener pastures. They had come by them via improved job opportunities as trade unionists in the 1930s and 1940s and, later, following the civil rights movement[37], in public sector jobs, such as at the huge Social Security headquarters in Baltimore County. They could also look forward to better schools in the counties and, hopefully, even greater job opportunities for their better educated children.[38]

For the majority of blacks, however, the story has worsened: broken families lacking in marketable skills or adequate educations, living in crowded, dilapidated houses, unprotected by housing code enforcement, atop a deteriorating infrastructure. As if this weren't bad enough, beginning with the 1930s, the appearance of packaged good stores, drugs, and,

*The Greater Baltimore Metroplitan Area, 1992*

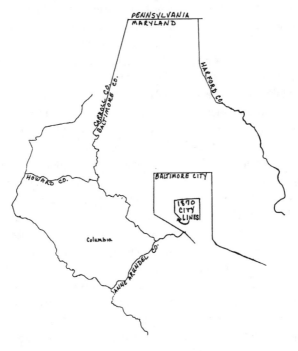

*Source: The Genuine C&P Yellow Pages (Baltimore, 1992).*

most recently, wanton violence made possible by the extraordinary availability of handguns have threatened to crush the internal cohesion of the inner city community.

Statistics bearing this out are reported on a regular basis. Like most older cities, Baltimore's population has declined from an all-time high of 950,000 in 1950 to 736,000 in 1990. A full sixty percent of the current population is African-American. Approximately one in five Baltimoreans lives below the poverty level. In 1989, the city's per capita income level of $8,647 was closer to that of rural Talbot County than, say, Tacoma Park ($13,905) or Hyattsville ($13,329) two of the older Maryland suburbs of Washington, D.C. Baltimore's infant mortality rate of 12.7 per 1,000 births and its rate of births to mothers aged 19 or younger (22.7 per 1,000 births) were the highest in the nation.  In 1985, city police recorded nearly 68,000 serious crimes, over 15,000 of them violent, and in 1990, it recorded 371 murders, eleventh highest in the U.S.  According to one unofficial estimate, 25 percent of black young men in Baltimore between the ages of 18 and 25 were either in prison or awaiting trial.[39]

City officials, who in bygone days had either acquiesced in these inequalities or actively promoted them, now find themselves with a limited number of options.  No longer able to utilize metropolitan annexation to cure the ills of the city, prior mayors and city councils, while sensitive to the need to provide direct assistance for housing, jobs, education, medical assistance and related needs, put most of their resources and creativity into restoring the downtown commercial center into a recreational and tourist attraction. Much heralded in the 1980s as the prototype for urban redevelopment projects, the Inner Harbor  has created jobs for blacks and whites in the construction industry and for managers of the various Harbor attractions: the National Aquarium, World Trade Center, Harbor Place mall, a science center, the Baltimore Convention Center, a new multi-million dollar baseball stadium, a score of large hotels, and so on.  While the Inner Harbor has succeeded in bringing tourists and suburbanites downtown in the evenings and on weekends, the city--or the state for that matter--has done little to address the problems of the mean streets which lie just on the outskirts of all the glitter. Fifty percent reductions in federal community development grants, employment and training funds, and various construction programs since 1981 have further tightened the noose around the  city's neck.[40]

Perhaps it is the scale of Baltimore's urban problem that seems to defy solution.  The city of Baltimore today is, after all, six times larger than the industrial town of 1870.  Because of decades of neglect and denial on the part of the body politic, Baltimore's racial problems, once confined to alleys, are now as big as the city itself and spilling over.  Neither the unprecedented improvement in the quality of  life enjoyed by  the new black middle class nor the growing installation of home security systems by whites in the surrounding counties can deny or conceal the waste in human spirit which is the reality of the inner city poor.   Not until we agree to look this issue in the face, acknowledging its severity, enormity and mutuality, and commit resources  and  will  power  to its resolution can we hope to do anything about it.

1. For an extended treatment of this subject see Joseph Garonzik, "The Racial and ethnic Make-up of Baltimore Neighborhoods, 1850-1870," *Maryland Historical Magazine*, 71 (Fall 1976): 392-402.

2. George E. Waring, Jr. *Report of the Social Statistics of Cities* (New York, 1970), 2:5-8; Clayton Colman Hall, ed., *Baltimore, Its History and Its People*, 2 vols. (New York, 1912), I:19-20, 44, 52; George Rogers Taylor, "American Urban Growth Preceding the Railway Age," *Journal of Economic History*, 27 (September, 1967): 311; Tench Coxe, *Aggregate Amount of Each Description of Persons Within the United States...in the Year 1810* (Washington, 1811), p. 53. Baltimore had already surpassed the town of Boston in size by 1800: Boston, 24,937; Baltimore, 26,514.

3. Thomas Courtenay Jenkins Whedbee, *The Port of Baltimore in the Making* (Baltimore, 1953), pp. 33-35; Joseph Austin Durrenberger, *Turnpikes: A Study of the Toll Road Movement in the Middle Atlantic States and Maryland* (Valdosta, 1931), pp. 65-70; Whedbee, *Port*, pp. 37-39, 41-43; Julius Rubin, *Canal or Railroad: Imitation and Innovation in Response to the Erie Canal in Philadelphia, Baltimore and Boston* (Philadelphia, 1961), pp. 9, 13, 64, 78; James Weston Livingood, *The Philadelphia-Baltimore Trade Rivalry, 1780-1860* (Harrisburg, 1947), pp. 97-98; Alan R. Pred, *The Spatial Dynamics of the United States Urban-Industrial Growth, 1800-1914: Interpretive and Theoretical Essays* (Cambridge, MA, 1966), pp. 20, 106.

4. Whedbee, *Port*, pp. 65-66, 41-43, 76-82; Hall, *Baltimore*, I: 138, 478, 523, 482; David T. Gilchrist, ed., *The Growth of the Seaport Cities: 1790-1825* (Charlottesville, 1966), pp. 170-73; Joseph C. G. Kennedy, *History and Statistics of the State of Maryland* (Washington, 1852), pp. 52-53; Census Office, *The Statistics of Wealth and Industry of the United States. . .Manufactures, Mining and Fisheries* (Washington, 1871), p. 673; Charles Hirschfeld, "Baltimore, 1870-1900: Studies in Social History," *Johns Hopkins University Studies in History and Political Science*, 59 (1941): 23. A comparison of published United States Census manufacturing reports indicates that only the industries of artificial flowers, band boxes, baskets, buttons, cages, and pyrotechnics failed to survive from 1850 to 1870. And in 1870 only the manufacture of sulfuric acid, smelted copper--as opposed to other forms of copper-roofing materials--and cotton goods had materialized during the generation.

5. J.D. B. DeBow, *Statistical View of the U.S. . . .Being a Compendium of the Seventh Census* (Washington, 1854), Appendix Tables I-III; Census Office, *Population of the United States in 1860*, pp. 453, 523, 589, 608-15; Census Office,

*The Statistics of the Population of the United States* (Washington, 1871), pp. 380-391.

6. George Rogers Taylor, "The Beginnings of Mass Transportation in Urban America," *Smithsonian Journal of History*, 1 (Summer and Autumn, 1966): 35-50, 31-54; Hall, *Baltimore*, I: 542-51. Although Baltimore led all American cities into the railroad age, it was the last of the big Eastern cities to develop the horse-car. Omnibus service in Baltimore began in 1844 but failed to provide the comfortable, speedy service necessary to generate an extensive system of intracity transportation. The movement to the western suburbs, well underway before the 1859 construction of railway tracks, is all the more remarkable in view of this. It may be that the original suburbanization entailed a combined business and residential movement, only to be transformed by a system of transportation which made commuting to the workplace far less onerous.

7. J. F. Weishampel, Jr., *The Stranger in Baltimore* (Baltimore, 1876), p. 59. No systematic measurement of commuting exists; however, a rough comparison of the location of businesses with those of the residences of persons employed in corresponding occupations indicates that a considerable commuting on a daily basis into the central business district had developed by 1870.

8. Joseph Garonzik, "Urbanization and the Black Population of Baltimore, 1850-1870" (Ph.D. diss., State University of New York at Stony Brook, 1974), pp. 7-35, 103-09. From 1850 to 1870 the city directories indicate that Episcopal and Presbyterian churches most closely followed the native migration to the north; Roman Catholic churces--except the German language ones--exhibited city-wide a peripheral expansion; Methodism, the most numerous denomination, expanded in all directions; the Reformed, United Brethren and Lutheran churches expanded outward more slowly and into the most German parts of the city; only the minority Protestant, Jewish, and all black churches showed very limited spread or growth.

9. Garonzik, "Urbanization and the Black Population of Baltimore," Appendix B, pp. 269-328. Two of the most densely populated alleys included Welcome Alley in South Baltimore and Happy Alley in East Baltimore. By 1870, the latter had been re-named Durham Street.

10. Garonzik, "Urbanization and the Black Population of Baltimore," Appendix C, pp. 329-54.

11. Ibid., Appendix D, pp. 355-81. On a per capita basis in 1870, Baltimore's German households were numbered among the city's solid middle class. Forty percent of the above owned property assessed at more than $500 compared with 36 percent of the British households, 34 percent, native; 24 percent, Irish; and 7

percent black. Native white Baltimoreans continued to dominate the upper class since 14 percent owned property in excess of $5,000, compared with 11 percent of the British; 7 percent, German; 5 percent, Irish; and no black households.

12. The total black population increased from 27,898 to 39,558 during the 1860s, an increment far too large for natural increase of the existing population to account for. In absolute numbers black live-in domestics grew more rapidly during the 1860s than the 1850s. The number of domestics per white household fell from .16 to .13 during the 1850s but rose to .14 by 1870.

13. The findings on pp. 10-14 of this article are based on a random sample of 385 black households in Baltimore enumerated in the 1850, 1860 and 1870 Federal Census Manuscripts. The number of households sampled per ward was stratified according to the share of the total number of households living in each ward. Besides property and work status, available census measurements consisted of age, sex, color, birthplace, school attendance, literacy and numbers of households under one roof. Over the twenty years under study, the sample population decreased slightly: 1,796 persons in 1850; 1,736, 1860; 1,763, 1870.

14. For purposes of greater detail, the major occupational headings were broken down as follows: *Unemployed*--None; *Unskilled Laborers*--Laborers (lLabor), Brickmoulders (lBrick), Stevedores (1Steve), Whitewashers (1WWash), Sawyers (1Sawyr), Miscellaneous laborers (1Other); *Unskilled Servicers*--Porters (2Portr), Draymen (2Draym), Day domestics (2Domes), Seamstresses (2Seams), Nurses (2Nurse); *Tradesmen*--Masons and blacksmiths (3Mason), Caulkers (3Caulk), Carpenters and other Woodworkers (3Woodn), Butchers, bakers and other provision tradesmen (3Provi), Barbers (3Barbr), Paper tradesmen (3Print), Musicians and actors (3Music), Textile tradesmen (3Textl); *Commercial Employees and Employers*--Seamen (4Marin), Clerical and supervisory personnel (4Cleri), Hucksters (4Hucks), Food proprietors (4Food), Other Proprietors (4Oprop); *Professionals*--Clergymen (4Minis), Physicians and dentists (4Phys), Druggists (4Apoth), Teachers and music teachers (4Teach), Lawyers (4Lawyr), Financiers (4Finan). The occupational category *None* refers to all heads or persons not credited with an occupation by the enumerators. This catch-all term embraces unemployed persons in the labor force, as well as those not in the labor force, whatever their reasons.

15. In terms of real purchasing power, only 1.2 percent of black heads owned more than $450 in 1860 compared with 2.5 percent who owned more than $600 in 1870. On the other hand, 16.6 percent of heads owned more than $90 in 1860 compared to only 10.6 who owned more than $120 in 1870.

16. While the 1850 and 1860 schedules classify persons simply as *literate* or *illiterate*, the 1870 schedules define individuals in terms of their separate abilities to read and to write. For consistency's sake, if an individual over the age of 19 lacked either of these skills, he or she was here classed *illiterate*. The literacy rate for blacks over the age of 19 doubled between 1850 and 1860 before returning to its pre-war level of 33 percent in 1870. School attendance among black youths, on the other hand, role from 21 percent to 38 percent during the second decade.

17. James M. Wright, *The Free Negro in Maryland* (New York, 1921), pp. 99, 104-06, 107, 118-22; Jeffrey Brackett, *The Negro in Maryland: A Study in the Institution of Slavery* (Baltimore, 1889), p. 153.

18. M. Ray Della, "An Analysis of Baltimore's Population in the 1850s," *Maryland Historical Magazine*, LXVIII (Spring 1973): 28; Brackett, pp. 123-24, 184-86, 203-05, 232-33; Grace Hill Jacob, "The Negro in Baltimore: 1860-1900" (M.A. Thesis: Howard University, 1945), 12-13.

19. Richard B. Morris, "Labor Controls in Maryland in the Nineteenth Century," *Journal of Southern History*, XIV (August, 1948): 392-393; Brackett, *Negro*, pp. 127-28, 130-33; Penelope Campbell, *Maryland in Africa: The Maryland State Colonization Society, 1831-1857* (Urbana, 1971), pp. 36-37, 109, 115, 175, 242, 292-95; *Seventh Annual Report of the Board of Managers of the Maryland Colonization Society* (Baltimore, 1839), p. 10; George F. Bragg, Jr., *Men of Maryland* (Baltimore, 1925), pp. 59-60; Wright, *Free Negro*, pp. 315, 326; August Meier and Elliott M. Rudwick, *From Plantation to Ghetto* (New York, 1966), pp. 97-98. John W. Blassingame, "The Recruitment of Negro Troops in Maryland," *Maryland Historical Magazine*, LVIII (1963): 21-24; Carter G. Woodson, *The History of the Negro Church* (Washington, 1921), p. 163.

20. Jeffrey R. Brackett, *Notes on the Progress of the Colored Peoples of Maryland Since the War: A Supplement to the Negro in Maryland, A Study in the Institution of Slavery* (Baltimore, 1890), pp. 10, 17-18; Jacob, *The Negro*, pp. 56-57, 66; Benjamin Quarles, *Frederick Douglass* (New York, pp. 1970), 250-51; Margaret Law Calcott, *The Negro in Maryland Politics: 1870-1912* (Baltimore, 1969), pp. 21-23, 24, 34-35, 57-60, 76-78. Only in 1899 did Baltimore not send a completely Democratic slate to Annapolis in that century. Political independents also sought gains for their fellow blacks. Black independents ran for the city council in 1860, 1882, 1885, and 1886. In the last year, S.G. Sanks entered the race for a U.S. congressional seat from Baltimore. All were defeated.

21. Jacob, *The Negro*, pp. 32-84, 86, 141; Calcott, *Negro in Maryland. Politics*, pp. 76-80.

22. Wright, *Free Negro*, pp. 234-37; Quarles, *Douglass*, p. 11; Daniel A. Payne, *History of the African Methodist Episcopal Church* (Nashville, 1891), p. 236.

23. Wright, *Free Negro*, pp. 213, 218, 227; Payne, *History*, pp. 13-15, 21, 109; John Thomas Scharf, *History of Baltimore City and County* (Philadelphia, 1881), p. 581; Noah Davis, *A Narrative of the Life of the Reverend Noah Davis* (Baltimore, 1859), p. 83. By 1870 other important Methodist congregations included Ebenezer AME Church on Montgomery Street (1848), Water's Chapel AME on Jefferson Street (1859), Tessier Street Chapel AME in northwest Baltimore (1869), Mount Zion AME church on Saratoga near Republican Street in west Baltimore (1860), and Orchard Street AME (1837).

24. Payne, *History*, 236; Wright, *Free Negro*, pp. 205-206; J.E.P. Boulden, *The Presbyterians of Baltimore, Their Churches and Historic Graveyards* (Baltimore, 1875), p. 132; Davis, *Narrative*, pp. 83-84, 9-13, 26-34, 44-53; George F. Bragg, Jr., *The First Negro Priest on Southern Soil* (Church Advocate Print, 1909), pp. 9-12, 14,19-25, 36-40; Jacob, *The Negro* pp. 53-54; William Joseph Fletcher, "The Contribution of the Faculty of Saint Mary's Seminary to the Solution of Baltimore's San Dominican Negro Problem, 1793-1852" (M.A. Thesis, Johns Hopkins University, 1951), pp. 18-19, 32-35, 41, 46, 49, 50-51. The black Presbyterian church on Madison Avenue had a small congregation but a large Sunday School enrollment. It began as the Baltimore African Association School on Paca Street with 89 students in 1818. Formally organized as a church by the Reverend John Watts, it met in the "Warfield Church" on Calvert Street until the congregation moved into its permanent home on Madison Avenue, formerly a white Baptist building. On the eve of the war, 240 pupils were attending its school while the resident congregation was a mere 69 members.

25. Richard C. Wade, *Slavery in the Cities* (New York, 1964), pp. 268-269; Jacob, *The Negro*, pp. 45-48, 73-74; Brackett, *History*, pp. 221-222; Wright, *Free Negro*, 252-253; W. A. Low, "The Freedman's Bureau and Education in Maryland," *Maryland Historical Magazine*, XLVII (1952): 32, 34-46; Koger, *Negro Baptists of Maryland*, (Baltimore, 1946), p. 7; Carter G. Woodson *The History of the Negro Church*, (Washington, D.C., 1926), p. 189; Calcott, *Negro in Maryland. Politics*, p. 65.

26. E. Franklin Frazier, *The Negro Church in America*, (New York, 1964), pp. 15-16; Bragg, *Priest*, pp. 35, 47-50; Wright, *Free Negro*, pp. 202, 232-33; Jacob, *The Negro* pp. 52, 77-79; Woodson, *History of Negro Church*, p. 150; Payne, *History*, pp. 182-83; Davis, *Narrative*, p . 84; James G. Fleming, "The Negro Publicly Supported Colleges in Delaware and Maryland," *Journal of Negro*

*Education* (Summer, 1962): 260-74.

27. Wright, *Free Negro*, pp. 236-37, 251; Bragg, *Priest*, pp. 26-30; Brackett, *Notes*, pp. 48-49.

28. Wright, *Free Negro*, p. 251; Brackett, *Notes*, p. 51.

29. Baltimore City Tax Ledgers, 1866; Jacob, *The Negro*, pp. 44-45; Brackett, *Notes*, pp. 30-31.

30. Brackett, *Notes*, p. 41; Bragg, *Men*, pp. 123-24; A. Briscoe Koger, *The Maryland Negro* (Baltimore, 1953), pp. 5, 16; Jacob, *The Negro*, pp. 98, 102-105, 106, 109, 144.

31. U.S. Census (1850). Schedule I (Population), Baltimore City; U.S. Census (1860). Schedule I (Population), Baltimore City; U.S. Census (1870). Schedule I (Population), Baltimore City; Jacob, *Ibid.*

32. The 1970s and 1980s witnessed a veritable renaissance in Baltimore history scholarship. The pre-eminent work was the first modern, scholarly history of the Monumental City in this century--Sherry H. Olson, *Baltimore: The Building of an American City* (Baltimore, 1979). This extraordinary blend of spatial analysis, politial culture, business history, and period photographs captures the cadence of urbanization along the Chesapeake Bay in a way that informs and challenges. Robert J. Brugger, *Maryland: A Middle Temperament, 1634-1980* (Baltimore, 1988) is an exquisitely written synthesis of Maryland politics and culture based on an exhaustive reading of the secondary literature, key Maryland newspapers, and government sources. No one can read this book without coming away with a fuller understanding of Maryland history as a product of its topography and peculiar location among the competing political cultures in the U.S. Researchers would also do well to read over the Fall 1976 (Volume 71) issue of the *Maryland Historical Magazine* for the following articles bearing on 19th century Baltimore: Bettye Gardner, "Ante-bellum Black Education in Baltimore," pp. 360-66; Michael S. Franch, "The Congregational Community in the Changing City, 1840-1870," pp. 367-80; Bettye C. Thomas, "Public Education and Black Protest in Baltimore, 1865-1900," pp. 381-91; and Edward K. Muller and Paul A. Groves, "The Changing Location of the Clothing Industry: A Link to the Social Geography of Baltimore in the Nineteenth Century," pp. 403-20. See also Elizabeth Fee, Linda Shopes & Linda Zeidman, eds., *The Baltimore Book: New Views of Local History* (Philadelphia, 1991); Jean H. Baker, *The Politics of Continuity: Maryland Political Parties from 1858 to 1870* (Baltimore, 1973); Bettye C. Thomas, "A Nineteenth Century Black Operated Shipyard, 1866-1884: Reflections upon Its Inception and Ownership," *Journal of Negro History*, 59 (1974): 1-12; Martha S. Putney,

"The Baltimore Normal School for the Education of Colored Teachers: Its Founders and Its Founding," *Maryland Historical Magazine* 72 (Summer 1977): 238-52; Suzanne E. Greene, "Black Republicans on the Baltimore City Council, 1890-1931," *Maryland Historical Magazine* 74 (Sept. 1979): 203-22; Joseph L. Arnold, "Suburban Growth and Municipal Annexation, 1745-1918," *Maryland Historical Magazine*, 73 (1978): 109-28; Edward K. Muller and Paul A. Groves, "The Emergence of Industrial Districts in Mid-Nineteenth Century Baltimore," *Geographical Review*, 69 (1979): 159-78; and D. Randall Beirne, "Residential Growth Stability in the Baltimore Industrial Community of Canton during the Late Nineteenth Century," *Maryland Historical Magazine*, 74 (1979): 39-51.

33. Olson, *Baltimore*, passim. At some point in the 1930s black churches petitioned the city government to ban the licensing of packaged goods stores in their neighborhods--to no avail.

34. Theodore Hershberg, "Free Blacks in Ante-Bellum Philadelphia; A Study of Ex-Slaves, Freeborn and Socioeconomic Decline," *Journal of Social History* V (Winter, 1971-72): 183-209; Allan H. Spear, *Black Chicago, The Making of a Negro Ghetto, 1890-1920* (Chicago, 1967), pp. 167-79, 223-29. Both of these studies underline the typicality of the two-parent black family in metropolitan areas as early as the 1830s and as late as 1920. The strength of family displayed itself despite far-ranging threats from white job competition and racism, with their attendant effects upon the economic conditions of the black communities in question.

35. Olson, *Baltimore*, pp. 326-27.

36. Beirne, "Residential Growth and Stability," pp. 39-51. As the metropolitan area expanded, it did so heterogeneously, so, for example, the northern and northwestern suburbs became primarily bedroom communities, while Brooklyn, to the south of the city, and Dundalk, to the east in Baltimore County, are industrial suburbs. To this day, Canton, situated just east of the 1870 city limits has a diversifed make-up and continues to house many persons of eastern and southern European descent whose turn-of-the-century fathers and grandfathers actually commuted away from the city to can factories and steel plants.

37. Olson, *Baltimore*, 368-70. The role of black activists in Baltimore throughout this century was an important one and, while local in its focus, enjoyed a dynamic interaction with others who worked for full equality at the national level. The contributions of Baltimore-born Thurgood Marshall, Lillie Jackson, and Mrs. Jackson's daughter, Juanita Jackson Mitchell, and her family in this regard were critical. As a result of their efforts, beginning in the 1960s the number of

professional and technical jobs held by blacks in Baltimore increased fivefold, clerical jobs trippled, and "pink collar jobs"--restaurant and hospital workers and the like-- tripled as well.

38. Olson, *Baltimore*, pp. 274-8, 364; Greene, "Black Republicans," 203-22. David J. Dent, "The New Black Suburbs," *The New York Times Magazine* (June 14, 1992): 18-25. The key point to understanding why the ghetto supplanted alleyway residential patterns is the sheer scarcity of housing open to the black community. What *was* available, owing to a gradually increasing white flight to the suburbs, restrictive real estate practices, housing codes, and the 1910-13 City Council Ordinances which threatened to fine any black family that moved into a white neighborhood, was more and more used housing. Interestingly, according to a recent newspaper account of a new affluent black suburb outside of Washington, D.C., the black middle class, like its 19th-century white ethnic counterpart, may prefer to live in racially homogeneous communities based upon the attainment of wealth--if given the choice.

39. *Baltimore Magazine* (May 1992): 34-39, 70-72. U.S. Department of Commerce, *County & City Data Book, 1988* (Washington, D.C., 1988), pp. 237-49, 658-65, 753.

40. Arnold, "Suburban Growth," pp. 117, 122-25. Garland L. Thompson, "The Cost of Dreams Deferred," *The Sun* (May 16, 1992), pp. 10a. As late as 1918, when the city's annexation of portions of Baltimore and Anne Arundel counties brought it to its present size, Baltimore was able to leverage the votes of suburbanites in referrenda on annexations because the city had services (water, sewerage, etc.) they wanted and were not able to procure from the rural-minded counties they had moved to. When the question of another annexation was taken up in 1967-68, during the state constitutional convention, it was defeated because the postwar growth of the counties had tipped the scales in favor of the suburbanites (over the farmers), who, therefore, no longer needed the city and who wanted no parts of the problems they thought they could leave behind.

# 9

# The Winnebago Urban System:
## Indian Policy and Townsite Promotion On the Upper Mississippi

### Kathleen Neils Conzen

In the late spring of 1848, the Winnebago Indians were once again reluctantly on the move. They had arrived in northeastern Iowa from Wisconsin only six years earlier, but now Iowa had become a state, and one of the terms of its admission was a Federal promise that all the native peoples within its borders would be removed. It took two weeks of intensive negotiations in Washington in 1846 before the Winnebagos consented to give up their Iowa land and move north to central Minnesota, and another year and a half more of government pressure before they actually could be dislodged. Their present country was as good as any they could expect to find, they argued; why should they have to move?[1] Some in protest melted away westward to join kindred tribes along the Missouri River. Others -- as many as 900 -- slipped back in small groups across the Mississippi to roam their original hunting grounds, much to the distress of the white settlers who had appropriated their lands.[2]

Young Henry Mower Rice, one of the Winnebago's licensed traders, won the removal contract. First, he and some of his men went up to the central Minnesota reservation site on the Crow Wing River to construct new agency buildings, and then scoured western Wisconsin for any of the wanderers they could find. In the meantime, the Winnebago's conscientious federal agent, Jonathan Fletcher, tried to convince skeptical tribal leaders that the move was inevitable. The Winnebagos, one of the traders worried in late May, "are getting unmanageable and refuse to go north. I am told that the troops ... had to be ordered out yesterday to keep them from leaving in a body for the Missouri."[3] Dragoons from Iowa's nearby Fort Atkinson--local volunteers, since the regulars had been called away by the Mexican War--certainly lent weight to Fletcher's arguments, as did his determination to pay the Winnebago annuity only in Minnesota. But when the recalcitrant tribe finally started north in early June, the buried caches of corn, axes, feathers, and kettles that they left behind bore witness to their confident plans for a return south once the annuity payments had been made.[4]

They travelled upriver in two unwieldy contingents. One, led by Rice and accompanied by volunteers from Prairie du Chien's Fort Crawford, went by canoe up the Mississippi. The other, with Fletcher, various licensed traders and agency personnel, and the Fort Atkinson dragoons, travelled by pony and wagon along the river's west bank, the wagons driven by sixty teamsters contracted to Rice. Along the east bank, outside of Indian territory and thus beyond federal jurisdiction, a gaggle of unlicensed whiskey traders kept pace with their thirsty customers. The two Winnebago contingents met by prearrangement about a week and a half into the journey at a Dakota village on the river's west bank in southern Minnesota. Here Wabasha, the Dakota chief, offered to sell the Winnebagos land if they cared to remain with his people. Rice in consternation jumped aboard a passing steamboat to seek aid from the federal garrison upriver at Fort Snelling. The garrison captain, Seth Eastman, quickly steamed south with two dozen of his men, some hundred Dakota allies, and the energetic Rice. Eastman, himself a talented artist, also invited along Henry Lewis, a St. Louis panoramist who happened to be working in the area, and the two men's sketches provide a vivid record of the ensuing confrontation.[5]

At Wabasha's prairie, beneath the picturesque bluffs lining the Mississippi, Eastman found perhaps 200 whites uneasily eyeing some seven or eight hundred raucous, well-armed and mounted Dakota and Winnebago warriors. He formed the caravan's wagons into a square closed along the riverbank by his munitions keelboat, and invited the Indians to a conference the next day. During the night, the Indians quietly brought horses and weapons into position around the makeshift fort. Eastman responded at dawn, moving out a line of troops with its center strengthened by two cannons and the sixty teamsters and its flank by his mounted men. The Indians charged Eastman's frightened lines with war whoops and shooting, only to pull back smartly and assure him with high humor that the whole had been no more than a chivalrous display in his honor. The formal conference, with much pipe smoking and speechifying, then took place as scheduled. The precarious peace almost came apart at one point when an Indian, insulted by a drunken volunteer, raised his gun, but before he could fire, it was knocked from his hand by the ever helpful Henry Rice, and the day was saved. Eastman assured the Winnebagos that if they found the new country not to their liking, they could return or find other land, and they finally agreed to continue north. Fletcher took one band off immediately by steamboat, leaving the remaining whites and Indians to face one another warily until its return. "I am *almost* used up, & can think of nothing but Indians," a weary Rice complained to Henry Sibley, his Minnesota business partner. "Wabashaw shall suffer for this. Tomorrow we shall move our camp a short distance in order to get out of the filth that has been accumulating around us for the last two weeks."[6] Wabasha did indeed suffer. Rice had him escorted to Fort Snelling under military arrest as a troublemaker, the Dakota chief laughingly prophesying that he would soon return, which two weeks later he did.

The sorry procession of Winnebagos, its numbers halved by constant quiet desertions, finally arrived on the east bank opposite its destination, 310 miles and 52 days from its Iowa starting-point. Here the Winnebagos faced one final obstacle. The Ojibwas whose land they were to occupy refused to yield possession, since Congress had unilaterally amended the purchase treaty. It took more than a week of negotiations, liberally oiled by the wares of the unlicensed whiskey traders and some $4-5,000 worth of Winnebago gifts and hospitality, before the Ojibwas finally consented, in Fletcher's words, to let the Winnebagos "cross over the Mississippi to take possession of the promised land."[7]

The 1848 Winnebago hegira is in many ways a familiar one, another of the "trails of tears" that recurred only too often in the course of nineteenth century Indian removals, more farcical and less tragic than many, perhaps, but still readily interpreted in accustomed historiographical terms. But it was also something more, something less commonly recognized. It was, I would like to argue, part of a large-scale urban speculation. The players in the speculative game were the Winnebago traders, agents, and their allies. What they were playing for were the federal funds that the Winnebagos represented, and the townsites and city lots into which those funds could be converted. For a decade and a half, the Winnebagos were perhaps the single most important source of development capital in the Upper Mississippi, and men like Henry Rice would capitalize the beginnings of a regional urban system upon their presence. Access to urban opportunity was linked to access to the Indian trade. That link fashioned the structure and early growth of the nascent urban system. Even more irrevocably it fashioned the fate of the Winnebagos themselves.

By the middle decades of the nineteenth century, the frontier mania for townsite speculation had become one of the most dramatic manifestations of the "urban transformation" of American society whose contours Eric Lampard has so compellingly charted.[8] Virgin soil still exerted its mythic lure, but western Americans had well learned that new cities were among its most lucrative crops. "This government land speculation is the surest," a Wisconsin investor observed in 1836, "but there is not so much to be made as there is in town property."[9] Some 700 townsites were reportedly platted in Minnesota alone in 1855; the town promoter had become the prototypical pioneer.[10] One result is well-known to urban historians: an urban system shaped as much by the assumptions, schemes, and boosting of rival speculations as by the logic of urban demand.[11] Another is less familiar, and the subject of this essay: the distortion of Indian policy and the manipulation of tribal fates that was also an early part of the urban transformation.

Cash, as ever, was the nexus binding cities and Indians on the mid-nineteenth century frontier, and it was the Indian trader who forged the bond. The Indian trader has had only a walk-on part in American urban historiography. He is a stock character in the early pages of many a city's biography, familiar and seldom problematized. Revered as the city's "first white (or part-white) settler," as the "founding father' whose vision confirmed the city's site and sometimes its name, he is at the same time generally discounted as an inexperienced and insignificant player in the game of town-lot speculation and city building that followed. Like Chicago's Gurdon Hubbard or John Kinzie, he might be able to convert his fortuitous presence into at least modest speculative wealth, but more often, like that same infant city's Madore Beaubien, he finds the new urban dispensation as culturally alien as do his Indian customers and kin.[12] The broader city-building role of the fur trade itself is similarly downplayed. Earlier in the century, to be sure, when profits were greater and the national economy was less well integrated, the trade could sustain a western city like St. Louis for a decade or two, and yield the wealth that John Jacob Astor went on to invest in New York real estate. But by the 1830s, historians agree, it was no longer an "important economic activity"; it could neither make profits for its participants nor generate appreciable regional economic development.[13]

The very structure of the standard urban narrative, it would seem, reflexively mirrors nineteenth century assumptions about the essential incongruity of Indians and cities, implicitly regarding urban life as "civilization" whose annals begin only when "savagery" is removed.[14] Even historians attuned to the echoes of minority voices find the comings and goings of indigenous predecessors largely irrelevant to the sweep of subsequent urban development.[15] As Bayrd Still observed in one classic urban biography, "neither Indian village nor transient trader could provide the basis of a really permanent community. In fact, it was the absence rather than the presence of the Indians that made possible urban beginnings in the Milwaukee area." [16]

But Indian traders often bore little relationship to the stereotypical urban history image of romantic traditionalists passively entangled in the coils of modernization. They were, after all, and had been since the seventeenth century, point men in a mercantile system linking the wilderness to the European world's city-based commercial core.[17] In the years after 1815, older French and Scottish traders and their offspring were joined in the Midwest by entrepreneurial Yankees who saw in the Indian business a chance for commercial opportunity, and who realized how the terms of the trade could be manipulated to improve their own position during the inevitable "*transit state*" to white settlement.[18] Successful townsite speculation, for example, required capital. Eastern businessmen seeking new outlets for investment provided one possible source.[19] But the Indian trade offered the west a source of development capital of its own. Richard Wade more than three decades ago called attention to the role of federal transfer payments in supporting early urbanization in the west.[20] It was the Federal Treasury, and not fur alone, that Indian traders after the 1830s used their customers to tap. Their complex, ingenious, frequently illegal, and generally unscrupulous strategies, western historians have argued, impoverished the Indians and hastened their removal from the path of white settlement.[21] But such strategies could also, the story of the Winnebago in the upper Mississippi suggests, prolong a local Indian presence, increase Indian exposure to urban influence, redirect the path of tribal migration, and help determine ultimate reservation location, all while laying the basis for a local urban system.

Several circumstances conspired to make the Winnebago-financed urban system in the upper Mississippi possible. One was the state of federal Indian policy. By the 1820s it was clear that American settlers would not coexist with Indian neighbors, and that it would be government policy to effect their removal. But it was equally clear that the government lacked both the will and the power to force wholesale removal through military force. Bribery in the form of tribal annuities and other payments was generally the most viable alternative. It preserved the illusion of compensation for the land the Indians relinquished, and when accompanied by additional monies for education and instruction in agriculture, it held out the hope of ultimate "civilization," particularly if a system of licensed traders could protect the Indians from the corrupting effects of the white man's whiskey. And because Indians were frequently in debt to their traders, who could exert considerable influence and were naturally reluctant to see them depart until their debts were cleared, payment of traders' debts was generally also a part of the treaty process, despite laws to the contrary after 1843.[22]

For the traders, the annuity system was a bonanza that promised all the profits of the fur trade with few of its market uncertainties. Already accustomed to extending credit to Indians in anticipation of the hunt, they could now extend that same credit in anticipation of federal payments, and collect at annuity time. They profited from the inflated prices they charged Indians for trade goods to cover bad debts. They profited again when they collected those bad debts at treaty time. They profited yet again when they sold annuity goods to government agents at marked-up prices; when they bought trust or allotted lands from Indians and resold them to whites; when they demanded compensation for Indian depredations; when they bid on contracts for Indian removal; when they charged Indians attorneys' fees for representing them in negotiations with the government; when they directed trust fund investments. And above all, they profited by selling illegal whiskey. Assuming that through all this they kept the Indians' trust, as many seem to have done, they could then move west with the tribe and begin the cycle anew. Only licensed traders could deal on Indian land, and the agents assigned to individual tribes to oversee the treaty relationship were also charged with insuring the honesty of the traders. Such a system was highly susceptible to political pressure and fraud, and even honorable agents often found their powers limited.[23]

This situation, arising from the peculiar combination of land hunger and conscience that motivated American Indian policy, offered unusual opportunity to the hard-dealing trader, and by the early 1840s, as the era of the fur trade gave way in the Upper Mississippi to what can be termed the era of the Indian business, there was no longer a dominant trading monopoly to control competition. This was the second important circumstance that shaped speculation in the Upper Mississippi. International depression and competition from the upstart Fort Wayne, Indiana, firm of W.G. and G.W. Ewing pushed the old American Fur Company into bankruptcy in the early 1840s and spun off a series of successor firms, the most important of which would ultimately be consolidated under the aegis of Pierre Chouteau, Jr. and Co. of St. Louis, and carry the old company's name. Only their close involvement with the business of Indian removal saved the Ewings from sharing the collapse of the A.F.C. They came west with their customers when the Indians of northern Indiana were removed to Iowa, Kansas, and Nebraska in the early 1840s, and found themselves in direct competition with the Chouteau group in its own back yard.[24]

Finally, the peculiarities of time and place also played their role. When Wisconsin entered the union in 1848, Minnesota was left to organize as a territory at a time when virtually its entire white population was involved in the Indian trade, and almost all of its land was still Indian country closed to white settlement. The Indians and their federal monies were the new territory's main resource, and there was little to counteract their wholesale exploitation.[25] A settler-dominated territory might be expected to press for Indian removal, but factions in a trader-dominated territory could be counted on to fight over their retention and location.

There was, to be sure, no single grand, carefully structured plot to convert Winnebago annuities into an urban system.  There were, rather, numerous actors scrambling to make money in a fluid situation, whose individual promotional activities added up to what became, in effect, both a town promotion scheme and an Indian policy.  But there was no man to whose mind the logic of the Winnebago system unfolded more clearly than Henry Mower Rice, and no man who did more to make it a reality. Rice is a hard man to pin down.  There can be few U.S. Senators who have more effectively covered their tracks.  His papers are a masterpiece of expurgation, and his story has to be pieced together from Indian Office records, scattered correspondence, and casual references in newspapers, memoirs, and local histories.  But its outlines are clear enough for present purposes.[26]

Rice, a young, academy-educated Vermonter with two years of legal training under his belt, had followed his prominent guardian's investments and family to the Michigan frontier in the boom years of the 1830s, where he presumably apprenticed in the essentials of successful land speculation. He did some state surveying and worked for a Kalamazoo mercantile house before heading further west on foot with a pack on his back --or so he later told the tale -- when times grew slack.  In 1839 he signed on with the A.F.C. as a sutler's clerk at Minnesota's Fort Snelling, and when troops were sent south the following year to keep an eye on the Winnebagos in Iowa, he took the sutler's post at the new Fort Atkinson.  Michigan tradition insists that he played a major role in the disreputable business of Potawatomi removal from the Kalamazoo area that summer; if so, he kept this fact from his later Minnesota hagiographers.  At any rate, he acquired a taste for the Indian trade, and a vision of the way that trade could open the path to wider opportunity.  "In a few years there will be a great opportunity for speculation," he wrote Henry Sibley from Fort Atkinson in 1841, "and we ought to be prepared to act.  I mean to be on the ground and invest at every opportunity .... Henceforth I will cast my lot in the Northwest and am confident I will never regret it."[27] Rice in 1842 abandoned his government post to sign on as Winnebago trader for the A.F.C.'s Western Outfit operating out of Prairie du Chien under the direction of Hercules Dousman.  Red-haired, ambitious, and reckless, with the vision to conceive grand projects and the charm to convince even the most cautious businessman that he might bring them to fruition, Rice was also, or so his enemies would charge, unscrupulous and duplicitous.  The thrill of the game seems to have meant as much to him as its profits.   "It is gratifying to me to know that my people are beating the opposition -- it makes one feel strong," he once observed; his maxim was, "If we make nothing, none else shall."[28]

Sibley, who had been the A.F.C.'s principal trader with the Dakotas in Minnesota since the early 1830s, was a different breed of man.  The son of a Michigan Supreme Court justice, he was both more cultured and yet more culturally at home in Indian country than his slightly younger colleague.  He was attracted to many of the values of the bi-racial trading community that he had joined at 18, and saw himself as a young patriarch or guardian to "his" people.  He fathered a Dakota daughter, revelled in the buffalo huntswhich he reported on to an eastern sporting journal under the nom-de-plume of "Hal, A Dakota" -- and found it difficult to believe that even a half century would see much change in primitive Minnesota life.  Rice would convince him otherwise.  As Sibley later recalled, "when Mr. Rice began investing tens of thousands of dollars in good American gold" -- originally paid out as Indian annuities, we might note, though Sibley did not -- "in claims and other ways, we were converted to his way of thinking."[29]

It was when pressure mounted to remove the Winnebagos from Iowa that Rice found himself in position to make his major play.  The Winnebagos were a Siouan people whose historic home was in east central Wisconsin.  For more than a century and a half, they had lived upon and helped construct what Richard White has termed the "middle ground," the cultural space within which Indians and whites mutually accommodated one another for trade and military alliance.  By the 1820s that middle ground was passing, as aggressive American settlers rejected its terms.  Established conventions for avoiding vengeance and covering the dead broke down, and the Winnebagos found themselves in a miniature "war" with the Americans in 1827 that ended with the surrender of a significant part of their territory and the acceptance in 1829 of their first annuity from the federal government.  It took two more treaties in 1832 and 1837, and further annuities, before the federal government, desperate to move them off their lead-rich Wisconsin land, finally got them to accept, at least in theory, an Iowa reservation that placed them as a buffer between the Sioux and their enemies, the Sacs and Foxes.[30]

Traders played a critical role in the protracted treaty process that left the Winnebagos relatively speaking "the richest tribe on the continent".

As Wisconsin's territorial governor, Henry Dodge, noted in 1840, "It is a fact well known to all conversant and acquainted with our Indian relations, that the agents of the Government are obliged, to a certain extent, to be dependent -- on the traders for the influence they exercise over the Indians committed to their charge; and such is the influence of the traders, that the Government of the United States cannot now make a treaty with the Indians, without securing to them important pecuniary advantages."[32] By 1846 the Winnebago, a tribe of fewer than 2600 members, was receiving roughly $93,000 annually in services, supplies, and gold.[33] "What a source of wealth, for so small a tribe," remarked the son of one of their early agents. "Truly may it be said, that with the slightest exertions on their part, and with a proper expenditure of their money, they need never want. But it is from the very amount of these resources that they must be protected. So large an amount being annually paid to them cannot fail of attracting a hoard of traders, peddlers, etc., whose only object will be to get their money for little or nothing."[34]

His prophecy proved correct. "Never," in the words of a later Minnesota historian, "did traders have fatter picking than did those among the Winnebago."[35] Those pickings both biased the removal process and promoted tribal degeneration. They swayed the small traders of Portage, Wisconsin -- "a set of loafers and whiskey sellers, who depend for a livelihood, on what they can *hook* from the Indians at the time they receive their annuities" -- to abet the Winnebagos in their reluctance to leave the region.[36] Large and small Wisconsin traders alike combined to thwart government efforts -- promoted by the Ewings -- to move the Winnebagos further west to the new Indian territory beyond the Missouri.[37] The 1837 treaty that provided for removal to Iowa was fraudulent in a triple sense: tribal members not authorized to engage in treaty negotiations were brought to Washington under false pretenses, compelled to remain until they feared for their families' well-being with the onset of winter, and then told that the treaty they were signing gave them eight years before moving, when they actually had only eight months.[38] Corrupt manipulation of the treaty's provisions for traders' claims and half-breed allotments -- the former involving the larger traders, the latter the treaty commissioners themselves -- further delayed Winnebago departure, helped create an enduring tribal split, provoked the tragic murder of one of their most popular traders, and helped bring down a subsequent Commissioner of Indian Affairs.[39]

The move to Iowa failed to remove the Winnebagos from the temptation of the traders. The east bank of the Mississippi across the river from Indian country was soon lined with independent transients operating small posts -- many of them little more than grog shops -- for the Winnebago trade, most drawing their supplies from reputable Prairie du Chien merchants like Dousman of the A.F.C. Others clustered just beyond the boundaries of the Iowa reservation, most notably at a site soon known as "Sodom."[40] One small east bank trader took in $1,000 in silver after the annuity payments in his first trading season.[41] The extent of the traders' profits were mirrored in the tribe's increasing dissipation and social disintegration. "It is no uncommon occurrence for an Indian to leave one of these dens of infamy stripped of his horse, gun, blanket, and indeed every thing belonging to him of the slightest value," one contemporary complained. "They neglected their hunts, and their cornfields; and when these resources failed them, they prostituted their wives and daughters in order to obtain the means of intoxication," observed another.[42]

It was a situation tailor-made for the talents of a man on the make like Henry Rice. The licensed trade at the Iowa agency itself was fiercely contested between Rice, representing the A.F.C., and the Ewings' man, David Olmsted.[43] It was Rice who succeeded best in gaining the trust of the Winnebagos, aided by the tribe's long-standing links with the A.F.C. and perhaps by his own familial relations with individual Winnebagos.[44] He supported the "treaty-abiding" segment of the tribe -- those who had removed to Iowa, as opposed to the "disaffected bands" who obstinately clung to the Wisconsin woods -- in its resistance to repeated federal proposals for a move west of the Missouri, and as early as 1844 began exploring for them an alternative northern site in Sioux country on Minnesota's Blue Earth River.[45] When in 1846 pressures for removal from Iowa finally became too great to withstand, this Minnesota lure was used to bring the Winnebagos to a treaty council. Accompanying them to Washington as their interpreter was Rice's former clerk and future partner, Sylvanus B. Lowry; Rice met them there.[46]

The Winnebago's federal agent later asserted that without Lowry's

influence there would have been no treaty; Rice's hand was even more in
evidence. The federal commissioners first repeated, for the fifth time in
four years, their offer of a Kansas reservation, but then came back
with the Minnesota alternative. Negotiations stuck at two points: the
Winnebagos wanted the land on the Blue Earth while the commissioners
wanted them farther from white settlements in the forests to the north,
and the Winnebagos demanded $400,000 in cash while the government
was willing to offer only $150,000, along with another $40,000 for
removal expenses and the first year's subsistence. "Your Great Father,"
the commissioners insisted, "has done making treaties for the Traders, or
at their dictation." But when negotiations resumed a few days later, there
was a new official delegate on the Winnebago side: Watch-ha-ta-kaw,
also known as One-Eye Decorah, was conveniently ill, and Henry Rice
had taken his place. Final terms now were quickly agreed upon: the
government's commitment remained at $190,000, $40,000 of which, it
was now stipulated, was to be used by the Winnebagos "to comply with
their present just engagements, and to cover the expenses of exploring
and selecting (by their own people, or by an agent of their own
appointment) their new home." As that clause suggested, the exact site of
the reservation was left for later determination. By whom? "We want
our friend (Mr. Rice) who has helped us to make this treaty to go along
and act for us when the country for our home is selected." Among the 24
"Winnebago" signatories of the treaty was Henry M. Rice.[47]

Rice selected for the Winnebagos neither the prairie tract in Sioux
country that they had wanted, nor the kind of isolated site that the
government had envisioned. Instead, he chose 890,700 acres of forested
Ojibwa land along the Crow Wing River on the west side of the Mississippi
in the central part of the territory.[48] His motives in choosing this site have
seemed inexplicable.[49] The Winnebago's new home, like their old, was
just across the Mississippi from legal territory for whiskey traders, stood
squarely in the path of development, and its thick brush bore little
resemblance to the prairies that the treaty bands had learned to hunt. From
Rice's perspective, however, the logic was clear. He was investing his
best asset where he could anticipate the greatest return. The Ewings had

pressed to move the Winnebagos into their trading territory along the Missouri, but they were temporarily discredited by shady dealings that lost them their Iowa trading licenses, and the most they could do was to fan the flames of Winnebago reluctance to move.[50] To move the Winnebago north to Minnesota, by contrast, was to move them and their funds directly into an area of A.F.C. dominance. To move them as far north as the Crow Wing was also, thanks to a series of maneuvers in 1846 and early 1847, to move them into an area controlled by Rice himself Upon Dousman's retirement, he and Sibley had divided the old A.F.C.'s upper Mississippi trade between them, Sibley retaining his Dakota interests and Rice taking over much of Dousman's Ojibwa as well as Winnebago business; by moving the Winnebagos into Ojibwa rather than Dakota territory, Rice insured that their annuities would remain with him, and strengthened his position in the Ojibwa trade.[51]

Rice reportedly never visited the country he acquired for the Winnebagos. He did, however, receive $3,000 from the tribe for his services in the matter. His overall assistance in negotiations and removal reportedly cost the Winnebagos $17,906.94 over and above his share of the $40,000 treaty-stipulated debt settlement with the traders. Lowry got a $1,000 bonus for assisting Rice and the others in convincing the Winnebagos to authorize these expenditures, and then billed them $614 for his interpreter's services during their move north.[52] If Rice felt his patience sorely tried by Winnebago footdragging at Wabasha's Prairie, it was small recompense for what he and his associates were costing them. As Rice moved to parlay these payments into real estate in Minnesota's newly rechristened east bank whiskey trader's community of St. Paul, the scope of the development vision that he had set in motion by removal began to emerge. The Winnebagos were to be his "California lode," as his admiring contemporaries soon put it.[53] Securely lodged in his mercantile backyard, their trade would be channeled into both licensed and unlicensed trading posts under his control. He would locate those posts at sites propitious for the Winnebago trade, to be sure, but he would also locate them with a view towards future townsite development, and he would make his land claims with that goal in mind. He would invest his Indian profits in townsites and city lots, and in the kinds of infrastructure necessary to promote their development, whether it was constructing hotels or mills, donating lots to churches, investing in a steamboat line, or promoting a railroad. And he would convert the local power so attained into political influence in Minnesota and Washington, through lobbying, elective office, and Democratic Party politics, to guarantee that his source of federal funds continued to flow. His initial investments may have been relatively small -- $40,000 by 1850 is one figure that appears in an early history -- but they provided the vital spark, his contemporaries agreed, that set Minnesota development in motion.[54]

Rice almost overreached himself in the initial exhilaration of this successful development strategy. As early as the autumn of 1848, playing what observers termed "a deep and strong game," he mounted a futile challenge against Sibley for the office of territorial delegate, using his new St. Paul real estate to reward potential supporters; even the Winnebagos up north on their reserve followed the contest, some of them siding with Sibley.[55] "He cannot floor me," he wrote darkly of Sibley; "I am anxious to get *ahead* of my enemies."[56] Emboldened perhaps by his success in wooing and winning a Richmond belle during a lobbying visit to Washington that winter, he next tried to bypass Sibley and make a private trading arrangement with Chouteau. Sibley in response initiated an investigation of Rice's books, the partnership collapsed in a welter of public accusations and lawsuits, and a humiliated Rice temporarily joined trading forces with the hated Ewings. What particularly enraged Sibley was the legal technicality that enabled Rice to treat as personal property the valuable St. Paul real estate that he had purchased with what Sibley regarded as company funds. Sibley estimated his losses at $25,000. Rice for his part was heard to vow that he "would live to ride over you all," and the ensuing feud gave Minnesota competing foci for political and economic development energies for over a decade.[57]

St. Paul was undoubtedly the centerpiece of the urban system that Rice sought to build. It was the head of reliable navigation on the Mississippi, the centerpiece for goods and settlers, the warehousing center for the territory's trade. Sibley had long been established on a low-lying island a few miles upriver beneath Fort Snelling; it took Rice to see the advantages of moving headquarters out of Indian country to a site with legal land titles and unregulated trade. In June of 1849 he floated his family down to St. Paul in a birchbark canoe to establish his home there, and was soon busy constructing warehouses and business blocks. In the debacle with Sibley, he made it a central object to "save my real estate for I have enough of that to make me well off." Two years later, he could note with satisfaction that "The town is growing unusually fast, I sold an unimproved lot yesterday for 800$ -- last week I sold one for 300$. I have about 80 left all good lots and am in hopes to sell most of them early in the Spring."[58]

But St. Paul's growth was not the only urban product of the new trading order. The Winnebagos' sojourn in western Wisconsin and Iowa had already created one local urban system. Prairie du Chien, of course, had a history as a fur trade center long antedating the Winnebago reserve in the area, but its growth had received a major fillip from the Winnebago presence, and Rice himself was a prominent early town lot investor.[59] La Crosse was a more direct beneficiary, originating as an unlicensed east bank post whose five small traders cooperated to insure that each was able to bid in his claim unopposed when federal land sales opened in 1848, and whose initial plat, additions, and town boosting were all the products of Winnebago trader initiative.[60] Even small posts like that at Trempealeau were located "more to hold the town site than for the purposes of trading with the Indians," an early trader recalled.[61] As settlement advanced, successful speculation enabled some traders to drop out of the Winnebago urban system, so to speak, and become local capitalists and town fathers. At Prairie du Chien Hercules Dousman--of whom one competitor dryly noted that he arrived "in the autumn of 1827 ... and has ever since steadily pursued what he appeared to have most taste for, the accumulation of wealth" --was one particularly prominent example; Joseph Levy of La Crosse was another. Levy, a London-born German Jew, entered the fur trade in St. Louis, worked next in Prairie du Chien, and was trading at the La Crosse site when settlement caught up with him; he went on to plat one of the first additions, opened a hotel, and died decades later after a satisfying career as forwarding and commission merchant, lumber and real estate dealer, banker, and three-term mayor.[62]

Now, as the Winnebagos moved to Minnesota, many of their unlicensed east bank traders from downriver hastened to repeat the process, setting up grog shops at every likely townsite along the east bank of the Mississippi from St. Paul to the northern boundary of the new Winnebago reserve. Thomas A. Holmes, for example, was already established at a prime river crossing near the reserve when the first Winnebagos arrived. Holmes was a colorful and even tragic character in the eyes of his acquaintances, a fifty-year-old Pennsylvanian with a *"demon of unrest"* unleashed by a beautiful wife too genteel for either the crude frontier or her mismatched husband. "While I can only just about write my name now," he once said of himself, "*I can skin a musk-rat quicker than an Indian.*" When his wife found refuge and then death in drug addiction, he had established an enduring relationship with a Dakota woman, and now, after an unsuccessful east bank venture at the site of Fountain City, was ready to try his luck on the next frontier.[63]

Rice was not content to leave either the Winnebago trade or its attendant townsite promotion to independents like Holmes and others of his ilk. On his way north to locate the agency site at the Crow Wing River reserve, for example, he stopped in La Crosse to pick up two of the old east bank traders, Asa White and Nathan Myrick. White remains a shadowy figure -- he was a 28-year-old Pennsylvanian who had been trading on a small scale with the Winnebagos in the La Crosse area for several years, and had taken as his wife "a most uncouth sample of a Winnebago squaw" -- but Myrick, two years younger, was already an important operator.[64] Academy-educated, the eldest son of a prosperous Lake Champlain area entrepreneur, he left home at 19 with his father's reluctant consent, $100 in savings, and $15 hidden by his mother in his bible. He began in east bank Winnebago trading in a small way, then used his father's credit to establish his own relationship with a New York supplier, becoming so successful that the A.F.C. was forced to buy him out. A markedly tall, nervous, and energetic man whose willingness to take business risks matched that of Rice -- a "rustler" in the parlance of the day -- he had already used his Winnebago profits to plat the townsite of La Crosse. During the trip north, Rice, as Myrick later recalled, "made me some propositions in regard to business enterprises which I thought best to accept."[65]

The upshot was that Myrick built a trading post for Rice on the east bank just south of the new Winnebago reserve, while White located a similar post at a busy ford a few miles north. Between them, they had claimed the two most likely sites for the Winnebago whiskey trade.[66] As licensed traders at the Long Prairie agency on the new reserve, Rice established his brother, Charles, and Sylvanus Lowry.[67] At least six other sites up and down the river were also claimed by Rice and his crew of dependent downriver Winnebago traders, including a post a few miles north of White operated by Edwin A. E. Hatch, a boyhood friend and sometime clerk of Myrick's, a man "of peculiar character" who had adapted readily to Indian ways and Indian women, and had assisted in the Winnebago removal.[68] In an audacious coup, Rice also convinced the army to locate its new Fort Ripley north of the Winnebago reserve where it could serve -- and be served by -- both his Winnebago and his Ojibwa posts, rather than to the south where it might have played some logical role in containing the Winnebagos on their land.[69]

At each trading site, Rice made sure that his men filed land claims. Successful sites tended to attract not only independent smallfry, but often a competing trader in the Ewing interest and, after the split between Sibley and Rice, a Sibley man as well. The result sometimes would be adjacent sites competing for ultimate urban honors; sometimes the competing interests vied to promote a single site. Newspapers, hotels, steamboat landings, sawmills, gristmills, stagecoach lines, mail contracts -- all were weapons in the competition, and all helped promote the growth and development of nascent cities and the profits of their proprietors. All three competitors, for example, underwrote trading ventures to secure the urban potential of Wabasha's picturesque prairie where the Winnebagos had staged their abortive revolt, though it was a fourth player -- the captain of a steamboat in which Rice held a share -- who secured what proved to be the actual site of the future city of Winona.[70] But some of the most dramatic maneuverings occurred below the southern boundary of the new Winnebago reserve, near the rapids at the mouth of the Sauk.

Myrick's initial Sauk Rapids site ended up in the hands of the Sibley group after the split (Olmsted traded there briefly also, in the Ewing interest), while Rice's men focused their attention on the Watab site established by White a few miles upriver. Well-situated for trade not only with the Winnebagos but with the developing pineries to the northeast and with Canada's Red River settlements to the northwest, one or the other of these trading posts seemed clearly destined to become a significant town, and their rivalry became intense.[71] Watab, with a better location and personal connections for the Winnebago trade, took the initial lead. After a season or two most Winnebago bands abandoned their Long Prairie agency site -- purposely located well away from the river and its tempting trading posts -- to camp across the river from Watab, and soon, recalled one of the early traders, were "roaming around looking for a chance to play poker or some other gambling game, at which many of them were

experts, or to obtain whiskey, for which they would give their last blanket."
Soldiers from Fort Ripley made periodic raids to destroy whiskey and
"break up arrangements for furnishing it" to the Winnebagos, and the
Winnebagos periodically broke into or fired warehouses when the liquor
flow was dammed. Lowry moved his main trading operations to Watab
in 1851, and soon became the infant townsite's principal promoter.[72]

But Sauk Rapids had advantages of its own. It was the last upriver
site that could be served by very shallow draft steamboats from St. Anthony
Falls above St. Paul, making it the logical entrepot for future white
settlement in the region, and its rapids promised waterpower. Equally
important was the fact that Sibley allies dominated the territorial legislature
when the time came to designate a county seat, and that Sibley was the
territorial delegate in Washington when the time was ripe to open a federal
land office in the area. Sauk Rapids gained both plums, despite Lowry's
campaigns for Watab, and as the end of the Indian era approached, the
A.F.C. traders there began developing the waterpower, printing a
newspaper, and encouraging friends and relatives from Michigan to
settle.[73] Watab responded with an attempt to snatch the county seat in
1856 once the Rice faction gained ascendancy in the territorial legislature,
and a new infusion of downstream money flowed in, but in vain; Sauk
Rapids, it seemed, simply was better situated for white settlement.[74] But
Lowry in the meantime began to develop another townsite across the
river that soon attracted other speculators, and it was this site, St. Cloud,
that would win the urban laurels in the end.[75] Lowry did not live long to
enjoy his triumph, dying prematurely in 1865 of a mysterious mental
illness and leaving his estate tied up in litigation for years. Raised among
the Winnebagos by his missionary parents, official Winnebago mouthpiece
at virtually every council through 1859, Lowry was "a man who has
nothing American about him, in morals, manners, dress, or habits of life,
except the characteristic traits of its savage, silent and stealthy Aborigines,"
as one political enemy scathingly observed. "In his haughty reserve, in
his low cunning, in his love for fire water and vulgar games of chance,
and in his treatment of women he is all the Indian." There may be no
better index of the depth of the region's urban speculative fever than the
way in which it so absorbed the attentions of such a man.[76]

As Henry Rice extended his sphere of operations deeper into Ojibwa
territory, and began to meddle also in Sibley's Dakota business, his urban

promotions moved with him. He acquired significant holdings at the future site of Minneapolis early in 1850, for example, while a fleeting visit to Traverse des Sioux in 1852 to test the Dakota trade led to yet another townsite claim.[77] In 1857 he became involved in a speculation at Breckenridge on the Red River, also in Dakota territory.[78] His plans for Ojibwa country culminated after 1853 in a grandiose promotion at Superior, Wisconsin, that entangled two Democratic presidential candidates in its complex web of railroad speculation and bribery before it collapsed in the Civil War crisis.[79] By this time, Rice himself was sitting in the Senate (he was one of the two first Senators sent to Washington after statehood in 1858), and Sibley had completed a term as Minnesota's first state governor. Like St. Cloud and Winona, some of the sites promoted by Rice and his associates and rivals would grow into significant regional towns. Others like Watab, or Itasca further downstream, would wither and disappear.[80] But the outlines of an urban system were being laid in a conscious conjunction of the Indian business and urban promotion, and never was truth so tersely told as in a satirical notice that appeared in a parody newspaper ostensibly printed at Rice's Watab post in 1851: "The Bank of Watab. Open daily from 10 a.m. until an indefinite hour of the night. Baptiste, pres't, One-Eye-Dacoffa, Cash."[81] Baptiste and One-Eye, needless to say, were Winnebago chiefs.

Winnebago money indeed remained a prime asset in these development schemes through the mid-1850s. The Winnebagos never accepted their new country. No sooner were they settled on their Minnesota reserve in 1848 than their agent, leaving for St. Louis by steamer to collect the annuity funds, found among his fellow passengers some of the very Indians whom he had just escorted north at such trouble and expense. "There was no Game in [the country] but frogs," objected One-Eye, and "the bush was so thick that a rabbit could not get through it." Nor did they appreciate having the relatively impoverished Ojibwas as neighbors, since traditional customs of gift-giving, they complained, meant that the Ojibwas ended up enjoying vastly more of their annuities than they did.[82] Soon Minnesotans became familiar with the nocturnal sight of Winnebago canoes drifting silently south under the walls of Fort Snelling, and distinctive Winnebago graves began to appear along the trails downriver.[83] First they drifted away from Long Prairie and toward the whiskey posts on the Mississippi, and then gradually southwards. By late 1853, only about 300 remained at the agency and a handful at the river; a year later, most were back in southeastern Minnesota and Iowa, in Wisconsin, or on the Missouri.[84]

The Winnebagos kept pressing for a new reserve so they wouldn't have to keep returning north to receive their annuities. The Ewings continued scheming to remove them to the Missouri, citizens of Wisconsin, Iowa, and southern Minnesota kept complaining of depredations by wandering Winnebagos -- and the Minnesota government and Minnesota traders kept insisting that the Winnebagos should be made to stay. The traders' interest was in the Winnebago debts. "The old Winnebago traders," the territorial governor noted, "intend to keep these Indians on the wing and discontented until they get what they call their *claims'* agst (sic) them."[85] Rice had even attempted to recoup his fortunes in 1851 with a government contract to remove to the Long Prairie agency, at $70 per person, any Winnebagos he could find who were not in their own territory. It was, the governor observed, a "pretty speculation," since even half that price would have yielded a good profit -- had Rice been able to find enough of the elusive Winnebagos to recoup his initial investment. There was public outcry and a congressional investigation -- instigated by Sibley -- of the political chicanery that had led to this contract, and it took Rice years to collect.[86]

But in general, there was wide support for efforts to keep the Winnebagos in the territory. When Rice and the Ewings briefly flirted with promoting Winnebago removal to Missouri in 1852, with the hope of profiting from the removal contract, for example, the territorial government exerted its full influence to block them. "Should the removal be effected it would work great detriment to the Territory," the administration maintained, "by diverting the large amount of payments made by the Government to the Winnebagoes."[87] In 1851, over and above the annuity goods and services they received, every Winnebago man, woman, and child was entitled to $35 annually in gold or silver, averaging from $175-350 per family, far more specie than most white settlers ever saw in a year. No other Indian tribe in the nation received even half as much in aggregate federal appropriations in 1852; the Winnebagos in that year received just under half of all moneys appropriated to Indian tribes. Even election bets were depressed in Minnesota when Winnebago annuities were late.[88] By late 1853, though most Winnebagos had effectively removed themselves, the territorial governor was still reminding Washington that "Minnesota in her infancy owed much of her prosperity to these same Winnebagos, that they were the pioneers -- that in their path the white man followed and settled the country -- that the time is not forgotten when the suspension or postponement of a Winnebago annuity payment was considered a public calamity, and that even now the removal of the Winnebago from Minnesota would be considered a serious drawback on her prosperity."[89]

In late 1853, Rice was still dependent enough upon his Winnebago bankers to stir up successful opposition both locally and in Washington when the territorial governor negotiated a treaty with the Winnebagos that would have legalized their de facto occupation of prairie land south of their reserve but that did not provide for traders' claims.[90] Within two years, however, circumstances had changed. Following the scandal-ridden Sioux and Ojibwa treaties of the early 1850s, for which they assiduously worked and which cleared many of their debts, Sibley and Rice both gradually withdrew from the Indian business for the now greener pastures of politics, pineries, and railroad promotion, and the Ewings too essentially closed down.[91] Lumberinen began coveting the accessible timber on Winnebago land, and the rising tide of white settlement caused town promoters to reevaluate the unsavory local consequences of dependence on the Indian trade. "There is a point beyond which forbearance ceases to be a virtue," a Watab grand jury charged in late 1852. "We submit that as American citizens, we have a right to demand that this drawback to our interests, welfare, and prosperity, this evil now become intolerable among the Citizens of this County should be removed without delay."[92] With major opposition thus removed, the Winnebagos in early 1855 were finally able to exchange their northern country for the land south of the Minnesota that they had wanted all along, and with no provision for traders' debts. White squatters in that area were furious, but the federal government was desperate for any solution that might induce the Winnebagos to congregate in one place, and Minnesota would still retain their annuities. After seven years of passive resistance, the Winnebagos had seemingly won. In mid-June "the entire Winnebago tribe, over two thousand strong," with Agent Fletcher again in the van, broke "like an avalanche" upon their new reserve. Moving with them, inevitably, were their current traders -- men like Asa White with familial and cultural ties to the tribe, or ambitious newcomers like Joseph Levy's former clerk, Isaac Marks, who had arrived too late to cash in on the earlier Winnebago frontiers.[93]

There was to be no happy ending for the Winnebagos on the Blue Earth, however. A significant proportion of the tribe's annuities were due to expire in 1859, and faced with imminent loss of income, the Winnebagos listened to their traders when they proposed yet another treaty. The 1855 treaty, in accord with prevailing federal Indian policy, foresaw the allotment of the new reserve into individual farms; the new 1859 treaty now provided for the sale of half the reserve to pay outstanding traders' debts and finance the establishment of individual farms, and for the individual allotment of the remainder -- "so as to give them an idea of individual property, and a greater incentive to personal exertion and industry," in the words of their agent, but also, in the minds of their traders, something more to sell. The 1859 treaty negotiations were the capstone to Sylvanus Lowry's productive career as official Winnebago interpreter.[94] Three years later, the Winnebagos petitioned Congress for permission to expend a lump sum from their trust fund so that they could delay land sales in hopes of a better market. Was this, one congressman inquired of his Minnesota colleagues, "a mere grab for some speculators to take money away from the Indians?" Cyrus Aldrich earnestly denied that this was the case. Congress laughed.[95]

Until the bloody Dakota revolt in the Minnesota valley in 1862, it looked as if the Winnebagos might actually settle down to successful farming on the Blue Earth. Few Winnebagos participated in the revolt; indeed, many of the most acculturated were serving in the Union Army at the time. But they were Indians, they occupied rich land, and their satisfied former traders had little further interest in defending their presence. Business leaders at the nearby townsite of Mankato, arguing that only removal would guarantee local prosperity, formed the semisecret "Knights of the Forest" to press for that end, and the Winnebagos were summarily swept along in the Dakota removal to a barren reserve at Crow Creek in South Dakota. Fifteen years earlier, on the Winnebago trek north from Iowa, Wabasha had responded to the lure of Winnebago gold with an offer to sell them some of his land; this time it was the Omahas of northeastern Nebraska, with whom many of the disaffected Winnebago bands had long hunted, who made a similar offer as the Winnebagos were escorted up the Missouri. When failed crops and a corrupt supply system took a cruel toll that first winter on Crow Creek, the Winnebagos simply did what they were now well accustomed to doing: they slipped away once again, downriver to take up the Omaha offer and finally buy a reserve of their own. Enough of the disaffected bands kept returning to Wisconsin that in 1874, they too were permitted to claim legal homesteads there if they wished.[96]

Even in these last sad stages of their upper Midwestern pilgrimage, the Winnebagos continued to serve as an urban development fund, though by now for smaller fry than Henry Rice. Wherever the Winnebagos had halted, some of their traders remained behind to cash in on the urban boom they left in their wake -- Dousman in Prairie du Chien, Joseph Levy in La Crosse, the Bunnells in Winona, Rice in St. Paul, Lowry in St. Cloud -- and now Asa White and Isaac Marks, among others, repeated the process at Mankato on the Minnesota.[97] Rice himself maintained some interest in Mankato townsite speculations.[98] Contractor for the removal to South Dakota was another familiar player, the Chouteau company; the special removal agent was none other than Edwin A. C. Hatch, Myrick's boyhood friend, assisted by others of the old downriver Winnebago traders.[99] Mankato businessmen may have wanted the Indians out of their immediate backyard, but managed to retain an effective lien on Winnebago funds, probably with the conscious assistance of the Republican appointee in charge of the Northern Superintendency, southern Minnesota businessman Clark W. Thompson. Not only were the Winnebagos' licensed traders two Mankato merchants -- one of them a trusted associate of Thompson -- but when charged to select a reservation site near the army's Fort Randall to insure easy supervision, Thompson chose one of the first sites upriver from that fort that could be logically supplied overland from Minnesota rather than via the Missouri, despite the site's complete lack of any other advantages to recommend it. Thompson then delayed supplying the new agency until it was too late in the season to reach it by water, guaranteeing that initial supply contracts went to Mankato merchants, who exulted in a "Minnesota System" worth, they estimated, $100,000 to $150,000 in annual business for the area. While the contracts proved profitable for Mankato-area suppliers and merchants, their overland winter expedition fell disastrously short of meeting the Indians' needs.[100] The Winnebago's first agent in Nebraska, a Winona druggist, was credibly accused of feathering his own nest at Winnebago expense, and retired to invest his profits in Omaha newspapering and real estate promotion; his successor promoted a Nebraska townsite of his own.[101]

The Winnebago urban system had clearly survived yet another transplantation. Little wonder, then, at how the Winnebagos reacted when a shanty town sprouted on the fringes of their reservation with the coming of the railroad in 1881: galloping their ponies into town at dawn, they gave the startled squatters no more than an hour to pack up and move over the line. Barely a board was left behind. [102]

"How solemn and beautiful is the thought," mused Mark Twain in 1883, "that the earliest pioneer of civilization, the vanleader of civilization, is never the steamboat, never the railroad, never the newspaper, never the Sabbath-school, never the missionary -- but always the whiskey!" Meditating upon the origins of the city of St. Paul, he grasped the central process that brought urban development to the Upper Mississippi. "Look history over, you will see. The missionary comes after the whiskey -- I mean he arrives after the whiskey has arrived; next comes the poor inmigrant, with axe and hoe and rifle; next the trader; next, the miscellaneous rush; next, the gambler, the desperado, the highwayman, and all their kindred in sin of both sexes; and next, the smart chap who has bought up an old grant that covers all the land; this brings the lawyer tribe; the vigilance committee brings the undertaker. All these interests bring the newspaper; the newspaper starts up politics and a railroad; all hands turn to and build a church and a jail, -- and behold, civilization is established forever in the land. But whiskey, you see, was the van-leader in this beneficent work. It always is." His inevitable conclusion: "Westward the Jug of Empire takes its way."[103]

It may be stretching the moral of my tale of the Winnebagos and the Indian traders too far if I attempt to elevate Twain's neglected frontier thesis into a new model of western urbanization. It is, first of all, impossible to estimate just how much Rice and the other traders really made from the Winnebagos. Traders like Rice and Sibley experienced constant financial ups and downs, a constant sense of being in debt. A good deal of their profits inevitably flowed downstream, to partners and suppliers like Dousman and Chouteau, and then eastward. The reach of Rice and the other traders extended beyond the Winnebagos to other Indian tribes, and their investments were never confined to purely urban targets of opportunity. Sibley, certainly, was always more involved with the Dakotas than with other Minnesota tribes, and never seemed as sophisticated or as single-minded in his town promotion schemes as his red-haired rival. Moreover, the exceptional degree of influence enjoyed by Rice and Lowry among the Winnebagos must have rested as much on nonreplicable personal ties as on factors pervading the entire Indian trading system. And the Winnebago system itself pales in comparison with the large-scale schemes for corporate extraction of Indian resources being hatched in Kansas at the time. [104]

Nevertheless, it can clearly be argued that the federal funding that flowed through the Winnebagos to their traders, employees, and suppliers, and then on into real estate investment, urban promotion, and railroad development, played a critical role as seed capital in the development of the Upper Mississippi urban system. Similar processes undoubtedly operated elsewhere, with other tribes and other traders. The expectation of profit, as much as profit itself, turned traders into townsite locators, transportation boosters, and migrant recruiters, insuring that a basic complement of urban services were in place before the first farmers ever arrived, and providing an immediate local market for their produce.[105] Trader initiative and long-standing Washington connections insured that Indian annuities became as significant a federal source of urban development capital to this frontier as were harbor improvements or military contracts elsewhere. Subsequent speculators may have reaped richer rewards, but in the Upper Mississippi at least, the Indian trader was more than a bit player in the urban drama; he shaped the opening act. Equally clear is the critical role in this process of the "Jug of Empire" itself. More reputable traders may have felt a certain discomfort about their direct or indirect reliance upon the whiskey trade -- Sibley even initiated a temperance program among his employees -- but there was no surer sluice for the flow of federal funds through Indian and into white hands. "Do you drink any firewater," Commissioner George W. Manypenny asked the Winnebagos at the 1855 treaty negotiations. "We all drink," Chief Little Hill replied, "even our women. The whites have brought it amongst us." "Will you quit drinking?" "As you ask, father," responded Little Hill, "I will tell you. We came here to ask for the country ... and, if you will give it to us, and keep the whites out, as we don't know how to make firewater, we will not drink any."[106] Rice -- now Senator

Rice -- in a tacit ex post facto justification of his business strategy, blamed the situation on the temptations of federal Indian policy. "Alas!" he lamented to a noted Indian sympathizer (and constituent of his) after the Dakota uprising, "the poor Indian is kept in a savage state by a great government -- and his condition renders him, not an object of pity, but of plunder."[107] Rice was being disingenuous. From the early 1840s onward, he spent almost as much time in Washington lobbying for Indian policy modifications, treaty

ratifications, appropriations, appointments, and claims approvals as he ever spent actually trading on the Mississippi. It is unlikely that Congress would have been nearly as forthcoming with Indian appropriations, as generous in financing the work of civilization and individual land allotment, had the traders' lobby not been assiduously at work, shaping government policy secure in the knowledge that Indian appropriations would soon be theirs. "Whiskey," Chief Winnesheik reportedly admitted to an old acquaintance as they steamed up the Missouri to Crow Creek, ".. . has brought us here."[108]

Thus the most significant impact of the Winnebago urban system was experienced by the Winnebagos themselves. There was ample room within the broad framework of national Indian policy and popular prejudice for regional development schemes to result in dramatically differing destinies for individual tribes. Ironically, the one part of the federal Indian program meant to mitigate the nation's naked land grab -- payments to be invested in turning the Indians into farmers -- was what swept them into the vortex of its urban transformation. Winnebago entanglement with "the trick and trap Indian trading interest" -- the phrase is that of a Minnesota governor -- influenced the pace and trajectory of their migration, detouring them to Minnesota and Nebraska instead of to Kansas and then Oklahoma with their neighbors.[109] It delayed removal, multiplied exposures to the devastation of the "transit state," and left the tribe with an enduring split. To be sure, it also gave them, for a time at least, allies of dubious value and a certain degree of leverage. A frustrated federal government could never really confine the wandering Winnebagos to any reservation; they were able to reject land they did not want, and to put a relatively high price on the land they were forced to yield. But they remained pawns in a traders' game, their lives and culture devastated by the jug that financed the system, their inability to resist their traders as they resisted the government negating any chance of effectively playing the few cards that they held.

Indian policy had become development policy in the broadest sense, supporting a western city-building process that the government had no direct way to fund. The notion of a "Winnebago urban system" that frames this essay is, of course, little more than a heuristic conceit. But it serves to call attention to the kinship among a cohort of towns that shared mutual godfathers and a common source of development capital, and it underlines the human agency and human consequences of constructing this local urban system. "Towns grow," Eric Lampard observed almost forty years ago, "only as they generate opportunity for the alert and enterprising to promote new business around a basic 'carrier' core."[110] In the Upper Mississippi, the Indian trade carried nascent urbanization in a dual sense. Servicing the trade generated the first proto-urban population concentrations; its profits underwrote their speculative promotion.

I wish to express my gratitude to Christopher Buckley, Alexandra Gillen, and Maureen Harp for research assistance with parts of this project, and to participants in the Chicago Historical Society Urban History Seminar, March 26, 1992, for their comments on an earlier version of this essay.

1. Documents Relating to the Treaty with the Winnebago at Washington, D.C., October 13,1846, in Bureau of Indian Affairs, "Documents Relating to the Negotiation of Ratified and Unratified Treaties with Various Tribes of Indians," National Archives Microfilm T 494, reel 4 (hereafter cited as BIA-Treaties).

2. Reuben Gold Thwaites, ed., "The Wisconsin Winnebagos: An Interview with Moses Paquette," *Collections*, State Historical Society of Wisconsin XII (1892), 407-8; Henry M. Rice to Commissioner of Indian Affairs, June 4, 1848, United States Bureau of Indian Affairs, Letters Received, Winnebago Agency, National Archives Microfilm 650 (hereafter cited as USBIA-LR/WA), reel 934.

3. B. W. Brisbois on board the "Doctor Franklin" to Henry Sibley, May 30,1848, Henry H. Sibley Papers, Microfilm, Minnesota Historical Society, St. Paul (hereafter cited as SP).

4. *Charles Philip Hexom, Indian History of Winneshiek County, Iowa* (Decorah, Iowa: A. K. Bailey & Son, Inc., 1913), n.p.32.

5. Hexom, *Indian History of Winneshiek County, n.p.; Return 1. Holcombe, Minnesota in Three Centuries* (St. Paul: The Publishing Society of Minnesota, 1908), 1:207-12; Henry Lewis, *Das Illustrirte Mississippithal* (Leipzig: H. Schmidt und C. Günther, 1923), 99-103, 108; John Francis McDermott, *The Lost Panoramas of the Mississippi* (Chicago: University of Chicago Press, 1958).

6. Rice to Sibley, 28 June 28, 1848, SP. For accounts of the confrontation see J. E. Fletcher to Superintendent of Indian Affairs, St. Paul, May 26, 1854, USBIA-LR/WA, reel 934; *An Illustrated Historical Atlas of the State of Minnesota* (Chicago: A. T. Andreas, 18 ), 263; Henry Lewis, *Illustrirte Mississippithal* , 99-103, 108; J. E. Fletcher to Alexander Ramsey, Sept. 22, 1849, USBIA-LR Minnesota Superintendency, reel 428; Holcombe, *Minnesota in Three Centuries*, I:212-18.

7. Chippewa Petition, Osaukis Rapids, July 25, 1848; Chippewa Petition, July 29, 1848; J. E. Fletcher to U.S. Indian Sub Agent, LaPointe, July 25, 1848; Agreement July 27, 1848; USBIA-LR/WA, reel 932; Peter Manaige to J.E. Fletcher, Dec. 1850, USBIA-LR/WA, reel 933; quotation, J.E.Fietcher, July 27,1848, USBIA-LR/WA, reel 932.

8. Eric E. Lampard, "Historical Contours of Contemporary Urban Society: A Comparative View," *Journal of Contemporary History* 4 (1969), 3.

9. E. W. Edgerton to Elisha Edgerton, August 31, 1836, quoted in Bayard Still, *Milwaukee: The History of a City* (Madison: State Historical Society of Wisconsin, 1965), 1.

10. David Hamer, *New Towns in the New World: Images and Perceptions of the Nineteenth-Century Urban Frontier* (New York: Columbia University Press, 1990), 35-36.

11. For the historiography of western urbanization, consult Oliver Knight, "Toward an Understanding of the Western Town," *Western Historical Quarterly* 4 (1973), 27-42; Lawrence H. Larsen, 'Frontier Urbanization," in Roger L. Nichols, ed., *American Frontier and Western Issues: A Historiographical Review* (New York: Greenwood Press, 1986), 69-88; Carl Abbott, "Frontiers and Sections: Cities and Regions in American Growth," in Howard Gillette, Jr., and Zane L. Miller, eds., *American Urbanism: A Historiographical Review* (New York: Greenwood Press, 1987), 271-90. David Ralph Meyer, "A Dynamic Model of the Integration of Frontier Urban Places into the United State System of Cities," *Economic Geography* 56 (1980), 12040, stresses the critical role of capital imported by early migrants; for the general role of merchant capital and enterprise in shaping the nascent urban systems of the west, see James E. Vance, Jr., *The Merchant's World: The Geography of Wholesaling* (Englewood Cliffs, N.J.: Prentice-Hall, 1970). "Urban system" as used here refers loosely to the evolving set of urban places that emerged to meet the needs of the new territory's developing economy. But the nascent cities under discussion also formed a system in a more specific sense: they were conceived and sited by their fur trader founders as an interconnected hierarchy of places monopolizing the urban services—and hence profits—required by future white settlement. As such, this "system" to some extent anticipated both the locational principles and the creative federal funding of the better-studied railroad towns; cf. John Hudson, *Plains Country Towns* (Minneapolis: University of Minnesota Press, 1985).

12. Lloyd Wendt, *Swift Walker: An Informal Biography of Gurdon Saltonstall Hubbard* (Chicago: Regnery Books, 1986); Jacqueline Peterson, "Goodbye, Madore Beaubien: The Americanization of Early Chicago Society," *Chicago History* 19 (1980), 89-111.

13. Glenn Holt, "St. Louis's Transition Decade, 1819-1830," *Missouri Historical Review* 76 (1982), 365-81; John Denis Haeger, *The Investment Frontier: New York Businessmen and the Economic Development of the Old Northwest*

(Albany: State University of New York Press, 1981), quotation, 62; see also James L. Clayton, "The Growth and Economic Significance of the American Fur Trade, 1790-1890," in Dale L. Morgan et al., *Aspects of the Fur Trade. Selected Papers of the 1965 North American Fur Trade Conference* (St. Paul: Minnesota Historical Society, 1967), 62-72.

14. See Hamer, *New Towns*, 204-21, for a perceptive discussion of the pervasiveness of this imagery in nineteenth-century urban thought.

15. E.g. William Cronon, *Nature's Metropolis: Chicago and the Great West* (New York: W.W. Norton & Company, 1991), 25-54; for the necessity of incorporating Native American voices, cf. George Miles, "To Hear an Old Voice: Rediscovering Native Americans in American History," in William Cronon, George Miles, and Jay Gitlin, eds., *Under an Open Sky: Rethinking America's Western Past* (New York: W.W. Norton & Company, 1992), 52-70.

16. Still, *Milwaukee*, 7.

17. Howard R. Lamar, *The Trader on the American Frontier: Myth's Victim* (College Station: Texas A & M Press, 1977); Richard White, *The Middle Ground: Indians, Empires, and Republics in the Great Lakes Region, 1650-1815* (Cambridge: Cambridge University Press, 1991).

18. The term (and the underlining) is that of Henry Sibley, himself one of those early Yankees attracted to the upper midwest; Sibley to Charles Trowbridge, Sept. 6, 1847, SP. The racial basis for the common stereotype of the unenterprising Indian trader becomes clear in the observations of an early Yankee trader, James H. Lockwood, whose own activities disproved his rule: "Indian traders, as a class, possess no enterprise, at least none that is of any advantage to the settlement and improvement of a country.... I have never seen a man who made money in the Indian trade, apply it to the ordinary improvements that foster and encourage the growth of a country -- they have made money in a certain routine of business, with which they are acquainted, and fear to invest it in some other business with which they are not familiar." Lockwood, *Early Times and Events in Wisconsin*, Collections, State Historical Society of Wisconsin, II (1 856), 114.

19. John D. Haeger, "Capital Mobilization and the Urban Center: The Wisconsin Lakeports,"*Mid-America* (60 (1978), 75-93; Haeger, *Investment Frontier*.

20. Richard D. Wade, *The Urban Frontier: The Rise of Western Cities, 1790-1830* (Cambridge: Harvard University Press, 1959).

21. Paul Wallace Gates, *Fifty Million Acres: Conflicts Over Kansas Land Policy 1854-1890* (Cornell: Cornell University Press, 1954); H. Craig Miner and William E. Unrau, *The End of Indian Kansas: A Study of Cultural Revolution, 1854-*

*1871* (Lawrence: The Regents Press of Kansas, 1978); Robert A. Trennert, Jr., *Indian Traders on the Middle Border: The House of Ewing 1827-1854* (Lincoln: University of Nebraska Press, 1981).

22. For the evolution of Indian policy during this period, see Robert A. Trennert, Jr., *Alternative to Extinction: Federal Indian Policy and the Beginnings of the Reservation System, 1846-51* (Philadelphia: Temple University Press, 1975); Francis Paul Prucha, *The Great Father. The United States Government and the American Indians* (Lincoln: University of Nebraska Press, 1984), 1:243-339; Robert M. Kvasnicka and Herman J. Viola, eds., *The Commissioners of Indian Affairs, 1824-1977* (Lincoln: University of Nebraska Press, 1979), 23-75.

23. James L. Clayton, "The Impact of Traders' Claims on the American Fur Trade," in David M. Ellis, ed., *The Frontier in American Development: Essays in Honor of Paul Wallace Gates* (Ithaca, N.Y., 1969), 299-323; Robert A. Trennert, Jr., "The Business of Indian Removal: Deporting the Potawatomi from Wisconsin, 1851," *Wisconsin Magazine of History* 63 (1979), 36-50; idem., "A Trader's Role in the Potawatomi Removal from Indiana: The Case of George W. Ewing," *The Old Northwest* 4 (1978), 3-24; ibid., *Indian Traders*; Jeanne P. Leader, "The Pottawatomies and Alcohol: An Illustration of the Illegal Trade," *Kansas History* 2 (1979), 157-65; Miner and Unrau, *Indian Kansas*; the practice of paying traders' claims did not really end until 1854 in the wake of the scandals accompanying the 1851 treaties with the Minnesota Sioux.

24. Trennert, *Indian Traders*, 59-83, 87-91, 116-17; Rhoda R. Gilman, "The Last Days of the Upper Mississippi Fur Trade," *Minnesota History* 42 (1970), 129-34; David Lavender, *The Fist in the Wilderness* (Garden City, N.Y.: Doubleday and Co., 1964).

25. For the connection between Minnesota territorial politics and Indian traders, consult William W. Folwell, *A History of Minnesota*, I (St. Paul: Minnesota Historical Society, 1921); Erling Jorstad, "Personal Politics in the Origin of Minnesota's Democratic Party," *Minnesota History* 36 (1959), 264-71.

26. The small collection of Rice Papers are at the Minnesota Historical Society, St. Paul.

27. This letter is reproduced in Holcomb, *Minnesota*, 11:98; for Rice's background, see Folwell, *History of Minnesota*, 1:239-41; *The National Cyclopaedia of American Biography* (New York: James T. White & Company, 1931), XXI:273-74; Matt Bushnell Jones, *History of the Town of Waitsfield, Vermont 1782-1908* (Boston, 1909), 250-51, 425-6; *History of Kalamazoo County, Michigan* (Philadelphia, 1880), 221, 77, 213-14; J. Fletcher Williams, A

*History of the City of Saint Paul and of the County of Ramsey, Minnesota* (St. Paul: Minnesota Historical Society, 1876), 186-89.

28. Folwell, *History of Minnesota*, 1:239-41; *The National Cyclopaedia of American Biography* , XXI:273-74; *History of Kalamazoo*, 221, 77, 213-14; Williams, *City of St. Paul*, 186-89; on the Potawatomi removal, see R. David Edmunds, *The Potawatomis: Keepers of the Flame* (Norman: University of Oklahoma Press, 1978), 268-71. This character sketch of Rice is built up from judgments expressed by others and the evidence of his letters and behavior as they appear in the Sibley Papers; for the two quotations, see Rice to J. H. McKenny, March 15, 1849; Rice to Sibley, Dec. 18, 1847, SP. For his hair color, Borup to Sibley, undated note, Sept. 1853; J. J. Nash to Sibley, Nov. 23, 1858; SP. See also the brief character sketch of Rice in Willis A. Gorman to Stephen A. Douglas, Nov. 25, 1853, Stephen A. Douglas Papers, Regenstein Library, University of Chicago (hereafter cited as DP; I am grateful to Maureen Harp for the citations from the Douglas Papers).

29. 1889 statement of Sibley, quoted in Holcombe, *Minnesota*, 1:99; Wilson Porter Shortridge, *The Transition of a Typical Frontier, with Illustrations from the Life of Henry Hastings Sibley* (Menasha, Wisconsin: The Collegiate Press, 1919); Theodore C. Blegen, ed.,"The Unfinished Autobiography of Henry Hastings Sibley," *Minnesota History* 8 (1927), 328-62; for a character sketch of Sibley that accords well with the man as he presents himself in his papers, see Roger G. Kennedy, *Men on the Moving Frontier* (Palo Alto: American West Publishing Company, 1969), 39-73.

30. White, *Middle Ground*:; Ronald Rayman, "Confrontation at the Fever River Lead Mining District: Joseph Montfort Street vs. Henry Dodge, 1827-1828," *Annals of Iowa* 44 (1978), 278-95; Martin Zanger, "Conflicting Concepts of Justice: A Winnebago Murder Trial on the Illinois Frontier," *Journal of the Illinois State Historical Society* 75 (1980), 263-76; J. A. Jones, Alice E. Smith, and Vernon Carstensen, *Winnebago Indians* (New York, 1974). For a history of the Winnebagos, see Nancy Oestreich Lurie, "The Winnebago Indians: A Study in Cultural Change," unpub. Ph.D. dissertation, Northwestern University, 1952.

31. The remark was made by the treaty commissioners during the 1846 negotiations; BIA-Treaties.

32. *Senate Documents*, 26th Cong., 2nd Sess. (1840-41), vol. 1, 334.

33. Report of the Commissioner of Indian Affairs, November 24, 1845, *Senate Documents*, 29th Cong., 1 st Sess., vol. 1, 460, 473.

34. "Report," N. Boilvin, Exploring Agent, St. Louis, Jan. 11, 1840, to Hon. T.

Hartley Crawford, Commissioner of Indian Affairs, Washington, D.C. (pamphlet, Everett D. Graff Collection of Western Americana, Newberry Library, Chicago), 3.

35. Folwell, *History of Minnesota,* 1:309.

36. Boilvin, "Report," 2-3, quotation 8.

37. Boilvin, "Report;" "Report from the Secretary of War," *Senate Documents,* 26th Cong., 1st Sess. (1840-41), vol. 1, 330; vol. 6, 1-3.

38. Lurie, "Winnebago Indians," 119-129; Henry Merrell, "Pioneer Life in Wisconsin," *Collections,* State Historical Society of Wisconsin, VII (1876; reprinted 1908), 393-4.

39. *Congressional Globe,* 26th Cong., 1st Sess. (1839-40), 499; John T. DeLaRonde, "Personal Narrative," *Collections,* State Historical Society of Wisconsin 7 (1876; reprinted 1908), 345-65; Merrell, "Pioneer Life," 366-404; John Weidman of Lebanon, Pennsylvania, February 22, 1855, "Rejoinder to the Defense Published by Simon Cameron, February 6th, 1855, to the Charges Made Against Him as Commissioner to Carry into Effect the Treaty with the Half-Breed Winnebago Indians" (pamphlet, Ayer Collection, Newberry Library); Robert A. Trennert, Jr., "Orlando Brown, 1848-50," in Kvasnicka and Viola, eds., *Commissioners of Indian Affairs,* 4147.

40. Morrison McMillan, "Early Settlement of La Crosse and Monroe Counties," *Collections,* State Historical Society of Wisconsin, IV (1859), 383-84; Reminiscences of Lafayette Houghton Bunnell in *History of Winona and Olmsted Counties* (Chicago: H. H. Hill and Company, 1883), 44-81; Nathan Myrick, "Reminiscences of Early Times, in *Biographical History of La Crosse, Trempealeau, and Buffalo Counties, Wisconsin* (Chicago: The Lewis Publishing Company, 1892), 541-69; Hercules Dousman to Henry Sibley, June 2, 1843, Oct. 19, 1844, Feb. 2, 1846, Feb. 24, 1846, SP; James Clarke, Iowa Superintendency of Indian Affairs, to Commissioner of Indian Affairs, October 3, 1846, in *Senate Documents,* 29th Cong., 2nd Sess., Vol. 1, 240-45; Hexom, *Indian History of Winneshiek County,* n.p.

41. Albert H. Sanford and H. J. Hirschheimer, *A History of La Crosse, Wisconsin 1841-1900* (La Crosse: La Crosse County Historical Society, 1951), 23.

42. *Senate Documents,* 29th Cong., 2nd Sess. (1846-47), vol. 1, 243; Boilvin, "Report," 3. While white observers cannot be regarded as unbiased judges of either the extent or the motivation of Winnebago alcohol usage, whiskey traders clearly regarded the market as a profitable one, and Winnebago seasonal camps definitely tended to gravitate towards the unlicensed rather than the licensed trading

posts, both in Wisconsin and Iowa and subsequently in Minnesota; cf. Nancy Oestreich Lurie, "The World's Oldest On-Going Protest Demonstration: North American Indian Drinking Patterns," *Pacific Historical Review* 40 (1971), 311-32; Jack Waddell, "Malhiot's Journal: An Ethnohistoric Assessment of Chippewa Alcohol Behavior in the Early Nineteenth Century," *Ethnohistory* 32 (1985), 246-68; Peter C. Mancall, "'The Bewitching Tyranny of Custom': The Social Costs of Indian Drinking in Colonial America," *American Indian Culture and Research Journal* 17 (1993), 15-42.

43. Trennert, *Indian Traders*, 87-91, 116-17, 141-47; J. E. Fletcher to Superintendent of Indian Affairs, St. Louis, June, 1848, USBIA-LR/WA, reel 932; Dousman to Sibley, June 2,1843, Feb. 10 and 24,1846, SP.

44. Rice and his partners took in $22-23,000 of the $31,000 paid out to the Winnebagos in the autumn of 1844, for example, leaving the Ewings and another trader to split the remainder; Dousman to Sibley, Oct. 19,1844, SP. Rumors of Rice's involvement with Indian women dogged his career. General John Pope in 1862 referred to him as a "reckless and ruined speculator and old Indian trader" with "a knowledge of Indians and Indian character, acquired during many years of unlimited concubinage with Indian women;" quoted in Richard N. Ellis, "Political Pressures and Army Politics on the Northern Plains," *Minnesota History* 42 (1970), 45; Ojibwa tradition attributed the poor terms they received in the Winnebago land cessions to the fact that Rice, one of the treaty commissioners, had a Winnebago wife; Roger and Priscilla Buffalohead, *Against the Tide of American History: The Story of the Mille Lacs Anishinabe* (Cass Lake, Minn.: The Minnesota Chippewa Tribe, 1985), 49. A light-skinned nephew of Chief Grey Wolf was pointed out to visitors of Nebraska's Winnebago Reservation in 1870 as the son of ex-Senator Henry M. Rice; clipping, "From the Winnebago Agency," scrapbook, Joseph Paxson Papers, Wisconsin State Historical Society. For analysis of the role played by such familial relationships in the upper Mississippi Indian trade, see Gary Clayton Anderson, *Kinsmen of Another Kind: Dakota-White Relations in the Upper Mississippi Valley, 1650-1862* (Lincoln: University of Nebraska Press, 1984).

45. B.W. Brisbois, Prairie du Chien, to Sibley, July 18, 1844, SP.

46. Lowry's exact status at this time is in some doubt. He later insisted that "though I have since been engaged in the Indian Trade at that time I was not interested in any Trading establishment nor in any manner connected with the Indian Trade" (S. B. Lowry to Commissioner of Indian Affairs, Feb. 22,1850; USBIA-LR/WA, reel 932). However, he seems to have been employed by Rice

as a clerk in 1844, and he was clearly working for him again in 1848 (Statement by Michael St. Cyr, Winnebago Agency, Nov. 25, 1850, USBIA-LR/WA, Reel 933; J. E. Fletcher to Superintendent of Indian Affairs, St. Paul, May 26,1854, USBIA-LR/WA, reel 934).

47. USBIA-Treaties; Charles J. Kappler, ed., *Indian Affairs: Laws and Treaties,* 2nd ed., (Washington, D.C.: United States Government Printing Office, 1904), 565; Edwin C. Bailey, *Past and Present of Winneshiek County, Iowa* (Chicago: S. J. Clarke Publishing Co., 1913), 1:46, 47.

48. The Ojibwa were induced to agree to the cession owing to a growing scarcity of game in the area and the promise that the Winnebagos would serve as a buffer against their enemies, the Sioux; Roger and Priscilla Buffalohead, *Against the Tide*, 48-49. Rice first negotiated the treaty as a private citizen, aided by the long-established contacts of his A.F.C. associates in the Ojibwa trade, then legalized the venture by getting himself appointed one of the two formal treaty commissioners; USBIA-Treaties, reel 4, "Documents Relating to the Negotiation of the Treaty of August 2, 1847, with the Chippewa of the Mississippi and Lake Superior Indians;" Dousman to Sibley, March 9,1846, SP.

49. Folwell, *History of Minnesota*, 1:310.

50. J. E. Fletcher to Superintendent of Indian Affairs, St. Louis, June 1848; David Olmsted to Commissioner of Indian Affairs, July 7 1848; USBIA-LR/WA, reel 932; Trennert, *Indian Traders*, 141-47, 172. The Ewings attempted in 1846 and 1847 to trade in Minnesota, but met with little success and withdrew at a loss in their general contraction of western operations.

51. This is an oversimplification of a complicated set of agreements and partnerships; see Dousman to Sibley, Feb. 24 and May 10, 1846; Brisbois and Rice to Sibley, July 13,1846; Dousman to Sibley Nov. 25, 1846; Rice to Sibley, July 4, 1847, May 13, 1848, SP. Sibley also knew that the Sioux were unwilling to sell land to the Winnebagos, and probably had little desire to see Rice use the Winnebagos as a wedge into his well-established Sioux trade; William Henry Forbes to Sibley, Dec. 8, 1846; Sibley to Charles Trowbridge, Sept. 6, 1847, SP.

52. J. E. Fletcher, Winnebago Agency, November 25,1850, USBIA-LR/WA, reel 933.

53. Charles N. W. Borup to Sibley, 2 May 1850, SP.

54. Holcombe, *Minnesota*, 1:99.

55. J. R. Potts to Sibley, Sept. 14, 1848, Oct. 31, 1848; William Dugast Forbes, Oct. 31, 1848; Joseph R. Brown to Sibley, Dec. 1, 1848; quotation H. L. Moss to Sibley, Oct. 20, 1848; SP. "Every constituents of the new town proprietor

is getting a lot or two according to suvices rendered & promises hereafter," wrote J. W. Ball to Sibley; "it reminds me of the Later day sants when they had the Imortal joe for thare leader;" Jan. 28, 1849, SP.

56. Rice to J. H. McKenny, Jan. 13,1849, SP.

57. Matilda W. Rice, "The 4th of July in the 1850s," *Minnesota History* 49 (1984), 54-55; Sibley to Chouteau, June 20, June 25, 1849; Chouteau to Sibley July 12, 1849; Sibley to Chouteau, August 8, 1848; C.N.W. Borup to Sibley, Sept. 4, Sept. 5, 1849; Sibley to Borup, Sept. 5, 1849; Sibley to Chouteau, Sept. 5, Sept. 28, 1849; Rice to Sibley, Oct. 1 1, Nov. 8, 1849; Sibley to Borup, Feb. 9, 1854, SP; Jorstad, "Personal Politics," 261-64; quotation, J. J. Noah to Sibley, Nov. 13, 1858, SP.

58. Rice to Dousman, Jan. 8, 1850, March 7,1852; *Green Bay and Prairie du Chien Papers*, Vol. 15, Letters, State Historical Society of Wisconsin, Madison (hereafter cited as GBPC); General C. C. Andrews, ed., *History of St. Paul, Minn.* (Syracuse: D. Mason & Co., 1890),314-17,394; T. M. Newson, *Pen Pictures of St. Paul, Minnesota, and Biographical Sketches of Old Settlers* (St. Paul: by the author, 1886), 1:131-32, notes that Rice induced friends from the South and elsewhere to invest in St. Paul.

59. Lockwood, "Early Times," 98-232; Rice to Dousman, July 7,1852, GBPDC.

60. Sanford and Hirshheimer, *History of La Crosse*, 40-47.

61. *History of Winona and Olmsted Counties* (Chicago: H. H. Hill and Company, 1883), 49, quotation 52; the author of this chapter is Lafayette Bunnell, who arrived in the area with his brother in 1842. When they first landed at La Crosse with a canoe-load of goods purchased at Prairie du Chien, one of the traders there urged them to "remain and help build up a city" (54).

62. The Dousman comment is from Lockwood, "Early Times," 175-76; for Levy, see Sanford and Hirshheimer, *History of La Crosse*, 32-47 passim; McMillan, "*Early Settlement of La Crosse and Monroe Counties*," 383-84; *History of La Crosse County*, 453-55.

63. N. H. Winchell, *History of the Upper Mississippi Valley* (Minneapolis, 1881), 343, 287; Helen McCann White, ed., *Ho! For the Gold Fields: Northern Overland Wagon Trains of the 1860s* (St. Paul: Minnesota Historical Society, 1966), 25; quotations LaFayette H. Bunnell, *Winona and its Environs on the Mississippi in Ancient and Modern Days* (Winona, 1897), 218, 224; also 193, 214-39 passim; Albert M. Goodrich, *History of Anoka County and the Towns of Champlin and Dayton in Hennepin County, Minnesota* (Minneapolis, 1905), 28-30.

64. *History of La Crosse County, Wisconsin* (Chicago: Western Historical Company, 1881), 459; Bunnell, *Winona and its Environs*, 228, 235, 262.

65. Myrick, "Reminiscences of Early Times," 541-69, quotation, 567; *Historical Atlas of the State of Minnesota*, 261; the personal description is from Newson, *Pen Pictures*, 1:85-6. Myrick's reminiscences are a rich descriptive source for the river trading system, despite Gary C. Anderson's plaint (*in Kinsmen of Another Kind*, 199) that little is known of Nathan Myrick and his brother Andrew -- the latter the trader who entered Minnesota legend when he was supposedly found dead with his mouth stuffed with grass during the Sioux Uprising of 1862, after having remarked that if the Sioux were hungry, they should eat grass; cf. Gary Clayton Anderson, "Myrick's Insult: A Fresh Look at Myth and Reality," *Minnesota History* 48 (1983), 198-206.

66. Myrick, "Reminiscences," 567; Winchell, *Upper Mississippi Valley*, 368; Bunnell, *Winona and its Environs*, 269; Sibley to Chouteau, Sept. 11, 1849, Borup to Chouteau, August 22, 1850, SP. Myrick was probably the "Merrick" charged with selling liquor to the Winnebagos early in 1849 (David Lambert to Sibley, Feb. 8, 1849, SP), while White clearly numbered among the "host of vagabonds" employed by Rice who so bothered the Sibley faction; they were particularly scandalized when he lost $75 gambling in a single night (Borup to Sibley, Sept. 15 and 29, 1849, SP).

67. J. E. Fletcher to Superintendent of Indian Affairs, Dec. 6, 1848, USBIA-LR/WA, reel 932; George Culver to Commissioner of Indian Affairs, Apr. 20,1852, ibid., Reel 933.

68. Winchell, *Upper Mississippi Valley*, 224-5, 275, 287, 294, 320, 370, 586; Goodrich, *History of Anoka County*, 39; Bunnell, *Winona and its Environs*, 266-69; Edwin A.C. Hatch and Family Papers, Minnesota Historical Society.

69. Robert Orr Baker, *The Muster Roll: A Biography of Fort Ripley, Minnesota* (St. Paul, n.d.), 11-16.

70. *History of Winona and Olmsted Counties*, 157-65.

71. For Rice's assessment of the advantages of the location, see Rice to Commissioner of Indian Affairs, June 27, 1850, USBIA-LR/WA, reel 932.

72. Quotations in William Bell Mitchell, *History of Stearns County Minnesota* (Chicago: H. C. Cooper, Jr., & Co., 1915), 627, and Minnesota *Chronicle* (St. Paul), Aug. 6, 1850, quoted in Baker, *Fort Ripley*, 20. The maneuverings to establish the two sites can be followed in USBIA-LR/WA, and correspondence in SP, with biographical research confirming the Sibley, Rice, or Ewing allegiances of the principal players; see, in particular, Sibley to Rice, Oct. 30, 1849, Sibley to

Chouteau Aug. 8, 1849, Sept. 11, 1849, SP; J. E. Fletcher to Alexander Ramsey, Sept. 30, 1850, USBIA-LR, Minnesota Superintendency, reel 428; A. W. Fridley to Superintendent of Indian Affairs, USBIA-LR/WA, reel 933; Depositions, March 15, 1850, USBIA-LR/WA, reel 932; J. E. Fletcher to Alexander Ramsey, Sept. 22, 1849, USBIA-LR, Minnesota Superintendency, reel 428, A. M. Mitchell to Commissioner of Indian Affairs, USBIA-LR/WA, reel 932; Winchell, *Upper Mississippi Valley*, 343-49, 368-70.

73. Mitchell, *Stearns County*, 418, 430, 627, 880, 1416-17; Lowry to Sibley, Sept. 20, 1852; Winchell, *Upper Mississippi Valley*, 342-49.

74. Wincholl, *Upper Mississippi Valley*, 341; Julia Sargent Wood, "Sauk Rapids Never Swiped the County Seat from Watab," clipping, Wood Family Papers, Minnesota Historical Society; Manuscript Territorial Census, 1857, Benton County, Minnesota Territorial Papers, National Archives microfilm T1175, reel 1.

75. Mitchell, *Stearns County*, 1434-46.

76. Mitchell, *Stearns County*, 181-2, 1080; Lawrence A. Lowry to Commissioner of Indian Affairs, May 15, 1849, USBIA-LR/WA, reel 932; his role as Winnebago interpreter can be traced through the Winnebago Agency papers; quotation, "Senex" in *St. Cloud Democrat*, Sept. 1, 1859.

77. Rice to Dousman, Jan. 23,1850, July 30,1852, GBPDC, Letters, Volume 17.

78. Geo. Brott, "The Life, Adventures, and Mistakes of a Business Man," St. *Cloud Journal-Press*, 1908, clipping in George F. Brott Biographical File, Stearns County Historical Society, St. Cloud, Minnesota.

79. Frank A. Flower, *The Eye of the North-West: First Annual Report of the Statistician of Superior, Wisconsin* (Milwaukee: King, Fowler & Co., 1890), 47-62; Rice to Stephen A. Douglas, Dec. 8, 1853, Box 3:2, DP. Rice was first attracted by the possibilities of the site when he came north to negotiate the Chippewa treaty in 1847, and after Michigan began breaking ground for the Soo canal in 1853, his townsite company successfully bested rival groups in claiming the area, thanks to his Washington connections, and to some 25 half-breeds and a few white men imported to make preemption claims for the group; Rice's brother located in the area that year with a trader's license to be on the spot. Hatch was involved with Rice in this speculation; see Hatch to Esteemed Friend, Aug. 29, 1854; Hatch to My Dear Lottie, Sept. 4, 1854, Hatch Papers.

80. A reporter nostalgically recalled in 1860 the "flush times" of Itasca five years earlier, when "Indian payments made money plenty, and every man in all

the region round about got some... Indian traders were as thick as blackberries, and so were Indians." But when the Winnebagos left, the "traders among them followed with their goods," and their buildings now stood "empty and forsaken;" *New Era* (Sauk Rapids, Minnesota), Feb. 9, 1860.

81. Watab *Reveille*, 20 January 1851, microfilm , Minnesota Historical Society.

82. Folwell, *History of Minnesota*, 1:311-12; Deposition of Peter Manaige, Interpreter, Winnebago Agency, December, 1850; USBIA-LR/WA, reel 933; J.E. Fletcher to Superintendent of Indian Affairs, St. Paul, Sept. 22, 1849, USBIA-LR, Minnesota Superintendency, Reel 428; Baker, *Fort Ripley*, 23; cf. Bruce M. White, "A Skilled Game of Exchange: Ojibway Fur Trade Protocol," *Minnesota History* 50 (1987), 229-40.

83. *New Era* (Sauk Rapids, Minn.), Feb. 23, March 29, 1860. Julia Sargent Wood, the paper's editor, recalled of the Winnebagos that "they were constantly on the go -- so the territorial road was always enlivened by fantastic groups of these children of nature, and the air vocalized with their loud songs of rejoicing and of lamentation;" ibid.

84. Willis A. Gorman to Commissioner of Indian Affairs, Sept. 19, 1853, USBIA-LR/WA, reel 933; Annual Report, J. E. Fletcher, Winnebago Agency, Sept. 12, 1854, USBIA-LR/WA, reel 934.

85. Willis A. Gorman to Commissioner of Indian Affairs, May 21, 1855, USBIA-LR/WA, reel 934.

86. Jorstad, "Personal Politics," 264-71; Folwell, *History of Minnesota*, 1:312-18, 367-72; Trennert, *Indian Traders*, 159; Frederic Sibley to Sibley, May 4, 19, June 8, Sept. 11, 1850, Olmsted to Sibley May 5, June 20, 1850, Alexander Ramsey to Sibley, June 3, 1850, Sibley to Chouteau, Sept. 3, 1851, Joseph A. Sire to Sibley, Oct. 12, 1850, May 24, 1851; quotation, Ramsey to Sibley, Apr. 10, 1850, SP; in comparison, an Ewing-backed contractor removed Potawatomis from Wisconsin to Kansas that same year for $55 per person, and made a direct profit of almost 50 per cent on the contract; Trennert, "Business of Indian Removal," 40, 49.

87. Alex. Wilkin to Millard Fillmore, Feb. 28,1852; quotation, Alex. Wilkin to Commissioner of Indian Affairs, Jan. 7,1852, USBIA-LR/WA, reel 933.

88. Alexander Ramsey to Commissioner of Indian Affairs, Nov. 20, 1851, USBIA-LR/WA, reel 933; 'Report of the Commissioner of Indian Affairs, Nov. 30, 1852,' *Senate Documents*, 32nd Cong., 2nd Sess. (1852-53), vol. 1, 301-6; Minnesota Pioneer (St. Paul), September 5, 1849, cited in William James Ryland, *Alexander Ramsey; A Study of a Frontier Politician and the Transition of*

*Minnesota from a Territory to a State* (Philadelphia: Harris and Partridge Co., 1941), 52.

89. Willis A. Gorman to Commissioner of Indian Affairs, Sept. 19, 1853, USBIA-LR/WA, reel 933.

90. Willis A. Gorman to Commissioner of Indian Affairs, August 11, 1853, USBIA-LR/WA, reel 933; Folwell, *History of Minnesota*, I:478-82.

9l. Trennert, *Indian Traders*, 172-85, 201.

92. Grand Jury at the U.S. District Court at Sauk Rapids, presentment December 16, Dec. 18,1852, USBIA-LR/WA, reel 933. Lumber interests reportedly played a major role in the 1855 treaty; Folwell, *Minnesota History*, 1:307.

93. Edmund J. Danziger, Jr., *Indians and Bureaucrats: Administering the Reservation Policy during the Civil War* (Urbana: University of Illinois Press, 1974), 99-100; Kappler, "Treaty with the Winnebago, 1855," 690-93; "Report of the Commissioner of Indian Affairs, Nov. 26, 1855," *Senate Documents*, 34th Cong., Ist and 2nd Sess. (1855-56), vol. 1, 323, 368-78; Hughes, *Blue Earth*, 60-62, 274, quotation 60. Nancy Lurie is clearly incorrect in stating that the Winnebagos were "forced to cede" their Long Prairie reservation; this was a cession they strove long and hard to effect; Nancy Oestreich Lurie, ed., *Mountain Wolf Woman, Sister of Crashing Thunder: The Autobiography of a Winnebago Indian* (Ann Arbor: University of Michigan Press, 1961), 112.

94. Kappler, "Treaty with the Winnebago 1859," 790-91; "Report of the Commissioner of Indian Affairs, Nov. 26, 1859," *Senate Documents*, 36th Cong., Ist Sess. (1859-60), vol. 1, 377-78, 476-80; quotation from "Report of the Commissioner of Indian Affairs, Nov. 30, 1857," *Senate Documents*, 35th Cong., Ist Sess. (1857-58), vol. 1, 290.

95. *Congressional Globe*, 37th Cong., 2nd Sess. (vol. 32), July 10, 1862, 3240. Removal from the state soon aborted the allotment process altogether.

96. "Report of the Commissioner of Indian Affairs, October 31, 1863," *House Executive Documents*, 38th Cong., Ist Sess. (1863-64), vol. 3, 151-52; Markku Henriksson, *The Indian on Capitol Hill: Indian Legislation and the United States Congress, 1862-1907* (Helsinki: Finnish Historical Society, Studia Historica 25, 1988), 143-44; Danziger, *Indians and Bureaucrats*, 117-28; William E. Lass, *The Removal from Minnesota of the Sioux and Winnebago Indians, Minnesota History* 38 (1963), 353-64; Bunnell, *Winona and its Environs*, 269-270.

97. East Prussian-born Marks became one of Mankato's leading merchants and officeholders, and was the first Mason to be initiated into its local lodge; *Mankato: Its First Fifty Years* (Mankato, Minn.: Free Press Printing Co., 1903), 271; Charles

S. Bryant, *History of the Minnesota Valley* (Minneapolis: North Star Publishing Co., 1882), 598.

98. R. G. Murphy to Stephen A. Douglas, Dec. 29,1857, Box 8:13, DP.

99. Lass, "Removal from Minnesota," 355, 360-63; Bunnell. Hatch owed the position to Rice; Ellis, "Political Pressures and Army Politics," 45.

100. Lass, "Removal from Minnesota," 354; William E. Lass, "The 'Moscow Expedition'," *Minnesota History* 40 (1965), 227-40; the speculation that Thompson's delay was deliberate is that of Lass. Following further the speculative trail blazed a generation earlier by Rice, these Mankato merchants in 1865 bought out the AFC's Upper Missouri Outfit for trade among the Sioux and Crow, and sought careers in Dakota politics and town promotion; John E. Sunder, *The Fur Trade on the Upper Missouri*, 1840-1865 (Norman: University of Oklahoma Press, 1965); Howard K. Lamar, *Dakota Territory*, 1861-1889: *A Study of Frontier Politics* (New Haven: Yale University Press, 1956).

101. J. Sterling Morton et al., *Illustrated History of Nebraska* (Lincoln: Western Publishing and Engraving Co., 1911), I:54, 44; 11:205, 325-26.

102. A. T. Andreas, *History of the State of Nebraska* (Chicago: Western Historical Company, 1882), 615; William Huse, *History of Dixon County, Nebraska* (Norfolk: The Daily News, 1896), 105, 207.

103. From *Life on the Mississippi*, in Charles Neider, ed., *The Complete Travel Books of Mark Twain* (Garden City, N.Y.: Doubleday and Company, 1967), 639-40.

104. Miner and Unrau, *End of Indian Kansas*; H. Craig Miner, *The Corporation and the Indian: Tribal Sovereignty and Industrial Civilization in Indian Territory, 1865-1907* (Columbia: University of Missouri Press, 1976).

105. Indeed, as white settlement progressed, Rice lobbied successfully to insure that bids for contracts to supply Minnesota Indians with food and other provisions were advertised for delivery locally rather than downriver, thereby giving Minnesota's pioneer farmers their own stake in the Winnebago "California lode"; Alexander Ramsey to Commissioner of Indian Affairs, Apr. 29, June 12, 1852, USBIA-LR Minnesota Superintendency, reel 428; Rice to Commissioner of Indian Affairs, Dec. 11, 1854, USBIA-LR/WA, reel 934.

106. "Documents Relating to the Negotiation of the Treaty of Feb. 27, 1855, with the Winnebago Indians," BIA-Treaties, reel 5.

107. Rice to Henry B. Whipple, Nov. 27, 1862, quoted in Prucha, *Great Father*, I:473.

108. Bunnell, *Winona and Its Environs*, 341; Bunnell had been involved in the

downriver trade in a small way in the mid-1840s, and was recruited by Hatch to assist in the removal to Dakota; his recollections are among the most vivid and unvarnished of the later fur trade era.

109. Quotation, Willis A. Gorman to Stephen A. Douglas, Nov. 25,1853, Box 3:2, DP.

110. Eric E. Lampard, "The History of Cities in the Economically Advanced Areas," *Economic Development and Cultural Change* 3 (1955), 116.

# 10

# Environmental Re-Reading
## Three Urban Novels

## Sam Bass Warner, Jr.

The goals of this essay are two. First, to encourage the re-reading of classic American fiction from the vantage point of our contemporary environmental concerns. Second, to direct readers attention to the richness of images, problems, and conflicts appropriate to today's environmental politics that are contained in classic American urban novels.

Today both popular and scholarly writing in America about the environment carry a strong animus towards cities. They express their ignorance and hostility by measuring present problems against pastoral and wilderness images. However, it is my contention that in the design of cities and in the improvement of ways of urban living there lies the answer to many of our environmental problems. My sense is that Eric Lampard shares this same outlook, or at least he did so in my favorite essay of his, "The Urbanizing World."[1]

Therefore what follows is an example of an urban historian's approach to the current American problems of humans' relations to their human and non-human environments.[2] The examples are drawn from the very largest fictive cities of our nineteenth and twentieth century authors. As the authors imagined their cities they resembled quite different environments in respect to city size, rates of growth, technological mix, and forms of capitalist institutions. The novels are: Herman Melville's *Redburn* (1849), William Dean Howells' *A Hazard of New Fortunes* (1890), and John Dos Passos' *Manhattan Transfer* (1925). I selected these because

I am an urban historian, and also because I think Americans are currently having a hard time reconciling their ideas of non-human nature with their metropolitan ways of living. Although the cities imagined are of many years ago, all of the environments the authors describe are analogous to those found around the world today. I don't think of these three novels as an exclusive selection; many other choices would serve as well.

In the past these novels have been read as commentary on the effects of urbanization, industrialization, and capitalism upon the social classes of the United States and England. I believe that they were written with that intention. The sensitivity and intelligence of the three novels makes them important responses to those social events, and has earned them their position as American classics. Today they can also be re-read as environmental fiction because, in the process of dealing with class relations, the novelists raise issues and tell stories that are of especial concern to anyone who was now trying to understand the implications of a modern culture which would simultaneously carry a concern for human well-being with a concern for the well-being of non-human nature.

### The Urban Environments

The novels are situated in two very different sets of urban technological environments. The stories in *Redburn* go forward amidst the social arrangements and machinery of paleotechnic[3] Liverpool. It was a time of the most narrow privatization of human affairs, a time of the least government management of cities, the least municipal infrastructure, and the most pervasive room crowding within jerry-built small houses, courts, and alleys. Periodic plagues of cholera appeared as crescendos to the droning rhythms of typhus, typhoid, tuberculosis and syphilis. In terms of mere human survival the large city of this era has been properly characterized as the place and time of "the slaughter of the innocents."[4] International immigrants from Germany, England, Scotland, and Ireland flooded the cities. The sailing ship, the horse and wagon, the canal, the steam engine, cast and wrought iron, textile and woodworking machinery, the cheap clock and the cheap gun characterize paleotechnic technology.

During this era (approximately 1820-1870) England and the United States experienced their most rapid rates of urbanization. Melville's novel matched this actuality. He told a story about his hero's (young Redburn Wellingborough) shock and dismay when he discovers the degree to which Liverpool had changed in 60 year's time. Redburn set out for a walking tour of Liverpool in the 1830's armed with his father's 1770 guide book:

> "Here, now, oh, Wellingborough, thought I, learn a lesson, and never forget it. This world, my boy, is a moving world; its Riddough's Hotels are forever being pulled down; it never stands still; and its sands are forever shifting. This very harbor of Liverpool is gradually filling up, they say; and who knows what your son (if you ever have one) may behold when he comes to visit Liverpool, as long after you as you come after his grandfather. And, Wellingborough, as your father's guide book is no guide for you, neither would yours (could you afford to buy a modern one today) be a guide to those who come after you." (p.224)

Sheer size, hugeness, was the barrier to comprehension in *A Hazard* and *Manhattan Transfer*, not the pace of change. Both were located in neotechnic New York City in the years from 1890 to 1921. In this technological era the very largest metropolises of the United States were growing more rapidly than smaller cities. Large staffs of municipal employees, public health campaigns to clean up food and milk, and huge investments in public water supplies and sewage systems had succeeded in making these metropolitan environments sufficiently safe so that the humans living there could reproduce themselves. It was the first time in history that large cities were so minimally compatible to the human organism. International immigrants continued to come from Germany and Ireland, but new waves were arriving from Italy, Austro-Hungary, Poland, Scandinavia, and Russia. Populations of large cities in the neotechnic era were now to be counted in the millions, not in the hundred thousands as they had been in the earlier paleotechnic.[5]

Coal and steel, railroads, steamships, electricity, electric street railways and subways, and mechanical inventions of all kinds characterized the technology of the era. In *Manhattan Transfer*, a novel whose stories span the years from 1896 to 1921, the telephone was portrayed as ubiquitous, the automobile appeared as the common taxi and as a machine of the rich, and air travel was by dirigible. Movies were briefly mentioned only, and the radio did not appear. The characteristic housing in *A Hazard* was the brownstone row house, and the Lower East Side five story tenement; in *Manhattan Transfer* it was the hotel, the apartment-hotel, the apartment house, and the five-story tenement.

All three constructed cities with steep social gradients from desperate poverty to luxurious wealth. All three fashioned places with demanding manners and sharp geographical segregation to hold one class apart from another. All three told stories in which their hero discovered these class divisions and extended his sympathies and even sometimes his actions across them.

For Melville the poor were slum dwellers, sailors, and German and Irish immigrants; for Howells the poor were immigrants and transit workers; for Dos Passos the poor were young people, immigrant and native born, who were trying to make their way in the city and who were being destroyed by its culture and politics. Melville's poverty was depicted as the most desperate, as was fitting for the ferocity of the paleotechnic city, but the isolation of the poor from the well-to-do appeared as a common theme in all three novels.

In constructing stories in this way the authors anticipated the demands of environmental writing today. They wished, as environmentalists do now, to press their readers to look beyond a narrow and immediate self-interest. They wanted people to stretch their moral concerns to distant and unfamiliar people and places. Their intention was to over come the barriers of social class. These novels, however, can now be read for their insights into the problems of human perception of the non-human environments as well as the human ones.

### The Location of Nature

Consider an essential question of environmental consciousness: "Where does nature reside? Is it within as well as without humankind? Or, are humans separate, and apart from nature?"[6]

The novels divide on this issue. For Melville people were nature embodied. Human nature in *Redburn*, varied and conflicting as he presented it, was nonetheless a part of nature. For Howells and Dos Passos, however, human nature stood apart from non-human nature: people, thunderstorms, and herring gulls may have coexisted, but they were not members of unified natural systems.

The expansion and intensification of the built forms of the city over the fifty to seventy-five years represented by Melville's Liverpool and Dos Passos' New York cannot account for the change in the authors' outlook. More bricks, more asphalt, and more concrete are not what separated humans from their sense of oneness with nature. Dos Passos, to be sure, described his city in a voice that is familiar to Americans in the 1990's. He made a specialty of evoking the harshness of the man-made environments, the buildings, streets, and signs of early twentieth century Manhattan. Melville, however, despite the smaller size of his Liverpool compared to Dos Passos' New York, was not backward in locating such settings. He singled out a new kind of man-made desert in Liverpool, the great port's warehouse district with its often-empty streets and its forbidding masonry walls. Here at Launcelott's-Hey he found a man-made barren as hostile to living creatures as New York's Wall Street at 2:00 a.m., or today's deserts beneath the expressway, or the blank expanses of shopping mall parking lots and their wind-swept concrete garages.

At issue in the shift in stories from unity to separation of man and nature was a change in the view of the interior of human beings. Melville, the Romantic, understood the forces of nature to lodge throughout the human organism. Human emotions, good and evil, taught and untaught, were, for him, elements of a sentient creature (p. 345).

Howells, a transitional author between Melville's Romanticism and Christian myths and Dos Passos' Naturalism and modern secular myths, wrote in a post-Darwin climate when many authors characterized natural and human environments as a struggle for the survival of the fittest. Howells' characters, therefore, are sociological, and take their shapes from their socio-economic settings. Beneath their social actions human characters still existed as a separate entity apart from society. It had the capacity for evil as well as loving kindness. Yet, this core being, in turn, was to be understood by still another human construct, conventional nineteenth century Christianity. Such a sociological focus isolated the humans in *A Hazard* from nature and natural processes (pp. 395, 412).

Dos Passos shared this idea of the separation of man from nature even though he mentioned the weather, the sunlight, and the presence of birds as often in his New York stories as Melville did in his descriptions of the Atlantic voyage of the *Highlander* in *Redburn*. In *Manhattan Transfer* the seasons and the weather appeared frequently either to amplify, or to contrast with the mood of the central character of the many stories (Spring, p. 35l, Summer pp. 240-4l, Fall p. 27l, Winter pp. 343-44). Also the port of New York was still, in the early twentieth century, a vital element of Manhattan so that the harbor, ocean liners, schooners, tugs, fogs, gulls, and views from ferries, and bridges appeared throughout the novel. Dos Passos' New York was not merely building facades, signs, and pavements.

He arranged his selections from non-human natural systems to stand apart from human beings. And he held to this separation despite his comprehension of the new understandings of psychoanalysis. He mentioned psychoanalysis in his novel as an important element in the culture of his young people (pp. 334, 343). Freud's view of personality, however, resembled Melville's: people were creatures in a world of other creatures. Dos Passos' humans were like Howells', organisms nourished only by a socioeconomic system and fragments of inherited culture.

The consequence of this long-term trend in story telling was to strip non-human nature from whatever protections can be provided by myths of harmony, imaginations of gardens of human and non-human spirits, and religious unities of all kinds. Nature, so set off in fiction, must now depend on the adequacy of secular imaginations.

The collapse of individual Christian morality as a device for appealing to the sympathies and moral sensitivities of the readers demonstrates the consequences of placing the realm of human beings apart from the realms of nature and nature myths. Melville believed that individual actions were significant and that a description and evaluation of the public world of the city could be meaningfully carried forward in terms of traditional Christianity. For example, the famous chapter of the starving woman and children in Launcelott's Hey, and Redburn's inability to save them, is a retelling of the parable of the Good Samaritan.[7] So, too, when Melville's stories turned to a description of the life of sailors as members of a permanent underclass, or to a description of the ill-treatment of immigrants, he reached out to his readers by reminding them of elements in their Christian tradition.

"And yet, what are sailors? What in your heart do you think of that fellow staggering along the dock? Do you not give him a wide berth, shun him, and account him but little above the brutes that perish? Will

you open your parlors to him; invite him to dinner? Or give him a
season ticket to a pew in your church? -- No. You will do no such
thing; but at a distance, you will perhaps subscribe a dollar or two for
the building of a hospital, to accommodate sailors already broken down;
or for the distribution of excellent books among tars who cannot read."

"But can sailors, one of the wheels of this world, be wholly lifted up
from the mire? There seems not much chance for it, in the old systems
and programs of the future however well-intentioned and sincere;..."

"But we must not altogether despair for the sailor; nor need those
who toil for his good be at bottom disheartened. For Time must prove
his friend in the end; and though sometimes he would almost seem as a
neglected step-son of heaven, permitted to run on and riot out his days
with no hand to restrain him, while others are watched over and tenderly
cared for; yet we feel and we know that God is the true Father of all,
and that none of his children are without the pale of his care." (pp. 204-
205)

Howells could not make his conventional individualistic nineteenth
century Christian religion work with any force either upon the actions of
the novel or to demand an equivalent attention from his readers. He
directed his attention to the large organizations of neotechnic metropolis
by setting up a strike of streetcar workers as the dramatic and moral climax
of the novel. The hero, Basil March, struggled to encompass within his
traditional Christianity what he saw to be a private war between the
workers and their employers. Basil March's individualistic religion failed
to encompass the circumstances of New York City.

There were two saintly characters in the novel, one Conrad Dryfoos
who got shot accidentally while trying to intervene in the police violence
of the strike, the other a beautiful society girl, Margaret Vance who became
an Episcopal nun. March understood their lives as examples of the human
impulse for atonement. March lectured his wife:

"Why should there be such a principle in the world? But it has been felt,
and more or less dumbly, blindly recognized ever since Calvary. If we love
mankind, pity them, we even *wish* to suffer for them. That's what has
created the religious orders in all times -- the brotherhoods and sisterhoods
that belong to our day -- as much as the medieval past." (pp. 409-10).

Like many Americans Howells' Basil March experienced the metropolis of 1890 as a perpetual conflict in which one man's gain was another man's loss. In such a world he could not find a moral path, despite his travels about New York listening to socialist orators and Sunday sermons of every point of view (p. 274). In yet another discussion with his wife Basil March set forth his understanding of the environment of New York:

> "But what I object to is this economic chance-world in which we live, and which we men seem to have created. It ought to be law, as inflexible in human affairs as the order of day and night in the physical world, that if a man will work he shall both rest and eat, and shall not be harassed with any questions as to how his repose and provision shall come. Nothing less than this ideal satisfies the reason. But in our state of things no one is secure in this. No one is sure of finding work; no one is sure of not losing it...At my time in life -- at every time of life -- a man ought to feel that if he will keep on doing his duty he will not suffer in himself or in those who are dear to him, except though natural causes. But no man can feel this as things are now; and so we go on, pushing and pulling, climbing and crawling, thrusting aside and trampling underfoot; lying, cheating, stealing; and when we get to the end, covered with blood and dirt and sin and shame, to look back over the way we've come to a palace of our own, or the poor-house, which is about the only possession we can claim in common with our brother-men, I don't think the retrospect can be pleasing" (p. 396).

Dos Passos' New York stories described the city the same way, except his novel lacked the easy-going warm and friendly relationships among a family of core characters. Dos Passos' New York was a city of isolates who must exist without love.

The idea that humans exist apart from nature also seems to have contributed to the weakening of the pastoral as a literary form within which authors might speculate about an alternative good society. Environmentalists attend to pastorals because these visions tell of an author's imagining of places beyond the conflicts of the city. Pastoral places are improved hybrids; they are tamed by the virtues of civilization and refreshed by primitivism and wilderness. In economic terms pastorals are places of human sufficiency and comfort, as opposed to places of struggle and greed.

In all three novels pastoral tales are very minor, and all reduced them to a domestic compass. Melville dallied with two pastoral scenes. One took the form of an embowered cottage in the country outside Liverpool, a cottage wherein dwelt three beautiful maidens whom Redburn imagined marrying (pp.290-93). The second pastoral Melville constructed out of the small single-handed work boats, Salt-droghers, that bobbed about in the Liverpool harbor.

> "It was diverting to observe the self-importance of the skipper of any of these diminutive vessels...What more could Caesar want? Though his craft was none of the largest, it was subject to *him*; and though his crew might consist of only himself; yet, if, he governed it well, he achieved a triumph, which the moralists of all ages have set above the victories of Alexander."
>
> "Yet small, low, and narrow as the cabin is, somehow, it affords accommodations to the skipper and his family. Often, I used to watch the tidy good-wife, seated at the open little scuttle, like a woman at a cottage door, engaged in knitting socks for her husband; or perhaps, cutting his hair, as he kneeled before her. And once, while marveling how a couple like this found room to turn in below; I was amazed by a noisy irruption of cherry-cheeked young tars from the scuttle, whence they came rolling forth, like so many curly spaniels from a kennel" (pp. 235-36).

Howells imagined a similar pastoral scene. The magazine promoter in *A Hazard* fell in love with a young woman at his boardinghouse, and he imagined domestic bliss to be his when he mowed the grass in the small Greenwich Village backyard garden the ladies of the boarding house had fashioned (p. 258).

The warm delicatessen of Madame Regaud (pp. 89-90) and Joe Harlan's watchman's shack (pp. 189-90) in *Manhattan Transfer* were portrayed as places of sufficiency and content, so they too might be read as minor continuations of the pastoral tradition. A more interesting possibility, however, lies in reading Dos Passos' treatment of proposals of marriage as evidence of where this ancient literary tradition had lodged

in the social imaginings of the twentieth century American metropolis.
On several occasions Dos Passos tells the story of wealthy men proposing
to the beautiful Ellen Thatcher (pp. l4l, 203, 375).

> "...You can't understand how lonely a man gets when year after year
> he's had to crush his feelings down into himself.  When I was a young
> fellow I was different, but what are you to do?  I had to make money
> and make my way in the world.  And so I've gone on year after year.
> For the first time I'm glad I did it, that I shoved ahead and made big
> money, because now I can offer it all to you.  Understand what I
> mean?...All those ideals and beautiful things pushed down into myself
> when I was making my way in a man's world were like planting a seed
> and you're the flower" (pp. 202-03).

In such a sequence of stories the ancient pastoral space of shepherds
and nymphs has been reduced first to Valentine cottages and city gardens,
and then to projections of fantasies upon women as the possible sites of
an alternative life to the socioeconomic environments of the paleotechnic
metropolis.

In addition  to the central issue of the location of nature within, or
outside human beings, the three novels possesses particular stories that
touch upon the urgent concerns for an environmentalist in the l990's.
Melville's universals, Howells' bureaucracy, and Dos Passos' sensory fog
are all stories of intense meaning today.

### Melville's Universals

One of the great pleasures in reading *Redburn* comes from the ease
in which Melville's imagination carried him from the interior of humans
outwards through all the scales of human experience.  In *Redburn* he
offered a few stories that were truly global yet at the same time rooted in
personal and everyday experiences.  At the outset of the voyage of the
*Highlander* from New York for Liverpool, on Redburn's first watch, he
heard the men sing as they pulled on the ropes to trim the sails.  At this
moment Melville introduced his readers to his first universal, music (pp.
93-94).

Later, on the return voyage, an Italian orphan boy, Carlo, who supported himself with a street organ, caught the emotions of the ship's diverse humanity with his tunes: officers and crewmen, whites and blacks, first class passengers and steerage, Irish and Germans. Soon thereafter Melville told the story of Harry Bolton, the frightened, effeminate, runaway English aristocrat who has become the pariah of the crew. Harry's beautiful voice and songs overcame their animosity:

> "So one night, on the windlass, he sat and sang; and from the ribald jests so common to sailors, the men slid into silence at every verse. Hushed, and more hushed they grew, till at last Harry sang among them like Orpheus among the charmed leopards and tigers. Harmless now the fangs with which they were wont to tear my zebra, and backward curled in velvet claws; and fixed their once glaring eyes in fascinated and fascinating brilliancy" (p. 364).

From universal spirit of the common sailors' music Melville turned to the significance of immigrant passengers traveling to the United States. Here the nation was imagined to be a congregation of the world. "Settled by the peoples of all nations, all nations may claim her for their own. You can not spill a drop of American blood without spilling the blood of the whole world" (p. 238).

And finally it was the genius of commerce, the trade of the world which vivified the community of mankind and the compass of the globe.

> "Surrounded by its broad belt of masonry, each Liverpool dock is a walled town, full of life and commotion; or rather, it is a small archipelago, and epitome of the world, where all the nations of Christendom, and even those of Heathendom, are represented...Here are brought together the remotest limits of the earth; and in the collective spars and timbers of these ships, all the forests of the globe are represented, as in a grand parliament of masts...Here, under the beneficent sway of the Genius of Commerce, all climes and countries embrace; and yard-arm touches yard-arm in brotherly love" (p. 234).

### *Howells' Bureaucracy*

In the working out of his narrative of the street railway strike Howells called forth a central modern problem: the uncontrolled, destructive bureaucracy that attacks its own citizens. Perhaps Howells was moved to raise this issue from his painful experiences in attempting to get pardons for the innocent men who had been wrongfully imprisoned and sentenced to death for the bombing and subsequent police riot at Chicago's Haymarket.[9]

However it may have been, he told his story cleverly by beginning with an impartial police officer, the very hope most citizens have for their police. Howells' story of the streetcar strike opened with an exchange between an angry, selfish artist, Angus Beaton, and a moderate policeman on the occasion of Beaton's discovering that there would be no horsecars to take him home.

> 'If I was a manager of the roads,' said Beaton, thinking of how much he was already inconvenienced by the strike...' I would see them starve before I'd take them back -- every one of them.'
> 'Well,' said the policeman impartially, as a man might whom the companies had allowed to ride free, but who had made friends with a good many drivers and conductors in the course of his free riding, 'I guess that's what the roads would like to do if they could; but the men are too many for them, and there ain't enough other men to take their places.' (p. 368).

The policeman had predicted trouble would come only when the police would later on begin "to move the cars" with strikebreakers (p. 367). Fighting did begin soon thereafter when the managers of the streetcar companies imported scabs from Philadelphia.

A New York State Arbitration Board then offered its services. The men rushed to give the Board their grievances; the managers declared that there was nothing to arbitrate (pp. 369-70). The strike then dragged on with repeated clashes between strikers on one side, and police and strikebreakers on the other (p. 374).

Basil March, the author's voice and principal character, wondered why such a private war was allowed to be carried on without the state intervening to protect the public interest (p. 370). March, although generally a timid man, wanted to experience the strike first hand. Thereupon he took a car filled with police and was carried into the midst of an ugly incident (p. 373). Strikers had attacked the street car where upon a patrol of police rushed up to club the strikers and drive them off. As they did so someone shot the saintly Conrad who was trying to make peace, trying to stop a policeman from clubbing Lindau, the old, one-armed white-bearded German socialist. On the corner Lindau is shouting at the police.

> "Ah, yes! Glup the strikers -- gif it to them! Why don't you co and glup the bresidents that insoalt your lawss, and gick your Boart of Arpidration out-of-toors? Glup the strikerss -- they cot no friendts! They cot no money to pribe you, to dreat you!" (p. 383).
>
> "The officer whirled his club, and the old man threw his left arm up to shield his head...The policeman stood there; he saw his face: it was not bad, nor cruel; it was like the face of a statue, fixed, perdurable; a mere image of irresponsible and involuntary authority" (p. 384).

Later in the novel Basil March ducked away from the implications of the incident. Yet it seems an important story for such a popular novelist as Howells to have told to his readers. The violent policemen of the neotechnic labor wars prefigured the growing twentieth century destruction of humans and their environments by agents of the nation state. Even as this is written, the American military is doing more damage to the environment than all the nation's chemical plants.[10]

### Dos Passos' Metropolitan Sensory Fog

The main axis of conflict in the many stories of *Manhattan Transfer* lay in the tension between the liveliness, hope, and emotional energies of the human beings in the city as opposed to the narrow confinement of self that was demanded by the processes of accumulation of wealth and power. A few characters in the novel succeeded at the cost of their liveliness; many, especially the young people seeking places in the city, were crushed by its harsh demands.

Dos Passos experimented with a new style in which to tell these stories. It was a style he later perfected for his trilogy, *U.S.A.* In this book he gave his readers a sense of a fast-paced urban environment by fragmenting the narrative and multiplying the characters and scenes. For example, in the first part of the novel, in the first hundred pages, two dozen named characters weave in and out of thirty-five different scenes. Many of the scenes compose continuing narratives, but others do not. The sense of the city full of motion is reinforced by snatches of popular songs, headlines from newspapers, advertisements, and signs, all interspersed with brief narratives that lend a sense of crowds in restaurants and cafés, and the flows of people along sidewalks, and moving on trains and ferries.

A flat-toned descriptive list was a special stylistic method of the novel. I understand it as a verbal imitation of a black and white photograph. Like the photograph it gave the reader a sense of authenticity since it was composed of actualities rendered as facts. The words were plain, often joined only by commas or "and" to make a list. Of course, like the photograph these descriptions were not actuality at all, but a pattern of selection that represented the artist's mood and focus.

For example Dos Passos told of his main character, Ellen Thatcher, stepping out with the man she loved:

> "He had his hand under her arm, she squeezed it tight against her ribs with her elbow. Aloof, as if looking through thick glass into an aquarium, she watched faces, fruit in storewindows, cans of vegetables, jars of olives, redhotpokerplants in a florist's, newspapers, electric signs drifting by. When they passed cross-streets a puff of air came in her face off the river. Sudden jetbright glances of eyes under straw hats, attitudes of chins, thin lips, pouting lips, Cupid's bows, hungry shadow under cheekbones, faces of girls and young men nuzzled fluttering against her like moths as she walked with her stride even to his through the tingling yellow night" (pp. 152-53).

It is helpful to an understanding of Dos Passos' narrative devices to recall his friendships to the Ashcan School painters who also took delight in portraying the commonplace of Manhattan during the early twentieth century. Dos Passos also knew of French symbolist poets (Mallarmé, Verlaine, and Rimbaud), and the Cubist painters so that his methods are complicated. His point of view mixed fragments of sights, smells, noises and gestures with more conventional descriptions.

These flat descriptive passages build up in time to make a panorama of Manhattan. Slowly, as you follow the characters moving always in this mass of little details, you come to realize that the crowds, the facades, the busyness of the rooms, the fast pace form a confusing fog of little particles that keep the characters from understanding either their city or themselves. As a reader reaches the end of the book he becomes aware that all those clearly identified details have spread a sensory fog over the entire island setting up a barrier between the characters and their need to penetrate the actualities of their environment. Dos Passos' New York characters are thus not only separated from nature, they are alienated from all aspects of their environments. As Karl Marx identified the situation years earlier, they are also alienated from themselves.[11]

The character who represented Dos Passos in this collection of stories, Jimmy Herf the *Times* reporter, closed the novel by leaving the city headed out to an undetermined somewhere else. He was just moving on. As he did so Herf departed in a sensory fog that obscured both his interior and exterior perceptions:

"Jobless, Jimmy Herf came out of the Pulitzer building. He stood beside a pile of pink newspapers on the curb, taking deep breaths, looking at the glistening shaft of the Woolworth. It was a sunny day, the sky was a robin's egg blue. He turned north to walk uptown. As he got away from it the Woolworth pulled out like a telescope. He walked north through the city of shiny windows, through the city of scrambled alphabets, through the city of gilt letter signs.

"Spring rich in gluten...Chuckful of golden richness, delight in every bite, THE DADDY OF THEM ALL, spring rich in gluten. Nobody can buy bread better than PRINCE ALBERT. Wrought steel, monel, copper, nickel, wrought iron. *All the world loves natural beauty.* LOVE'S BARGAIN that suit at Gumpel's best value in town" (p. 351).

"Jimmy Herf is walking alone up South Street. Behind the wharfhouses ships raise shadowy skeletons against the night. 'By Jesus I admit that I'm stumped,' he says aloud. All these April nights combing the streets alone a skyscraper has obsessed him, a grooved building jutting up with unaccountable bright windows falling onto him out of a scudding sky. Typewriters rain continual nickleplated confetti on his ears...one of two inalienable alternatives: go away in a dirty shirt or stay in a clean Arrow collar. But what's the use of spending your whole life fleeing the City of Destruction? What about your inalienable right, Thirteen Provinces? His mind unreeling phrases, he walks on doggedly. There's nowhere in particular he wants to go. If only I still had faith in words" (p. 366).

Surely in these three cities we can recognize our modern urban environments. And surely in the telling of their stories -- in Melville's seeking for universals, in Howell's collision with a destructive bureaucracy, and with Dos Passos' confused and impenetrable metropolis -- we meet the conflicts within our own environmentalism.

**References to the Novels:**

The page numbers given in the essay refer to the location of the quotations in the following editions of the three novels: Herman Melville, *Redburn, His First Voyage* (London: Penguin Group, 1986). William Dean Howells, *A Hazard of New Fortunes, A Novel* (Oxford: Oxford University Press, 1990). John Dos Passos, *Manhattan Transfer* (Boston: Houghton Mifflin, 1953 edition. It appears to be a photocopy of the first, 1925, edition.)

1. Eric E. Lampard, "The Urbanizing World," in H. J. Dyos and Michael Wolff, *The Victorian City, Images and Realities,* I (London: Routledge & Keegan Paul, 1973), 3-57. Cited also by Raymond Williams, *N.Y. Times Review,* Nov. 4, 1973, 6.

2. Lowell W. Adams & Daniel L. Leedy, eds., *Wildlife Conservation in Metropolitan Environments* (Columbia, Md.: National Institute for Urban Wildlife, 1991); and Wolfgang Haber, "Using Landscape Ecology in Planning and Management," in Isaak S. Zonneveld & Richard T. T. Forman, eds., *Changing Landscapes: An Ecological Perspective* (New York: Springer-Verlag, 1990), 217-232.

3. The terms "paleotechnic" and "neotechnic" were coined by the botanist-city planner Patrick Geddes and popularized by Lewis Mumford in his *Culture of Cities* (New York: Harcourt, Brace & Co., 1938), 495-496.

4. George Rosen, *A History of Public Health* (New York: M. D. Publications, 1958), 139.

5. Tertius Chandler, *Four Thousand Years of Urban Growth, An Historical Census* (Second Edition, Lewiston, N.Y.: Edwin Mellen Press, 1987), 521.

6. Clarence J. Glacken, *Traces on the Rhodian Shore* (Berkeley: University of California Press, 1967), 550.

7. Luke, 10:30-35.

8. Donald Worster built the structure of his intellectual history of modern ecology around the tensions between pastoral ideas, which he calls "arcadian," and their scientific opposites in *Nature's Economy* (Cambridge: Cambridge University Press, 1977).

9. William Dean Howells, Letter to the Editor, "Clemency for the Anarchists," *New York Tribune,* November 6, 1887.

10. Michael Renner, "Assessing the Military's War on the Environment," in Lester R. Brown, ed., *State of the World: 1991* (New York: W. W. Norton, 1991), 132-152.

11. Karl Marx, "Estranged Labor," in Robert C. Tucker, ed., *The Marx-Engels Reader* (Second Edition, New York: W. W. Norton, 1978), 72-75.

# 11

# On Urban Types:
## Comic and Social: from Egan to Mayhew

## Peter G. Buckley

In *The Idea of Poverty: England in the Early Industrial Age*, Gertrude Himmelfarb carefully prepares social historians for some disappointments. One by one, those nineteenth century writers who have remained influential in setting the terms and questions for recent work on the urban working class fall short of an honest engagement with the problem of "poverty." Carlyle, Cobbett, and of course Marx and Engels, wrote according to ideological, rhetorical and indeed personal requirements.

Himmelfarb reserves her most extended treatment, however, for Henry Mayhew, author of the four volume *London Labour and the London Poor* (1861), and not someone who has traditionally ranked high in the canon of social and poverty sciences. She asks why the urban poor became a heightened object of critical and literary attention in a decade when the "condition-of-England" question had already moved from the center of public debate and "poverty," as a national reality, had received some amelioration. The answer is that Mayhew was interested in a culture of poverty (before Oscar Lewis), rather than its economic basis, and that this was because he was "primarily a journalist, not, as we have come to think of him, a sociologist or historian." The main problem, indeed, is Mayhew's preoccupation with street-folk — a preoccupation that led him to ignore many honest indoor trades and never to fulfill the early promise to produce a "cyclopaedia" to life in London.[1]

How we have come to think of Mayhew as a "systematic empirical investigator" Himmelfarb finds easy to trace.[2] She is concerned to detail

Mayhew's haphazard methods and to place him as a popular or "Bohemian" thinker, only because of the way in which he has been advanced as a serious social critic by E.P. Thompson, among other social historians surveyed in the footnotes. To challenge Mayhew is therefore to cast suspicion on the whole tradition of "left" writing about urban labor. Eileen Yeo, in particular, has argued that at the level of detail and in his direct focus on the relation of poverty to wage levels, Mayhew "completely transcended the London low life genres" in which he began his writing career.[3]

Himmelfarb is surely right on one count. Mayhew was indeed unsystematic about his choice of trades. He was also something akin to an entrepreneur of poverty-writing with his cadre of stenographers, cabmen and experts.[4]    Above all Himmelfarb is convincing when she argues that he was not as much in control of his material as he professed to be. His vision remained circumscribed within his early comic work for *Figaro* in London and *Punch*, to the extent that he focused on the visual excitements of the street and melodramatic vignettes of degradation rather than on the realities of political economy.[5]

Yet behind this strong criticism lies another premise. Himmelfarb advances a Victorian assumption that it is impossible to have a seriousness of purpose without a heaviness of manner. In emphasizing Mayhew's debt to popular tradition and his Bohemian temperament, she discounts the cultural significance of this general preoccupation with the street. From the other camp, Yeo finesses Mayhew's attention to street-folk by stating that costermongers and their ilk are only a particular case of a sub-culture, set aside from the world of the manufacturing trades. Both then, expend much intellectual effort in separating comic sketching from social analysis, and as a result neither provides a satisfactory account for Mayhew's interest in the costermonger, or the over-representation of street types in his census of the city's poor (or the way the sections relating to costers were brought forward from their later placement in the *Morning Chronicle* series to providing a portal to the world of *London Labour*). Why are street vendors the group that opens the whole category of "those who will work," in volumes one and two, when they have the most irregular habits and the most uncertain income? Do these writings presage, as Yeo suggests, a new sociological interest in subcultures, or do they provide positive proof that Mayhew follows earlier delineations of London low-life?

Here I wish to argue that Mayhew neither transcends, nor is trapped within, the popular genres of low-life London, but rather that comic sketching prepares the way for social analysis in the Anglo-American tradition of urban writing. There are, of course, many other sources that have already received the attention of historians, especially the work of the various Select Committees of Parliament, the Voluntary Statistical Societies and health reformers. The occasion of Mayhew's entry into the field of social reportage for the *Morning Chronicle* in 1849 was the cholera outbreak of that year. However, the confluence of the comic, low-life sketch and Carlyle's notion of a writer's responsibility to the social "environment" in the works of such figures as Mayhew, Dickens or even Thackeray, helps to characterize the particular output of the late 1840s; moreover it engaged a wider section of the public in the sentiments of reform than earlier efforts had achieved.

Comic types became social types for two related reasons. The comic low-life sketch had traditionally emphasized the oddities of occupation and behavior as departures from a vision of society in which ideal, undifferentiated social actors stood above private desires. Comedy appeared in lapses from civility, statesmanship and disinterest. As metropolitan centers increased their geographies and range of employments, and as higher rates of social mobility broke "rank" as an operative category, what had been merely "comic" now became the norm. One might say, at the risk of reification, that the early nineteenth century city overwhelmed previous representations of social order.

The second reason has less to do with writing *about* society than the changing place of literature within it. The vogue for urban "typing" occurred within a vastly expanded market for literature, the graphic arts and cheap theatre. Popular authors may still have felt a vocation, of religious dimensions, for their work, yet they also gained "careers" (a word still usefully retaining its origin in chariot racing) which were pulled by the popular market toward depictions of common life. Writers used the resources of the comic sketch to gain an imaginative purchase on the heterogeneity of the urban scene. Those authors who worked with comic urban types were well prepared both to expose the "realities" of poverty and to invoke a crowd of readers for them (see below, n. 17).

This is not just a preparedness that we can detect only in Mayhew. Many of those writers, artists and actors who had specialized early in their careers in delineating the urban heterogeneity, in either the gothic or comic mode, found a more active engagement with "the social question" in and through the 1840s. The three main "mystery and misery" writers — Eugène Sue for Paris, G.W.M. Reynolds for London and E.Z.C. Judson for New York — never finished their mammoth productions but ended up at the head of crowds and as editors of papers addressed to the needs of urban workers.[6]   The social investigators, Mayhew in London and George Foster for New York, both began an active dialog with laboring "correspondents" and addressed workers meetings; and the poet Thomas Hood gave up his *Comic Annuals* that he been editing since 1829 to found *Hoods Own Monthly* in 1844, a magazine dedicated to the interests of laboring classes.

Political forces are the significant key to the shape and timing of this engagement. Crowds had a habit of becoming angry in 1848 and 1849. Few writers, like the population at large, remained indifferent to the Chartist March on London, or more importantly, the February and June days in Paris. Yet the ethical and literary quality of this engagement remains at issue. Himmelfarb sees Mayhew stuck at the desk of popular literature, pouring out lively vignettes, whereas Yeo believes that through the experience of the survey Mayhew encountered the reality of a degradation so vast that he became a hostile critic of the emerging capitalist order.

Though there is no convenient half-way house of interpretation between these two positions, another look at the centrality of the jovial costermonger in Mayhew's urban panorama may help to locate the nature of his engagement with the street vendors at other levels. As Yeo notes, in contrast to others working in the "curiosities of London life" genre, Mayhew used more direct transcription of the words of his "informants," seldom theatricalized the labor process, and generally steered way from first person moralizing when faced with scenes of debauchery. However, for all of his efforts at journalistic objectivity — detailing the terms of each trade, the capital employed, and net wage estimates — "labour" remains a cultural rather than an economic phenomenon. Labor markets are curiously localized with a welter of placing detail and they are hedged in by custom and heredity. Mayhew views trades as ethnographic units, usually "tribes," which possess their own geographies, clothing, physical appearances, habits and pastimes. Such portraits retain the literary force and interest of the caricature though they additionally acquire the ideological force of opening a frontal attack on classical economics. In contrast to Adam Smith's "supply and demand" model for the operation of labor markets, Mayhew's workers are largely trapped within a culture of local ignorance and inelastic custom. Even life expectancy and rates of infant mortality — of universal significance to the contemporary statisticians — become indices to craft particularity.

The costers, however, form less of a distinct tribe than the coal-heavers, rag-pickers, street-sweepers and so forth who are to follow in the four volumes. Mayhew suggests that they are recruited from a wide range of previous employments, that they have the most extended of geographical rounds and that they possess higher rates of social mobility. Their knowledge of London's folkways is unmatched. They are certainly the most expressive of all the street traders, and most immediately appealing in their crafty patter and banter. As such they become mediating "characters" between the author and audience, between the desk and the street. Together with their iconographically close transatlantic cousins --New York's Bowery B'hoys--they serve as the engaging narrative vehicle which will allow the reader to descend into the unknown metropolis of degradation and despair. Both types are "comic" to the extent that they ape and mimic manners above or beyond their social station, but who are "social" in the way that they figure the relations of the new popular culture of print.

Not surprisingly therefore, though he spends much time detailing the terms and conditions of the trade, Mayhew returns again and again to the coster's relationship with this popular commercial culture. He is ambivalent, in a very studied way, about the social effects of their consumption of "penny dreadfuls" and popular illustration: whether their appetites attest to the "improvability of the class" or whether they serve to enforce ignorance:

> 'The costermongers,' said my informant, 'are very fond of illustrations. I have known a man, what couldn't read buy a periodical what had an illustration a little out of the common perhaps, just that he might learn from some one, who could read what it was all about. They have all heard of Cruikshank, and they think *everything funny is by him* - funny scenes in a play and all. His "Bottle" was very much admired. I

heard one man say it was very prime, and showed what "lush" did, but
I saw the same man,' added my informant, 'drunk three hours
afterwards.'[7]


For Himmelfarb, such reported scenes speak to a "confusion of
identity" in Mayhew's handling of the costers. Are they members of the
deserving poor who elicit our sympathy, or should they be classed with
the undeserving, as irredeemably bound to their vigorous and vicious
subculture? There is however a prior "confusion" or problem (of which,
one suspects, Mayhew was well aware) that produces a studied, rather
than simply confused, ambivalence. What is the relationship between
the author or illustrator and the popular classes he seeks to reach, either
as audience or charitable subject? Here, the most popular pictorial and
didactic narrative of social declension, George Cruikshank's "Bottle," is
viewed by costers as a comic, theatrical performance (which it indeed
became in certain "transpontine" stage versions) [PLATE I].[8] "The bottle,"
and its successor "The Drunkard's Children" engages the coster's interest
in reading yet does nothing to change the behavior it seeks to reform. No
doubt Mayhew's informant actually recorded a "real' conversation, though
it is telling that this scene reproduces, in a low tavern, a debate that had
been active in literary offices. Mayhew, among others, had already seen
Cruikshank's reworking of Hogarth's "progress" narratives as insufficiently
"radical" since the drunkard's road to ruin began in the merriment of social
and domestic life rather than in the poverty of the slum. The joke finally
was on George, for "The Bottle" did nothing to repudiate his own
reputation for drunkenness and fast living first gained through his
illustrations for Pierce Egan's *Life in London*.[9]

The whole literary and graphical tradition of urban comic typing had
been re-engerized by the publication Egan's work in 1821, the full title
being *Life in London, or, The Day and Night Scenes of Jerry Hawthorn,
Esq., and his Elegant Friend Corinthian Tom, accompanied by Bob Logic,
the Oxonian, in their Rambles and Sprees through the Metropolis*. Egan
established the novel claim to see all of London, from the Corinthian
Capital to the low life base [PLATE II]. The scrapes are amusing enough
and the material is sufficiently salacious still to be a good read, yet they
achieve their comic effects to the extent that they depart from classical
ideals of civility and learning. The Corinthian column suggests

architectural perfection and political order yet the base, the foundation, rests on what Tom terms "rich bits of low life." This comic subversion of civic humanism is unremitting. Language is larded with slang from the markets, the turf or the ring: so much so that the original editions have mock footnotes set in one of the three type faces used in the text.[10]

The many character types Tom encounters do not fit any known model of the ideal citizen or subject. They are all interested in some way, in drink, in sex, or in cash. They are all embedded in some form of exchange. There is no actor who is elevated enough to serve as a rational political agent in the way Enlightenment thinkers might have demanded. Egan makes sure that his reader gets this point, by frequently invoking the traditions of academic history and landscape painting, especially Reynolds' discourses on subjects fit for public art and discussion. "The Metropolis is now before me: POUSSIN never had a more luxuriant, variegated, and interesting subject for a landscape; nor had SIR JOSHUA REYNOLDS finer characters for his canvas."[11]

Egan gained his own Poussin and Reynolds in the form of the Cruikshank brothers, and the narrative, in quite a new way, is subservient to the illustration, devoting long passages to the woodcuts' explication. The illustrations, in fact, outdistanced the text in stressing the equality and promiscuity of people at pleasure. The plates aimed at delineation of "life" somewhere between, in George's own words, "the sublime and the ridiculous"[12] [Plate III].

Of course, low-life literature had a long tradition especially within humanist circles, and collections of vulgarisms are as old as print culture itself. But writing in 1820, Egan encountered a much broader public of readers, and perhaps had a hand in forging newer markets since he was a pioneer in inexpensive serial publication. Louis James has counted sixty-seven derivative publications of *Life in London* that appeared within three years of its arrival.[13] In less than two months a stage version, by Montcrieff, called *Tom and Jerry*, the title of which would require an essay to itself, became a standard afterpiece in popular London theatres, and was to remain so until the 1850s. Through plagiarism and popular marketing, Egan effectively lost control over his own creations. His types became the common property not only of other illustrators, writers and dramatists, but also of tailors who catered to the mania for Corinthian dressing.

There is reasonable evidence that Egan's work accelerated the vogue for "slumming" among upper-class blades and certainly it stood as a model for writing (and living) for authors as different in social background as Dickens and Thackeray.

Egan was understandably disappointed that he had not reaped the financial benefits of such popularity -- "We have been *pirated*, COPIED; traduced; but, unfortunately, not enriched by our indefatigable exertions": in addition, he did not like the way that Tom was changing in others hands or pens. It was not that the pace of the sprees were any more frenetic or the action more bawdy. Corinthian Tom, like Egan himself, was a member of the fancy set -- a gentleman who consciously descends the social ladder to take his pleasures. The action of *Life in London* remained picaresque in the sense that however roving Tom might have been in his quest for pleasure, he carried out his sprees in the niches of a relatively fixed order. But the new Toms or their equivalent were lower in rank and more socially presumptuous. In 1827 Egan published a sequel called a *Finish to Tom and Jerry* which did not have the effect demanded by the title. It is obvious, for instance, that Sam Weller, the loquacious cockney in the *Pickwick* papers, takes on, in a more benevolent fashion, where Tom leaves off.[14]

Translations, or transpositions, also take place across the Atlantic. As early as 1823, an African-American theatre company stages a *Life in New York*, of which we have few records, unfortunately, other than the title, though we know that the British actor, Charles Mathews, attended a performance and later incorporated a black dandy in his American "At Home" polymonologues, (ironically re-importing Tom in blackface back to the London stage). By 1827, New York's Park Theatre begins the annual custom of staging a *Life in New York* for the volunteer firemen's benefit night, in which an American Tom appears in top hat wearing the firemen's red shirt. Indeed, the protean figure of the New York's Bowery B'hoy begins to take shape in these productions to arrive fully-fledged (or iconographically fixed) in Benjamin Baker's *Life in New York in 1848* at the Olympic Theatre [PLATE IV]. Though Baker claimed to have modeled his Bowery B'hoy on figures seen on New York street, local plebeian swells had already adopted the gregarious costumes seen in earlier productions of Montcrieff's version of *Tom and Jerry*.[15]

After the success of Egan and his imitators, the notion of "seeing" the city will be written out, sketched out or played out by popular writers and dramatists for whom classical visions of urban order and civility were neither available nor made sense. The Corinthian architecture and scaffolding to the city disappears while Tom becomes more plebeian or localized. He stands as a figure whose origin is *of* the street, rather than one who steps into it from a coach. The story of an urban know-it-all introducing the sights to his rural friend remains, but the narrative force of the sketch is no longer solely dependent on the idea of social descent. The author is thus bound in ever more tight relations with the popular audience he invokes.

The results initially are still only comic. Through the 1830s a number of monthly publications appear that specialize in deflating and satirizing the fashionable enthusiasms of the metropolis. They usually take their names from the smart subversives and servants of previous literatures -- *Punch, Figaro* and *Charivari*. A generalized social radicalism appears here: aristocrats in *Punch* are always rendered as snobs, and the producing classes usually pretentious and opportunistic. Yet such magazines do form a remarkable training ground for those who will find ways to extend the circumscribed sketches of urban life. In *Punch* alone we have Thackeray, Henry Mayhew and the poet Thomas Hood, all of whom will break out into more extended treatments of social relations still based on typing.

In New York the development is somewhat different, given the early appearance of a cheap, unstamped and almost totally unregulated daily press. Here the know-it-all flaneur who will introduce the common reader to the intricacies of city life is the journalist, who from the start is remarkably unembarrassed about introducing his fashionable persona into the story. A century and a quarter before Tom Wolfe reinvented the new journalism a young Walt Whitman paraded himself in lower Manhattan, surveying the extremes of social life and the variety of occupations and functions:

> Then finding it impossible to do anything either in the way of "heavy business," or humor, we took our cane (a heavy dark beautifully polished, hook ended one) and our hat, (a plain, neat fashionable one from Banta's, 130 Chatham street, which we got gratis, on the strength of giving him this puff) and sauntered down Broadway to the Battery. Strangely enough, nobody stared at us with admiration -- nobody

said "there goes the Whitman of the Aurora!" -- nobody ran after us to
take a better, and second better look -- no ladies turned their beautiful
necks and smiled at us -- no apple women became pale with awe - no
newsboys stopped, and trembled, and took off their hats, and cried
"behold the man that uses up the Great Bamboozle [Park Benjamin]!
no person wheeled out of our path deferentially -- but on we went,
swinging our stick (the before mentioned dark and polished one) in our
right hand -- and with our left hand tastily thrust in its appropriate
pocket,  in our frock coat (a gray one)[16]

This kind of writing in popular press served to characterize the city
by 1840 as a realm of accident and idiosyncrasy, a crowd of different
interests, occupations and appetites that amounted to a parody of Smith's
division of labor. For what had been to the eighteenth century a fathomless
crowd, a crowd with no possible political will, becomes a rich array of
socially individuated types.[17] The types are predictable, but they are also
purposive.  They are avatars of urban desire.  The popular writer had
reached out to the crowd as an audience, and in so doing had made it a
public in a political and commercial sense, investing it with will.

It is in the 1840s that such schemata achieve something else through
the political pressures that forge ever closer alliances between comic
authors and audiences.  The author of the crowd is tempted or persuaded
to become something more than a sketcher or dandy, but tribune, savior
or reformer as well.  Social engagement allowed writers, especially those
trained in the comic, sketching tradition to elaborate and extend what had
previously been reductive.  The inequalities of urban society now offered
their own plot, no longer requiring the know-it-all flaneur to set the
narrative in motion.[18]

Yet in this new and serious engagement with the poor, the comic
shadows of Tom remain.  For Mayhew, the flamboyant, bawdy costers
provide the entrance into the world of London labour, not because they
are typical of pauperized workers, or even a defined subculture, but
because they mirror, and offer a self-reflexive commentary upon, the
position of an author seeking an "extensive acquaintance" with the growing
city.  "Considered economically," Mayhew's fascination with costering
lies in the very novelty of urban markets, that between producers and
consumers there lies a vast range of types introducing the "two great

classes" (in James Mill's sense of producers and consumers) to each other mainly through patter and flash work. Street traders, it appears, are chiefly entrepreneurs of words rather than of tangible goods. Mayhew, with approval, quotes a regular bred coster who knows that the public pays first for the talk and then for the produce. For all of the latter tales of hardship and degradation, Mayhew's opening interest lies in the psychology of how the coster, like the author, approaches his market, with fear or with assurance. Yet, as the quotation from Walt Whitman shows, the popular writer remains a figure in the street, not one born to the street, reaching out to the crowd as patron while at the same time surveying it as subject: forever moving between "heavy business" and "humor."[19]

Plate 11.1

*Plate 11.2*

Plate 11.3

*Plate 11.4*

F S CHANFRAU IN THE CHARACTER OF 'MOSE'

PLATE I   The third scene from "The Drunkard's Children," glyphograph by George Cruikshank, 1848.

PLATE II  Frontispiece from *Life in London* designed and etched by I. R. and G. Cruikshank (London: Sherwood, Neely, and Jones, 1821)   Here, the three central characters of Tom, Jerry and Bob are placed in the middle of the column, raising their glasses, appropriately enough, for it is drink that will lubricate their acquaintance with the nobility, the merchant, the mechanic and the rag-tag and bobtail.

PLATE III  "Midnight. Tom and Jerry at a Coffee Shop near the Olympic" from *Life in London.*

The accompanying text reads "This group (which the Plate so correctly delineates, and in point of character, equal to any of HOGARTH's celebrated productions) displays a complete picture of what is termed "LOW LIFE" in the Metropolis; drunkenness, beggary, lewdness, and carelessness, being its prominent features. It is, however, quite new to thousands in London. TOM and JERRY have just dropped in, by way of a finish to the evening, in their route towards home, and quite prime for a lark."

PLATE IV   "F.S. Chanfrau in the Character of "Mose"" E & J. Brown lithograph, New York 1848. Library of Congress.   The most popular stage delineation of New York's version of the Coster, the butcher and volunteer fireman "Mose," the Bowery B'hoy.  Both Whitman and E.Z.C. Judson had a hand in manufacturing the type.

1. Gertrude Himmelfarb, *The Idea of Poverty: England in the Early Industrial Age* (New York: Random House, 1983). A similar assessment of Mayhew's work had already been offered by H. J. Dyos in "The Slums of Victorian London," *Victorian Studies* 13 (September 1967).

2. The phrase is from Eileen Yeo's "Mayhew as a Social Investigator," in E.P. Thompson and Eileen Yeo, *The Unknown Mayhew: Selections from the Morning Chronicle, 1849-1850* (London: Penguin, 1973), 56.

3. Yeo, unlike Himmelfarb, claims that there are "two" Mayhews: the "unknown" Mayhew of the *Morning Chronicle* and the more commercially driven writer of the later *London Labor and the London Poor* (1861).  Himmelfarb's critique opens with Mayhew's better known writings, reserving her remarks about the Chronicle essays until after Yeo and Thompson's enthusiasm for them appears misplaced.

4. Augustus "Gus" Mayhew, Henry's younger brother, certainly conducted many interviews and had a hand in writing them up; so did Richard Knight, who had

been a paid employee of the London City Mission, and one Henry Wood, about whom not much is known. Yeo stresses that Mayhew supervised all of the work with care, pointing out that current social investigation is often undertaken by groups, whereas Himmelfarb characterizes the outfit more as a species of popular amusement.

5. One has to note that Mayhew has not fared any better of late on the literary left and in cultural studies. Mayhew's use of metaphors of "race" is seen as an attempt to construct a stable place for the bourgeois observer before the sight of the unregulated poor. See, for instance, the comments of Peter Stallybrass on the ideological consequences of Mayhew's typing in "Marx and Heterogeneity: Thinking the Lumpenproletariat", *Representations* 31, (Summer 1990), 71.

6. Not by chance, for Mayhew, are the costers supporters of Reynolds after his sudden insertion into Chartism during the debacle in Trafalgar Square: "What they love best to listen to -- and indeed, what they are most eager for -- are Reynolds' periodicals, especially the 'Mysteries of the Court'. 'They've got tired of Lloyd's blood stained stories,' said one man, who was in the habit of reading them, 'and I'm satisfied that, of all London, Reynolds' is the most popular man among them. They stuck to him in Trafalgar Square, and would again. They all say he's 'a Trump', and Feargus O'Connor's another trump with them.'" *London Labour and the London Poor* (London: Griffin, Bohn and Company), Vol.1:27. This is deliberately contrasted with their reception of Cruikshank; see below.

7. Mayhew, *London Labour and the London Poor*, Vol. 1:28

8. The 'Bottle,' and its successor 'The Drunkard's Children', were Cruikshank's most successful works in terms of sales, with 100,000 copies distributed within two weeks. He had hoped that by reworking Hogarth's "progress" narratives that he could effect a popular transformation of British drinking habits, and thus set a price, at eight plates for a shilling, that he thought would be within everyone's reach.

9. Thus Dickens wrote: "At Canterbury yesterday I bought George Cruikshank's "Bottle". I think it very powerful indeed: the last two plates most admirable....I question whether anybody else living could have done it so well.... The philosophy of the thing, as a great lesson, I think all wrong; because, to be striking, and original too, the drinking would have to begin in sorrow, or poverty, or ignorance, the three things in which, in its awful aspect, it does begin. The design would thus have been a double-edged sword -- but too "radical" for good old George, I suppose." Dickens to Forster, December 17, 1847, quoted in Blanchard Jerrold, *The Life of George Cruikshank* (London, 1879). For recent work on Cruikshank

see Michael Wynn Jones, *George Cruikshank: His Life and London* (London: Macmillan, 1978) and Robert L. Patten (Ed.) *George Cruikshank; a Re-evaluation* (Princeton N.J: Princeton University Press, 1974), a reprint of material in the Princeton University *Library Chronicle* 35 (1973). I have so far not discovered any scholarly survey of the explosion in the illustration of London low life that appears to occur during the 1820s, nor the re-appreciation of Hogarth's work that proceeds in the same period as, for instance, in Charles Lamb's essay "On the Genius and Character of Hogarth (*Reflector*, 3, 1811). For new approaches to the illustration of the period see John Barrell's "The Private Comedy of Thomas Rowlandson," *Art History* 6 (December, 1983).

10. For a fine discussion of Egan's place within the development of English literary humor see Roger B. Henkle, *Comedy and Culture, 1820-1900* (Princeton: Princeton University Press, 1980)

11. Egan, *Life in London*, (London, 1821),15

12. George Cruikshank's own account of how he came to draw "life" in a manner opposed to the academic tradition rings true: "There was in the neighbourhood in which I resided a low public-house; it has since degenerated into a gin palace. It was frequented by coal heavers only, and it stood in Wilderness lane. To this house of inelegant resort, which I regularly passed in my way to and from the Temple, my attention was one night especially attracted by the sounds of a fiddle, together with other indications of festivity; when, glancing towards the tap-room window, I could plainly discern a small bust of Shakespeare placed over the chimney-piece, with a short pipe stuck in its mouth. This was not clothing the palpable and the familiar with golden exhalations from the dawn, but was reducing the glorious and immortal beauty of Apollo himself to a level with the commonplace and the vulgar. Yet there was something not to be quarreled with in the association of ideas to which the object led. It struck me to be the perfection of the human picturesque. It was a palpable meeting of the sublime and ridiculous..... I thought of what the great poet had himself been, of the parts that he had played, and the wonders he had wrought within a stone's throw of that very spot; and feeling that even he might have well wished to be there, the pleased spectator of that lower world, it was impossible not to recognise the fitness of the pipe. What a picture of life was there! It was as though Death were dead! It was all life. In simpler words, I saw on approaching the window and peeping between the short red curtains a swarm of jolly coal-heavers! Coalheavers all - save a few of the fairer and softer sex - all enjoying the hour with an intensity not to be disputed, and in a manner singularly characteristic of the tastes and propensities

of aristocratic and fashionable society ...The living Shakespeare, had he been there, would but have seen a common humanity working out its objects. *"George Cruikshank's Omnibus* (London: 1841) No 1, p 2.

13. Louis James, *Fiction for the Working Man, 1830-1850: A Study of the Literature Produced for the Working Classes in Early Victorian Urban England* (London: Penguin, 1963).

14. In the *Finish*, Egan removes Jerry Hawthorne and the fat, benevolent figure of Sir John Blubber, via a coach ride from Piccadilly to the small Somerset town of Pickwick; thus Dickens almost exactly begins his career in fiction where Egan's finishes. For more on Egan see J.C. Reid, *Bucks and Bruisers: Pierce Egan and Regency England* (London: Routledge and Kegan Paul, 1971)

15. The dramatist Paul Preston remembered that *Tom and Jerry* in New York "was as keenly appreciated here as in the latitude for which it was indicated. Corinthian Tom was as much of a New York character as he was a type of London swell, and I am certain that a dozen counterparts of a Bob Logic could be scared up at a day's notice without going more than a block away from the Olympic's portico, especially when Charley Abel's bar room was tolerably well filled." Newspaper clipping in an extra-illustrated edtion of Joseph N. Ireland, *Records of the American Stage* (New York: T.H Morrell, 1866), Volume 2, Harvard Theatre Collection.

16. Walt Whitman, "Walks on Broadway" *New York Aurora*, February 23, 1842.

17. The word "type" only appears to have gained a sociological meaning in the early nineteenth century. It is instructive how many words now used commonly to designate a human quality at first possessed a more restricted meaning within the graphic arts and theatre. A *person*, for instance, originally came from persona, as in a mask used by a player, though it became a general term for a human being by the 14th century; *character*, first an engraving instrument (from the Greek), became a sign or mark, usually on the face, of inner humor, while in a different 18th century development it stood for a written testimony to someone's social standing. In Franklin's Philadelphia, for instance, a character was equivalent to a reputation. Only in the mid-nineteenth century did character, personality and type come to mean a lively personal identity, something in one's private possession. What seems striking is the way that masks and graphic signs proceed metaphorically to stand for internal qualities though they usefully retain, in an age of popular communication, their sense of legibility and display. See Raymond Williams, *Keywords: A Vocabulary of Culture and Society* (London: Fontana, 1976), 196.

18. Jonathan E. Hill, "Cruikshank, Ainsworth and Tableau Illustration," *Victorian Studies* 23 (Summer 1980) 429-459.

19. Even for Thackeray, who never set out to survey the poor, the sketch ascends to become a moral tale with the change of title from *Pen and Pencil sketches* of *English Society* to *Vanity Fair, A Novel without a Hero* in 1847. Rising expectations of "literature" allowed authors to capture the complexity of social relations.

# 12

# Cohorts and Communities:
## A Personal Note*

## Leo F. Schnore

### *I*

My first acquaintance with the work of Eric E. Lampard was in 1955 when I was still a neophyte in my own field, but one with a general and quite naive interest in "urban studies" writ large. This original concern was mainly limited to studies of the U.S.A. but extended to international comparisons of levels and rates of urbanization in different nations and territories. (My own work had a special focus on "sociological human ecology" as developed by Amos R. Hawley and Otis Dudley Duncan, stressing spatial patterns in and around cities.) The Lampard essay was his seminal article in *Economic Development and Cultural Change*.[1]

This essay had the carefully developed and compact style, rich in hypotheses, that I admired so much in the works of Hawley and Ronald Freedman, my mentors in demography and human ecology at the University of Michigan, and Duncan, whom I met when I was still a graduate student in Ann Arbor.[2] Moreover, my undergraduate training at Miami University (Ohio) had prepared me for a minor in anthropology at the M.A. level, an interest that I have never lost.

As a sociologist, all that I knew of Lampard initially was that he was an economic historian and that he was affiliated with Smith College. I knew nothing of his background, especially of his lengthy service in the Royal Marines during World II (1941-46) on behalf of England, his native land, and his prewar and postwar training at the London School of Economics before he came to the United States in 1948. Here he was strongly influenced (as I learned later) by the work of the late Abbott Payson Usher, the internationally renowned Harvard economic historian of Europe.[3]

My second and even more impressive contact with his work came with his contribution to a highly regarded study sponsored by the Resources for the Future -- *Regions, Resources and Economic Growth* -- coauthored by Harvey S. Perloff, Edgar S. Dunn, Eric E. Lampard and Richard F. Muth.[4] Lampard's contribution was based on the U.S. Census of Population and Housing and (above all) it was very readable, rendering major "regional" differences in important social and economic characteristics in a way that immediately caught the attention of an amateur statistician like me. (Clarity of expression has always been important to me.)

I finally met the man in person in 1958 when I was invited to join a Committee on Urbanization sponsored by the Social Science Research Council in New York City. That group met at least three times a year for six years, 1958-1964, and in the seventh year brought forth *The Study of Urbanization.*[5] I came to feel that I was privileged to hold a kind of postdoctoral education in urban studies. And in meeting Lampard face-to-face, I learned something of the character of this thoughtful gentleman. Upon reflection, my opinion is that his chapter on "Historical Aspects of Urbanization" in that book, and especially his distinctions between "Primordial" and "definitive" and "classic" and "industrial" urbanization, represents the most original contribution to a rather uneven series of essays that might be expected from any multidisciplinary group.

Eventually, I am happy to say that he was persuaded to leave the east and return to the University of Wisconsin-Madison, where he had received his Ph.D. under the direction of Vernon Carstensen and the strong influence of Merle Curti, the eminent social historian; here Lampard wrote a prize-winning dissertation on the rise of the dairy industry in Wisconsin.[6]

Although we had become close personal friends over the course of seven years, it turned out that we collaborated on only one essay, "Social Science and the City: A Survey of Research Needs," in a volume on *Urban Research and Policy Planning.*[7] In addition we both served for a time as adjunct professors of urban and regional planning on the Madison campus.

In that period we also developed a "Seminar in Urban History" open to students in all of the social sciences. My contribution was to send up broad and sweeping generalizations from "classical" urban sociology and anthropology. His role was to bring down these balloons with a barrage of empirical studies, ranging over national (U.S.) or international data, whether fully "comparative" or based on case studies of particular cities. He would indicate, for example, (1) refinements such as *variations* in territorial patterns with such staples of sociological and ecological analysis (including the anthropological literature) as size of the city, its rate of growth, regional location, age of the city, its political status, etc. or (2) outright *rejection* or disconformation of "theory" as I then understood it. I soon came to regard him as "the walking bibliography." He read widely through all of the social sciences as well as urban history, and unlike many of us he retained what he had read.

Our final "collaboration," albeit at a distance, came out of a conference project at the University of Wisconsin-Madison, supported by the Mathematical Social Science Board, and underwritten by the Center for Advanced Study in the Behavioral Sciences, which led to the publication of *The New Urban History: Quantitative Explorations by American Historians.*[8] The greatest value of this book, in my view, lies in the magisterial essay, "Two Cheers for Quantitative History: An Agnostic Foreword," in which Lampard brings some degree of order into the work of historians, economic historians and social and economic geographers, efforts which are widely divergent in theory and method. Stepping across disciplinary lines was never as much a problem for Lampard as it was for me. He always had the ability to present an integrative view of the subject at hand, and I regarded his move to the State University of New York at Stony Brook as a grievous loss to the University of Wisconsin-Madison.

## *11*

Now we might turn to the matter of the main title of this brief note, indicating ways in which I might have been of some utility to Lampard, if only as a "conduit" of ideas and concepts developed by sociologists, and especially by demographers and sociological human ecologists.

*Cohorts.* In demographic circles, a "cohort" is a subpopulation experiencing a particular change of experience in its "life course" that occurs within a given time period, usually taken as a calendar year.

Examples of such subsets are births (as in the familiar notions of "the baby boom" and "baby bust" in the U.S. and elsewhere), marriages, divorces, and entries into and separations from the labor force. These are only examples. The cohort approach has long been employed in life-table analysis, upon which insurance policies are based. For a more formal definition we might offer that set out in a highly influential essay by Norman B. Ryder, another former colleague at the University of Wisconsin-Madison:

> A cohort may be defined as the aggregate of individuals (within some population definition) who experienced the same event within the same time interval..... The cohort record is not merely a summation of a set of individual histories. Each cohort has a distinctive composition and character reflecting the circumstances of its unique origination and history. The lifetime data for one cohort may be analyzed and compared with those for other cohorts by all the procedures developed for a population in temporal cross section.[9]

In fact, demographers have had no monopoly on the concept; many years ago, Louis 1. Dublin and A. J. Lotka, in *The Length of Life*, reported that the cohort based life-table approach had been regularly used for many years in testing material products such as light bulbs and washing machines with regard to length of useful service.[10] The life-table approach has also been a staple for life insurance companies for decades, as I have noted above.

These facts struck me with the simple idea that *the concept of the cohort might be usefully employed in the analysis of urban communities* by taking note of the dates of settlement *or* incorporation *or* state charter *or* whatever measure of the "birth" of individual cities of a given size one might employ.

The effort at identifying the "age" of cities is not as simple as it might seem in empirical terms. I have experimented with a number of measures over the years. "Cities" in the U.S. are creatures of the states in which they are located; they are also unlikely to "hold still" for the observer. *Annexation* of territory by cities is common in most parts of the country, and *detachments* of parts of cities have occurred from time to time, although such a political move is rather rare. One of the most influential of the earlier sociological human ecologists was sensitive to this and other relevant issues; I refer to the appendices to R. D. McKenzie, *The Metropolitan Community*.[11]

I have also found numerous instances in which "suburbs" *have* changed their boundaries by annexation, and there is always the vexing problem of *enclaves*--politically independent islands of territory surrounded by major cities in the course of their growth and development. (McKenzie's work, together with that of James A. Quinn,[12] expresses the different approaches that stemmed directly from the works of the original developers of sociological human ecology--Robert E. Park and Ernest W. Burgess--at the University of Chicago in the late 1910s, 1920s and early 1930s). Other investigators, including Hawley, Donald J. Bogue, Avery M. Guest and I have attempted to use variations on the familiar "Burgess hypothesis" with mixed results. My approach has been to simplify the familiar "Burgess Zonal Hypothesis," which holds that socioeconomic status tends to rise with distance from the center of the urban complex. In the course of my work, I developed an "evolutionary hypothesis" describing the changing patterns of socioeconomic status differences between cities and suburbs. Three stages are recognized: (1) one in which the elite resided very near the center of the city, with the disadvantaged located at the periphery; (2) one in which both the highest and lowest strata were overrepresented in the central city; (3) one in which the inner city is dominated by the lowest strata, and the higher "social classes" are found in suburbia and beyond. The last stage, of course, is the one on view in most of the older and larger urban agglomerations in the U.S. The sheer age of the city seems to be a powerful factor in predicting the overall distribution of socioeconomic strata in the entire urban complex, best represented by the Urbanized Area in the U.S. Census of Population and Housing.

Long ago I decided that detailed comparisons by "distance zones" were fruitless, and despite the ready availability of data for entire *counties* --whether they are called Standard Metropolitan Areas (SMAs), *or* Standard Metropolitan Statistical Areas (SMSAS) *or* Metropolitan Statistical Areas (MSAS) *or* simply Metropolitan Areas (the next likely step in Federal nomenclature), I decided that the Urbanized Area (UA) -- which is a more specialized density-based unit of urban analysis that uses "Census Tracts" in the main, and that is *not* strictly based on building blocks comprised by county and town(ship) political lines--is more appropriate for research *and* planning purposes. (In its own way, this note constitutes a plea for the continued delineation of Urbanized Areas in future censuses for the use of sociologists, historians, economists, geographers, planners, and others engaged in urban studies.)

Now let us turn to the second of the two notions that have preoccupied sociological human ecologists over the decades, which is also represented in the main title of this essay: the concept of "community." This turned out to be a large undertaking for me, since so many writers in the field of sociology (as well as in others) have expressed so many views over the decades that diverge sharply from the tradition of sociological human ecology.

In 1967, 1 was invited to prepare a chapter on "Community" for what turned out to be a widely used textbook in introductory sociology. The request from the editor--another former colleague, Professor Neil J. Smelser of the University of California at Berkeley--specified (1) that the chapter should be conceived as one of several "basic social structures" and (2) that it should accommodate both (a) static or cross-sectional as well as (b) longitudinal or historical aspects. Having considered several conceptions of the basic idea of community as it evolved over the years, I offered the following as my own:

> Since we have briefly reviewed the development of the community concept, and have examined some of its applications and the issues they raise, I now offer a working definition designed to serve the main purposes of this chapter. I do this with some hesitancy, but it is essential that I make clear at the outset just what I regard as "the community." If the review of research undertaken here is to have meaning, some boundaries must be established, and this is most readily accomplished by means of a working definition. In other words, we need to delineate a manageable area of inquiry.

> For the purpose of this chapter, then, I shall regard "the community" as *the localized population which is interdependent on a daily basis, and which carries on a highly generalized series of activities in and through a set of institutions which provides on a day-to-day basis the full range of goods and services necessary for its continuity as a social and economic entity.*

As we shall see, this kind of omnibus definition encounters some difficulties in use. One difficulty is that communities differ in the extent to which they depend upon other populations: some communities are virtually "independent" entities, while other are involved in a complex network of relations with still other communities. Nevertheless, the terms in this definition refer to variables whose meanings are reasonably straightforward. Following Hawley and [Talcott] Parsons, the restriction of attention to "daily" interaction clearly excludes regional and global applications. The emphasis on "a highly generalized series of activities" means that the term cannot be properly applied to such "total institutions" as prisons and mental hospitals, where activities are narrowly focused. Reference to "a set of institutions which provide on a day-to-day basis the full range of goods and services" also serves to exclude these single-purpose establishments. Finally, the stress upon "continuity as a social and economic entity" brings out the salient fact that the life span of the community normally exceeds that of its members and suggests that it is a unit in its own right, with a history that is something more than the sum total of its inhabitants' biographies.

This definition advances no judgments concerning the extent to which residents of the community share a common culture, or--more particularly --the extent to which they experience some kind of "we-feeling" or sense of uniqueness. I contend that these matters are better left open for empirical assessment. At our present state of knowledge, these features are more properly regarded as variables, with some populations exhibiting them quite clearly and others failing to display manifestations of these particular psychological traits in any significant degree.

However, one remaining issue that has yet to be seriously confronted in the sociological literature is the extent to which communities, as defined here, might contain other social units that are *themselves* properly regarded as communities. Specifically, are such areas as New York's Harlem, Chicago's Bronzeville, and San Francisco's Chinatown to be regarded as "communities" in their own right? These are localized populations which seem to display many, if not all, of the characteristics that I have specified in my definition. Moreover, they display a high degree of visibility and persistence over time.

The thin literature dealing with these areas, and others like them, suggests a wide degree of variation in the extent to which they should be regarded as communities *per se*. In many instances, it is difficult to discern any substantial degree of agreement concerning their boundaries, and the extent to which their constituent institutions fully provide for the daily needs of their members remains open to question.

One solution, although not a fully satisfactory one, is simply to regard these areas as distinctive *subcommunities*, the unity and integrity of which may vary from case to case. These areas are something more than

> "neighborhoods," but something less than communities in the fullest sense of the term. That is, they are parts of a larger whole; while they may be amenable to the same kind of analysis as the community at large, they are not the same kind of "complete" social unit...[13]

With this conception in mind, my own thinking from the same general period can be more fully understood. In a collection of my early articles, I used as many as 200 *Urbanized Areas* (UAs) centered on cities (or combinations of cities) of 50,000 or more; most of this work employed 1960 Census data.[14] Several of my graduate students have subsequently tested the evolutionary hypothesis, using 1950, 1960, and 1970 Census materials, using metropolitan area designations for those years *or* UAs.[15] Now (in the 1990 U.S. Census) we have 366 Metropolitan Statistical Areas (MSAS) *and* Urbanized Areas centered on cities (or combinations of cities) of 25,000 and over. *This opens the opportunity for a more adequate statistical basis for historical analysis.*

It is my present feeling that the Urbanized Area (UA) seems to offer a more appropriate empirical representation of "the city" *and* its suburbs than what the 1990 Census calls the Metropolitan Statistical Area (MSA). The UA in its totality *is* the contemporary American city as it is perceived as one approaches it while passing through it or over it by modern means of transportation, whether over land or by air. For all its many merits, we may have been deluded, or at least unduly influenced, by the notion of "megalopolis," introduced in this country by the famous Belgian geographer Jean Gottmann.[16] Compared to the UA, the MSAs (and combinations thereof) are simply much more convenient to the investigator; counties are required by Federal and State authorities in each locality to report on an enormous variety of economic and social topics.

In my own work on the socioeconomic status of cities and suburbs, as well as in that of my graduate students, we have employed *both* the UA and the metropolitan area unit in use at the time, depending upon the problem at hand. We have also used only a limited list of variables--(a) *size* of city *or* of the Metropolitan Statistical Area *or* the UA, (b) *age of the city* (the number of decades that have passed since a city reached a particular size), (c) *region and division*, as set out by the U.S. Bureau of the Census; the latter pair designates a combination of States. (d) Finally, variations in *location* with respect to oceans, rivers, and railroads ("site features" along with topography in the geographer's vocabulary) were considered. This yielded a *"minimalist"* framework, or a kind of lattice to which other variables might be added, as suggested by other scholars, most notably John J. Harrigan, a political scientist, and sociologists Joel Smith and Harold F. Goldsmith and his various colleagues in sociology . Only Smith used data for the UA; the others relied on the SMSA. [17]

In my own case, in the course of working with 1950, 1960, and 1970 census materials, along with my graduate students, I came to see some evidence of a very *slow* "evolution" through certain "stages" in which various socioeconomic status categories (especially as measured by educational attainment) relocate in apparent response to (1) *economic forces*: (a) the shifting location of the labor force in response to the relocation of jobs in industry and services (as depicted so clearly in the works of John D. Kasarda, another student of Hawley's) as well as (b) the changing market linkages of the central city, (2) *social and political impulses* (as in the abandonment of certain areas to (a) avoid or (b) seek contacts with various ethnic groups) and (3) *geographic features* such as (a) "situational" factors including changing transport access to other cities and regions--and in more recent years--(b) the buildup of certain areas according to the various "amenities" they have offered, as in the growth of "sun belt" cities and suburbs at the expense of urban areas in other regions. The *ethnic dimension* has received overwhelming attention since the 1950s and 1960s, but America has always been a "racist" society, as any Native American Indian can attest. Subsequent social movements have learned a great deal from that period, as we shall observe below.

It has been often noted in the sociological and economic literature, of course, that upper-status individuals and families have the wherewithal to locate wherever they wish; and the trek to "suburbia," so widely noted in the U.S.A., results from the elite leading the way to the outlying promised land, and even beyond to "exurbia," only to be followed by the broad "middle class" (the latter being a popular notion that has yet to be precisely defined). In my view this is an interesting approach with much merit, but it relies too much on dubious assumptions, often without data in support of them, and altogether connotes a "microsociological" approach. The problem of *changes* in population distribution can be just as well taken as the basis for the kind of "macrosociological" analysis as in Hawley's and Duncan's earlier works. This strategy also underlies some of Lampard's work, as we shall observe below.

In a conference at Leicester (England), I once expressed the idea that American cities seem to be evolving in the direction I have indicated.[18] I put this idea forth as simply a hypothesis to be tested by replications, but scholars from France and Germany, well versed in the history of cities on the European continent, indicated that nothing of the sort could be observed in the major cities therein. (I have always learned from negative as well as positive critiques by my colleagues in the entire field of urban studies.) My response was that I would be very pleased if the evolutionary hypothesis held for the U.S. or (on a more grandiose scale) for a least *some or even all* of the English-speaking world. I was very pleased and encouraged only a few years later to find the following concluding passage in the work of an eminent geographer, R. J. Johnston, in a chapter devoted to "The Changing Social Topography":[19]

> Schnore's [evolutionary] model has been considered in some detail because it probably represents the most significant development in the field since Burgess and [Homer] Hoyt.

Johnston holds that the evolutionary pattern is clearly evident not only in larger cities in the U.S., but also in those found in Canada, the United Kingdom, Australia, New Zealand, and South Africa. It should be noted, however, that his approach relies heavily on "Social Area Analysis," a form of factor analysis, or "Factorial Ecology," which I have never regarded as satisfactory, since I was schooled in a day in which hypotheses were derived from theory and set forth as "if-then" propositions to be tested by empirical evidence. This is clearly *not* the case with Social Area Analysis.

To return to one of the main themes of this note, I was one of the earliest of those to advocate the POET scheme devised by Otis Dudley Duncan in "Human Ecology and Population Studies" in Philip M. Hauser and Duncan (editors), *The Study of Population: An Inventory and Apraisal*.[20] That frame of reference--"The Ecological Complex"--holds that there are four main axes along which ecological analysis might proceed, not only in the study of urban areas but even "primitive" populations in what is now called "the Third World" and those in developing nations, as well as in developed nations like the U.S.A. A number of anthropologists and other social scientists have done field work that can be interpreted in these terms. (The POET notion is an acronym that stands for *population, organization, environment* and *technology*. Each of the four axes is held to be influenced by the other three according to Duncan's highly original exposition.)

The conception of "technology" as a distinct parameter (or more properly as a cluster of more specific and measurable variables) must certainly include the means of transportation and communication *and* what is now fashionably labeled as the community's "infrastructure." As Hawley has noted,

> Human ecology begins with the obvious fact that human life is lived on the ground, so to speak, and that it is all mixed up with soil, tools, food, raw materials, buildings, and other material externalities. A social system is reared upon those profane foundations and it never disassociated from them, not even in its more rarefied moral and sacred aspects. [21]

Lampard seems to have found such ideas useful, at least for a time.[22] The POET scheme is obviously a variation on Hawley's basic idea that social organization or "the social system" stands between a given population and its environment; this was his central argument set forth in 1950 in his classic treatise *Human Ecology: A Theory of Community Structure*[23] and repeated as recently as 1992 in an essay on sociological human ecology as a form of macrosociology.[24] Hawley's basic idea is that technology is merely "an aspect of organization." To repeat the point stated above, if we look closely at the anthropological findings on cities and surviving "primitive" communities in "the Third World," as well as reports on "developing nations" by anthropologists and other social scientists around the world, one could very well argue that *organization is an aspect of technology*. In any case, much of Lampard's more recent efforts still imply that technological factors are truly critical in urban analysis, although other variables must be introduced in order to yield a fuller understanding of the contemporary urban scene.

Lampard became much more than an economic historian in the narrow sense over the course of his long career. Even after he left the University of Wisconsin-Madison in 1969 1 followed his writings closely. His expanding horizons are well represented in three papers from the 1970s: (a) "The Dimensions of Urban History: a Footnote to 'the Urban Crisis'," *Pacific Historical Review*, 39 (August, 1970), pp. 261-278; (b) "The Pursuit of Happiness in the City: Changing Opportunities and Options in America," *Transactions of the Royal Historical Society*, 5th Series, 23(1973), pp. 175-220; and (c) "Figures in the Landscape: Some Historiographical Implications of Environmental Psychology," *Comparative Urban Research*, 5 (1977), pp. 20-31. The very titles suggest the wider canvas of his work. The psychological and moral dimensions of urban community life have long been ignored by those of us working in the mainstream of sociological human ecology, and we have born the brunt of critical attacks for maintaining this macrosociological position over the years.

As I indicated above, Lampard's sole 1970 essay was devoted to "The Dimensions of Urban History: a Footnote to 'The Urban Crisis'", an insightful paper in which he showed the historical roots of the "problematic" aspects of urban living in the U.S.A. "Race Riots" were obviously at the forefront of American thinking in the late 1950s and 1960s. It is my present feeling that these outbreaks of violence--sparked by the Civil Rights movement under the leadership of *many* prominent figures--that spread so quickly over college and university campuses in the U.S.A. from border to border and coast to coast (along with parallel protests over the War in Viet Nam) set the pattern for subsequent social movements of the 1970s and 1980s to the present. I refer, of course, to the movements on behalf of women's rights (again with a wide variety of ideological leaders) to the current concerns over gay and lesbian rights. These topics are usually regarded as beyond the ken of demographers and human ecologists, but the numerous works of Donald J. Bogue, Nancy Denton, Otis Dudley Duncan and Beverly A. Duncan, Reynolds Farley,

Freedman, Hawley, Stanley Lieberson, Douglas Massey, Alma F. Taeuber and Karl E. Taeuber must be regarded as providing vital background data on the *ethnic* dimensions of the long-standing urban chaos again being brought to daily public view in the 1990s through the persistent efforts of the print and electronic media.

Demographers and sociological human ecologists have been traditionally wary of projections into future time, at least until the age of computers. For invaluable perspective on the question of the spatial segregation of major "color" categories in and around American cities, see Karl E. Taeuber, "Residence and Race: 1619 to 2019," Center for Demography and Ecology, University of Wisconsin, *CDE Working Paper* 88-19, April 1988, 49 pp. As for my own view of the whole range of major problems facing U.S. cities at the beginning of the 1960s, see my paper on "Social Problems in an Urban-Industrial Context," *Social Problems*, 9 (Winter, 1961-62), pp. 228-240. While I claim no gift for prophecy, many of the trends observed in that essay have come to pass. The "urban crisis" continues to haunt our cities to this day.

My only other effort at moderately long-range prognostication was in "The Journey to Work in 1975," in Donald J. Bogue (editor), *Applications of Demography: The Population Situation in the United States in 1975*, Oxford, OH and Chicago: Scripps Foundation for Research in Population Problems, Miami University, and Population Research and Training Center, University of Chicago, 1957, pp. 73-75. The modest predictions set out in that paper were subsequently verified in some degree by the decision of the U.S. Bureau of the Census to create "separate" Metropolitan Areas in Nassau and Suffolk Counties within the Greater New York Metropolitan Area.

In general, however, I share with Lampard a certain unease about projections of even the most obvious historical trends into future time. It is difficult enough to make sense of the past, *after the fact*, as it were. I feel that we must avoid the easy temptation to be cast in the role of soothsayers as students of urban history, whether our interests are purely domestic or international in scope.

In the late 1970s and early 1980s, Lampard seemed to have reverted for a time to an interest in "morphological" or "ecological" concerns. In his 1978 paper, "Some Aspects of Urban Structure and Morphology in the Historical Development of Cities in the United States," in *Cahiers*

*Bruxellois: Revue d'histoire urbaine*, Brussels, 1978, pp. 73-115, Lampard used the work of urban geographers, urban land economists, demographers and sociological human ecologists, as well as transportation historians, economic historians and more conventional urban historians in order to reconstruct the story of U.S. urbanization from the sixteenth to the twentieth century. Further evidence of Lampard having been influenced by "morphological" or "ecological" thinking is provided in one of his more recent and ambitious undertakings. I refer to his essay on "Mutations of Cities in the Industrializing Era: An Ecological Perspective on Urbanization in the U. S. A." *Essays from the Lowell Conference on Industrial History 1982 and 1983* (Lowell, MA, 1985), pp. 194-249.

In "The Nature of Urbanization," a 1983 paper prepared for Derek Fraser and Anthony Sutcliffe (editors), *The Pursuit of Urban History*, [25] Lampard again showed a sensitivity to the role that changing areas (as measured in square miles) might play in comparing city growth in Europe and America. To me, this is the single most impressive essay produced by Lampard in the 1980s. Its value is suggested by its being used (*sans* statistical data) as the introductory chapter in a wide-ranging and impressive collection of essays edited by William Sharpe and Leonard Wallock (editors), *Visions of the Modern City: Essays in History, Art, and Literature.*[26]

I was first sensitized to the issues of annexation, consolidation and detachments of territory in major American cities in connection with my doctoral dissertation research at Ann Arbor in 1954-55. (See *Patterns of Decentralization: A Study of Differential Growth in the Metropolitan Areas of the United States, 1900-1950, xxx+ 416 pp.*) Building upon McKenzie's reports for 74 cities, I assembled information on city areas (in square miles) by surveying the Departments of Civil Engineering and related offices in all of the metropolitan centers recognized in 1950 in order to acquire data which were then retrojected to 1900. 1 pursued this matter in three subsequent papers: (1) "The Timing of Metropolitan Decentralization: A Contribution to the Debate," *Journal of the American Institute of Planners*, 26 (November, 1959), pp. 200-206; (2) "Municipal Annexations and the Growth of Metropolitan Suburbs, 1950-1960," *American Journal of Sociology*, 67 (January, 1962), pp. 406-417; and (3) Schnore and Vivian Z. Klaff, "Suburbanization in the 'Sixties: A Preliminary Analysis," *Land Economics*, 48 (February, 1972), pp. 23-33.

Klaff later went on to explore the effects of annexation on the growth of nonmetropolitan as well as metropolitan centers, studying all places of 2,500 and over in the course of two decades. See Klaff and Glenn V. Fuguitt, "Annexation as a Factor in the Growth of U.S. Cities, 1950-1960 and 1960-1970," *Demography*, 15 (February, 1978), pp. 1- 12. In this important paper, the authors conclude that the role of annexation should be taken into account in all subsequent studies of population redistribution. I regret to say that this good advice was not followed, and that it led to some of the misunderstanding of the "nonmetropolitan population turnaround" of the 1970s.

Other recent studies of annexation by sociologists include David Bromley and Joel Smith, "The Historical Significance of Annexation as a Social Process," *Land Economics*, 49 (August, 1973) pp. 294-309, John D. Kasarda and George V. Redfearn, "Differential Patterns of City and Suburban Growth in the United States," *Journal of Urban History*, 2 (August, 1975), pp. 43-66, and Joel Smith, David Bromley and Kenneth Manton, "Changes in the Coincidence of the Boundaries and Populations of Central Cities," *Social Forces*, 57 (March, 1979), pp. 931-951. Fortunately, the U.S. Bureau of the Census now maintains a data file on intercensal annexations, consolidations and detachments of territory by municipal governments of all sizes. This constitutes an invaluable source of information for urban-historical analysis.

Lampard's essay in the Sharpe-Wallock volume is profoundly ecological throughout, viewing "modern" urbanization as a process of population redistribution that has been responding (since the beginning of the nineteenth century to the present) to technological and organizational changes, both viewed as affected by important innovations--whether under private or public auspices--and thereby simultaneously creating and responding to an everwidening physical and social environment or ecosystem. Two phases of urbanization are recognized: (1) a *centripetal* period of city building, and (2) a *centrifugal* era in which selective dispersal of population and broadly socioeconomic functions have to be recognized. In the case of the U.S. the shifting role of municipal, state and federal levels of government are given due attention. As a political economist in the classical sense of that term, Lampard offers critical insights into the role that policy planning might play, and emphasizes the limits that social and economic realities set for the social engineers, who seem to prescribe placebos as often as they offer panaceas for our continuing urban ills. (In my reading of history, cities seem always to have been in one or another kind of trouble from the beginnings of civilization until today.)

The introductory essay in the Sharpe-Wallock collection (by the editors) is entitled "From 'Great Town' to 'Nonplace Urban Realm': Reading the Modern City." The former phrase is taken from a very influential essay by a Berkeley urban and regional planner, Melvin M. Webber, in Melvin M. Webber *et al* (editors), *Explorations in Urban Structure*, Philadelphia, 1964. Webber also developed the concept of "community without propinquity" to describe the current urban scene; both Hawley and Kasarda have employed this notion in their ecological works. Webber's notion of the "nonplace urban realm" parallels Kasarda's conception of a "polycentric ecological field" in which the traditional urban center is merely "one specialized node in a multinodal multi-connected ecological field of interdependent activity centers." (See John D. Kasarda, "The Implications of Contemporary Redistribution Trends for National Urban Policy," *Social Science Quarterly*, 61, (December, 1980), pp. 374-400.)

Hawley's more recent views are well represented in his *Urban Society: An Economical Approach*, New York, 1971, revised edition, 1981. As I see it, this theoretically-oriented work will provide another whole generation of sociological human ecologists and other students of urban affairs with a wide array of testable hypotheses. Some of this work has been accomplished by John D. Kasarda, one of Hawley's outstanding students. For a summary of Kasarda's views on U.S. development, see his essay on "Urban Economic Transitions," in Edgar F. Borgatta, (editor), *Encyclopedia of Sociology*, New York, 1992, Volume 4, pp. 2195-2198. See also Lee J. Haggerty's article on "Urbanization," in the same encyclopedia, Volume 4, pp. 2198-2203. Haggerty's views are also in the mainstream of sociological human ecology.

Finally, Lampard has produced another essay demonstrating the sweep of his interests and the catholicity of his views in his introductory essay on "Structural Change" in William R. Taylor (editor), *Inventing Times Square: Commerce and Culture at the Crossroads of the World*.[27] It is highly doubtful that any other living scholar could have accomplished this *tour de force*. Other contributions that Lampard has made in the past to my own field are very evident. For example, he was the first (in 1968) to predict "the nonmetropolitan population turnaround" of the 1970-1980 intercensdal decade that so preoccupied rural sociologists and demographers for a time.[28] Lampard has also been fully aware that the "nonmetropolitan turnaround" represented but a "blip" in the long-term course of the urbanization of our society since its colonial beginnings.[29]

## III

My own principal sociological interests have always been theoretical, but with the quantitative testing of hypotheses derived from ecological theory. My current stance may be more fully understood by reference to my article entitled "Notes on the Conduct of Urban Historical Research."[30] Needless to say, continuous direct exposure to Lampard's thinking and writing over the course of a decade exerted a profound influence upon my theoretical and empirical work, and I have continued to find his work most exciting since that time. His major contribution to my own understanding of American cities is the wealth of information he has amassed suggesting that the sheer age of the urban agglomeration is a critical variable with respect to changing forms of social and economic organization which are simply reflected in evolving spatial patterns.

At an international conference on urban history at Leicester (England) held in 1966, 1 proposed a modest agenda for urban-historical research to cover four distinctive aspects of the processes of urbanization and suburbanization. These were (1) the demographic, (2) the ecological, (3) the organizational, and (4) the behavioral (or social-psychological) facets. I saw these as a set of research foci that were deliberately ordered from the easiest to the most difficult, and I regarded them as candidates for joint efforts by all the social sciences involved in the broad area labeled "urban studies," as well as by professional historians *per se.*[31] With his eldritch ability at intellectual synthesis, it would appear that Lampard has single-handedly managed to enhance our understanding of all of these four aspects of urbanization and suburbanization, especially in the United States, but in other parts of the developed world as well. At the same time, he has produced a large part of the research he himself called for in his very influential essay on "Urbanization and Social Change."[32]

In all of the above discussion I have tried to convey some of the importance of Lampard's work *outside* the field of "urban history" *per se*, for he has consistently been making distinctive contributions to urban sociology, urban economics, urban geography, "urban psychology," the study of urban politics, and urban policy planning for over forty years. He has always managed to give unity to his work with materials from diverse data sources. And to rework a well-worn cliché, he has remained the consummate gentleman as well as the dedicated scholar, truly deserving the world renown he has achieved. Such a towering figure in any specialized field comes but once in a lifetime, always in the vanguard, and like a certain comet approaching us on this planet, such a man appears but once in a generation. Cheers, chum!

* This essay owes much to the critical scrutiny and comments of my esteemed colleague Merle Curti, Frederick Jackson Turner Professor of History emeritus, as well as to former colleagues at the University of Wisconsin and elsewhere. As always, I owe a special debt of gratitude to Richard L. Forstall of the Population Division, U.S. Bureau of the Census.

1. Eric E. Lampard, "History of Cities in the Economically Advanced Areas," *Economic Development and Cultural Change*, 3 (January, 1955), pp. 81-156. I received my own Ph.D. in that year and was teaching at Brown University in Providence RI at the time.

2. My essay on "Social Morphology and Human Ecology," *American Journal of Sociology*, 63 (May, 1958), pp. 620-634, reflects the heavy influences of both Hawley and Duncan.

3. Lampard's autobiography is given in brief in Bruce M. Stave, "A Conversation with Eric E. Lampard," *Journal of Urban History*, 1 (August, 1975), pp. 440-472. My own even shorter attempt to summarize my own career and my developing interest in urban history appears in the same journal; see Schnore, "Urban History and the Social Sciences: An Uneasy Marriage," *Journal of Urban History*, I (August, 1975), pp. 395-408.

4. Baltimore, 1960; reprinted Omaha, NE, 1965.

5. Philip M. Hauser and Leo F. Schnore (editors), New York, 1965.

6. Lampard, *The Rise of the Dairy Industry in Wisconsin, 1820-1920: A Study in Agricultural Change*, Madison, 1963.

7. Leo F. Schnore and Henry Fagin (editors), Beverly Hills, CA, 1967.

8. Princeton, NJ, 1975.

9. "The Cohort as a Concept in the Study of Social Change," *American Sociological Review*, 30 (December, 1965), pp. 843-861; the quotation is from p. 845.

10. Louis I. Dublin and A. J. Lotka, *The Length of Life: A Study of the Life Table*, New York, 1936.

11. New York, 1933.

12. *Human Ecology*, Englewood Cliffs, NJ, 1950.

13. Leo F. Schnore, "Community," in Neil J. Smelser (editor), Sociology: An Introduction, New York, 1967, pp. 79-150 (first edition); the quotation is from pp. 95-96.

14. Leo F. Schnore, *The Urban Scene: Demography and Human Ecology*, New York, 1965, especially Part Four, Chapters 11 and 12, on "The Socioeconomic Status of Cities and Suburbs" and "Urban Structure and Suburban Selectivity."

See also Leo F. Schnore and James R. Pinkerton, "Residential Redistribution of Socioeconomic Strata in Metropolitan Areas," *Demography*, 3 (1966), pp. 491-499; Leo F. Schnore and Joy K. Jones, "The Evolution of City-Suburban Types in the Course of a Decade," *Urban Affairs Quarterly*, 4 (June, 1969), pp. 421-442; and Leo F. Schnore and Juliette L. Redding, "The Evolutionary Hypothesis Reconsidered: Two Decades of Change in City-Suburban Status Differences," unpublished manuscript, 1985. See also James R. Pinkerton, "The Changing Class Composition of Cities and Suburbs," *Land Economics*, 49 (November, 1973), pp. 462-469.

15. In his article entitled "Another Look at the Burgess Hypothesis: Time as an Important Variable," *American Journal of Sociology*, 76 (May, 1971), pp. 1084-1093, Lee J. Haggerty applied Markov chain analysis to changes in the socioeconomic characteristics of Census Tracts, 1940-1960, and found "a trend toward a *direct* relationship between socioeconomic status and distance from city centers even within cities which show an *inverse* cross-sectional relationship" at the outset of the time period under observation. The quotation is from p. 1084, with italics added. A Markov chain (or process) is one in which the future values of a random variable are statistically determined by contemporary events and dependent on the events immediately preceding. It is named after the Russian mathematician Andrei Andreivich Markov (1856-1922), who developed it, and who is widely regarded as the father of modem probability theory in statistics. For a master overview of research in the "classical" tradition, see Avery M. Guest, "The City," in Michael Micklin and Harvey M. Choldin (editors), *Sociological Human Ecology: Contemporary Issues and Applications*, Boulder CO and London, 1984, pp. 277-322. Trends from 1950 through 1990 are stressed in Leo F. Schnore, "The Ecology of American Cities: Quantitative Studies in Urban History," unpublished manuscript, 1991.

16. Jean Gottmann, *Megalopolis: The Urbanized Northeastern Seaboard of the United States*, New York, 1961; see also Gottmann and Robert A. Harper (editors), *Metropolis on the Move: Geographers Look at Urban Sprawl*, New York, 1966, and Gottmann, *Megalopolis Revisited: 25 Years Later*, College Park, MD, 1987.

17. John J. Harrigan, "A New Look at Central City-Suburban Differences," *Social Science*, 51 (Autumn, 1976), pp. 200-208. Joel Smith, 'Another Look at Socioeconomic Status Distributions in Urbanized Areas,' *Urban Affairs Quarterly*, 5 (June, 1970), pp. 423-453. Harold F. Goldsmith and S. Young Lee, "Socioeconomic Status Within the Older and Larger 1960 Metropolitan Areas," *Rural Sociology*, 31 (June, 1966), pp. 207-215; Harold F. Goldsmith and Edward

G. Stockwell, "Occupational Selectivity and Metropolitan Structure," *Rural Sociology*, 34 (September, 1969), pp. 387-395; Goldsmith and Stockwell, "Interrelationship of Occupational Selectivity Patterns Among City Suburban and Fringe Areas of Major Metropolitan Centers," *Land Economics*, 45 (May, 1969), pp. 194-205. See also Reynolds Farley, "Suburban Persistence," *American Sociological Review*, 29 (February, 1964), pp. 38-47. A valuable overview as of the end of the 1960s is provided in James R. Pinkerton, "City-Suburban Residential Patterns by Social Class: A Review of the Literature," *Urban Affairs Quarterly* 4 (June, 1969), pp. 499-519.

18. Leo F. Schnore, "Problems in the Quantitative Study of Urban History," in H. J. Dyos (editor), *The Study of Urban History*, London, 1968, pp. 189-208.

19. R.J. Johnston, *Urban Residential Patterns*, London and New York, 1971, Chapter IV, pp. 126-14 1; the quotation is from p. 141. Johnston employs "Social Area Analysis," a form of Factor Analysis. "Factor Analysis" is a statistical research method that is widely employed in the social sciences and in certain related fields, such as "the communication arts." It purports to reduce a large number of variables to a much smaller number of categories or "factors" that can account for the correlation (if any) between the original variables. Both "Factorial Ecology" and "Social Area Analysis" are forms of Factor Analysis. Scholars employing the latter strategy (such as the sociologists, Eshref Shevky and Wendell Bell) have identified three factors in their studies of selected large cities in the United States; these are (1) the socioeconomic status dimension, (2) the familial dimension and (3) the ethnic dimension. Mainstream sociological human ecologists within sociology have tended to be suspicious of the entire approach. See Amos H. Hawley and Otis Dudley Duncan, "Social Area Analysis: A Critical Appraisal," *Land Economics*, 33 November, 1957), pp. 337-344. See also Leo F. Schnore, "Another Comment on Social Area Analysis," *Pacific Sociological Review*, 5 (Spring, 1962), pp. 13-16. Johnston gives surprisingly little attention (pp. 83, 94-96) to the famous Harris-Ullman multiple nuclei theory of urban structure, perhaps because it is not well suited to historical or longitudinal analysis. Chauncy D. Harris (1914-) and Edward L. Ullman (1912-1976) were colleagues in urban geography at the University of Chicago in the 1930s and early 1940s when sociological human ecology--first enunciated by Robert E. Park (1864-1944) and Ernest W. Burgess (1886-1966)--became a dominating view in American sociology and when Homer Hoyt's competing theory of urban residential structure (the "sector" model) was first set out. (See Homer Hoyt, *The Structure and Growth of Residential Neighborhoods in American Cities*, Washington DC,

1939). Hoyt deliberately posed his theory as an alternative to the Burgess model. For the original Harris-Ullman statement, see "The Nature of Cities," *Annals of the American Academy of Political and Social Science*, 242 (November, 1945), pp. 7-17. Insight into its development is provided in Chauncy D. Harris's Foreword to Ronald R. Boyce (editor), *Geography as Spatial Interaction* (Seattle, 1980), a collection of Ullman's most influential essays. Incidentally, Ullman's treatment of the role of "amenities" in changing patterns of population redistribution antedated the politically-inspired popular distinctions between "sunbelt" and "snowbelt (or "rustbelt")" cities that dominated conventional social and urban history in the 1980s.

20. Otis Dudley Duncan, "Human Ecology and Population Studies,' in Philip M. Hauser and Otis Dudley Duncan (editors), *The Study of Population: An Inventory and Appraisal*, Chicago, 1959, pp. 678-716; see especially pp. 681-685. Another important contribution in the same era was Duncan's "Population Distribution and Community Structure," *Cold Spring Harbor Symposia on Quantitative Biology*, 22 (1957), pp. 357-371. For a fascinating application of the POET framework to a pressing urban-environmental problem, see Duncan "From Social System to Ecosystem," *Sociological Inquiry*, 31 (Spring, 1961), pp. 140-149. See also Duncan's essay on "Social Organization and the Ecosystem," in Robert E. L. Faris (editor), *Handbook of Sociology*, Chicago, 1964, pp. 36-82.

21. Amos H. Hawley, "Sociological Human Ecology: Past, Present, and Future," in Michael Micklin and Harvey Choldin (editors), *Sociological Human Ecology: Contemporary Issues and Applications*, Boulder, CO and London, 1984, pp. 1-19; the quotation is from p. 3.

22. See Lampard, "Some Aspects of Social Structure and Morphology in the Historical Development of the United States," cited in the text. See also his more recent contribution, "Mutations of Cities in the Industrializing Era: An Ecological Perspective of Urbanization in the U.S.A.," in Robert E.-Weible (editor), *Essays from the Lowell Conference on Industrial History 1982 and 1983*, Lowell, MA, 1985, pp. 194-249. The terms "morphology" and ecology are virtually identical in Lampard's vocabulary. They register "ecosystem" functioning.

23. New York, 1950.

24. Amos H. Hawley, "The Logic of Macrosociology," *Annual Review of Sociology*, 18 (1992), pp. 1-14.

25. London, 1983. See Table 1-5 in the section on "Urbanization at full stretch and the morphology of space-time convergence," pp. 41-53, the concluding portion

of this very instructive chapter. As noted above, "ecology" and "morphology" are used as virtually identical terms throughout Lampard's writings.

26. New York, 1983. The value of the collection is suggested by its being republished (Baltimore and London, 1987) only four years later.

27. New York, 1991, pp. 15-35 and 372-375 (notes).

28. This fact is acknowledged in the most thorough review of the literature on the topic; see Glenn V. Fuguitt, "The Nonmetropolitan Population Turnaround," *Annual Review of Sociology*, 11 (1985), pp. 259-280. See also Franklin D. Wilson, "Urban Ecology: Urbanization and Systems of Cities," *Annual Review of Sociology*, 10 (1984), pp. 283-307 for an equally capable review of recent developments in my chosen field of study. Some readers may wonder about the role of "new towns," developed under the auspices of the Federal Government during the 1970s, in the period of the "nonmetropolitan population turnaround." Only four were actually completed. At the introductory level, the best treatment of "new towns" (all built at some distance from major urban centers in the U.S.A.) is to be found in Edward W. Hassinger and James R. Pinkerton, *The Human Community* (New York, 1986), Chapter 14, "Intentional Communities: Nineteenth-Century Utopian Communities and Contemporary Communities," pp. 379-409, and Chapter 15, "New Towns as Intentional Communities," pp. 410-435. An unknown factor in the 1970-1980 period is the rise of the three thousand-odd "communal" living arrangements found in all parts of the U.S.A. See Bennett M. Berger, *The Survival of a Counterculture: Ideological Work and Everyday Life Among Rural Communards*, Berkeley, CA (1981) for a thorough case study.

29. See Richard L. Forstall, "Is America Becoming More Metropolitan?" *American Demographics*, 3 (December, 1981), pp. 18-22. Forstall shows that, although it grew more rapidly than metropolitan areas during the 1970s, the nomnetropolitan sector actually lost some seven million people while metropolitan areas gained some thirty million. The reason behind this apparent paradox involves growth differentials by size (and probably age) of metropolitan areas, and (b) the formation and recognition of new metropolitan areas. See also Richard A. Engels and Richard L. Forstall, "Metropolitan Areas Dominate Growth Again," *American Demographics*, 7 (April, 1985), pp. 23-25.

30. *Essays in Human Ecology*, 3 (1990), pp. 32-47.

31. Leo F. Schnore, "Problems in the Quantitative Study of Urban History," in H.J. Dyos (editor), *The Study of Urban History*, London, 1968, pp. 189-208.

32. In Oscar Handlin and John Burchard (editors), *The Historian and the City* Cambridge, MA, 1963, pp. 225-247.

*Professional Publications: 1954-1991.*

1954:   *Urbanization and Economic Growth: A Case for Research in Economic History* (Philadelphia: Committee on Research in Economic History, 1954), pp. 100.

1955:   "History of Cities in the Economically Advanced Areas," *Economic Development and Cultural Change,* 3 (January, 1955), pp. 81-156. (Reprinted: Bobbs-Merrill *Reprints in Demography & Human Ecology,* S440; John Friedmann and William Alonso, eds. *Readings in Regional Development and Planning* (MIT Press, 1964).

1957:   *Industrial Revolution: Interpretations and Perspectives* (Washington, D.C., American Historical Association, 1957), pp. 50.

1960:   "Balance of Payments Estimates for the United States: A Comment," *Trends in the American Economy in the 19th Century,* W.N. Parker, ed. (Princeton: NBER *Studies in Income and Wealth,* 34, 1960), pp. 711-16.

"The Price System and Economic Change," *Journal of Economic History,* 20 (December, 1960), pp. 617-37.

*Regions, Resources and Economic Growth* (Baltimore, Johns Hopkins University Press, 1960), pp. 716. With Harvey S. Perloff *et al.* (Reprinted: Bison Books No. 319, University of Nebraska Press, 1965.)

1961:   "Urbanization Problems," *Research Needs for Development Assistance Programs* (Washington, D.C.: Brookings Foreign Policy Studies Program, 1961), pp. 1-63, with Leo F. Schnore.

"American Historians and the Study of Urbanization," *American Historical Review,* 67 (October, 1961), pp. 49-61. (Reprinted: Bobbs-Merrill *Reprints in American History* H. 121.)

1963:   "Urbanization and Social Change," *The Historian and the City,* Oscar Handlin and John Burchard, eds. (Cambridge, Mass.: Harvard-MIT Press, 1963), pp. 225-47. (Reprinted: Peter Orleans, ed. *Social Structure and Social Process,* 1970.)

*The Rise of the Dairy Industry in Wisconsin: A Study of Agricultural Change, 1820-1920* (Madison: State Historical Society of Wisconsin, 1963), pp. 446. Awarded David Clark Everest Prize in Economic History

"City," *Encyclopedia Britannica* (1963 edn.), V, pp. 809-11.

1965:     "Historical Aspects of Urbanization," *The Study of Urbanization*, Philip M. Hauser and L. F. Schnore, eds. (New York: John Wiley, 1965), pp. 519-54.

          "Urbanization and Urban History," *Colloquium No. 4* (John Wiley, New York), Fall, 1965, pp. 12-22.

          "Antebellum Urbanization: A Comment," *Journal of Economic History*, 25 (Dec., 1965), pp. 612-14.

1967:     "The Social Impact of the Industrial Revolution," *Technology in Western Civilization*, Melvin Kranzberg and C. W. Pursell, Jr., eds. (New York: Oxford University Press, 1967), Vol. 1, pp. 302-22.

          "Social Science and the City," *Urban Research and Policy Planning*, Leo F. Schnore and Henry Fagin, eds. (Beverly Hills: Sage Publications, 1967), pp. 21-47. With Leo F. Schnore. (Reprinted: In Leo F. Schnore ed., *Social Science and the City: A Survey of Urban Research*, 1968).

1968:     "The Evolving System of Cities in the United States: Urbanization and Economic Development," *Issues in Urban Economics*, Harvey S. Perloff and L. Wingo, eds. (Baltimore: Johns Hopkins Press, 1968), pp. 81-139.

          "The Study of Urban History: A Review," *Urban History Newsletter No. 11* (Leicester, December, 1968), pp. 20-3.

          "Periodical Literature of the U. S., Canada, and Other Americas," *Economic History Review*, 21-26, 1968-1973, annual reviews.

1969:     "Historical Contours of Contemporary Urban Society: A Comparative View," *Journal of Contemporary History*, 4 (August, 1969), pp. 3-25.

1970:     "The Dimensions of Urban History: a Footnote to 'The Urban Crisis'," *Pacific Historical Review*, 34 (August, 1970), pp. 261-78.

1971:     "The Plain People of Boston: An Afterword," in Peter R. Knights, *The Plain People of Boston 1830-1860: A Study of City Growth* (New York: Oxford University Press, 1971), pp. 187-96.

1972:     *Freedom of Choice in Housing: Opportunities and Constraints* (Washington, D. C.: National Research Council, National Academy of Sciences, 1972), pp. 62. With Amos Hawley *et al*.

1973:     "The Pursuit of Happiness in the City: Changing Opportunities and

Options in America," *Transactions of the Royal Historical Society*, 5th Series, Vol. 23, 1973, pp. 175-220. (The Prothero Lecture, RHS, Oxford, 1972).

"The Urbanizing World," *The Victorian City: Images and Realities*, H. J. Dyos and Michael Wolff, eds. (2 Vols. London: Routledge & Kegan Paul, 1973), I, pp. 1-57.

1974:      "Urban Development in Britain: Population Trends and Housing: A Comment," *Urban History Yearbook 1974* (University of Leicester Press, 1974), pp. 90-3.

1975:      "Two Cheers for Quantitative History," *The New Urban History: Quantitative Explorations by American Historians*, L. F. Schnore, ed. (Princeton: Princeton University Press, 1975) pp. 12-48.

"Conversations on Urban History," *Journal of Urban History*, 1 (August, 1975), pp. 440-472. (Reprinted: Bruce Stave, ed. *The Making of Urban History*, 1977.)

1976:      "Dairy Industry," *Dictionary of American History* (New York: Charles Scribner's Sons, 1976), Bicentennial Edition, II, pp. 279-282.

1977:      "Figures in the Landscape: Some Historiographical Implications of Environmental Psychology," *Comparative Urban Research*, 5 (1977), pp. 20-31.

1978:      "Some Aspects of Urban Social Structure and Morphology in the Historical Development of Cities in the United States," *Cahiers Bruxellois*, 22 (1977), pp. 37-115. (For the International Commission for the History of Towns, XIVth International Congress of the Historical Sciences, San Francisco, 1975).

"Urbanization and Social Change," *Proceedings of the Seventh International Economic History Congress*, Michael W. Flinn, ed. (2 Vols. Edinburgh University Press, 1978), II, pp. 533-40.

1980:      "Urbanization," *Encyclopedia of American Economic History*, G. Porter, ed. (New York: Charles Scribner's Sons, 1980), III, pp. 1028-57.

1980:      "City Making and Mending in the United States: On Capitalizing A Social Environment," in *Urbanization in the Americas: The Background in Comparative Perspective*, Woodrow Borah, Jorge Hardoy, and G. R. Stelter, eds. (Ottawa, National Museum of Man, 1980), pp. 105-18; reprinted as 'Construccion y Refaccion de Ciudades en los Estados

Unidos de America, Sobre la Capitalizacion de un Medio Social' *Revista Interamericana de Planificacion*, XIV (1981), pp. 156-188.

1981: "The Survival of Industrial Cities," *In Modern Industrial Cities: History, Policy, Survival*, Bruce Stave, ed. (Beverly Hills: Sage, 1981), pp. 267-82.

1982: "Urbanization of the United States: The Capitalization and Decapitalization of Place," *Villes en mutation XIXe et XXe Siècles* (Brussels: 10e Colloque international, Crédit communal de Belgique, 1982), pp. 147-200.

1983: "The Nature of Urbanization," *The Pursuit of Urban History*, Derek Fraser and Anthony Sutcliffe eds. (Edward Arnold: London, 1983), pp. 3-53.

"The Nature of Modern Urbanization," *Visions of the Modern City*, William Sharpe and L. Wallock, eds. (Proceedings of the Heyman Center for the Humanities, Vol. 1, Columbia University, New York, 1983), pp. 47-96.

1984: "New York, New York: Nr. 1 in den U.S.A.," *Die Zukunft der Metropolen: Paris, London, New York, Berlin* (3 Vols: Internationale Bauaustellung, Berlin, 1984) I, *Aufsätze*, pp. 204-14.

1985: "Mutations of Cities in the Industrializing Era: An Ecological Perspective on Urbanization in the U.S.A.," *Essays from the Lowell Conference on Industrial History, 1982 and 1983*, Robert Weible, ed. (Lowell National Historical Park, 1985), pp. 194-249.

1986: "The New York Metropolis in Transformation: History and Prospect. A Study in Historical Particularity," *The Future of the Metropolis: Economic Aspects*, Hans-Jürgen Ewers *et al.*, eds. (Berlin-New York: Walter de Gruyter, 1986), pp. 27-110.

"The City in History: Urbanization as Capital Formation," The 1986 Denman Lecture in Land Economy, Department of Land Economy, Cambridge University.

1987: "The Nature of Urbanization," *Visions of the Modern City: Essays in History, Art, and Literature*, William Sharpe and Leonard Wallock, eds. (Baltimore: Johns Hopkins University Press, 1987), pp. 51-100. (revised edition of 1983 publication).

1991: "Structural Changes: Introductory Essay," *Inventing Times Square:*

*Commerce and Culture at the Crossroads of the World*, Wm. R. Taylor, ed. (New York: Russell Sage Foundation, 1991), pp. 15-35, 372-75. Republished by Johns Hopkins University Press, Baltimore, 1996.